MYP Physics

A concept-based approach

Years **4&5**

William Heathcote

OXFORD
UNIVERSITY PRESS

OXFORD
UNIVERSITY PRESS

Great Clarendon Street, Oxford, OX2 6DP, United Kingdom

Oxford University Press is a department of the University of Oxford. It furthers the University's objective of excellence in research, scholarship, and education by publishing worldwide. Oxford is a registered trade mark of Oxford University Press in the UK and in certain other countries

British Library Cataloguing in Publication Data
Data available

978-0-19-837555-5

10 9 8 7 6 5 4 3 2 1

MIX
Paper from
responsible sources
FSC® C007785

Paper used in the production of this book is a natural, recyclable product made from wood grown in sustainable forests. The manufacturing process conforms to the environmental regulations of the country of origin.

Printed in Great Britain by Bell and Bain Ltd. Glasgow

Acknowledgements

We are grateful to the authors and publishers for use of extracts from their titles and in particular for the following:

Kuldip Acharya and Dibyendu Goshal: 'Flower Inspired Thunder Protecting Umbrella' published in the 2016 Proceedings of the International Conference on Modeling, Simulation and Visualization Methods (MSV'16); EDITORS: Hamid R. Arabnia, Leonidas Deligiannidis, Fernando G. Tinetti; CSREA Press; ISBN: 1-60132-443-X, 2016.

Sabine Begall et al: 'Magnetic alignment in grazing and resting cattle and deer' from Proceedings of the National Academy of Sciences of the United States of America, volume 105 (36), 13451-13455, 09/09/2008. Copyright (2008) National Academy of Sciences, U.S.A. Reproduced by permission of PNAS.

The publishers would like to thank the following for permissions to use their photographs:

Cover image: Shutterstock.
p2 (T): Science & Society Picture Library/SSPL/Getty Images; p2 (B): Author photo; p3 (T): Mopic/Alamy Stock Photo; p3 (B): Mopic/Shutterstock; p4: Aurora Photos/Alamy Stock Photo; p5 (T): DR GARY SETTLES/SCIENCE PHOTO LIBRARY; p5 (B): The Print Collector/Alamy Stock Photo; p6: World History Archive/Alamy Stock Photo; p12: Science Photo Library/Alamy Stock Photo; p15 (R): E.R. Degginger/Alamy Stock Photo; p15 (L): GARY DOAK/Alamy Stock Photo; p16: Ivica Drusany/Shutterstock; p17: Irina Falkanfal/Shutterstock; p20: Corbis; p21: Science History Images/Alamy Stock Photo; p23: Peter Probst/Alamy Stock Photo; p24 (B): Gianluca Curti/Shutterstock; p24 (T): Herrndorff/Shutterstock; p25 (T): Joyfull/Shutterstock; p25 (B): Stefan Pircher/Shutterstock; p26: Michael Taylor/Shutterstock; p27 (TR): Andrey Armyagov/Shutterstock; p27 (L): Photodisc/Getty Images; p28: Granger Historical Picture Archive/Alamy Stock Photo; p30 (C): Jorisvo/Shutterstock; p31: Mironov/Shutterstock; : Boris Rabtsevich/Shutterstock; p33: Tim UR/Shutterstock; p35: Haryigit/Shutterstock; p37: Room the Agency Mobile/Alamy Stock Photo; : Anna Omelchenko/Shutterstock; p42: J HIME/Shutterstock; p44: EADWEARD MUYBRIDGE COLLECTION/ KINGSTON MUSEUM/SCIENCE PHOTO LIBRARY; p45 (TR): Igorstevanovic/Shutterstock; p45 (TL): MIDDLE TEMPLE LIBRARY/SCIENCE PHOTO LIBRARY; p45 (B): NK Sanford/Alamy Stock Photo; p46: DAVID PARKER/Shutterstock; p49: DoodleDance/Shutterstock; p54: Cleanfotos/Shutterstock; p55: Egyptian Studio/Shutterstock; p57: NASA/ESA/STSCI/HIGH-Z SUPERNOVA SEARCH TEAM/ SCIENCE PHOTO LIBRARY; p59: EMILIO SEGRE VISUAL ARCHIVES/AMERICAN INSTITUTE OF PHYSICS/ SCIENCE PHOTO LIBRARY; p60: Paul Fleet/Shutterstock; p62: Art Directors & TRIP/Alamy Stock Photo; p63 (TL): Joao Virissimo/Shutterstock; p63 (TR): Andrey N Bannov/Shutterstock; p63 (B): MIKKEL JUUL JENSEN/SCIENCE PHOTO LIBRARY; p64: Oliver Hoffmann/Alamy Stock Photo; p65 (T): LilKar/Shutterstock; p65 (B): Cyo Bo/Shutterstock; p66: Christopher J. Morris/ Getty Images; p67: FRANS LANTING, MINT IMAGES/SCIENCE PHOTO LIBRARY; p68: WENN Ltd/Alamy Stock Photo; p69 : Maros Bauer/Shutterstock; p70: William Heathcote/ JOEL AREM/SCIENCE PHOTO LIBRARY; p75 (TL): Andrea Paggiaro/Shutterstock; p79 (TR): Kevin Smith/ /Design Pics/Corbis; p79 (TL): Tristan3D/Shutterstock; p80: NASA/ESA/STSCI/J. CLARKE, U.MICHIGAN/ SCIENCE PHOTO LIBRARY; p81: Arto Hakola/Shutterstock; p82: Richard Peterson/Shutterstock; p84 (T): Karen Kaspar/Alamy Stock Photo; p84 (B): 3Dstock/ Shutterstock; p85 (T): SAKARET/Shutterstock; p85 (B): Archive Image/Alamy Stock Photo; p85 (B): Shutterstock/Fedorov Oleksiy; p87 (C): Kajornyot/Shutterstock; p86: Zoia Kostina/ Shutterstock; p87 (BL): FloridaStock/Shutterstock; p87 (BR): Ulrich Willmunder/ Shutterstock; p88: Triff/Shutterstock; : Pascal Goetgheluck/Science Photo Library; p89: Galina Barskaya/Shutterstock; p93 (T): Kotenko Oleksandr/Shutterstock; p93 (B): KPG_Payless/ Shutterstock; p94: Photodisc/Getty Images; p95: Photodisc/Getty Images; p97 (T): Andrew Lambert Photography/Science Photo Library; p97 (B): Nattakit Jeerapatmaitree/Shutterstock; p99: Denis Scott/Corbis; p102: Giedre vaitekune/Shutterstock; p103: Vicspacewalker/ Shutterstock; p106 (T): Tatiana Popova/Shutterstock; p106 (B): Aslysun/Shutetrstock; p107 (T): Javarman/Shutterstock; p107 (B): Shutterstock; p108: Chris Howes/Wild Places Photography/Alamy Stock Photo; p109 (T): PjrStudio/Alamy Stock Photo; p109 (B): Triff/ Shutterstock; p111 (TL): E+/Getty Images; p111 (TC): Getty Images; p111 (TR): Photodisc/ Getty Images; p112: OUP; p114: Alamy Stock Photo; p113: Steve Noakes/Shutterstock; p115 (T): Jake Rennaker/Shutterstock; p117 (TL): Ken Tannenbaum/Shutterstock; p117 (TR): Alamy Stock Photo; p117 (C): Kokhanchikov/Shutterstock; p115 (B): World History Archive/ Alamy Stock Photo; p117 (BL): withGod/Shutterstock; p117 (BR): Kampol Taepanich/ Shutterstock; p118 (L): Shutterstock; p118 (CT): Miki Simankevicius/Shutterstock; p118 (CB): Tawansak/Shutterstock; p118 (TR): Jonathan Larsen/Diadem Images/Alamy Stock Photo; p116: Lola1960/Shutterstock; p118 (B): Eric M. Jones/NASA; p120: Racefotos2008/ Shutterstock; p123: MBI/Alamy Stock Photo; p122: Marythepooh/Shutterstock; p127 (L): Kryvenok Anastasiia/Shutterstock; p127 (LC): Mubus7/Shutterstock; p127 (RC): Shutterstock; p127 (R): Lasse Kristensen/Shutterstock; p131: Andrei Nekrassov/Shutterstock; p133: Shutterstock; p134 (L): Shutterstock; p134 (R): Iceink/Shutterstock; p135 (TL): Alamy Stock Photo; p135 (TR): Shutterstock; p135(B): Shutterstock; p136: RGB Ventures/SuperStock/ Alamy Stock Photo; p137 (TL): Stocktrek Images, Inc./Alamy Stock Photo; p137 (BR): INTERFOTO/Alamy Stock Photo; p138 (TL): Changsgallery/Shutterstock; p138 (BR): NASA Archive/Alamy Stock Photo; p139: Everett Historical/Shutterstock; p142 (B): Chronicle / Alamy Stock Photo; p142 (T): Sheila Terry/Science Photo Library; p143 (TL): Phoenix Photosetting/Q2A Media; p143 (BL): Paul Fearn / Alamy Stock Photo; p143 (BR): Lukasz Janyst/Shutterstock; p144: Georgios Kollidas/Shutterstock; p150 (T): Stocktrek Images, Inc./ Alamy Stock Photo; p151 (T): Granger Historical Picture Archive/Alamy Stock Photo; p151 (B): Mark Garlick/Science Photo Library; p156 (T): Marykit/Shutterstock; p156 (B): yousang/ Shutterstock; p157 (T): solarseven/Shutterstock; p157 (B): Everett Historical/Shutterstock; p159 (B): Aija Lehtonen/Shutterstock; p159 (T): Nicku/Shutterstock; p158: Haloviss/ Shutterstock; p161: Petar An/Shutterstock; p166: Collection Abecasis/Science Photo Library; p169 (L): Shutterstock; p169 (R): Gun/Shutterstock; p170: Sciencephotos / Alamy Stock Photo; p171: Stockphoto Mania/Shutterstock; p171: Stockphoto Mania/Shutterstock; : Willyam Bradberry/Shutterstock; : Nuwat Phansuwan/Shutterstock; p173 (T): William Heathcote; p173 (B): Deklofenak/Shutterstock; p174: Wearset Ltd; p178 (T): Sergio Gutierrez Getino/Shutterstock; p178 (B): Juan Aunion/Shutterstock; p 179 (T): PRISMA ARCHIVO/Alamy Stock Photo; p 179 (B): Andrey Armyagov/Shutterstock; p180: Science History Images/Alamy Stock Photo; p181 (T): Andrey VP/Shutterstock; p181 (B): ArchMan/Shutterstock; p182: World History Archive/Alamy Stock Photo; p183: Corbis; p184: SCIENCE SOURCE/SCIENCE PHOTO LIBRARY; p186 (T): ROYAL ASTRONOMICAL SOCIETY/SCIENCE PHOTO LIBRARY; p186 (B): Caltech/MIT/LIGO Lab/SCIENCE PHOTO LIBRARY; p187: ROYAL ASTRONOMICAL SOCIETY/ SCIENCE PHOTO LIBRARY; p189 (T): Roland Oster/Shutterstock; p189 (B): GIPhotoStock/ SCIENCE PHOTO LIBRARY; p190: ANDREW LAMBERT PHOTOGRAPHY/SCIENCE PHOTO LIBRARY; p192: Roberto Lo Savio/Alamy Stock Photo; p193: Pedrosala/Shutterstock; p194: Notety/Shutterstock; p197: GIPhotoStock/SCIENCE PHOTO LIBRARY; p198: CyberEak/ Shutterstock; p199: NYPL/SCIENCE SOURCE/SCIENCE PHOTO LIBRARY; p200: Asharkyu/ Shutterstock; p201: Waldenstroem/Shutterstock; p203: Asharkyu/Shutterstock; p204 (TL): William Heathcote supplied; p204 (TR): Thinkstock/Getty Images; p204 (B): MIchael Crawford-Hick/Alamy Stock Photo; p205 (T): Fotokon/Shutterstock; p205 (B): MARK SYKES/ SCIENCE PHOTO LIBRARY; p206: W.A. Sharman/Milepost 92 ½/Corbis; p207 (T): Jeff Gynane/ Shutterstock; p207 (B): Tappasan Phurisamrit/Shutterstock; p208 (L): Cpphotoimages/ Shutterstock; p208 (R): Ian Woolcock/Shutterstock; p209: TV/Shutterstock; p210 (T): WitR/ Shutterstock; p210 (B): IM_photo/Shutterstock; p211: Corey Ford/123RF; p212: William Heathcote supplied; p213: Rich Carey/Shutterstock; p214: Paulo Oliveira/Alamy Stock Photo; p218: Gameover/Alamy Stock Photo; p221 (TL): Outdoorsman/Shutterstock; p221 (TR): Danita Delimont/Alamy Stock Photo; p222 (TR): ModeList/Shutterstock; p222 (BL): Image Point Fr/Shutterstock; p223: Damsea/Shutterstock; p225 (TR): Nick Stubbs/Shutterstock; p225 (BL): Martin Parratt/Shutterstock; p226: Duncan1890/iStockphoto; p228: Christopher Elwell/Shutterstock; p232 (TL): Science History Images/Alamy Stock Photo; p232 (BR): Hulton Archive/Getty Images; p233 (T): Shutterstock; p233 (B): Vladimir Wrangel/ Shutterstock; p234: Anyaivanova/Shutterstock; p235 (T): Kostsov/Shutterstock; p235 (B): Thelefty/Shutterstock; p237 (BL): Dmitry Yashkin/Shutterstock; p237 (BR): Melis/ Shutterstock; p238 (TL): Nitr/Shutterstock; p238 (TR): Jovan Vitanovski/Shutterstock; p238 (BL): Mark Herreid/Shutterstock; p238 (BR): Kaband/Shutterstock; p239 (TR): Gan Chaonan/ Shutterstock; p239 (CL): Dmitri Melnik/Shutterstock; p239 (B): Photodisc/Getty Images; p241: Singkham/Shutterstock; p243 (CL): Andrew M. Allport/Shutterstock; p243 (CR): Kajornyot Wildlife Photography/Shutterstock; p244: Cephas Picture Library/Alamy Stock Photo; p248 (TL): Anat Chant/Shutterstock; p250: Bertold Werkmann/Shutterstock; p251: Markus Gann/Shutterstock; p252: Francesco R. Iacomino/Shutterstock; p254: Kaitong Yepoon/Shutterstock; p256 (TL): William Heathcote; p256 (TR): Margaret/Shutterstock; p256 (B): Eky Studio/Shutterstock; p257 (BR): Elenaburn/Shutterstock; p257 (BL): Kichigin/ Shutterstock; p258: Science History Images/Alamy Stock Photo; p259 (TL): Apiguide/ Shutterstock; p259 (CR): Eveleen/Shutterstock; p259 (B): William Heathcote; p260 (L): Rattiya Thongdumhyu/Shutterstock; p260 (C): Armin Rose/Shutterstock; p260 (R): Corbis; p261 (B): Ilya Andriyanov/Shutterstock; p262: MilanB/Shutterstock; p265 (BL): William Heathcote; p265 (BR): William Heathcote; p266: Reload Design/Shutterstock; p267 (B): Science Photo Library; p269: itsmejust/Shutterstock; p270: Aleksandr Yu/Shutterstock; p277: Vlad1988/Shutterstock; p280: MarcelClemens/Shutterstock; p282: Deco/Alamy Stock Photo; p285: Sergey Nivens/Shutterstock; p286: Overcrew/Shutterstock; p289: NASA/ESA/STScI/ SCIENCE PHOTO LIBRARY.

Artwork by Aptara Corp. and OUP.

Contents

Introduction

The MYP Physics course, like all MYP Sciences, is inquiry based. To promote conceptual understanding, the MYP uses key concepts and related concepts. Key concepts represent big ideas that are relevant across disciplines. The key concepts used in MYP Sciences are change, relationships and systems. Related concepts are more specific to each subject and help to promote more detailed exploration. Each chapter is focused on one of the twelve related concepts and one key concept.

Each chapter opens with ways in which the related concept is explored in other disciplines. This structure will help to develop interdisciplinary understanding of the concepts. After the interdisciplinary opening pages, the concepts are introduced more deeply in relation to the specific content of the chapter.

The objectives of MYP Science are categorized into four criteria, which contain descriptions of specific targets that are accomplished as a result of studying MYP Science:

A. Knowing and understanding

B. Inquiring and designing

C. Processing and evaluating

D. Reflecting on the impacts of science

Within each chapter, we have included activities designed to promote achievement of these objectives, such as experiments and data-based questions. We also included factual, conceptual and debatable questions, and activities designed to promote development of approaches to learning skills. The summative assessment found at the end of each chapter is framed by a statement of inquiry relating the concepts addressed to one of the six global contexts, and so is structured similarly to the MYP eAssessment.

For those students taking the eAssessment at the end of the MYP programme, the International Baccalaureate Organization provides a subject-specific topic list. Great care has been taken to ensure all of topics from the list are covered within this book.

Overall, this book is meant to guide a student's exploration of Physics and aid development specific skills that are essential for academic success and getting the most out of this educational experience.

How to use this book

To help you get the most of your book, here's an overview of its features.

Concepts, global context and statement of inquiry

The key and related concepts, the global context and the statement of inquiry used in each chapter are clearly listed on the introduction page.

Activities

A range of activities that encourage you to think further about the topics you studied, research these topics and build connections between physics and other disciplines.

Worked examples

Worked examples take a step-by-step approach to help you translate theory into practice.

Experiments

Practical activities that help you prepare for assessment criteria B & C.

Data-based questions

These questions allow you to test your factual understanding of physics, as well as study and analyse data. Data-based questions help you prepare for assessment criteria A, B & C.

ATL Skills

These approaches to learning sections introduce new skills or give you the opportunity to reflect on skills you might already have. They are mapped to the MYP skills clusters and are aimed at supporting you become an independent learner.

 A conceptual question   A debatable question

Summative assessment

There is a summative assessment at the end of each chapter; this is structured in the same way as the eAssessment and covers all four MYP assessment criteria.

Glossary

The glossary contains definitions for all the subject-specific terms emboldened in the index.

Mapping grid

The MYP eAssessment subject list for Physics consists of six broad topics:

Forces and energy · Heat, light and sound

Electromagnetism · Waves

Astrophysics · Atomic physics

These topics are further broken down into sub-topics and the mapping grid below gives you an overview of where these are covered within this book. It also shows you which key concept, global context and statement of inquiry guide the learning in each chapter.

Chapter	Topics covered	Key concept	Global context	Statement of inquiry	ATL skills
1 Models	Atomic structure, particles, charges and masses Longitudinal and transverse waves Wave equation	Relationships	Scientific and technical innovation	A good model can simplify and illuminate our understanding of complex phenomena.	**Communication skills:** Understanding and using standard form **Affective skills:** Practicing resilience
2 Interaction	Gravity and gravitational fields Electric fields Static electricity	Relationships	Identities and relationships	The way in which the universe changes is governed by fundamental interactions of matter.	**Thinking in context:** How does weight shape our identity?
3 Evidence	Measurement in science **The Big Bang theory**	Relationships	Identities and relationships	Experiments and measurements provide evidence to support or disprove scientific claims.	**Communication skills:** Presenting data in a graph **Communication skills:** Using and interpreting a range of discipline-specific terms and symbols **Transfer skills:** What constitutes evidence?
4 Movement	Speed, motion graphs Magnetism, magnetic fields	Change	Orientation in space and time	Movement enables humans and animals to change their surroundings for the better.	**Thinking in context:** How can magnetism help us to navigate?
5 Environment	States and properties of matter, kinetic theory Condensation and evaporation Density	Systems	Globalization and sustainability	Changes in our environment require all living things to adapt in order to survive.	**Thinking in context:** Why is rain important?
6 Function	Forces and effects of forces Forces and motion, newton's laws Current, voltage, power Electric circuits	Systems	Fairness and development	The development of machines and systems has changed the way in which human beings function.	**Communication skills:** Using subject-specific terminology **Thinking in context:** What happens to the Earth when you jump up in the air? **Creative thinking skills:** Proposing metaphors and analogies **Thinking in context:** How can we use electricity to drive machines?

Chapter	Topics covered	Key concept	Global context	Statement of inquiry	ATL skills
7 Form	The solar system Planets and satellites	Systems	Identities and relationships	Determining the form of objects can help us to understand how they behave.	**Communication skills:** Understanding and using units **Thinking in context:** How have our identities been shaped by the stars? **Thinking in context:** What happens when science challenges our identity? **Collaboration skills:** Encouraging others to contribute
8 Consequences	Electric and magnetic fields Electromagnetic forces and induction AC & DC Generation and transmission of electricity Sound waves	Change	Personal and cultural expression	The consequences of actions are predicted by the laws of physics.	**Thinking in context:** What are the consequences of personal expression
9 Development	Measurement in science Wave phenomena including reflection, refraction, diffraction	Systems	Fairness and development	The development of science and technology gives us the possibility of changing the world for the better.	**Critical thinking skills:** Considering ideas from multiple perspectives **Information literacy skills:** Publishing a scientific paper **Communication skills:** Plotting graphs
10 Transformation	Pressure Thermal physics Heat transfer	Change	Scientific and technical innovation	Scientific innovation can transform our human existence.	**Communication skills:** Organising and depicting information logically **Critical thinking skills:** Formulating counterarguments
11 Energy	Work and power, efficiency Transfer and transformation of energy, conservation of energy Energy sources and resources, fuels and environmental impact	Change	Globalization and sustainability	The need for sustainability is changing the way in which we produce and use energy.	**Communication skills:** Interpreting discipline-specific terms **Media literacy skills:** Seeking a range of perspectives from multiple sources
12 Patterns	Electromagnetic spectrum, imaging and applications Radioactivity and decay, forms of radiation, uses and dangers	Relationships	Identities and relationships	Patterns can demonstrate relationships between events and shed light on how they are caused.	**Information literacy skills:** Using mnemonics to remember sequences **Thinking in context:** Color and identity **Collaboration skills:** Building consensus **Media literacy:** Demonstrating awareness of media interpretations of events **Reflection skills:** Considering ethical implications

1 Models

Models are simplified representations of more complex systems.

Modeling the many different processes in the economy is complicated. Economists use models to help predict the consequences of changes in government policy, foreign trade and domestic expenditure. In this machine, developed by Bill Phillips in 1949, water flows between different tanks representing financial transactions. Changing factors such as taxes, interest rates or the amount of government lending, are modeled by opening and closing different valves. The amount of water held in different tanks represents the amount held in banks or by the government. Are there any other processes which can be modeled with water?

Understanding the development of the brains of babies is complicated by the fact that they cannot tell you what they are thinking. Developmental psychologists use models to simplify infants' development into stages. The baby's brain also uses progressively improved models to understand the world around it. This baby's brain is just learning about object permanence – the idea that hidden objects still exist. What would this baby think about a game of hide and seek?

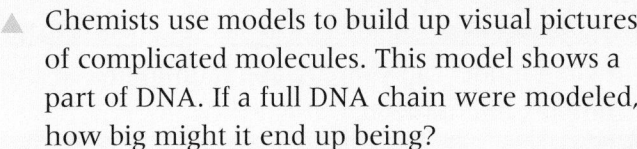

Astronomers use models to explain how the solar system might have formed. One such model is the solar nebular model which depicts how planets were formed from the same collapsing gas cloud that formed the Sun. It successfully explains why the planets all orbit in the same direction and in nearly circular orbits. If the solar nebular model suggests that the process which forms stars also forms planets, what does that say about the likelihood of finding life on another planet?

> **All models are wrong but some are useful.**
>
> **George Box**

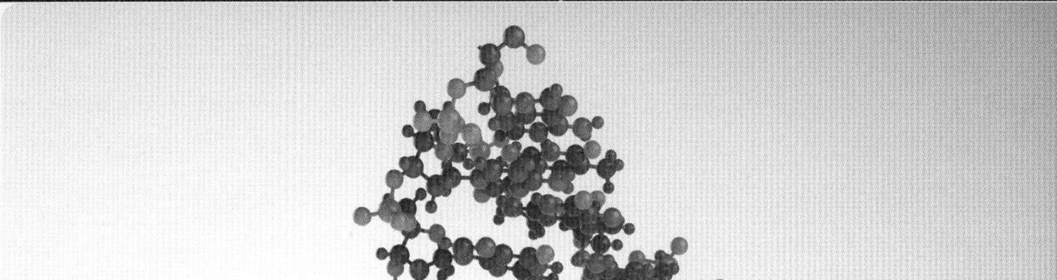

Chemists use models to build up visual pictures of complicated molecules. This model shows a part of DNA. If a full DNA chain were modeled, how big might it end up being?

Key concept: Relationships

Related concept: Models

Global context: Scientific and technical innovation

Introduction

The human brain is highly sophisticated but we struggle to envisage the sheer size of the universe. We find it difficult to conceive the vast distances of space in our heads without using scale models to help us to visualize them.

One of the greatest skills of the human brain is that of intuition. Through experience and perception, we build up patterns and we learn what to expect. If we see something balanced precariously, then we know that it is likely to fall over without having to calculate the forces on it.

▼ Our intuition tells us that the tightrope walker is unstable without us having to calculate the forces involved

Statement of inquiry:

A good model can simplify and illuminate our understanding of complex phenomena.

We can employ our intuition to help with complicated physics by using models. A good model can take something that we do not understand, simplify it and liken it to a more familiar concept. It can enable us to make predictions about how something will behave, which we can then test. A good model may make predictions which agree with experimental results, or it might highlight shortcomings in our understanding.

This chapter investigates how models of atoms and waves can simplify our understanding of what matter in the universe is made from and how it interacts. The key concept of this chapter is relationships.

Knowledge of the fundamental nature of matter fueled a technological revolution in the 20th century and today many scientific innovations arise from our better understanding of the nature of matter and its interactions and so the global context of this chapter is scientific and technical innovation.

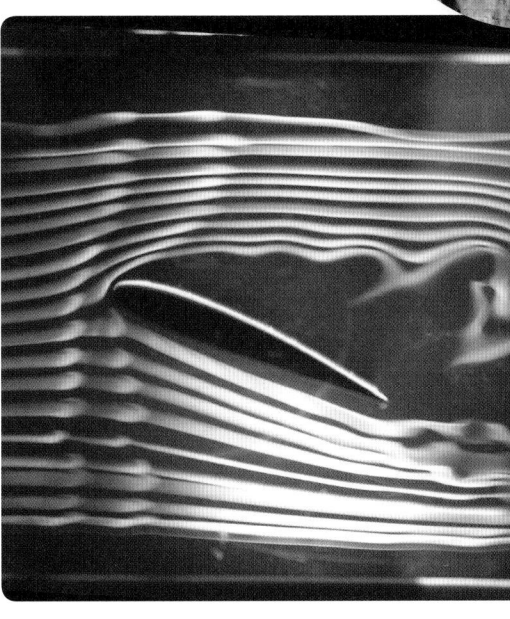

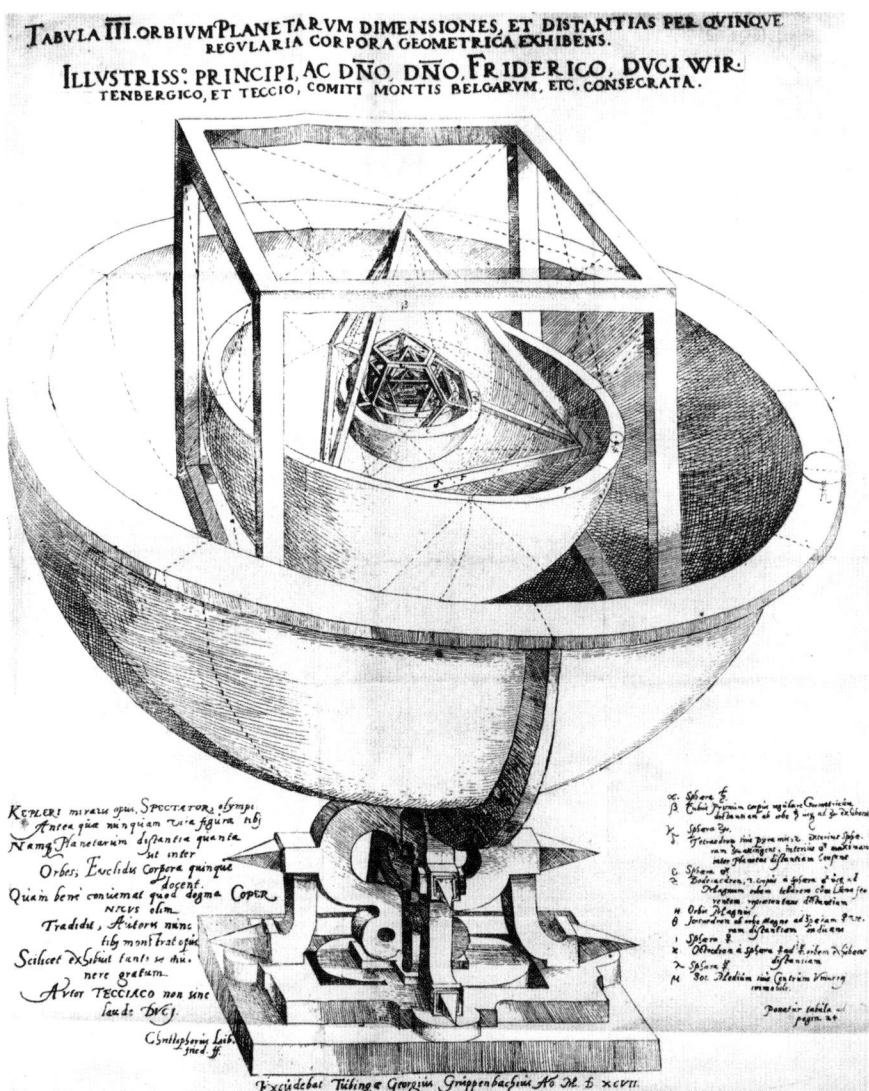

The way air flows around the wing of an airplane is a complex system. Testing a model wing in a wind tunnel can help engineers to understand how well the wing is working

Early models of the solar system allowed astronomers to predict and explain how the planets move in the sky. In this model, Kepler (1571–1630) attempted to explain the size of the gaps between the orbits of the six planets known at the time using the five regular polyhedra (cube, tetrahedron, dodecahedron, icosahedron and octahedron). Kepler abandoned this model because it was not sufficiently precise to match his measurements. Since there are only five regular polyhedra, this model explained why there were only six planets. What would have happened to this model after the discovery of Uranus in 1781?

What is an atom?

In one of his famous physics lectures in the 1960s, the Nobel Prize-winning physicist Richard Feynman considered a conundrum: if there were to be some cataclysmic event and all scientific knowledge were to be destroyed, what single sentence would contain the most information? His sentence described atomic theory: "That all things are made of atoms".

The ancient Greeks first developed the idea of atomic theory and thought of atoms as being the smallest building blocks of matter. They considered the idea of taking an amount of a substance, such as water, and dividing it into smaller portions. They knew that when a cup of water was poured into two smaller cups, the two smaller portions of water would have the same properties as the initial cup – it would still be the same substance. However, they thought that there would be a limit to how many times you could go on dividing the water. Eventually, they concluded, you would have the smallest amount of water possible that could not be divided any further while still having the properties of water.

They called this smallest amount an atom. The word atom itself derives from the Greek meaning "indivisible". We still use the word atom and their ideas of atoms today, however, the ancient Greeks did not know what types of atoms there could be – they thought that all matter was made from air, earth, fire and water.

▶ This 1660 model of the solar system shows the Earth in the center and the planets orbiting around it. Surrounding the Earth are what were thought to be the other three elements at the time: water, air and fire. What other models feature in this picture?

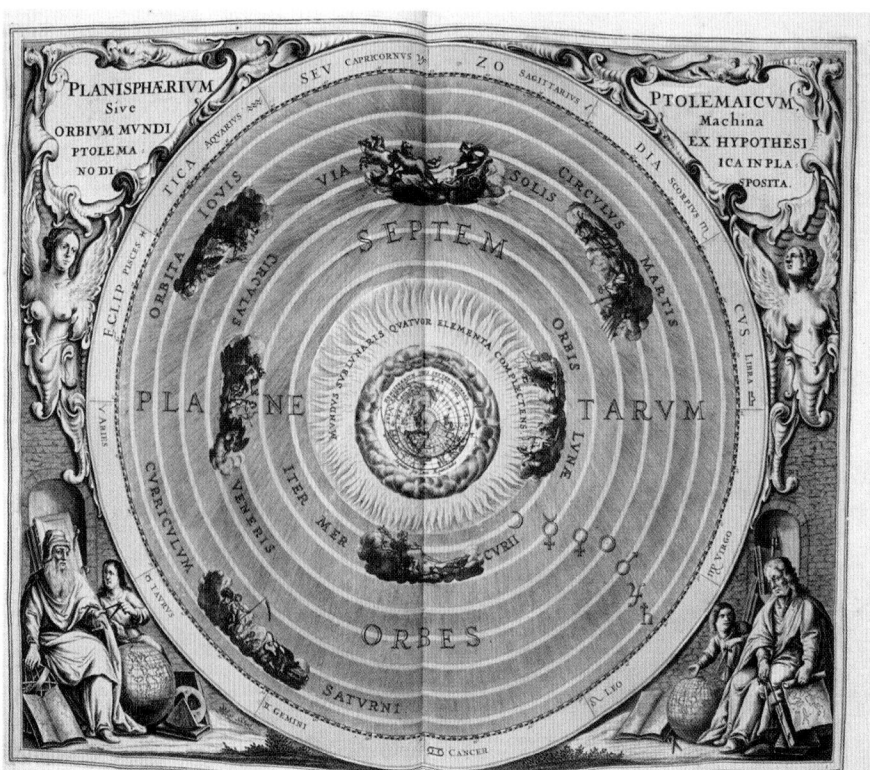

In the late 18th century, chemists studied the quantities of matter used in chemical reactions and realized that the relative amounts of matter involved were always in fixed ratios. This led to them drawing the conclusion that the fixed ratio of chemicals was due to the fact that the chemicals came in discrete quantities – atoms. Chemists were then able to classify substances as being either a compound, involving two or more different types of atom, or an element, matter which only had one type of atom. At the time they knew of only about 30 different elements, but over the next century, they discovered around another 50.

Chemists put the elements into an arrangement that they called the periodic table. This is a useful model: the position of an element in the table is related to its chemical properties. This means that you can predict how an element might behave in chemical reactions from where it appears in the periodic table. In the 19th century, gaps in the table were used to predict the existence of more elements: this led to the discovery of germanium and gallium.

Elements

			K = 39	Rb = 85	Cs = 133	–	–
			Ca = 40	Sr = 87	Ba = 137	–	–
			–	?Yt = 88?	?Di = 138?	Er = 178?	–
			Ti = 48?	Zr = 90	Co = 140?	?La = 180?	Tb = 231
			V = 51	Nb = 94	–	Ta = 182	–
			Cr = 52	Mo = 96	–	W = 184	U = 240
			Mn = 55	–	–	–	–
			Fe = 56	Ru = 104	–	Os = 195?	–
			Co = 59	Rh = 104	–	Ir = 197	–
			Ni = 59	Pd = 106	–	Pt = 198?	–
H = 1	Li = 7	Na = 23	Cu = 63	Ag = 108	–	Au = 199?	–
	Be = 9, 4	Mg = 24	Zn = 65	Cd = 112	–	Hg = 200	–
	B = 11	Al = 27, 3	–	In = 113	–	Tl = 204	–
	C = 12	Si = 28	–	Sn = 118	–	Pb = 207	–
	N = 14	P = 31	As = 75	Sb = 122	–	Bi = 208	–
	O = 16	S = 32	Se = 78	Te = 125?	–	–	–
	F = 19	Cl = 35, 5	Br = 80	J = 127	–	–	–

Position of germanium and gallium

▲ Mendeleev's original periodic table enabled chemists to predict the existence of missing elements

Up to this time, the atom was considered to be a fundamental particle, that is it could not be split into anything smaller. However, the discovery of the electron in the late 19th century showed that this did not seem to be the case. Scientists later determined that the electron was part of the atom and was much smaller and lighter than an atom. This meant that an atom was not the smallest unit of matter possible.

What is an electron?

An electron is a tiny particle, in fact it is so small that it behaves as if it were a point with no size. Scientists believe that it is a fundamental particle, that is, it is not made up of any smaller particles.

An electron's mass is also tiny: 9.1×10^{-31} kg. This is much smaller than the masses of the other particles in an atom, and so the mass of the electrons makes up a tiny proportion of the total mass of the atom. In fact, the mass of the electrons in an atom contributes less than one tenth of a percent (0.1%) to the total mass of an atom.

An electron also has a charge. Charge is a fundamental property of matter, just as mass is (this is discussed in more detail in Chapter 2, Interaction). Charge is the property which is responsible for electrostatic forces and electricity. The charge of an electron is negative and is -1.6×10^{-19} C. The unit of charge is the coulomb which has the symbol C.

ATL Communication skills

Understanding and using standard form

People regularly have to communicate large or small numbers and our language has words such as million or thousandth that help us to do this. The International System of Units, referred to as the SI system, also has prefixes which help communicate large or small units. For example, a kilometer is one thousand meters and a microgram is a millionth of a gram.

Some other prefixes used with SI units are shown below.

exa	E	$\times 10^{18}$	milli	m	$\times 10^{-3}$
peta	P	$\times 10^{15}$	micro	μ	$\times 10^{-6}$
tera	T	$\times 10^{12}$	nano	n	$\times 10^{-9}$
giga	G	$\times 10^{9}$	pico	p	$\times 10^{-12}$
mega	M	$\times 10^{6}$	femto	f	$\times 10^{-15}$
kilo	k	$\times 10^{3}$	atto	a	$\times 10^{-18}$

Scientists often need to express numbers which are beyond this scale. The mass of an electron is 0.91 thousandths of a yoctogram (the prefix yocto means 10^{-24} and is so small that it is rarely used) and so you would need about one million million million million million electrons to make a kilogram. Neither of these numbers is easy to communicate. Standard form makes it easier to represent large or small numbers. In standard form, we would write that the mass of an electron is 9.1×10^{-31} kg and so you would need just over 1×10^{30} electrons to make a kilogram.

1. Express these numbers in standard form:

   a) The probability of shuffling a pack of cards and finding that they had ended up in sequential order is one in eighty million million million million million million million million million million million.

   b) The number of insects on the Earth is estimated to be ten million million million.

   c) The number of protons in the universe is thought to be about one hundred million million million million million million million million million million million million million.

Because electrons are fundamental particles and cannot be divided into smaller parts with smaller charges, a charged object has a total charge that is a multiple of 1.6×10^{-19} C as it will have gained or lost a whole number of electrons. Scientists call this the elementary charge and label it e. An electron has a charge of $-e$ and an object that has gained two electrons would gain a charge of $-2e$. On the other hand, a previously uncharged object which loses an electron would be left with a charge of $+e$.

What else is inside an atom?

The discovery of the electron prompted scientists to rethink their ideas about the atom. If an atom had electrons which were negatively charged but the atom as a whole appeared to have no charge, then there must be a positive charge somewhere in the atom.

At first they thought that perhaps the electrons were dotted around inside the atom in a sea of positive charge. Because this resembled the fruit in a popular pudding of the time, this model was called the plum pudding model.

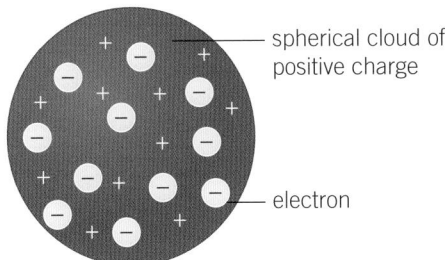

spherical cloud of positive charge

electron

The plum pudding model enabled scientists to explain the idea of electrons in an atom. However, it could not explain the results of Rutherford's scattering experiment

Ernest Rutherford was a physicist working in the early 20th century. He proposed an experiment where particles were fired at a thin sheet of gold. The experiment was carried out by Hans Geiger and Ernest Marsden. The particles fired at the gold were called alpha particles; these are positively charged and although they are about 50 times lighter than an atom of gold, they are more than 7,000 times heavier than the electrons in the atoms of gold. Since the alpha particles were heavier than anything known to be inside the gold atoms and traveling at a significant speed, Rutherford expected all of them to pass straight through.

Indeed, the vast majority of them did, but Rutherford was hugely surprised at Geiger and Marsden's finding that a very small number of alpha particles bounced back, since the plum pudding model of the atom did not have any particle heavy enough to deflect the alpha particles. He deduced that the alpha particles must be bouncing off something much heavier than themselves. He also deduced that whatever the alpha particles were deflecting off must be small, since very few particles were deflected.

Modeling the Geiger–Marsden experiment

For this activity you will need some lightweight balls such as table tennis balls, a blindfold and a football suspended from the ceiling. (You could put the football on a table if this is easier.)

From a couple of meters away, while wearing the blindfold, throw the table tennis balls towards the football. (You could have several people throwing table tennis balls at the same time.)

1. How many of them hit the football? What happens?

2. What would happen if you threw table tennis balls at a smaller object?

3. If you threw tennis balls at a balloon, how many would bounce back?

4. In the Geiger–Marsden experiment, some alpha particles bounced back but very few (about one in a million). Using your model, what does this suggest about the target that the alpha particles deflected off?

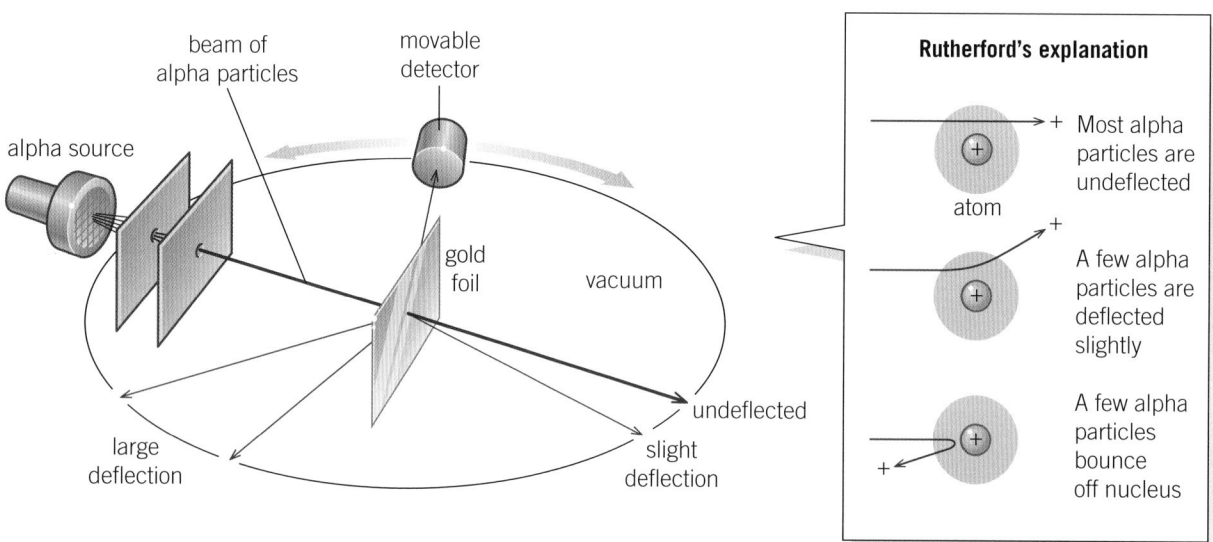

▲ The Geiger–Marsden experiment observed a small number of alpha particles were deflected through a large angle

Rutherford had discovered the nucleus of an atom. The nucleus is positively charged and contains almost all of the mass of an atom, but is also very small. If an atom were blown up to be the size of the Earth, then the nucleus would still only be about 100 meters in diameter. In later experiments, Rutherford showed that the nucleus contained positively charged particles called protons.

Making a model atom

A gold atom has a diameter of about 3.32×10^{-10} m. The nucleus inside the atom is only about 1.46×10^{-14} m across.

Make a scale model of a gold atom. Find a field or a large room to represent the size of the atom and work out what size the nucleus should be on this scale.

The discovery of isotopes – atoms with nearly identical chemical properties but different atomic masses – suggested that nuclei could vary not only in the number of protons but also in some other way. Since a variation in the number of protons would result in a different element altogether, Rutherford suggested that there was another particle in the nucleus with no overall charge. The discovery of the neutron in 1932 confirmed that the nucleus of an atom is composed of two different particles: protons and neutrons.

Protons and neutrons both have a similar mass: the mass of a proton is 1.673×10^{-27} kg and a neutron has a mass of 1.675×10^{-27} kg. These masses are much bigger than the mass of an electron (by about 1,830 times). Often relative masses are used where the mass of a proton or neutron is just counted as one.

Protons have a positive charge of $+e$, in other words they have the same sized charge as an electron, but are positive rather than negative. Neutrons have no charge.

	Electron	Proton	Neutron
Charge (relative units)	−1	+1	0
Mass (relative units)	0.00055	1	1

Rutherford's model of the atom consisted of protons and neutrons in a nucleus at the center of the atom with the electrons orbiting around the nucleus.

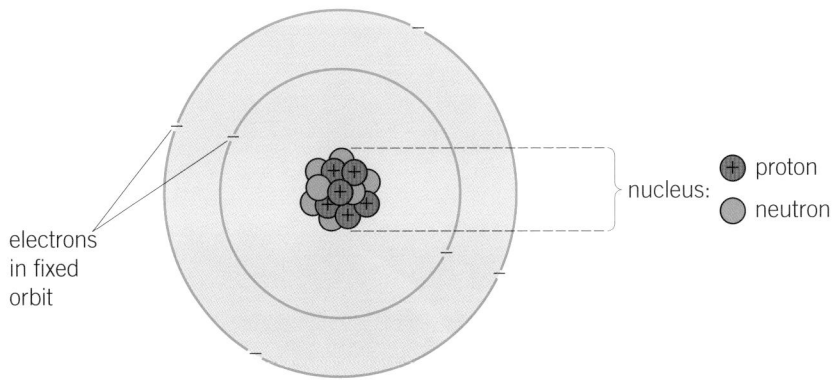

electrons in fixed orbit

nucleus:
⊕ proton
◯ neutron

In Rutherford's model of the atom, the nucleus consists of protons and neutrons, and the electrons are in fixed orbits around the nucleus. The overall atom has no charge, since there are the same number of electrons as protons

1 Why do you think that the electron was the easiest of these three particles to discover?

2 Why do you think the neutron might have been the hardest of these particles to discover?

3. Any given atom will have the same number of electrons as protons. For light elements it is likely to have the same number of neutrons as protons. For example, an atom of nitrogen taken from the air has seven protons and seven neutrons in its nucleus, and there are seven electrons which orbit around the nucleus. What proportion of the particles in the atom are electrons? What fraction of the mass is in the electrons?

What are isotopes?

The nucleus of the atom contains essentially all the mass of an atom, but it is about a hundred thousand times smaller than the whole atom. It is the electrons orbiting the nucleus which determine the size of the atom, and how it interacts with other atoms if they collide. This means that the electrons determine the chemical properties of an element. In fact almost all of what is studied in chemistry can be explained by the interaction of the electrons on the outside of atoms.

Atoms have an overall neutral charge, so an atom must have the same number of protons and electrons. An atom with more protons in its nucleus has more electrons, and these electrons experience a greater attractive force holding them around the nucleus. The electrons repel each other (see Chapter 2, Interaction, for why this is so) and some end up closer to the nucleus and some further away. This positioning of the electrons, their configuration, affects how atoms interact with each other. To summarize, atoms with different numbers of protons in their nucleus have different electron configurations, therefore they have different chemical properties.

The number of neutrons does not affect the number of electrons required to maintain a neutral charge, nor does it affect how the electrons interact with the nucleus. As a result, additional neutrons do not affect the configuration of the electrons and so there is no change to the chemical properties of the atom. The only difference is that the atom has a different mass on account of the additional neutrons.

▼ Analysis of rock from the Moon that was gathered during the Apollo missions shows that they have an almost identical mixture of the oxygen isotopes $^{16}_{8}O$, $^{17}_{8}O$ and $^{18}_{8}O$ to rocks on Earth. Since rocks from elsewhere in the solar system, such as asteroids, have different mixtures of these isotopes, this evidence points to the Moon and the Earth having a common origin. Astronomers believe that the Earth suffered a huge collision which blasted material into space and later formed the Moon. This model of the Moon's formation is called the giant impact hypothesis

Atoms of the same element, that is, with the same number of protons in the nucleus, but with differing numbers of neutrons are called isotopes. As a result of having the same number of protons, they have the same number of electrons and therefore the same chemical properties. The different number of neutrons gives them a different mass but does not affect the chemical properties.

1. The table below shows the numbers of particles in some different atoms.

Atom	Number of electrons	Number of protons	Number of neutrons
A	1	1	0
B	3	3	3
C	6	6	6
D	6	6	8
E	6	7	6

   a) Which two atoms are isotopes of each other?

   b) Which atom is charged (is an ion)?

   c) Which of these atoms is the most common in the universe?

   d) Which atom has the greatest mass?

What is atomic notation?

ATOMS

Elements are classified according to their chemical properties. As we have seen, these properties are governed by the configuration and number of the electrons which in turn are determined by the number of protons in the nucleus. The number of protons in the nucleus is called the atomic number.

The number of protons and neutrons in a nucleus determines the mass of an atom (since the electrons barely contribute to the mass). The total number of protons and neutrons is called the mass number.

A useful shorthand for describing the constituents of an atom is to use atomic notation. In atomic notation, the element is abbreviated to its chemical symbol and the atomic number and mass number are given in the format $^A_Z X$.

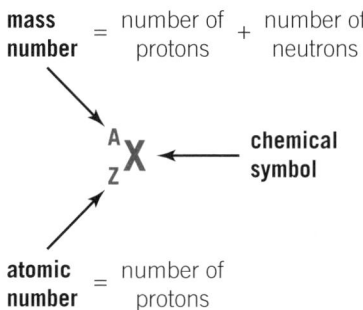

◀ Atomic notation

For example, the oxygen in the air has eight protons in its atomic nuclei.

- Most of these oxygen atoms will also have eight neutrons. This gives the oxygen an atomic number of 8 and a mass number of 16. We would write this in atomic notation as $^{16}_{8}O$.

- A very few atoms of oxygen (one in 2,700) have an extra neutron; these atoms are written as $^{17}_{8}O$. This is an isotope of oxygen since it still has eight protons and hence the eight electrons which give oxygen its chemical properties, but the number of protons (8) plus the number of neutrons (9) is now 17.

- About one in 500 oxygen atoms have ten neutrons; this isotope is written as $^{18}_{8}O$.

1. Here are some atoms written in atomic notation: $^{14}_{7}N$, $^{14}_{8}O$, $^{13}_{6}C$, $^{14}_{6}C$.

   a) Which atom has more protons than neutrons?

   b) Which atom has the most neutrons?

   c) Which two atoms are isotopes of each other?

   d) In a radioactive process, $^{14}_{6}C$ changes one of the neutrons in its nucleus into a proton. Which atom has it turned into?

ATOMS ## Is this atomic model correct?

The notion of atoms explains, among many other things, how gases exert pressure and why chemicals react in certain quantities. As a result, this model of atomic theory has been successful and scientists are happy with the idea that matter is made up of atoms. But is the Rutherford model of the atom correct?

The idea of a model being perfectly correct or not does not really matter, since the purpose of a model is to simplify a concept to make it easier to understand. Our idea of protons and neutrons in the nucleus with electrons orbiting around it helps us to explain why the electrons interact with other atoms and cause chemical reactions while the nucleus remains in the center of the atom and does not affect these. The masses of protons and neutrons enable us to explain isotopes. However, in simplifying the atom into an understandable model, it is inevitable that there will be some things which are lost in the simplification.

It turns out that electrons, and in fact all particles, can behave as waves as well as particles. The electrons in an atom act like a wave rather than a well-defined particle. Indeed, it is impossible to predict where an electron will be at any given time; we can only establish probabilities. This is quantum theory and it requires a more sophisticated model of the atom in which the electrons are waves.

The electron is a fundamental particle; that is, it cannot be split into anything smaller. Physicists have discovered that the proton and the neutron are not fundamental particles, but that they are made up of three quarks. During the 20th century, physicists discovered six different types of quarks as well as other electron-like particles. Just as chemists developed the periodic table and used this model to predict where elements were yet to be discovered, physicists developed a similar model of these fundamental particles. We call it the standard model and it has been used to predict the existence of particles such as the Higgs boson. It is the most successful theory of the universe that we have and yet it is only a model; for example, it cannot explain gravitation.

More complicated models of the atom using quantum mechanics are required to explain why different metals exhibit particular colors in a flame test

The Higgs boson

Peter Higgs used the standard model to predict the existence of a particle which was responsible for the other particles having mass. He predicted this particle's existence in 1964, but it was not discovered until 2012. In 2013 he was awarded the Nobel Prize along with François Englert.

Some Nobel prizes in physics are awarded for developing new models (often referred to as theories or laws), while others are for discoveries or technological innovations.

1. Research the Nobel prizes that have been awarded in physics and try to find one that was awarded for developing a model. Write a brief explanation for what the model explained.

2. Can you find two Nobel prizes that were awarded for other discoveries that are mentioned in this chapter?

ATL Affective skills

Practicing resilience

At many times, the existing model of the atom has been shown to be wrong. It would have been tempting to throw away the model and to start again. However, a simple model of an atom is still useful even if it is known to have limitations. A more complicated model may be harder to use but may not be necessary in many applications.

When faced with evidence which contradicts their models, scientists need resilience. Sometimes new discoveries are made when an existing model fails to explain an experimental result, therefore failure is an important process in science.

Can you think of a time when you have failed and been able to learn from the experience?

WAVES

What is a wave?

The complicated way in which electrons behave in an atom requires physicists to be able to model matter as sometimes being wave-like and sometimes particle-like. Particle-like behavior has been explained by the atomic model, but what is a wave and how do waves behave?

Sometimes in a football stadium, spectators create a Mexican wave by standing up and waving their arms at the right time. The effect is that a wave appears to move around the stadium quickly, but the spectators have not moved around the stadium, they have only moved up and down and remained in the same seat.

A Mexican wave is a good example of a wave. Waves transfer energy without transferring matter. This transfer of energy means that waves are also able to transfer information. We can see the wave move around the stadium; however, no matter has been transferred as the spectators all stay put in their original seats.

Light and sound are other examples of waves. In order to see and hear, when light and sound waves reach you, your eyes and ears need to detect the energy that is transferred. Just as with Mexican waves no matter is transferred, and so as you receive these waves, you do not get heavier.

▼ A Mexican wave

What types of wave are there?

There are two types of wave:

- transverse waves

- longitudinal waves.

In transverse waves the matter (or whatever medium the wave is traveling in) moves at right angles to the direction in which the wave is traveling. Waves on water are a good example of this (as are the Mexican waves discussed previously). When ripples travel across a pond, the surface of the water moves up and down but the wave travels along the surface of the pond at right angles to this. Once the ripple has passed, the water is left in the same position as it was before the wave came along because the water itself is not transferred by the wave. Electromagnetic waves (which are discussed in Chapter 12, Patterns), such as radio waves, X-rays and visible light, are transverse waves, as are the S-waves from earthquakes and waves which travel along strings or other surfaces.

In a longitudinal wave the matter moves parallel to the direction in which the wave travels. Sound is an example of this type of wave. When sound travels through air, a pressure wave is created. The particles of air are moved backwards and forwards in the same direction as the sound is traveling. After the wave has passed, the air particles are left in approximately their original positions because the wave has transferred energy through the air but not the actual air itself. Other compression waves, such as P-waves from earthquakes, are also longitudinal.

◀ In these waves on the surface of the pond, the water moves up and down but the wave travels along the surface of the water at right angles to the direction in which the individual molecules of water move

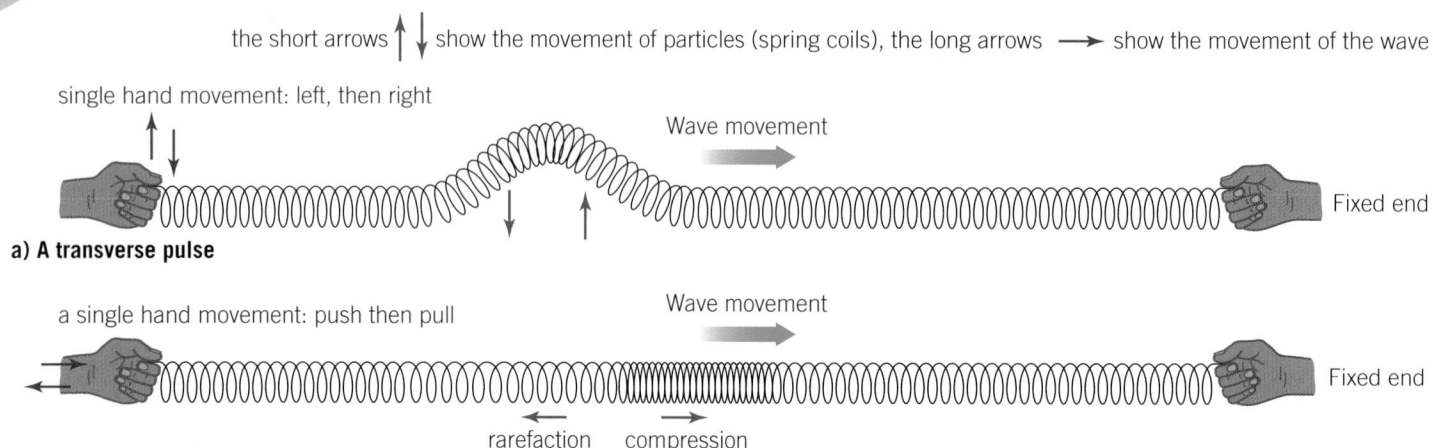

the short arrows ↑↓ show the movement of particles (spring coils), the long arrows ⟶ show the movement of the wave

single hand movement: left, then right

Wave movement

Fixed end

a) A transverse pulse

a single hand movement: push then pull

Wave movement

Fixed end

rarefaction   compression

b) A longitudinal pulse

▲ A slinky may be used to produce transverse and longitudinal waves. Moving your hand at right angles to the slinky creates a transverse wave pulse. As the pulse travels down the slinky, the individual coils move at right angles to the direction of the pulse. A push and pull motion, on the other hand, will create a longitudinal wave where the slinky coils move parallel to the direction of the wave

How do we measure waves?

▶ The amplitude of a wave is measured from the equilibrium position to the peak while the wavelength can be measured from peak to peak or from trough to trough

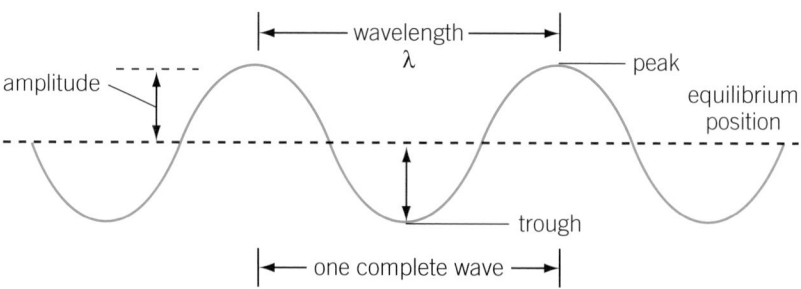

A typical wave is shown in the diagram – it could be a ripple on a pond. The dashed line shows the level of the pond's surface if there were no wave present. This is called the equilibrium position. The length of one complete wave is called the wavelength. This could be measured from the peak of one wave to the peak of the next, or from trough to trough. The maximum displacement that the wave has from the equilibrium is called the amplitude.

This picture only shows one moment in time; the wave will travel along the surface of the pond and as it does so the surface of the pond will move up and down. The time it takes a part of the pond's surface to complete an entire cycle of its motion (upwards, downwards and back to its original position) is called the time period of the wave.

The number of waves that pass by a given point in one second is called the frequency. Frequency is measured in Hertz (Hz) where

one Hertz means one wave per second. The frequency can also be calculated using the equation:

$$f = \frac{1}{T}$$

where f is the frequency and T is the time period.

The frequency of a wave and its wavelength are also related – longer waves take longer to pass and so the frequency is lower. The equation which relates these quantities is:

$$v = f\lambda$$

where v is the speed of a wave, f is the frequency and λ is the wavelength.

Observing waves on a slinky

With a partner, stretch a slinky along a long table or on the floor. Try sending these types of waves down the slinky.

- A longitudinal wave with a high frequency.

- A longitudinal wave with a small amplitude.

- A longitudinal wave with a low frequency and a high amplitude.

- A high-amplitude, low-frequency transverse wave.

- A low-amplitude, high-frequency transverse wave.

- A high-amplitude, high-frequency transverse wave.

- A low-amplitude, low-frequency transverse wave.

Experiment

For this experiment you will need a rectangular tray or plastic box, a stopwatch and a ruler.

Method

- Fill the tray with just enough water to cover its base to a depth of a couple of millimeters. Measure the depth of the water with a ruler.

- Give the side of the tray a sharp tap and observe the ripple travel across the tray. Measure the time it takes for the ripple to cross the tray. Repeat your measurements three times and take an average.

- Measure the length of the tray and use this to calculate the speed of the ripple across the tray.

- Repeat your measurements for different depths of water. Record your values of depth, time for the wave to cross the tray and wave speed in a table.

- Plot a graph of your results.

How does the speed of waves change in different depths of water?

1. The graph below shows the depth of water in a harbor as a wave passes through.

    a. From the graph, measure the wavelength of the wave.

    b. Determine the amplitude of the wave.

    c. The speed of the waves is 1.4 m s^{-1}. Calculate how long it takes a wave to pass a given point.

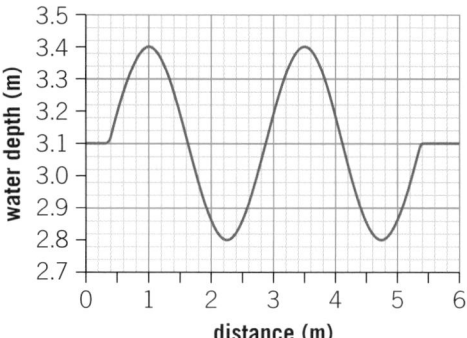

▲ Hokusai's 'The Great Wave off Kanagawa' is one of the most iconic images of a wave

Summative assessment

Statement of inquiry:

A good model can simplify and illuminate our understanding of complex phenomena.

Introduction

A nucleus is so tiny that is hard to study experimentally; it is impossible to use conventional techniques such as a microscope. This assessment is based on experiments to determine the size of the nucleus in atoms.

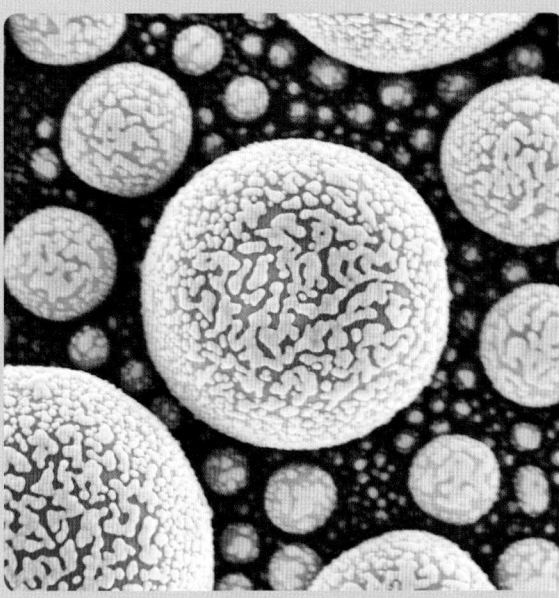

In this image, electrons with a small wavelength have been used to see the atoms of gold with a scanning electron microscope. Electrons with a much smaller wavelength would be required to observe the nuclei of these atoms

 Probing the atom

As a general rule, waves can only be used to see objects that are larger than the wavelength of the waves. Since the wavelength of visible light is about a thousand times larger than an atom, an optical microscope cannot be used to see individual atoms.

The nuclei of atoms are much smaller still and so we require waves with very small wavelengths to probe the nucleus of atoms. Electrons demonstrate both a wave-like and a particle-like behavior and since the wavelength of high energy electrons can be very small, they can be used to probe the nuclei of atoms.

In an experiment to measure the size of the nucleus of a gold atom, the wavelength of the electrons is 2×10^{-16} m and they are traveling at 3×10^8 m s^{-1}.

1. Calculate the frequency of the electron wave. [2]

2. Calculate the time period of the electron waves. [1]

3. The target nucleus in the experiment was gold which has a mass number of 197 and an atomic number of 79.

   a) Describe this nucleus in atomic notation. (The chemical symbol for gold is Au.) [2]

   b) How many neutrons are in the gold nucleus? [2]

4. Another isotope of gold has a mass number of 200. Explain what is meant by an isotope and how these nuclei differ from the gold-197 nuclei. [3]

5. Explain why the two gold isotopes have similar chemical properties. [3]

6. The electron waves are transverse. Describe the difference between a transverse wave and a longitudinal wave. [2]

 ## Investigating the nuclear radius

A series of experiments is designed to investigate other nuclear radii.

7. Explain which of the following you think would be the most suitable independent variable for the experiment:

   atomic number   mass number   number of electrons. [3]

8. Write a suitable hypothesis for this experiment. [4]

9. One suggestion is to investigate and measure the different radii of the isotopes of gold. Discuss whether this is a good suggestion. [5]

10. Explain why it might be important to use the same wavelength of electrons when measuring the differing nuclei. [3]

 ## The liquid drop model of the nucleus

11. The graph below shows the nuclear radius of some nuclei in femtometers (1 fm = 1 × 10⁻¹⁵ m).

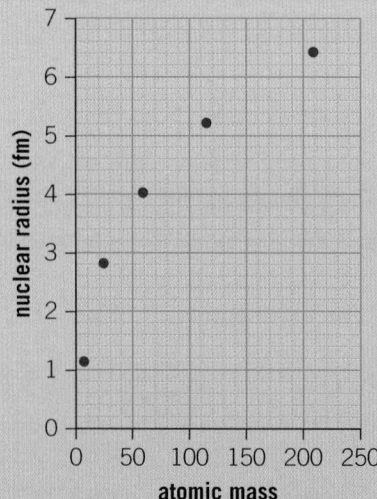

   a) Would you classify the trend of the graph as directly proportional, linear or non-linear? [1]

b) Draw a line of best fit on a copy of the graph. [1]

c) Use the graph to predict the radius of a nucleus of tungsten-184. [2]

12. A model of the nucleus called the liquid drop model suggests that the volume of a nucleus is directly proportional to the number of protons and neutrons in it.

A graph of the volume of nuclei against mass number is shown below.

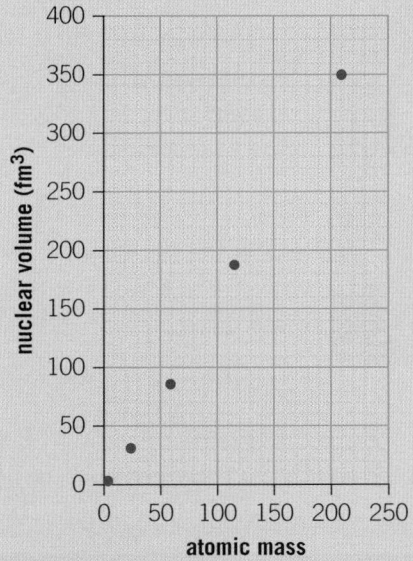

a) Using your value of the radius of tungsten-184 from the first graph, calculate the volume of this nucleus. (Assume that the nucleus is a sphere.) [4]

b) How would you classify the trend of this graph? [1]

c) Add this data point to a copy of the graph. [1]

d) Discuss whether the liquid drop model of the nucleus appears to be a good model. You should refer to the graph in your answer. [5]

 ## Describing the atom

13. The experiment described in this section can be described as nuclear physics since it is the study of the nucleus. However, the words "nuclear" and "atomic" are sometimes thought to refer to nuclear weapons and can cause fear as a result. Write a short paragraph explaining the structure of an atom without using the words "nuclear" or "atomic". [5]

14. Our increased knowledge of the structure of the atom and its nucleus have been a significant advance in scientific understanding. Identify the benefits and limitations that these scientific advances have brought us and justify whether this progress has been beneficial to humankind. [10]

The emblem of the International Atomic Energy Agency (IAEA) features a diagram of the Rutherford model of the atom. The IAEA promotes the safe, secure and peaceful use of nuclear science and technology

2 Interaction

◀ The social interactions we experience when we are young can shape our personality later in life. How is modern technology affecting the way in which we learn to interact with each other?

▼ In all music, interaction between the musicians is essential. In jazz music the musicians may be improvising, but by interacting with each other they are able to make a coherent piece of music. How do the musicians interact and communicate without speaking?

▲ A basic model in economics consists of the interaction between people and companies. People get jobs and form part of the workforce and consume goods while companies employ a workforce and supply goods. What happens when one part of this interaction fails?

◄ Animals can interact in different ways; some are predators while other animals are hunted. Other interactions between animals can be symbiotic where both animals gain from the relationship. The reef shark allows other fish near it to feed on parasites and dead skin. The fish get food and in return the shark gets a good clean. Are there any examples of humans forming symbiotic relationships with other animals?

Key concept: Relationships

Related concept: Interaction

Global context: Identities and relationships

Introduction

Without interactions, the universe would be a very dull place. Nothing could possibly change without interactions to cause that change to take place. However the universe started out would be how the universe would remain, forever. A universe with interactions, on the other hand, is a complex system of many objects all interacting and influencing each other. For this reason, the key concept of this chapter is relationships.

Scientists believe that all forces in the universe can be explained through only four fundamental interactions: electromagnetism, gravity, the strong interaction and the weak interaction. The strong and the weak interactions have an extremely short range – the strong interaction only acts over a few femtometers (1 femtometer is 10^{-15} m) and the weak interaction only acts over ranges about 100 times smaller than that. The short range of the weak and the strong interactions make them very hard to observe directly. The electromagnetic and gravitational interactions, on the other hand, have an unlimited range (although they get weaker at larger distances). This makes them easier to study.

The electromagnetic interaction accounts for the way light is emitted and the way we see it. It accounts for magnetism and electromagnetic induction. In this chapter we shall investigate electrostatic forces which are another part of the electromagnetic interaction.

▼ Physicists strive to explain the fundamental interactions of matter. This particle collision in the Large Hadron Collider is part of the ongoing experiments to unravel how these interactions take place

Statement of inquiry:

The way in which the universe changes is governed by fundamental interactions of matter.

Our experience of the universe often takes gravity for granted. For much of history humans have dreamed of escaping gravity and flying, and technology has enabled us to do so, however we often forget that the force of gravity is our most fundamental interaction with the planet upon which we live.

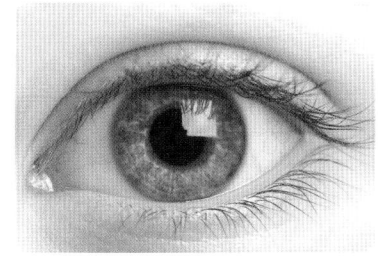

▲ The electromagnetic interaction allows us to see and interact with the outside world

▲ This picture shows the first unattached spacewalk which took place in 1984. The Earth still exerts a gravitational force on the astronaut but, because there are no other forces acting, he feels weightless. The sensation would be much like freefall, but with no air resistance and no frame of reference to show that he is falling

While electrostatic and gravitational interactions cause forces which are observable, the mechanism by which they work is invisible to us. This makes it hard for scientists to explain how these interactions work. Indeed even today, explaining how gravity and electromagnetism are related is one of the toughest challenges facing theoretical physicists.

We interact with the outside world through the electrostatic forces and gravity. Because these forces govern our perception of the world and our interaction with it, the global context of the chapter is identities and relationships. The interactions we experience throughout our lives with the outside world shape our relationship with it and so create the identities within which we live.

How does an apple help to explain gravity?

▶ This 19th century engraving depicts the story of Newton sitting under an apple tree and an apple landing on his head. The story is popular despite the fact that it almost certainly did not happen!

NEWTON AND HIS PIPE.

There is a story that Isaac Newton was sitting under an apple tree when an apple fell on his head. It is suggested that this event caused him to think about gravity and how the force that pulled the apple downwards was the same force that was responsible for keeping the Moon in orbit around the Earth and the planets in orbit around the Sun.

This event is unlikely to have actually happened and Newton never wrote of it at the time, although he seems to have developed the story and embellished it later in his life. However, the story was helpful to Newton in explaining how gravity worked. He reasoned that an apple fell directly downwards towards the center of the Earth because the Earth must exert a force. He also concluded that the apple should also draw the Earth up towards it, although the apple, being much smaller, would have a tiny and unmeasurable effect.

The importance of Newton's idea about gravity was that he thought that the same force that pulled the apple down to the ground also affected the way the planets moved. This meant that one force was able to account for many different effects over a large range of scales.

In order to account for the way in which gravity could cause the planets to orbit the Sun, Newton deduced that gravity's interaction would get weaker as it extended outwards away from the Earth. He reasoned that the force of gravity must be an inverse square law, that is, the force of gravity is inversely proportional to the square of the distance between the centers of mass of the two objects. This means that doubling the distance between two objects would cause the force of gravity between them to fall to a quarter of its initial strength.

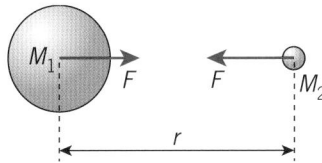

▲ The gravitational force between two objects is proportional to the two masses, M_1 and M_2, and inversely proportional to the square of the distance between their centers of mass

Newton's law of gravitation can be written as:

$$F = \frac{GM_1M_2}{r^2}$$

where M_1 and M_2 are the masses of the two objects between which the force of gravity F is acting, r is the distance between the centers of mass of the two objects and G is a constant with a value of $6.67 \times 10^{-11} \text{ m}^3 \text{ kg}^{-1} \text{ s}^{-2}$.

1. Use Newton's law of gravitation to calculate the force of gravity that would act between you and someone standing next to you. What does the size of this force say about how we notice the interaction of gravity?

2. The graph below shows how the force acting on a 1 kg object changes with its height above the Earth's surface. How high above the Earth's surface would you have to go for the gravitational force to have halved from its original strength on the ground?

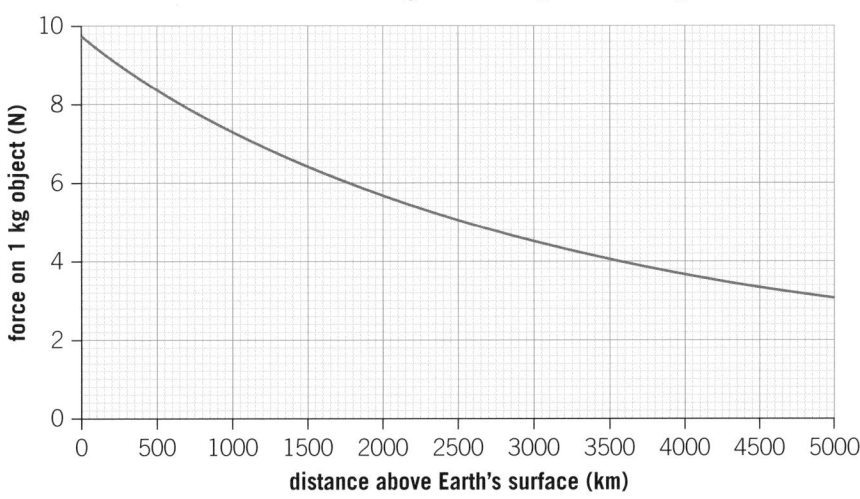

Comets

The Bayeux tapestry depicts the events leading up to the Norman conquest of England. The comet shown here maybe intended to foretell that the conquest wouldn't end well for King Harold: he was killed at the Battle of Hastings in 1066

Throughout history, comets have been associated with bad news. In 1664 a bright comet appeared over London. The following year, the plague struck, followed by the Great Fire of London.

In 1682 Edmund Halley observed a comet. Halley thought that the comet he saw was the same comet that had appeared in 1531 and again in 1608. Using Newton's law of gravitation and how this accounted for planetary orbits, Halley calculated the comet's orbit and this enabled him to demonstrate that the comets of 1682, 1608 and 1531 were indeed the same. He concluded that the comet returned periodically and that it was the same comet that is shown in the Bayeux tapestry. Halley predicted its return in 1758 and, although it was seen at the end of that year, Halley did not live to see it.

1. What is the length of time between appearances of Halley's comet?

2. Is this length of time always the same?

3. If the comet was seen in 1066 and 1682, how many times would it have been seen between these years?

4. Use your answer above to calculate an average for the length of time between appearances of Halley's comet.

5. When was Halley's comet last visible? When will it next be seen?

What is affected by gravity?

What Newton had realized was that gravity is a force between any two objects with mass. However, the interaction between everyday objects is so tiny that it is hardly detectable. Unless at least one object is planet-sized or heavier, the forces go unnoticed.

Any object creates a gravitational field around it. A field is a volume of space in which objects experience a force, in this case the force of gravity. For small objects, this gravitational field is undetectable; however, when an object is sufficiently large (such as a planet or a star) its gravitational field is large enough to be measurable. Any object with a mass that is in this gravitational field will experience the force of gravity. It is because of the Earth's gravitational field that objects around it are pulled downwards to the ground.

The gravitational forces between the Earth and other objects can act over large distances, although the force gets weaker the further the object is from the Earth. By the time you get as far away as the Moon, the gravitational field from the Earth is only about 3% of what it is at the surface of the Earth, but it is still strong enough to hold the Moon in orbit and stop it drifting away into space.

The Moon is also a large mass so it has an observable gravitational field of its own. Although this gravitational field is weaker than the Earth's, it still interacts with us even at that great distance. The force of the Moon's gravity causes tides in the oceans to rise and fall.

The Sun is many times more massive than the Moon: 27 million times heavier. Its gravitational field dominates the solar system and pulls all planets, asteroids and comets into orbits around it.

However, even the Sun's gravitational field is dwarfed by that of the galaxy. The center of the galaxy is about 25,000 light years away. At the center of the galaxy, there are many stars as well as the supermassive black hole Sagittarius A* which is about 4 million times heavier than the Sun. Despite being so far away, the gravitational field of these objects keeps the Sun in its path around the galaxy. The gravitational field stretches out even further and interacts with the nearest galaxies to us, even though some of them are millions of light years away.

▼ Even though the Andromeda galaxy is 2.5 million light years away, gravity causes it to be dragged towards our galaxy, the Milky Way. What will happen to the force of gravity between the two galaxies as they get closer?

ATL Thinking in context

How does weight shape our identity?

Our weight is the gravitational interaction of our bodies with the Earth. Because people are different sizes, they have different weights and this interaction can shape our identity. While it is important to be a healthy weight, our own perception of our weight is also important. When this perception is not healthy, it can cause anxiety or eating disorders which can be dangerous.

FORCES

What do we mean by weight?

On the surface of the Earth, we are always almost the same distance from the center of the Earth: about 6,400 km. Even the highest mountain is only a thousandth of this distance. As a result the gravitational field at any point on the Earth's surface is approximately the same. We call this a uniform gravitational field which means that all objects interact with the Earth's gravitational field with the same strength and in the same direction.

The Earth's gravitational field is approximately 9.8 N kg^{-1}, meaning that every kilogram of mass has a force of 9.8 N acting on it. The force of gravity upon an object is called its weight and can be calculated using the equation:

$$W = mg$$

where W is the weight, m is the mass of the object and g is the gravitational field strength.

Of course, if we were not on the Earth, the gravitational field strength would be different. On Mars, $g = 3.7$ N kg^{-1} and on the Moon it is only 1.6 N kg^{-1}.

1. Calculate your weight on Earth.

2. What would your weight be on Mars where $g = 3.7$ N kg^{-1}?

How would we evolve in different gravitational fields?

Life on Earth has evolved in a uniform gravitational field of 9.8 N kg^{-1}. Newly discovered exoplanets (planets that orbits a star other than the Sun) have potentially habitable environments but different gravitational fields. Trappist-1c is predicted to have a gravitational field of about 8 N kg^{-1}.

1 How might the evolution of life forms be affected by a different gravitational field?

What is the difference between weight and mass?

People often confuse the terms mass and weight. When we weigh an object we are really measuring its downwards force due to gravity. However, a set of weighing scales does not give you a reading in Newtons as it should; instead it gives an answer in grams or kilograms which is the unit of mass.

The difference is more easily seen if you think about objects on a different planet or even in space. As an example, consider a brick which has a mass of 3 kg. On Earth its weight is $3 \times 9.8 = 29.4$ N. On the Moon where $g = 1.6$ N kg^{-1} the brick will still have a mass of 3 kg, but its weight is now only $3 \times 1.6 = 4.8$ N. On Earth this is equivalent to the weight of an object with a mass of only 0.5 kg (as 0.5×9.8 is approximately 4.8). The brick still has the same amount of matter and hence the same amount of mass, but it is not being pulled downwards as much because the Moon's mass is less than that of the Earth.

If you took the brick deep into space, away from any planets or stars, so that the gravitational field was essentially zero, then the brick would be weightless and it would not experience any downward force. It would still have 3 kg of mass though. In this situation you could do an easy experiment to see the difference between mass and weight. You could float up to the brick and, if you thought that mass and weight were the same, you might be persuaded to give the brick a big kick. You would hurt your foot because although the brick is weightless, it still has mass and hence inertia!

Data-based question: Making bread on the Moon

A recipe for bread has the following ingredients:

- 500 g flour
- 330 g water
- 40 g oil
- 7 g salt
- 7 g yeast

Suppose that in the future, astronauts going to the Moon take this recipe and a set of weighing scales in order to make bread when they arrive. They know that gravity on the Moon is about six times weaker than on Earth.

1. They decide that they should they still measure the same mass of flour on the Moon rather than the same weight. Will this give them the same sized loaf of bread?

2. They know that their weighing scales measure weight but give a measurement of mass. Adapt the recipe's amounts so that they can use their weighing scales from Earth to make a similar loaf of bread on the Moon.

3. Will the weaker gravity affect any other parts of the baking process?

Data-based question: Dark matter

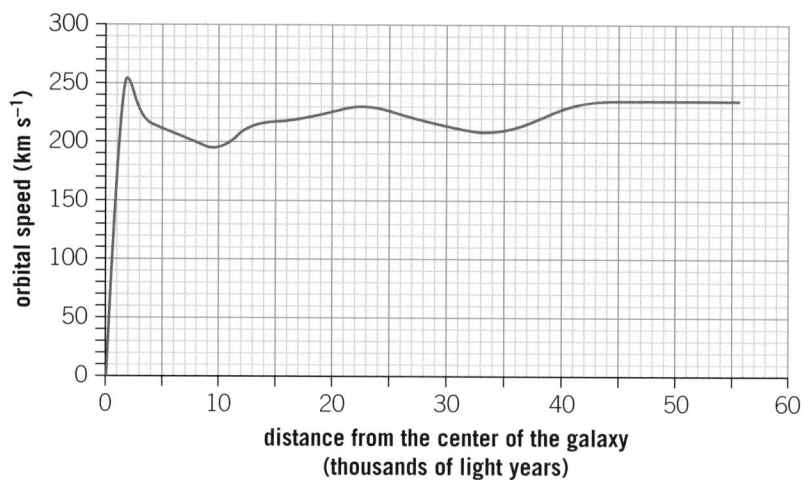

The graph shows the orbital speed of stars in the Milky Way galaxy at different distances from the centre of the galaxy.

1. The Sun is about 25,000 light years from the center of the galaxy. Use the graph to determine the Sun's orbital speed.

The mass which causes an object to orbit can be found using the equation:

$$M = \frac{rv^2}{G}$$

where M is the mass which is causing things to orbit it, r is the radius of the orbit, v is the orbital speed (in m s^{-1}) and G is a constant with a value of 6.67×10^{-11} m^3 kg^{-1} s^{-2}.

2. One light year is 9.5×10^{15} m. Find the distance from the Sun to the center of the galaxy in meters.

3. Use this value and the equation above to calculate the mass causing the Sun to orbit around the galaxy.

4. It is estimated that the mass of stars keeping the Sun orbiting the galaxy is about 5×10^{10} solar masses (1 solar mass = 2×10^{30} kg). Calculate the mass of stars in the galaxy.

5. How does this answer compare to the total mass you calculated in the galaxy?

In order to explain the Sun's fast motion around the galaxy, there must be extra mass causing a larger gravitational field. Despite accounting for stars, planets, clouds of gas and black holes, scientists still cannot find enough mass. Hence, there must be something else in the galaxy that we cannot see or detect: dark matter. It's estimated there is about five times more dark matter than normal matter in the universe and yet we cannot detect it!

Does gravity account for all interactions between matter?

Any object with mass interacts through gravity. Since almost everything in the universe has mass, this means that almost everything is affected by gravity. Even photons of light, which have no mass, can be deflected by a strong gravitational field. However, there are other ways in which matter can interact.

You can stick a balloon to a wall or ceiling by rubbing a balloon on a sweater. This requires an interaction other than gravity. The force responsible for this is the electrostatic force, a part of the electromagnetic interaction which acts between objects which have a charge.

Most objects are neutrally charged, at least most of the time, and so we do not often directly experience electrostatic forces; however, we sometimes experience the interactions which occur when charges build up. Sometimes, walking across a certain type of carpet in certain shoes will cause you to experience a small electric shock when you touch a door handle. You might experience similar effects if you jump on a trampoline or get out of a car. The interaction of your feet on certain surfaces or car tires on the road causes an electric charge to build up and you can feel it discharge; you may even see a small spark which is further evidence of an interaction between the two.

Knowledge of electrostatic force dates to at least ancient Greece. The ancient Greeks were aware that rubbing amber (fossilized tree resin) against fur enabled it to attract small objects such as a hair to it. The ancient Greek word for amber is "electron" and it is from this that we get the word "electricity".

▼ Rubbing a balloon on a sweater can cause it to become charged. As a result, it is able to deflect the stream of water from the tap

Later investigations showed that different materials responded differently to being rubbed against each other. In general, natural materials such as leather, fur and indeed human hair or skin, when rubbed against plastic such as polystyrene, polythene or rubber provide a strong electrostatic interaction.

How does rubbing two objects together charge things up?

In all of the examples above, two different materials come into contact and interact with each other. When two objects come into contact, electrons on the outside of atoms at the surface can be removed from their atoms (see Chapter 1, Models, for more on the structure of the atom). The electrons are negatively charged and the atoms, which were originally neutral, are left with a positive charge.

If two materials come into contact with each other, one of these materials is likely to gain electrons from the other. The material which gains electrons becomes negatively charged while the material which loses electrons becomes positively charged. Both materials have the same magnitude of charge because for every electron gained by one material, an electron is lost by the other. The number of electrons transferred depends on the nature of the two materials and how they interact. Rubbing two surfaces together increases the interaction between the two materials and increases the number of electrons transferred.

Some materials are conductors. In these materials, electrons can move easily. It is for this reason that electricity flows through metal wires. If two conducting materials are rubbed together then any electrons transferred between them quickly flow back and the two materials do not become charged.

Other materials do not allow electrons to move through them as easily; these materials are called insulators. If two materials that are insulators are rubbed together any electrons that are transferred from one material to the other stay there. This leaves one material with an excess of electrons so it is negatively charged. The other material is lacking in electrons and is positively charged.

The protons and neutrons in the nucleus of the atom do not normally get moved in this process. They are much heavier than the electrons and are therefore harder to move.

The triboelectric series

The triboelectric series is a list of different materials ranked in order of how good they are at snatching electrons off another material. Materials which acquire a negative charge are good at taking electrons whereas materials which acquire a positive charge easily lose electrons. Natural materials tend to give up electrons whereas plastics tend to acquire electrons.

Become positively charged								Neutral	Become negatively charged			
Human hands	Rabbit fur	Glass	Human hair	Nylon	Wool	Silk	Cotton		Rubber	Polyester	Polythene	Silicone rubber

1. You take off a polyester sweater in the dark and notice some sparks. Why does this not happen to the same extent with a woolen sweater?

2. Human hands are very good at acquiring charge; however, a little bit of moisture or sweat stops this effect. Why is this?

3. When you jump up and down on a rubber trampoline, friction can cause you to become positively charged and the trampoline becomes negatively charged. Which surface has gained electrons and which surface has lost some electrons?

◀ Jumping on a trampoline causes charge to be moved. As a result, these girls have gained a charge

How do charged objects interact?

If you rub a balloon on your hair, you transfer charge between the balloon and your hair. According to the triboelectric series, the balloon becomes negatively charged and your hair becomes positively charged. You should also notice a small force between your hair and the balloon; your hair is attracted to the balloon and the balloon might even stick to your hair. The reason for this is that there is an electrostatic force between your hair and the balloon.

Once two objects are charged, they interact with each other through the electrostatic force. This force depends on how far apart the charged objects are: the closer they are, the stronger the force. The electrostatic force also depends on the amount of charge the objects have. If the objects have more charge, then the force is greater.

The electrostatic force depends on whether the charges are positive or negative. In the case of rubbing a balloon against your hair, your hair becomes positively charged and the balloon becomes negatively charged. Whenever two objects have opposite charges, the force is attractive. On the other hand, two objects with the same type of charge (both positive or both negative) will repel each other. You may notice that even without the balloon nearby, your hair may stand up on end a little. This is because each hair has a slight positive charge so your hairs repel each other. They stand up as they try to separate from each other.

How can charged objects attract to neutrally charged objects?

If you rub a balloon against your hair or against a woolen sweater, you may be able to stick it to the ceiling. This may seem puzzling as although the balloon has charge as we have seen, the ceiling does not and so there should not be a force between the two.

The balloon is able to induce a charge in the ceiling through an effect called induction. The balloon is negatively charged and when it is brought close to the ceiling, the electrons in the ceiling are repelled from the balloon because they are also negatively charged. The electrons are not able to move very far unless the ceiling is a conductor, however they are able to move a little bit. Since the negatively charged electrons are now a little bit further away from the balloon than the positively charged nuclei, their repulsive force is less than the attractive force between the nuclei and the balloon. The balloon and the ceiling now have a small attractive force.

Van de Graaff generator

A device which makes use of charging objects is a Van de Graaff generator. This has two rollers with a rubber band stretched between them. In some designs, the roller at the bottom is made of nylon

and the top roller is made of polythene. When the rubber belt rolls over the nylon roller it becomes negatively charged and carries the negative charge upwards. When the band rolls over the polythene roller, the negative charge is transferred to the polythene roller. In this way, negative charge is moved upwards from the nylon roller to the polythene roller.

The polythene roller is connected to a metal dome. The electrons are able to move through the metal dome and so the charge builds up on the outside of it.

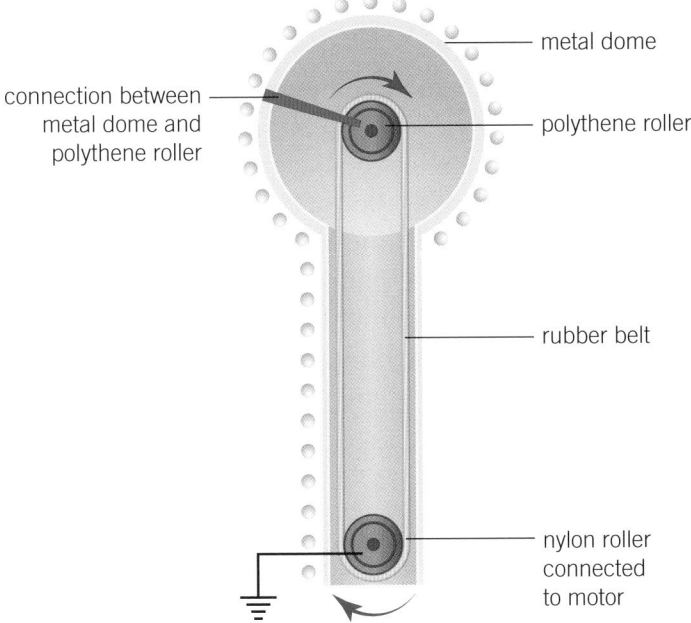

▲ Van de Graaff generator

As the charge builds up, the forces on the atoms in the air around the dome increase. The electrons in the atoms get repelled from the negatively charged dome while the positively charged protons in the nucleus are attracted to the dome. If the force from the dome is small, then the attractive force between the protons and electrons is big enough to hold the atom together. However, if the dome has a high enough charge, the outermost electron will be dragged off the atoms in the air and these atoms become ionized.

When this happens a spark is formed. The positive ions drift towards the dome (they are heavier than the single electrons therefore they move more slowly). When they reach the dome, they take one of the electrons from the dome and become neutrally charged atoms. The electrons travel to a nearby object; this is the spark. The nearby object will have a small positive charge through the process of induction described above so the electrons will be attracted to it. The nearer the object, the greater the induced charge will be on it and so the electrons will be more attracted to nearer objects. This is why sparks tend to travel to the nearest object.

What links the electromagnetism and gravity interactions?

In this chapter, you have seen how gravity causes masses to interact with each other and how electrostatic forces cause an interaction between charges. In many ways, these fundamental interactions are similar, but there are also some key differences. Electrostatic forces can attract and repel objects, but gravity can only ever attract. This is because charge can be positive or negative, but we only ever find things with positive mass (even antimatter has a positive mass). This causes scientists to ask why mass has to be positive.

Another major difference between the two interactions is their relative strengths. Simply rubbing a balloon on your sweater can be enough to stick it to the ceiling. This small electrostatic force is therefore strong enough to overpower the gravitational pull of the entire Earth on the same balloon. This causes scientists to question why gravity is seemingly so weak. One puzzling solution is that there may be more dimensions of space than the three dimensions we experience. If gravity spread into these dimensions but other forces did not, this could account for gravity's observed weakness.

Although scientists believe that electromagnetism and gravity interactions are related, to investigate this requires accelerating particles to high energies in particle accelerators and colliding them. Experiments like the Large Hadron Collider at CERN look for evidence for these theories.

1 Can you describe any other similarities or differences between electrostatic and gravitational forces?

2 Investigating these fundamental interactions requires huge experimental collaborations like CERN, which involves 22 countries and has an operating budget of about $1 billion per year. Discuss the economic arguments for and against spending such vast sums of money on scientific research.

Summative assessment

Statement of inquiry:

The way in which the universe changes is governed by fundamental interactions of matter.

Introduction

Lightning is one of the most powerful and impressive weather phenomena. Even though it occurs on a large scale, the principles of how lightning works are essentially the same as the way in which a Van de Graaff generator produces a spark. In this assessment we will investigate some of the processes involved in lightning.

How does lightning occur?

Inside a thunder cloud, ice crystals collide and transfer charge between themselves. Even though the ice crystals are made of the same material, heavier crystals tend to acquire a negative charge while smaller ice crystals become positively charged. The larger, negatively charged ice crystals sink to the bottom of the thunder cloud and the positively charged ice crystals float to the top.

When the bottom of the thunder cloud has enough charge, it starts to induce a positive charge in the ground underneath it. Atoms in the air experience opposite forces on them as the electrons are pulled towards the ground, while the protons in the atomic nucleus are pulled upwards. When these forces are large enough to pull an electron off the atom, a spark occurs. On this large scale, the spark is a bolt of lightning.

▲ Charged thunderclouds can cause lightning

1. When lightning strikes, the bottom of the thunder cloud is negatively charged. Determine the direction in which the electrons will travel. [2]

2. Explain why the electric field will pull the electrons and the nuclei of air molecules in different directions. [3]

3. The presence of the negatively charged thunder cloud causes the ground to acquire a positive charge by a process caused induction. Explain how this works. [5]

4. A thunder cloud may have a mass of about 2×10^6 kg. Calculate the weight of this thunder cloud. (Use $g = 9.8$ N kg^{-1}.) [2]

5. Two thunder clouds with an electric charge will interact with each other through electrostatic and gravitational forces. Which of these interactions would you expect to exert the larger force? Justify your answer. [2]

6. If the thunder clouds both had the same charge, determine whether they would attract or repel. [1]

▲ A Van de Graff generator

Thunder and lightning

A student wants to investigate the link between thunder and lightning. They design an experiment with a Van de Graaff generator. They plan to measure the loudness of the sound of the spark and compare it with the distance that the spark travels.

7. What is the dependent variable in this experiment? [1]

8. Suggest one control variable for this experiment and justify the reason for your choice. [3]

9. Formulate a hypothesis for this experiment. Explain the reasons for your hypothesis. [5]

10. Write a method for this experiment including any measurements that should be taken. [6]

An experiment to model lightning

The table below shows data for an experiment with a Van de Graaff generator. The Van de Graaff generator was charged and a spark crossed from its dome across to another smaller dome which was earthed. The student changed the distance between the two domes and measured the number of sparks that occurred in a minute.

Distance (cm)	Number of sparks per minute		
2	31	27	22
4	9	16	13
6	9	6	12
8	5	8	7
10	5	5	6

11. Plot the data and draw a line of best fit on your graph. [4]

12. Explain why is it important to take repeats in this experiment. [2]

13. Determine the distance between the domes at which you would expect to get one spark every 10 s. [2]

14. Describe the trend of the results and comment on the reliability. [3]

15. Identify one limitation of this experiment and suggest how it might be improved. [4]

Avoiding lightning

16. The taller a building is, the greater the risk of a lightning strike. What solutions to this problem are there? [2]

17. Carrying an umbrella in a thunderstorm is dangerous, particularly on flat open spaces. Write a paragraph to explain the dangers of this using scientific language in a way that a non-scientist could understand. [2]

The following text comes from a paper by Kuldip Acharya and Dibyendu Goshal entitled "Flower inspired thunder protecting umbrella". It was published on page 136 of the journal "Proceedings of the International Conference on Simulation and Modeling Methodologies, Technologies and Applications" on 1 January 2016.

The present study has dealt with an innovative idea regarding thunder protecting umbrella. The proposed umbrella can be folded and unfolded smoothly, and an animation algorithm is made to mimic the blooming of flower petals. The proposed umbrella is capable of protecting the user from any thunderstorm or lightning of any magnitude by providing a shielded conducting chord from the apex of the umbrella to the conducting spikes fitted at the bottom most layer of the shoe. The use of such an umbrella may be expected to provide a sound protection of the user to move within frequent thunder fall and lightning. The function of the proposed umbrella has been shown through computer animation. The movement of the user is easy in the presence of long flexible thin cable with appropriate connector jacks. The proposed design if manufactured at an industrial level may find some commercial utility also.

18. Give a reference for this paper that would be suitable for a bibliography. [1]

19. Describe the problem that is being solved here. [2]

20. Describe the advantages and disadvantages of this solution [4]

21. The text states that the function of the umbrella "has been shown through computer animation". Explain why it might be that the umbrella has not been tested in real life, and comment on the ethics of testing this umbrella with people. [4]

Evidence

▲ A popular question of interest in the 1870s was whether horses ever had all four hooves off the ground at the same time when running. Artists often painted horses with their front legs pointing forwards and their rear legs backwards, but no-one knew if this actually happened. Photographer Eadweard Muybridge decided to gather evidence to answer this question by setting up a series of cameras that were triggered by a thread as a galloping horse passed. The resulting images show that all four of the horse's hooves do leave the ground, but only when the hooves are underneath its body, not outstretched as the artists had been depicting. The evidence caused artists to change the way in which they drew horses. Why is photographic evidence compelling?

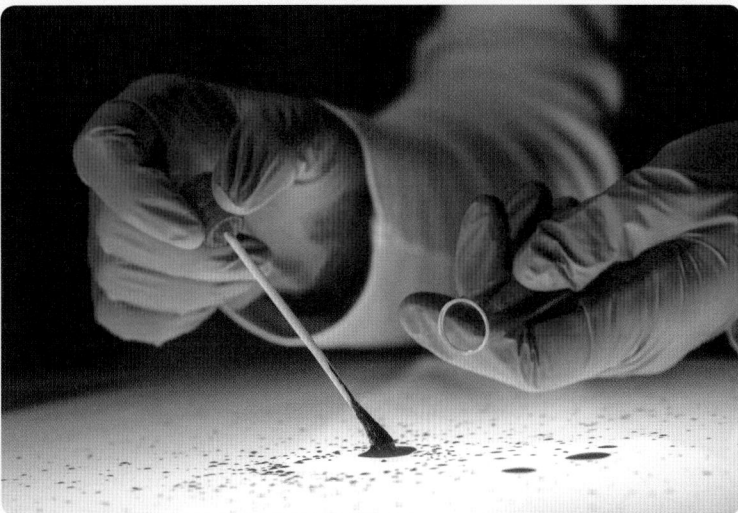

▲ DNA traces left at the scene of a crime can provide evidence in a trial. What does the DNA evidence actually prove?

◄ The giant squid has been the subject of myth for thousands of years, yet almost nothing was known about it as the only evidence of its existence was from dead specimens washed up on the shore or fragments found in the stomachs of sperm whales. The first observation of live animals did not occur until the beginning of the 21st century. Was it necessary to see a live animal in order to prove its existence?

▲ The possibility of climate change is a major threat to the human race. Many people believe that climate change is caused by humans; however, providing conclusive evidence that can persuade all scientists and politicians alike has proven difficult, and so the issue remains controversial. Why might scientists and politicians be persuaded by different forms of evidence?

Key concept: Relationships

Related concept: Evidence

Global context: Identities and relationships

▼ In the 1960s scientists theorized the existence of the Higgs boson; however, the theory could not be confirmed until the particle's discovery in 2012. Nobel Prizes cannot be awarded until there is sufficient evidence, so the prize was not given until 2013

Introduction

Scientists try to explain how and why things happen. In physics, we are concerned with the way the universe works, and physicists develop theories to explain the underlying mechanisms of nature. Some theories and hypotheses may seem to be common sense whereas other theories may make claims that seem bizarre. The test of the truth of these theories is whether there is sufficient evidence to support them.

Theories make predictions about the outcome of experiments and suggest how one factor may change another. It is important to measure the extent and the nature of these effects. In this chapter we will see some of the different ways in which variables can be related. For this reason, the key concept of this chapter is relationships.

In this chapter, we will also see how scientific evidence has changed the way we think about the universe. Rather than a never-changing emptiness, we now believe that the universe exploded into existence in the Big Bang and has been expanding ever since. Because scientific evidence caused us to rethink the identity of the universe, the global context is identities and relationships.

Statement of inquiry:

Experiments and measurements provide evidence to support or disprove scientific claims.

Why do we do experiments?

One of the most important aspects of science is that of developing ideas or theories and then testing them with experiments. In Chapter 9, Development, we see how to design an experiment with a view to testing a hypothesis, but how do we draw conclusions from the results of an experiment?

Most experiments involve measurements. Rather than looking at a table of measurements, it is often helpful to plot a graph of them as this makes it easier to spot a trend in the data. Usually we plot the independent variable (the quantity which you actively change) on the x-axis and the dependent variable (the one which you are investigating how it changes) is plotted on the y-axis.

Imagine an experiment in which you investigate how the mass of a ball bearing affects the time it takes for it to roll down a slope. You might make a hypothesis that a heavier ball bearing will roll down the slope in less time than a lighter one because the force of gravity is greater on the heavier ball bearing.

The results of your experiment might look like this:

Mass of ball bearing (g)	Time taken (s)
1	1.07
2	0.96
5	1.04
10	0.99
20	1.01

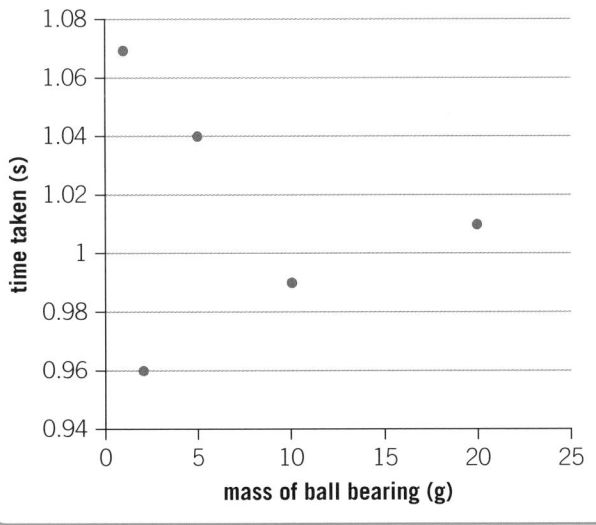

The results of the experiment are the evidence which either supports or contradicts the hypothesis. If you look at the values on the y-axis you can see that all of the balls rolled down the ramp in about one second. So does this mean that the mass of the ball bearing has no effect on the time taken for it to roll down the slope? The experiment suggests that this might be the case, but the evidence is not very strong.

Presenting data in a graph

The scale of a graph does not necessarily have to start from the origin; however, the graph will appear very different if this is the case. The graph in the example on the previous page could be plotted with the *y*-axis starting from zero and it would look like this:

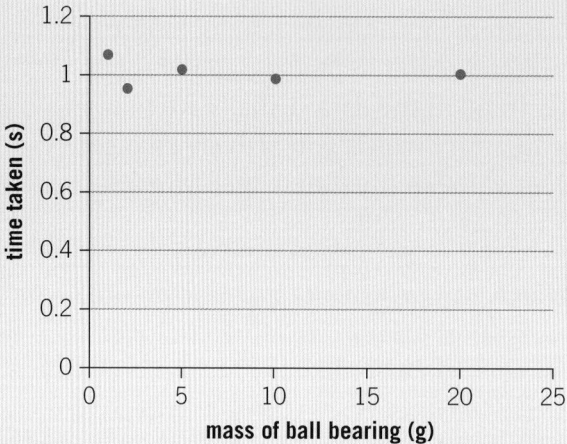

It is clearer that all the balls rolled down in about one second, but it is harder to see any trends within that range as most of the graph is empty.

Scientists often choose the axes of graphs to make the points spread over most of the graph but they are not the only ones to communicate data using graphs. Many communicators choose the axes of graphs to emphasize a point.

For example, if a magazine sold 91,000 copies in a month and its nearest rival sold 83,000 copies, different axes can make the sales look very different at first glance.

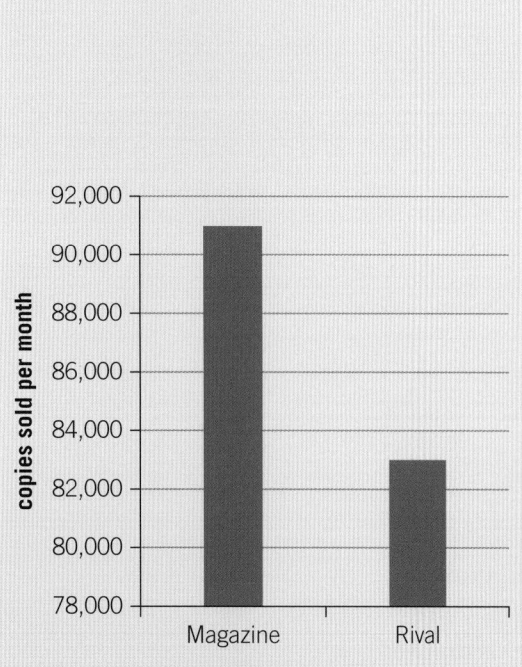

▲ In this chart it appears that the magazine has vastly outsold its rival

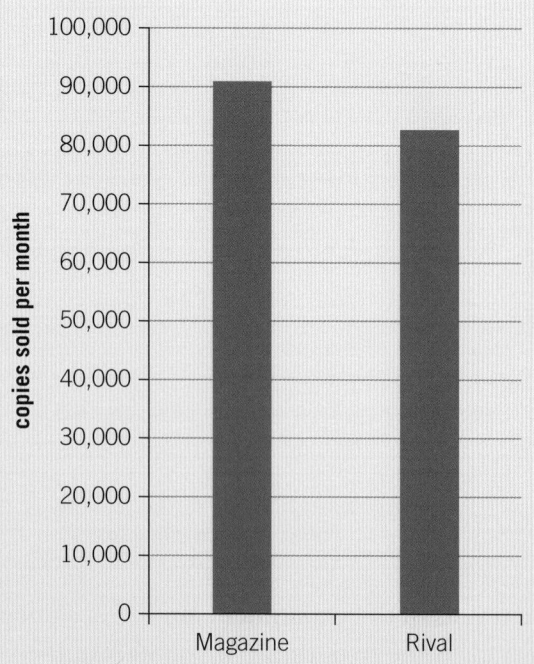

▲ If the origin is included, then it becomes clear that both magazines sold very similar numbers of copies

Presenting data

Two rival companies publish their yearly sales revenue (in millions of US dollars). The figures for the previous years are shown in the table below.

Year	Company A	Company B
2012	439	507
2013	472	486
2014	508	459
2015	524	452
2016	556	493
2017	587	574

1. Imagine that you work for Company A. Try to present the data in such a way that emphasizes that your company is the best.

2. Now imagine that you work for Company B. How might you change the presentation to show your company to be more successful?

3. Why is it important for scientists to try to present their data in as unbiased a way as possible?

What constitutes strong evidence? MEASUREMENT

Testing a die

With a perfect die you should have an equal chance of rolling any of the numbers on its faces. A weighted die has an increased chance of rolling one of the numbers (often a six). If you take a die and roll it once, does this tell you anything about whether it is weighted or not?

If you now roll it six times, the chances that each roll will give you a different number are about 1.5%. Does this mean that the die is weighted?

If you then roll the die more times and record the results in a table, how many times would you need to roll the die before you had enough evidence to say whether or not the die is weighted?

When evaluating the strength of evidence scientists consider its reliability and validity.

Validity is whether the experiment properly investigates the variables it set out to in a fair way. In order for an experiment to be valid, the independent variable should be investigated over a suitable range and all the relevant control variables should be accounted for.

If we had only investigated ball bearings of masses 10 g, 11 g and 12 g, then the investigation would not have given valid results because the range of masses would have been too limited and would not have enabled a sound conclusion to be drawn. If we had not kept the length of the ramp the same, then the measured times would have been longer for longer ramps and the results would have been invalid as the ramp length would have affected the measured times.

Reliability is a term used to describe whether subsequent experiments are likely to agree with the original experiment. A reliable experiment would always give similar results. We can consider reliability in two ways:

- Reliability of the trend: If all your data follow a good trend with no data points far off your line of best fit, then it would be reasonable to assume that if you took another data point it would also lie close to the trend line. This means that the trend is reliable.

- Reliability of the data: It is important to repeat the experiment. If you took a certain data point three times and got similar results each time, then we could assume that if we repeated the experiment a fourth time, the results would probably also be similar. The data can therefore be described as reliable. On the other hand, if your results vary significantly each time, then they are not reliable.

Our earlier experiment on rolling different balls down a ramp seems to be valid, but we cannot say if the results are reliable or not unless we repeat our measurements. If we do this, we might get data like this:

Mass of ball bearing (g)	Time taken (s)			Average
	1st reading	2nd reading	3rd reading	
1	1.09	1.02	1.05	1.053
2	0.94	1.07	1.02	1.01
5	1.09	1.02	0.95	1.02
10	1.02	0.93	0.98	0.977
20	1.04	0.95	0.95	0.98

We are now able to see that the data are in fact reasonably reliable. The variation in each set of readings is between 0.07 and 0.14 s which is much smaller than the measured times which are all about 1 s. This variation is about the same as the total variation in the times between all the different ball bearings. The evidence does not show a significant variation in the time taken for the different ball bearings to roll down the slope, and so the evidence contradicts the hypothesis.

This experiment is similar to one conducted by Galileo in which he dropped balls from the Leaning Tower of Pisa. Galileo's experiment showed that balls of different masses fell at the same rate. Similarly, the different ball bearings roll down the slope at the same speed. Even though a ball bearing with twice the mass of another has twice the weight pulling it downwards, using Newton's equation $F = ma$, we can see that if the force is doubled and the mass is also doubled, then the acceleration will remain the same. As a result, the ball bearings will all roll down the slope with the same acceleration and will reach the bottom in the same time.

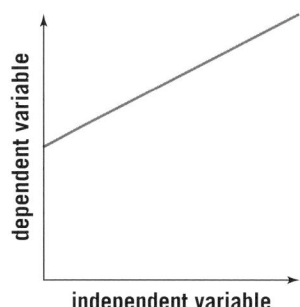

▲ Linear: The graph is a straight line but does not pass through the origin

Data-based question: Car testing

A car manufacturer is testing a new design of car. They want to know how much CO_2 is emitted for every kilometer it drives. They test it three times and get measurements of 147 g km^{-1}, 157 g km^{-1} and 143 g km^{-1}.

1. What is the average amount of CO_2 emitted per kilometer driven?

2. The manufacturer states that the car emits less than 150 g km^{-1}. Is this a reliable statement?

Measuring height

In your class, ask three people to independently measure the same person's height using a meter rule. Do all three measurements agree? How reliable are your measurements?

You may have noticed that in the ball bearing experiment there appears to be a slight downwards trend in the data. Even though the times do not vary by very much, the lighter ball bearings seem to take longer to roll down the slope. To investigate this further, you would need to be able to show a difference in the time taken by the lightest ball bearings and that taken by the heaviest ones. Since the difference in times is only about 0.07 s, you would need a timer that is capable of timing to the nearest millisecond. Light gates connected to a data-logger can do this. An electromagnet which releases the ball bearing at the exact time the timer starts would also help to make the timing more accurate. If you were to do this then you might be able to verify that the lighter ball bearings do indeed roll down the slope a little bit more slowly. This is because the air resistance acts on them and slows lighter ball bearings more than the heavier ball bearings.

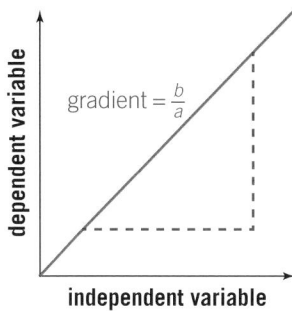

▲ Directly proportional: The graph is a straight line through the origin

Of course, different experiments would give different graphs showing different trends. Sometimes a graph of your data will show a straight line trend. Such a trend is described as linear. If your graph has a linear trend, then the gradient of the graph is the same at all places. This makes it easy to find the gradient and also the intercept with the y-axis.

Sometimes, the straight line trend passes through the origin (or at least very close to it). Such a trend is described as directly proportional.

Other experiments might give a trend which is not a straight line. Such trends can be described as non-linear. In these cases you could further describe whether the gradient of the graph is increasing or decreasing.

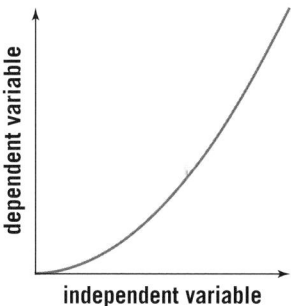

▲ Non-linear: The graph is curved

Experiment

A student makes a hypothesis that the time between the first and second bounce of a ball is proportional to the height from which it is dropped.

Design and carry out an experiment which gathers evidence to test this hypothesis. Using the evidence, establish whether or not the hypothesis is correct.

ATL Communications skills

Using and interpreting a range of discipline-specific terms and symbols

When quoting experimental measurements or any other numerical result, two important considerations are precision and accuracy.

Accuracy refers to whether the measurement is right or not. An accurate result will reflect the true value. Sometimes in experiments it is hard to assess whether a measurement is accurate if you do not know what the result is meant to be. However, the equipment you use can be tested for accuracy. For example, you could measure a known mass on a balance to test if the balance is accurate.

Precision refers to the number of significant figures given in your measurement. If you were asked the time and said that it was about ten to eleven, this is a relatively imprecise answer. On the other hand, 10:51 and 14 seconds is a very precise answer.

Numerical answers can be both precise and accurate or inaccurate and imprecise. They can be precise but inaccurate, or indeed imprecise but accurate.

1. Assess the following statements to determine their accuracy and precision.

   - The world's population is about ten billion people.

   - The Moon orbits the Earth every 27.322 days.

   - The speed of light is 289,792,458 m s^{-1}.

   - There are over a million different languages spoken on Earth.

What is the Doppler effect?

Scientists interpret the evidence from experiments to compare the experimental results to hypotheses made from scientific theories. However, gathering evidence and data can be a challenge.

In 1842, a physicist named Christian Doppler made a hypothesis that waves which were emitted from a source would have a different wavelength if the source were moving. He thought that this might explain why stars in the sky were different colors. (It didn't!) He predicted that the effect of moving the source would change the observed wavelength and frequency by a fraction that was proportional to the relative velocity of the source and the observer. This is now called the Doppler effect.

In 1845, a young physicist named Christoph Buys Ballot attempted to demonstrate this effect. He lived near a railway and was familiar with the idea that the whistle of a steam train changed pitch as it went past. However, gathering convincing evidence was hard. The train's whistle varied naturally in pitch so he could not reliably rule this cause out. Nor did he have the measuring equipment that we have today to measure the frequency of sound waves.

Instead, he used musicians. Since a change in the frequency of a wave would cause the pitch to change, musicians who were well trained in recognizing the pitch of notes were good detectors of the change of frequency of sound. He obtained the use of a steam train for a day and hired six trumpeters. He stood three trumpeters on the platform and put the three others on the train. He got the trumpeters on the train to take it in turns to play a note as the train went past the platform: when one played a note, others were able to verify that the note was at a constant pitch. The trumpeters on the platform had to listen to the note played, although it was quite difficult to hear the trumpet over the sound of the train. Timing the trumpeter so that he played one note as he went past the station was also difficult. Regardless, the trumpeters on the platform agreed that when the train was moving towards them, the trumpet sounded at a higher pitch, and when it was moving away from them, it sounded lower.

◀ Buys Ballot's evidence of the Doppler effect was convincing because it was observed by musicians who were independent of the scientific process

Buys Ballot gathered sufficient evidence to show that the Doppler effect did indeed occur, although he was not able to show that the change in frequency was proportional to speed. Nowadays it is easy to observe the Doppler effect, for example by listening how the sound of the siren on a passing ambulance or police car will change in pitch as it goes by. This is because the Doppler effect shifts the sound upwards in pitch (higher frequency) when the vehicle is coming towards you and when it is moving away from you, the pitch is lower (lower frequency).

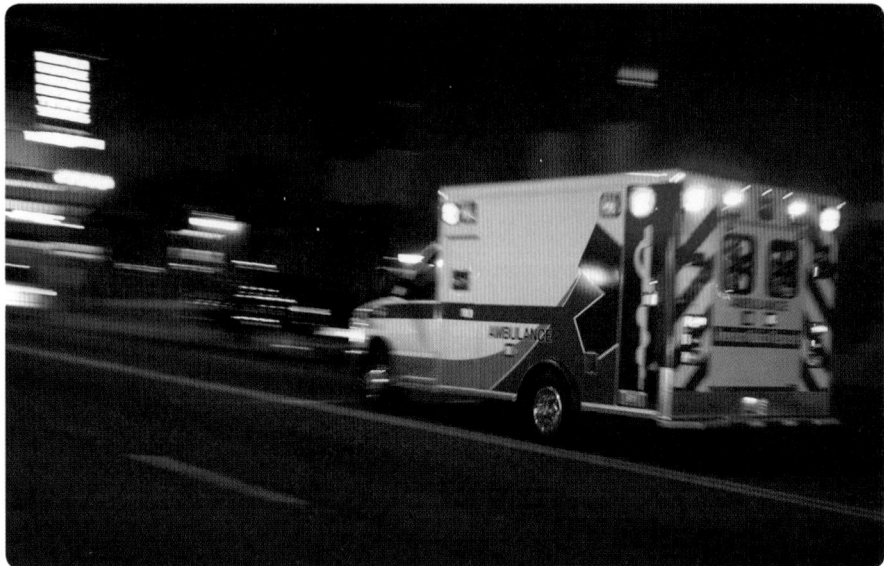

▲ As an ambulance passes at high speed, the pitch of the siren may appear to change. This is due to the Doppler effect

1. The trumpeters played a note with a frequency of 698 Hz. If the speed of sound is 340 m s^{-1}, using the physics you learned in Chapter 1, Models, calculate the wavelength of the sound waves coming from the trumpet.

2. Calculate the time period between successive waves.

3. The train traveled at 16 m s^{-1}. How far would the train travel in the time of one time period?

4. For a person standing on the station, the wavelength of the waves (calculated in question 1) would be shorter by an amount calculated in question 3 because each successive wave is emitted at a closer distance by that much. Calculate the wavelength of the waves as heard by a person on the station.

Hubble's law

In 1919, an astronomer named Edwin Hubble started working at the Mount Wilson Observatory in California. The telescope there had just been completed and, at the time, was the biggest telescope in the world. One of his first discoveries was that there were other galaxies. At the time the universe was thought only to extend to the edge of our own galaxy, the Milky Way.

Ten years later, astronomers knew of almost 50 galaxies. Hubble made measurements of their distances and, using the Doppler effect, the speed at which they were traveling away from us.

Stars consist mainly of hydrogen. Because they are hot, the hydrogen emits light of a certain color. This is very similar to the way a flame test can be used to identify elements in chemistry. A certain color of light corresponds to a particular wavelength of light, and Hubble could measure the specific wavelengths of light emitted from these distant galaxies. If the galaxy were moving towards us, the frequency of the waves would be higher and the light would be shifted towards the blue end of the spectrum. On the other hand, if the galaxy were moving away from us, the light's frequency would be lower and the light would appear to be red-shifted.

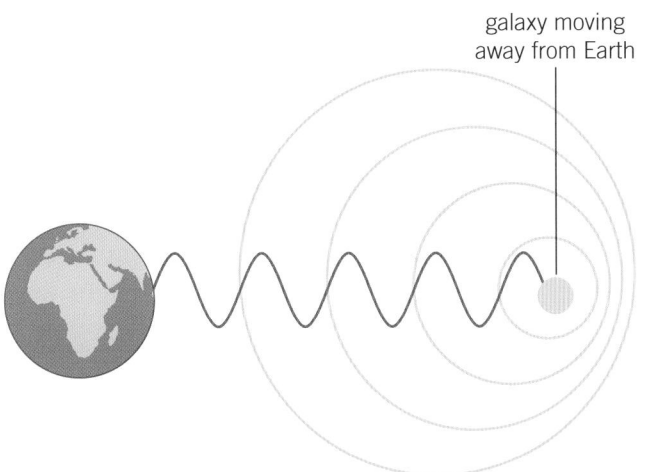

galaxy moving away from Earth

▲ As distant galaxies move away from the Earth, their light is red-shifted. Measuring this red-shift enables astronomers to determine the galaxy's speed

Hubble discovered that the light from most galaxies was red-shifted. He was able to measure the amount by which the light was red-shifted and could therefore determine the velocity at which the galaxies were moving away. He discovered that the velocities of the galaxies are directly proportional to the distance that they are from us. This is now known as Hubble's law.

▲ In 2004, the Hubble telescope took this picture of the most distant galaxies in the universe. These galaxies are moving away from us at very fast speeds as the universe expands. As a result, the light from these galaxies is significantly red-shifted

1 megaparsec or Mpc is 3.09×10^{16} m or 3.26 million light years.

Data-based question: Edwin Hubble's data

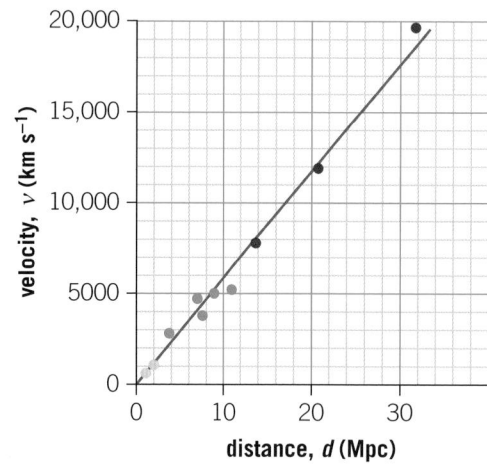

▲ This is a graph of Edwin Hubble's original data. The gradient of this graph is called Hubble's constant. It has units of $km\,s^{-1}\,Mpc^{-1}$

1. Find the gradient of this graph.

2. Comment on the reliability of the trend.

3. The accepted value of Hubble's constant is $72\,km\,s^{-1}\,Mpc^{-1}$. What does this suggest about the validity of Hubble's original experiment?

ATL Transfer skills

What constitutes evidence?

In physics the strength of evidence can be assessed through statistics. In order to consider an experimental result to have proved something, the chances of getting that result through random chance has to be shown to be less than 1 in 3.5 million. This is often called the 5–σ test (sigma σ is the Greek letter s so this test is also referred to as the 5-sigma test) where σ is the standard deviation. The probability of finding something five standard deviations from the average is so rare that this is set as the definition of scientific proof.

As an example, a person five standard deviations above the average height would be about 210 cm tall.

Many different subject disciplines deal with evidence and have different ways of assessing what constitutes strong or weak evidence. Think about and research what might constitute strong or weak evidence in the following subjects:

● mathematics

● history

● philosophy.

▲ A supernova (lower left) appears as bright as the rest of its galaxy for just a few weeks

A supernova is the explosive end to a star's life. For a few weeks, the dying star outshines its galaxy. Supernovae are useful tools for astronomers because they can be used to calculate the distance to that galaxy. Measurements of the red-shift of the light coming from the galaxy can then be used to test Hubble's law.

The table below shows the distance in megaparsecs to some supernovae as well as the speed at which the galaxy is moving away.

1. Plot a graph of the data with distance in Mpc on the x-axis and speed in $km\,s^{-1}$ on the y-axis.

2. Describe the trend of the data.

3. Add a line of best fit to your graph. The gradient of the graph is the Hubble constant. Find the value of the gradient.

4. Comment on the reliability of the trend.

Supernova	Distance (Mpc)	Speed (km s^{-1})
SN2007s	66.4	4,500
SN2008l	75.0	5,670
SN2007au	87.2	6,270
SN2007bc	93.3	6,570
SN2008bf	97.6	7,530
SN2007f	109.1	7,260
SN2007co	116.1	7,980
SN2007bd	131.1	9,600
SN2008af	142.6	10,230
SN2007o	156.4	10,980

What does Hubble's law say about the origin of the universe?

At the time of Hubble's investigations, most astronomers believed in a static universe. In that model, the universe was unchanging and had existed forever. Hubble's discovery, on the other hand, showed that the universe was expanding. This implied that at an earlier point in the universe's history, it would have been smaller and denser, and, as a result, hotter.

Because the velocity of galaxies was found to be directly proportional to their distance from us, this was consistent with the idea that the universe started from a single event. Galaxies that were twice as far away were found to be traveling at twice the speed which meant that they had been traveling for the same time.

Hubble's discovery led to the development of the Big Bang model of the universe. In this model, all of space and time started from an infinitesimally small point and exploded outwards into the universe that we see today.

What other evidence is there for the Big Bang?

Although Hubble's law provided good evidence for the Big Bang, it was only one piece of evidence and some astronomers were not convinced that the universe had to have started in this way. Some believed that matter was created in some parts of the universe and used up in other parts so that although galaxies were moving away from us, the universe was not expanding overall. To settle this dispute further evidence was required.

The Big Bang model of the universe predicts that at earlier times in the universe's history, it was more compact and therefore hotter. Evidence of hotter, earlier stages in the universe's history would support the Big Bang theory.

In 1964, Arno Penzias and Robert Woodrow Wilson were testing sensitive microwave receivers when they found an unexplained signal. Since this signal was detected all the time, regardless of the direction in which they pointed the receiver, they assumed that this was background noise and was due to some faulty wiring in the detector. They checked the wiring and everything else that could account for this signal but found no cause. Having ruled out all possible sources of the noise from Earth, they concluded that the microwave signal was coming from outer space.

Penzias and Wilson had detected the radiation given off by the hot universe at a much earlier stage in its history. About 400,000 years after the Big Bang, the universe had cooled to about 3000 °C. At this stage the universe became transparent and the light emitted from the hot universe was able to travel through space. Since then, the universe has expanded significantly and the wavelengths of the photons have been stretched along with it. What would have been visible or infrared light when it was emitted has now been "stretched" into microwaves.

What will happen in the universe's future?

ASTROPHYSICS

If the universe had a distinct beginning in the Big Bang, then it is reasonable to ask what the future of the universe will be. This is harder for scientists to answer definitively since the future is yet to happen. This does not stop scientists from measuring and making predictions based on their measurements.

If there is enough matter in the universe, then the gravitational pull on this matter could cause the universe eventually to collapse back in on itself in a Big Crunch. On the other hand, if there is not enough matter, perhaps the universe would expand outwards forever.

In 1998, astronomers measuring distant supernovae came to a different conclusion. Their measurements suggested that the universe was accelerating. The mysterious force which causes this acceleration is referred to as dark energy but its nature is not known. The nature of dark energy and indeed whether it even exists at all is one of the most important questions in modern physics.

Summative assessment

Introduction

Some speed cameras make use of the Doppler effect in radar guns to provide evidence of cars breaking the speed limit. This assessment will examine the physics of radar guns and the strength of the evidence that they provide.

Using the radar gun

The radar gun emits radio waves of a known frequency. These bounce off the moving car and back to the radar gun which detects them. The frequency of these waves is measured. If the car is moving towards the radar gun, the detected frequency is higher than the original frequency.

1. State the word used to describe what happens when waves bounce off a surface. [1]

2. The radar gun uses radio waves with a frequency of 1.8×10^{10} Hz. The radio waves travel at the speed of light (3×10^8 m s^{-1}). Calculate the wavelength of these radio waves. [2]

3. The Doppler shift of the radio waves depends on the speed of the car compared to the speed of the radio waves. A 100% change in frequency occurs if the car is traveling at the same speed as the waves; a 50% change occurs if the speed of the car is half that of the radio waves. Explain why only a very small change in frequency would be expected to be detected from this radar gun. [4]

   a) A car is traveling towards the radar gun at 50 km h^{-1}. Express this as a fraction of the speed of light. [2]

   b) The change in the detected frequency will be this fraction of the original frequency. Calculate the change in frequency. [2]

   c) Describe how the wavelength of the received radio waves has changed from the emitted wavelength. [2]

   d) Describe how the change in frequency would be different if the car was traveling away from the radar gun. [2]

▲ This speed camera uses radar to detect speeding cars

Calibrating the speed camera

The radar gun is tested on cars traveling at known speeds. The graph below shows the frequency of the detected radio waves against the speed of the car.

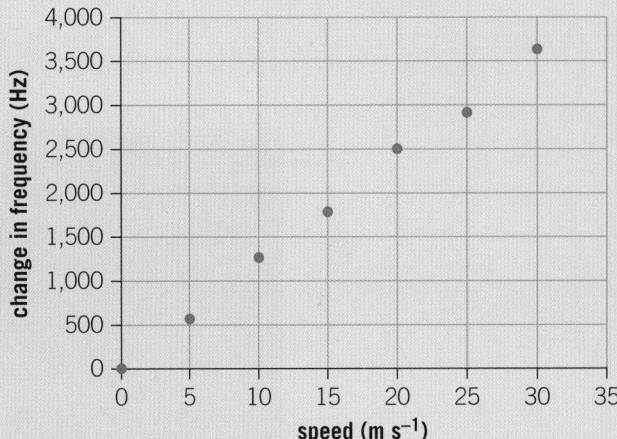

4. **a)** Describe an experiment that might be used to produce this graph. [6]

   b) Identify one suitable control variable in this experiment and explain how it might be controlled. [2]

5. Explain why the radar gun could not be used to measure the speed of the car. Describe a different method that could be used to establish the car's speed. [5]

6. Describe the trend of this graph. [1]

7. Comment on the reliability of the data. Explain how might the reliability be improved. [4]

8. Find the gradient of the graph. [3]

9. The detector is only capable of measuring the frequency of the waves to the nearest 100 Hz. If the speed limit is 20 m s^{-1}, what speed would the radar gun have to detect in order to be confident that the car was going faster than this speed limit? [4]

10. A car causes the radar gun to detect a shift of 1800 Hz (measured to the nearest 100 Hz). The speed limit is 40 km h^{-1} but it is normal not to prosecute a speeding driver unless their speed is 10% greater than this. Evaluate the evidence and decide whether there is enough evidence to suggest that the car was speeding. [5]

 ## Avoiding being caught by speed cameras

Some motorists install radar detectors to detect the radio waves coming from the radar gun. This warns them if there is a speed trap ahead and gives them time to slow down to avoid being caught.

11. Discuss how you might design a radar gun to avoid this problem. [5]

12. Comment on the ethics of avoiding speed cameras. [4]

13. Many speed cameras have a back-up measurement of the speed. This works by taking two photos separated by a known interval of time. Lines on the road, a set distance apart, help to determine the position of the car in each picture.

   a) Explain why it is important to have a back-up measurement when gathering evidence of a car exceeding the speed limit. [3]

   b) Describe, using scientific language appropriately, how the two photos may be used to determine the speed of the car. [3]

4 Movement

Movement is the act of changing from one place or situation to another.

▲ The Helios probes were launched in the 1970s to orbit and study the Sun at close range. Their orbits pass closer to the Sun than Mercury, so they get very hot. As they fell into their orbit, the Sun's gravity accelerated them to high speeds. The probes set the speed record for the fastest man-made object at 252,792 km h^{-1}. By contrast, the fastest speed attained on the surface of Mars is only 0.18 km h^{-1}. What are the challenges of traveling at high speeds on other planets?

▲ The growth rate of plants can be very slow. This saguaro cactus may grow to over 18 m, but it may take centuries to reach its full height growing at a rate of only a couple of centimeters per year. Which plants grow the fastest?

▲ Some motion is imperceptible. The movement of the atoms in this molten gold gives it its heat but the distance that the atoms travel is so small that we cannot see it. The speed at which the light travels to our eyes is the fastest possible speed in the universe, so fast that the time taken for the light to reach us is imperceptibly small. As this gold cools down, how will the atoms' motion change?

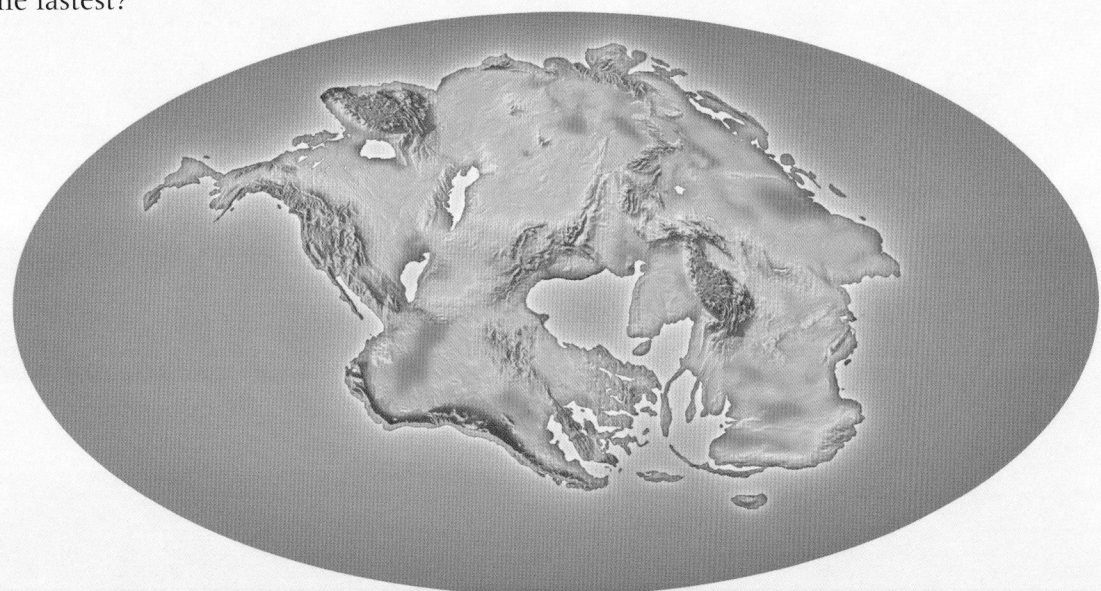

▲ Plate tectonics causes continental drift which occurs at just a couple of centimeters per year. Sometimes all the continents move together and form one big supercontinent such as the continent Rodinia which is thought to have broken apart about 700 million years ago. The last time that all the land was linked in one land mass was about 200 million years ago when the supercontinent Pangaea was surrounded by an ocean called Panthalassa. In about 200 million years' time, the continents may once again join together to form this configuration called Pangaea Ultima. What evidence do we have that the continents were once all joined together?

Introduction

Movement has been central to human progress over the centuries. We have crossed oceans to reach new continents, and navigated across land and sea to find food and resources, or just to explore the unknown.

Human migration and invading armies have caused the movement not just of people, but also of language, culture and technology. As a result they have shaped the world around us. Movement also requires navigation so that we do not get lost. In this chapter we will look at how we measure and describe motion, and how humans and other animals use magnetic fields to keep track of where we are. Because movement and navigation are linked, the global context of this chapter is orientation in space and time.

Movement is the change from one state of being to another. For a moving object, it is the location that might change or its orientation if the object is rotating. Such a change in position will also occur over a period of time. Therefore, the key concept for this chapter is change.

Key concept: Change

Related concept: Movement

Global context: Orientation in space and time

▼ This magnetic liquid moves in response to a magnetic field. The spikes form along the field lines

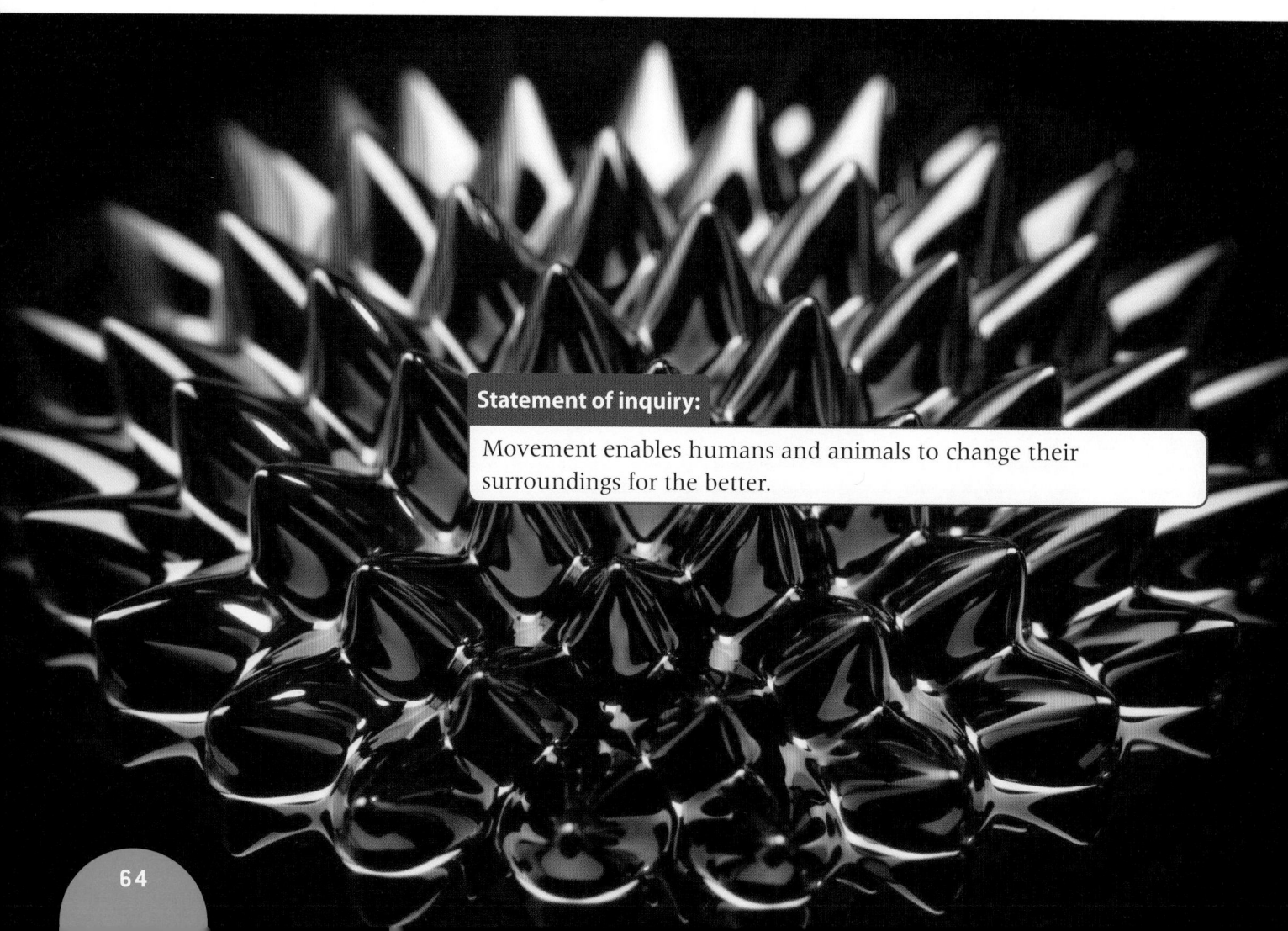

Statement of inquiry:

Movement enables humans and animals to change their surroundings for the better.

Scientists have shown that honey bees can sense magnetic fields. Other insects, birds, mammals, fish and even bacteria appear to be able to sense magnetic fields. Some scientists even believe that humans have the capability of detecting magnetic fields

The Shanghai Maglev Train is capable of reaching speeds of up to $350\,km\,h^{-1}$. Instead of running on wheels, it uses magnetic fields to lift it above the tracks and propel it along

How do we quantify movement?

Speed is defined as the rate at which an object covers distance. It can be calculated using the equation:

$$\text{speed} = \frac{\text{distance}}{\text{time}}$$

In the 2009 World Championships Usain Bolt broke the world record for the 100 m. He ran the race in 9.58 s, which using the equation for speed, gives an average speed of 10.4 m s^{-1}.

▲ Usain Bolt, who set the world record for the 100 m in 2009

Worked example: Calculating Usain Bolt's speed

Question

Usain Bolt ran 100 m in 9.58 s, calculate his speed and convert this to km h^{-1}.

Answer

Using the equation:

$$\text{speed} = \frac{\text{distance}}{\text{time}}$$

$$= \frac{100}{9.58} = 10.4 \text{ m s}^{-1}$$

To convert this to km h^{-1}, we must convert meters into kilometers and seconds into hours.

There are 60 seconds in a minute so Bolt would travel 60 times further in a minute. This gives 624 m min^{-1}. Multiplying again by 60 gives 37,440 m h^{-1}.

There are 1,000 meters in a kilometer and so his speed is 37.44 km h^{-1}.

In the 2016 Olympic Games, another world record was set when Wayde van Niekerk ran the 400 m in 43.03 s. His average speed is therefore 9.30 m s^{-1}.

When people or things move, it is important to consider the direction of motion as well as the distance they move. A quantity which has a direction as well as a magnitude (size) is called a vector quantity. Other quantities do not have a direction associated with them; these are called scalar quantities.

Physicists use the word "distance" to refer only to how far something has moved so it is a scalar quantity. We use the word "displacement" to define an object's distance and direction so displacement is a vector quantity.

In a similar way, speed tells us how fast something is moving but not the direction, so speed is a scalar quantity. The vector quantity is called velocity.

Vectors and scalars

A scalar quantity is one which only has a magnitude or size.
A vector quantity has a direction associated with it.

Sort the following quantities into scalars and vectors:

- density
- force
- magnetic field
- mass
- momentum
- temperature
- volume
- weight.

Velocity can be calculated using a similar equation to speed, but using the vector quantity of displacement instead of distance:

$$\text{velocity} = \frac{\text{displacement}}{\text{time}}$$

or using symbols:

$$v = \frac{d}{t}$$

Because Usain Bolt ran the 100 m in a straight line, his displacement over the course of the race was 100 m (that is, the finish line was 100 m from the start) and so his velocity was 10.4 m s^{-1} in a forward direction. However, the 400 m is run as one circuit of the track. This means that Wayde van Niekerk completed one lap and finished approximately where he started. The distance he ran was 400 m, but his displacement at the end was zero. As a result, his average velocity was also zero!

In fact, since Wayde van Niekerk ran in lane 8 (the outside lane), he had a staggered start which meant that he started about 53 m from the finish line. His total displacement was therefore 53 m in 53.03 s giving him an average velocity of about 1 m s^{-1} backwards! This shows that he could have started the race and walked directly to the finish line at a leisurely pace to arrive at the finish line at the same time as he did in the actual race. While this is a much easier way to achieve the same average velocity from the same start and end points, it is not allowed under the rules of athletics and could not be used to set 400 m world records!

1. The Berlin marathon is one of the fastest marathon courses; many world records have been set there. In 2014 Dennis Kimetto ran the 42.195 km in 2 hours, 2 minutes and 57 seconds. What was his average speed?

2. How fast would he have completed a 100 m race if he ran at the same pace?

3. If Usain Bolt were to be able to maintain his world record 100 m pace over a marathon, how long would it take him?

4. The start and finish lines of the Berlin marathon are only 860 m apart. By considering this displacement, what was Dennis Kimetto's average velocity?

▲ A giant Galapagos tortoise only travels at about 0.4 km h^{-1}. What is this speed in m s^{-1}? How long would it take this tortoise to complete 100 m?

MOTION

How do we change speed?

Not all objects travel at a constant speed or velocity. Objects can get faster or slower and/or change direction. As velocity is a vector quantity, direction is important, so if an object maintains a constant speed but changes direction, such as the runner going around a 400 m track, its velocity is changing.

Whenever there is a change in velocity, there is acceleration (or deceleration if the velocity is getting slower). Acceleration is calculated using the equation:

$$acceleration = \frac{change\ in\ velocity}{time}$$

or

$$a = \frac{v}{t}$$

A common example of acceleration is when objects fall under gravity (see Chapter 1, Models). Near the Earth's surface, falling objects accelerate at about $9.8\,m\,s^{-2}$ as long as they do not experience too much air resistance. This means that for every second they are in free fall, their speed increases by $9.8\,m\,s^{-1}$.

▶ The Bloodhound car is a project which is attempting to break the land speed record. Its aim is to break $1,600\,km\,h^{-1}$

1. On Earth, the acceleration of an object in free fall is $9.8\,\mathrm{m\,s^{-2}}$. How fast would an object be traveling after 3 s of free fall if it started from rest?

2. A cheetah can accelerate from rest to $25\,\mathrm{m\,s^{-1}}$ in only 2.5 s. What is its acceleration? How does this compare to the acceleration it experiences if it fell out of a tree?

3. On Io (a moon of Jupiter) the acceleration of free fall is $1.8\,\mathrm{m\,s^{-2}}$. After 3 s of free fall, how fast would an object be traveling if it started from rest?

(A)(B)(C)(D) Experiment

In this experiment you are going to measure the motion of a ball rolling down a ramp and measure its acceleration.

Method

- Set up a ramp that a ball bearing or marble can roll down. The ramp can be made of a half-pipe such as a length of guttering, or with something that has a square profile such as electrical cable trunking. The ramp should be about 1 m long.

- Release the ball bearing or marble from rest 10 cm from the end of the ramp. Let it roll to the bottom and time how long it takes with a stopwatch.

- Repeat this from 20 cm from the end, then in 10 cm increments until the ball rolls down the full 1 m ramp. Record your results in a table.

- Repeat the experiment twice and take averages of your data.

Questions

1. In this experiment identify one control variable.

2. Plot a distance–time graph to show the ball's motion (plot time on the x-axis).

The average speed of the ball over each distance d can be found using the equation:

$$v = \frac{d}{t}$$

Assuming that the ball is accelerating at a constant rate, the final speed of the ball at the end of the ramp is twice this:

$$v_{\text{final}} = \frac{2d}{t}$$

3. Use this equation to add a column to your table showing the final speed.

4. Plot a velocity–time graph for the ball's motion (also plot time on the x-axis).

5. Use the graph to find the acceleration of the ball.

Extension

- Suggest one improvement to the experiment.

- Using this apparatus design an experiment to investigate a factor which might affect the acceleration of the ball down the ramp.

How can we depict an object's motion?

It is very useful to be able to predict an object's future motion. With practice, our brains can do it well. It enables us to cross a road safely by judging how long we have until a car would reach us, assuming it does not change speed. It enables us to catch or hit objects assuming that they continue along their trajectory.

Sometimes we need to accurately predict an object's motion rather than just rely on intuition; one way of doing this is with a graph.

A displacement–time graph plots an object's displacement against time. The velocity is the rate of change of the displacement, that is, the change in displacement divided by the time taken. This can be found from the gradient of the graph.

A straight line graph with a constant gradient indicates that in any given time period, the change in displacement is the same. Therefore, the object has a constant velocity.

▲ When juggling, there are more balls than you have hands. It is impossible to watch every ball in order to track its movement; however, our brains are very good at intuitively understanding the motion of the balls.

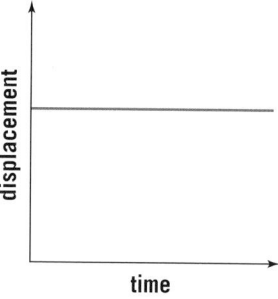

▲ Displacement is not changing so the object is stationary

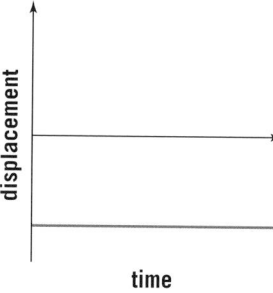

▲ This shows a negative displacement – this shows that the object is behind the observer

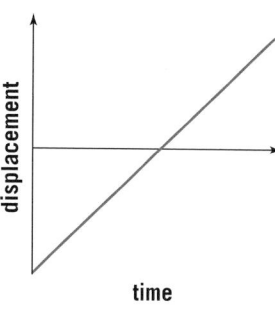

▲ Object is moving away at constant velocity. It starts behind the observer and then moves past

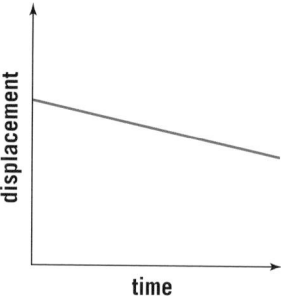

▲ Object is moving towards you at constant velocity

If the displacement–time graph is curved, then this shows that the speed is not constant and so the object is accelerating or decelerating.

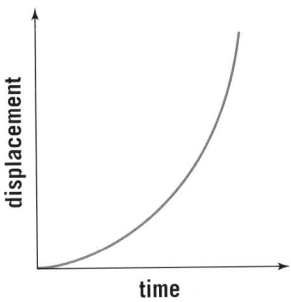

▲ Object is accelerating away from you

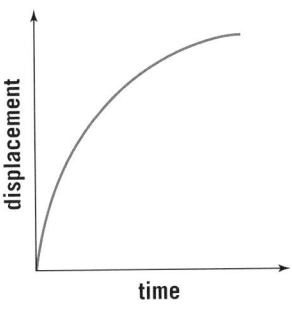

▲ Object is moving away but decelerating

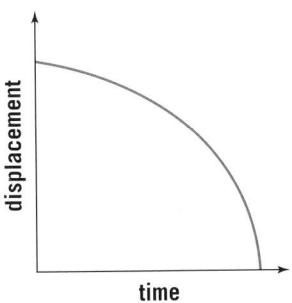

▲ Object is accelerating towards you

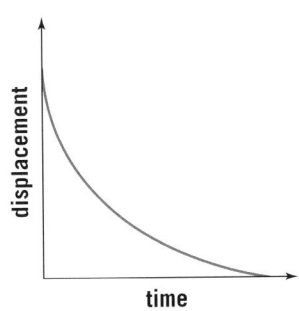

▲ Object is coming towards you and decelerating

Data-based question: Analyzing constant velocity

Which of the following displacement–time graphs represents the fastest speed?

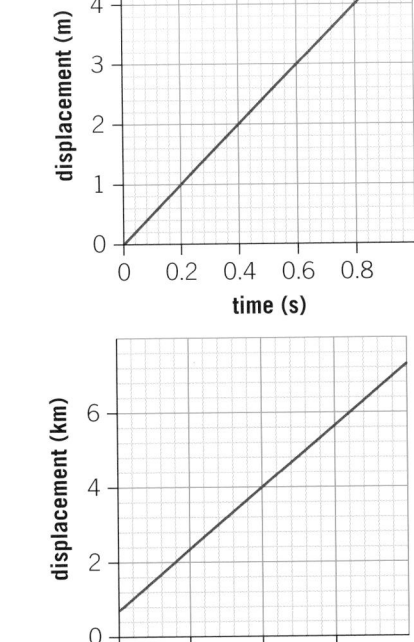

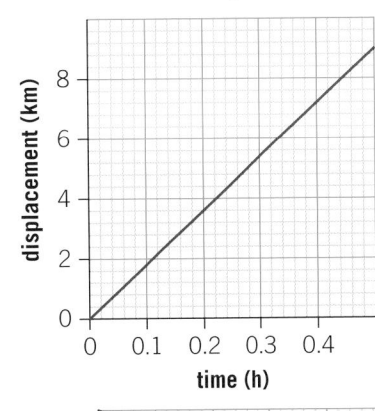

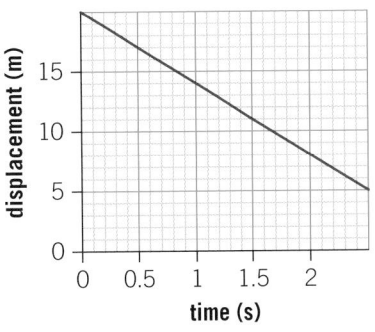

1. Here is the displacement–time graph for an object in free fall on the surface of Mars.

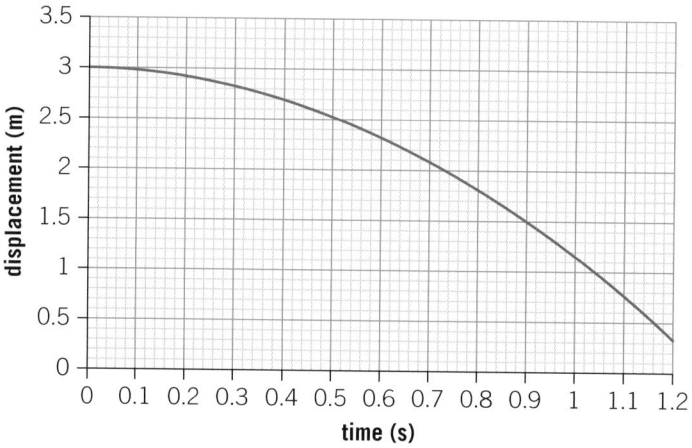

a) How can you tell that the object was dropped from rest?

b) What was the average speed over the first 0.9 s?

c) By drawing a tangent on the graph, estimate the speed of the object after 1 s.

d) What is the acceleration of free fall on Mars?

Another way of showing an object's motion is by plotting a velocity–time graph. Here velocity, rather than distance is plotted against time. In this case, the gradient of the graph represents the acceleration.

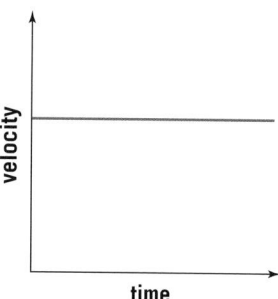

▲ Object is traveling at a constant velocity

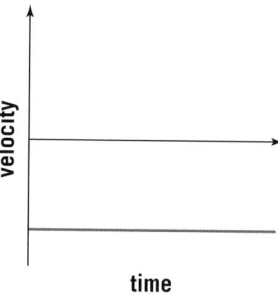

▲ The object is still traveling at a constant velocity but this time the negative value indicates that it is traveling backwards. It could still be in front of the observer, though

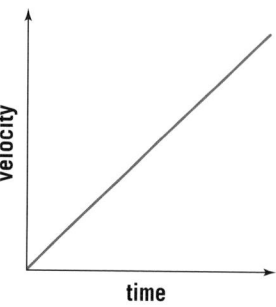

▲ Object is accelerating from rest at a constant rate

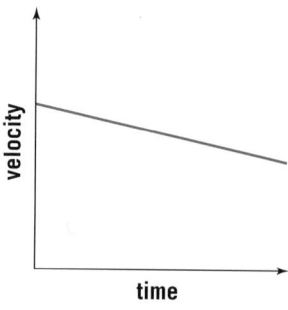

▲ Object is decelerating, but still moving forwards

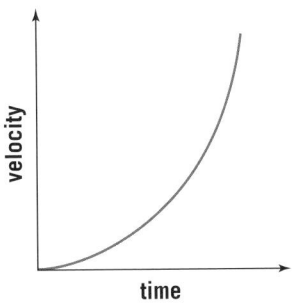

▲ Object is accelerating at an increasing rate

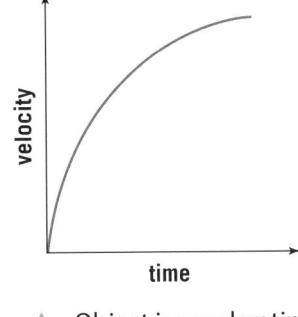

▲ Object is accelerating at a decreasing rate

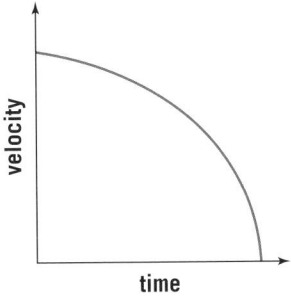

▲ Object is decelerating at an increasing rate

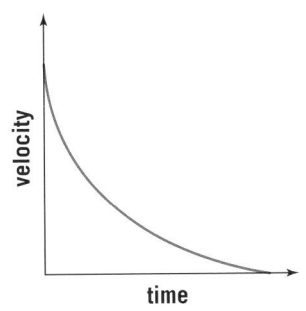

▲ Object is decelerating at a decreasing rate

The area under a velocity–time graph indicates the distance traveled.

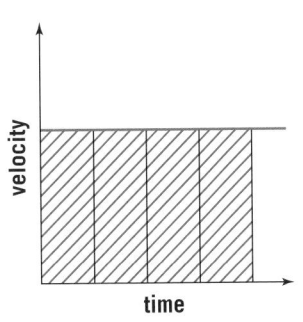

▲ Equal areas in equal periods of time show that the distance traveled in any given time is the same. The object is moving at constant velocity

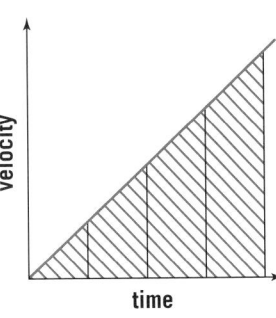

▲ In equal periods of time, the area under the graph gets bigger. The distance traveled is increasing and so the object is accelerating

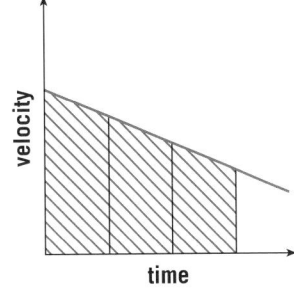

▲ In equal periods of time, the area under the graph gets smaller. The distance traveled is decreasing and so the object is decelerating

1. The velocity–time graph for a subway train journey between two stops is shown below.

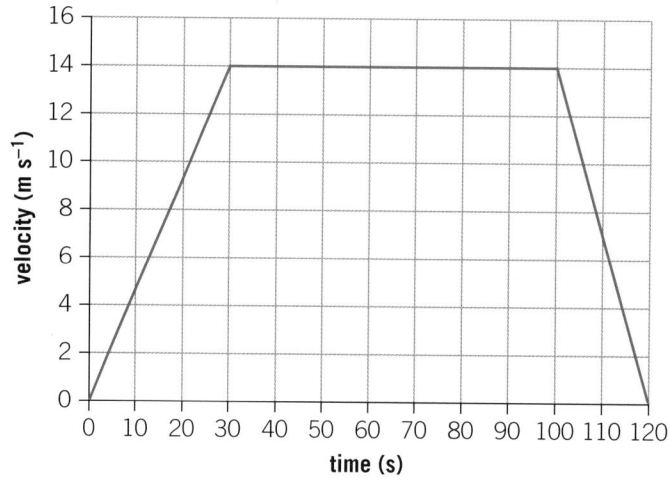

a) What was the maximum velocity of the train?

b) What was the distance between the two stations?

c) Calculate the average speed of the train over the entire journey.

d) Determine the initial acceleration of the train.

e) The greater the acceleration or deceleration, the harder it is to stand steady on the train. Explain why you can see from the graph that it is hardest to stand up when the train decelerates coming into the station.

MAGNETISM

What makes something magnetic?

Certain metals, most commonly iron but also nickel and cobalt, can be made magnetic. This is a result of the way their electrons are arranged.

A magnet made of one these materials has two poles: the north-seeking and south-seeking, or just north and south for short.

If the two poles of two magnets are brought together, there is a force between them. If both poles of the magnets are the same then the magnets repel each other, but if the south pole of one and the north pole of the other are brought together then they will attract.

> This gives us a simple law of magnetic forces:
> - like poles repel
> - opposite poles attract.

Thinking in context

How can magnetism help us to navigate?

Lodestone is a type of rock which is found naturally on Earth. It is a magnetic material and can attract small iron objects. Early Chinese navigators used it as an early compass to determine their direction of travel and to keep track of where they were traveling.

How else can we navigate and find out where we are?

▲ This reproduction of an ancient Chinese compass points south rather than north

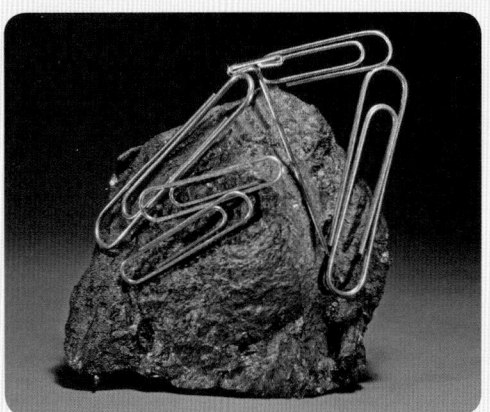

▲ Lodestone is a naturally magnetic mineral

A magnetic material is made up of tiny areas, each of which behaves like a little magnet. These areas are called domains. Normally they are aligned randomly, and so their different magnetic fields cancel each other out. However, if the domains can be aligned, then their magnetic fields will add together and produce a net magnetic field.

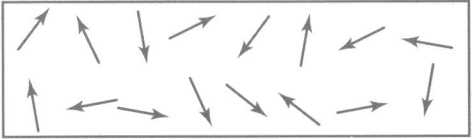

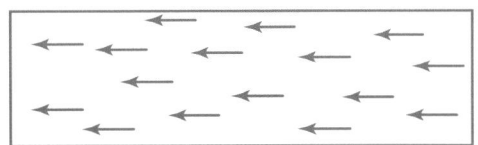

▲ In this magnetic substance, all the domains are misaligned. As a result, the individual magnetic fields each act against each other and so there is no overall magnetic field

▲ In this magnetic substance, the domains have all been aligned. The magnetic fields all add together to create a magnetic field

1 Using domain theory explain:

a) what happens if you cut a bar magnet in half

b) why hitting a magnetized iron rod with a hammer reduces the strength of its magnetic field

c) why heating a magnet sufficiently can reduce its magnetism.

 **Experiment**

Measuring the strength of a magnetic field

You can measure the strength of a magnet in different ways. Smartphones have an inbuilt magnetometer, a device which measures the surrounding magnetic field, and there are various free apps which enable you to measure the strength of a magnetic field. Alternatively, you could measure the strength of the magnetic field by finding out how many staples it could lift (or other small objects). Use one of these methods to carry out the experiment below.

Method

- Take a small iron rod or large nail. Can you detect any magnetism?

- Stroke it with a bar magnet in the same direction 20 times to align the domains. Can you detect any magnetism?

- Hit the rod or nail with a hammer. Does this affect its magnetism?

- Magnetize the iron rod or nail by stroking it with a bar magnet again. Measure how magnetic it is. Now heat it in a Bunsen burner flame until it is hot. Cool it down again (you can do this by dipping it into water). Does this affect its magnetism?

MAGNETISM ## What is a magnetic field?

The region around a magnet exerts a force on other magnetic materials. The extent of this force and its region of influence is described as a magnetic field. You can trace the magnetic field around a bar magnet using a small compass.

▶ The magnetic field lines around a bar magnet. Where is the magnetic field strongest?

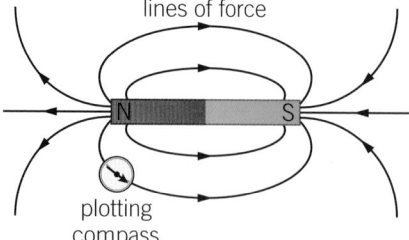

Magnetic field lines indicate the direction that a compass needle would point if it were placed at that point in the field. The field lines obey certain rules:

- they go from the north pole to the south pole

- they cannot cross each other

- they cannot stop or start anywhere other than at the pole of the magnet so there cannot be any breaks in them
- the closer the field lines are together, the stronger the magnetic field is at that point.

The shape of the magnetic field of a bar magnet is shown above. A uniform field can be created using two bar magnets by bringing the north pole of one magnet close to the south pole of the other magnet. The field lines go straight from the north pole to the south pole. They are equally spaced and this shows that the magnetic field is equally strong anywhere in this region.

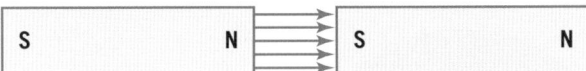

▲ The magnetic field between two bar magnets is uniform. This can be seen from the fact that the field lines are equally spaced and parallel which shows that the magnetic field is the same

Experiment

Tracing the magnetic field of a bar magnet

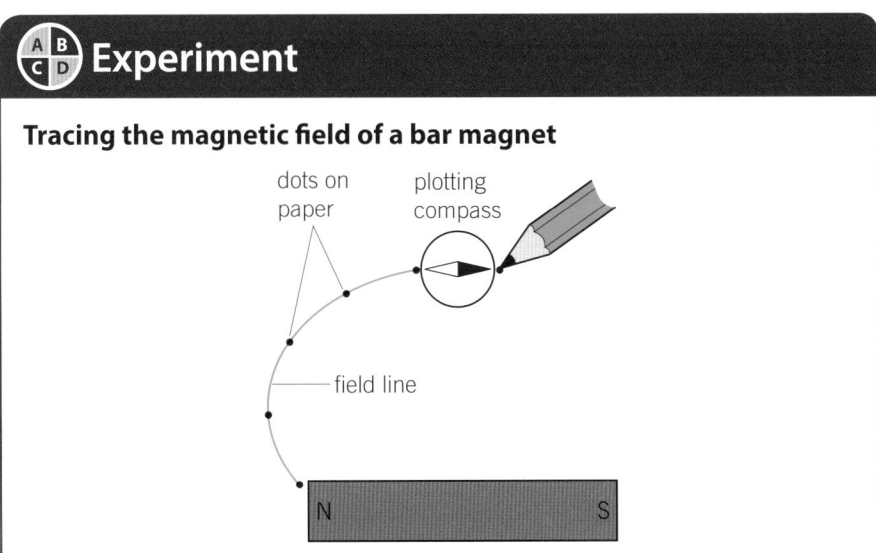

You can trace the magnetic field around a bar magnet using a small compass.

Put a bar magnet on a piece of paper. Place a small plotting compass near one of the poles and mark a small dot with a pencil where the compass points. Move the compass so that the other end of the needle lines up with your pencil dot and mark again where the needle is pointing. Continue this process to create a sequence of dots going from one pole of the magnet to the other, then join the dots to form the field line. Trace the field lines from different positions to draw the magnetic field.

What is the Earth's magnetic field?

The Earth itself has a magnetic field. It is believed that this is caused by the Earth's spinning iron core. The magnetic field of the Earth is very similar to that of a bar magnet. It is tilted a bit so that the magnetic poles do not perfectly align with the geographic poles. The magnetic North Pole is currently located in the north Canadian Arctic and the magnetic South Pole is off the coast of Antarctica.

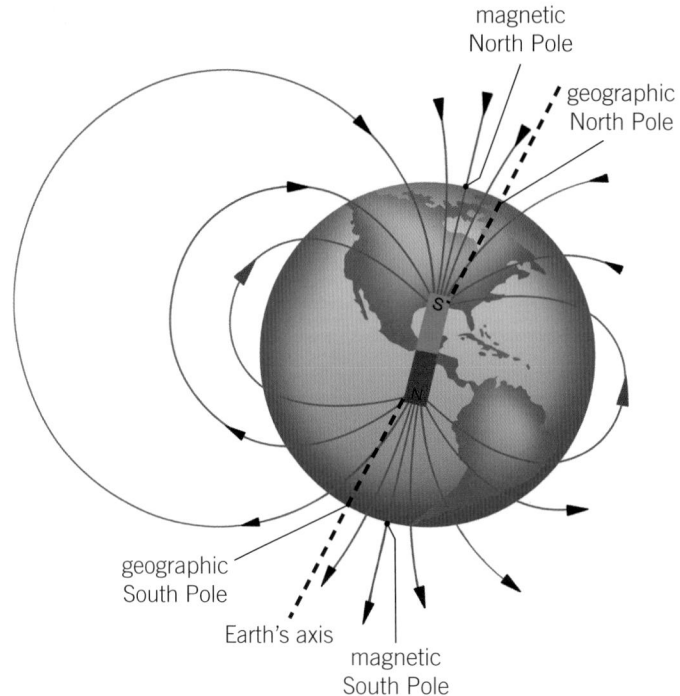

magnetic
North Pole

geographic
North Pole

geographic
South Pole

Earth's axis

magnetic
South Pole

▶ The Earth has a magnetic field. Compasses align themselves to the Earth's magnetic field and the north-seeking pole will point to the magnetic North Pole

We can use the Earth's magnetic field to navigate. A compass can be made from a small bar magnet which is able to move and orientate freely. The north pole of this magnet is attracted to the magnetic North Pole. Note that because opposite poles attract, this means that the magnetic North Pole is the south-seeking pole of the Earth's internal magnet.

The magnetic poles are not stationary; instead they move by about 50 km every year. This makes navigation by compass impossible near the magnetic poles. Fortunately, the magnetic poles are in places on the Earth where there are very few inhabitants.

Every so often (a few times in a million years), the Earth's magnetic field completely flips. This process seems to happen randomly and occurs very quickly, perhaps within 100 years.

How does the Earth's magnetic field protect us?

Aside from the benefits of navigation, the Earth's magnetic field is very important for life on Earth.

The Sun produces many charged particles which stream away from the Sun in what is called the solar wind. Some of these travel

towards the Earth at high speed. If these charged particles hit the outer layers of the Earth's atmosphere they would strip it away, but when they encounter the Earth's magnetic field, a long way above the atmosphere, they are deflected. Some of these charged particles follow the field lines around to the poles where they finally enter Earth's atmosphere. As the charged particles enter the atmosphere they cause auroras, spectacular displays of glowing light.

▲ It is thought that the lack of magnetic field on Mars has allowed the solar wind to strip away much of its atmosphere. The ice caps, visible at the top of this picture, suggest that Mars might once have had an atmosphere with water

▲ This spectacular aurora, seen over Alaska, is caused by charged particles from the Sun interacting with the Earth's atmosphere

Are there magnetic fields elsewhere in the solar system?

MAGNETISM

The fact that magnetic fields protect the Earth's atmosphere and, therefore, protect life on Earth means that scientists are interested in other planets and moons that have magnetic fields as it might be possible for them to harbor life as well.

Mercury, Venus and Mars all have weaker magnetic fields than Earth. The gas giant planets (Jupiter, Saturn, Uranus and Neptune) have large magnetic fields and aurora have been seen on these planets, but as they have no solid surface, they are not considered candidates for sustaining life. Some of the moons of the gas giants, however, orbit close enough to their parent planet that they are protected by their planet's magnetic field. One such example is Titan, the largest moon of Saturn. It has a substantial atmosphere, and it is possible that its atmosphere is protected from the solar wind by Saturn's magnetic field.

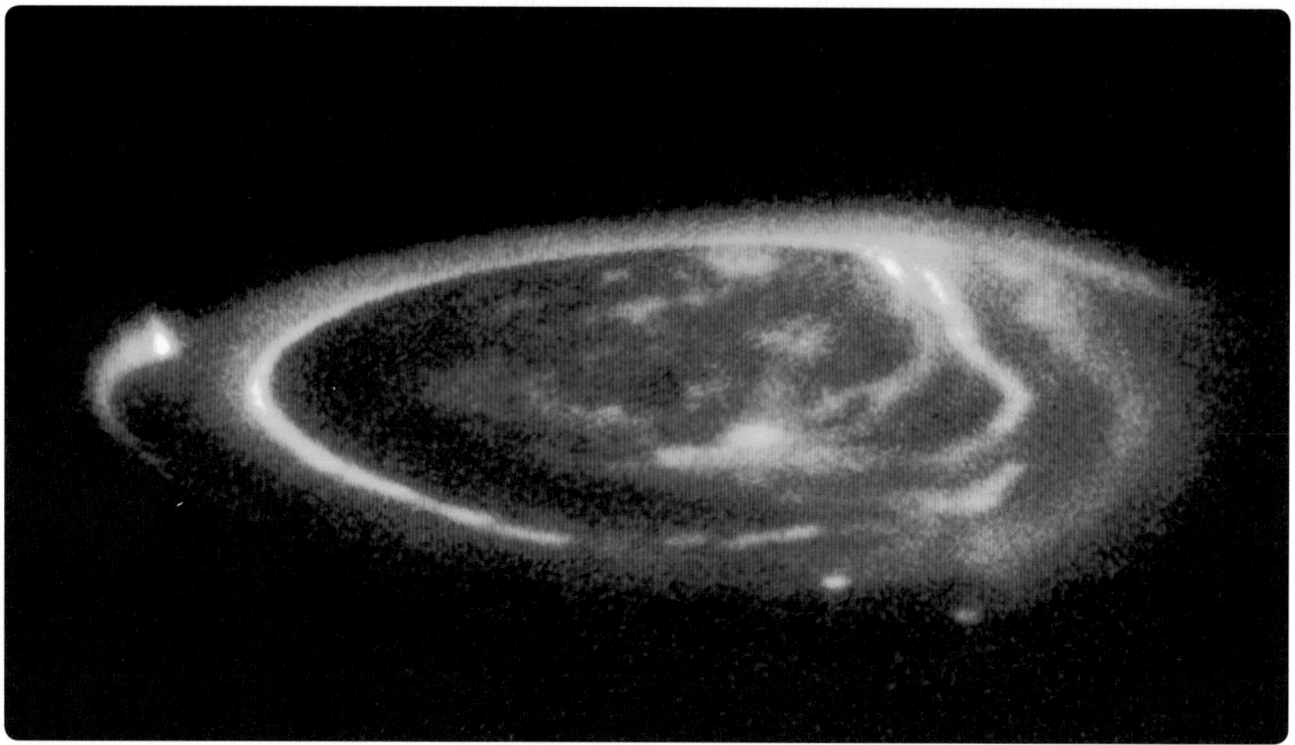

▲ Jupiter has a strong magnetic field and charged particles from the Sun interact with it in the same way as they do with the magnetic field on Earth. This picture shows the aurora on Jupiter

Summative assessment

Statement of inquiry:

Movement enables humans and animals to change their surroundings for the better.

Introduction

The theme of this assessment is animal movement.

 Bird migration

1. During the northern hemisphere's summer, Arctic terns nest in the most northern parts of the globe, such as Iceland and Greenland, as well as in other parts of northern Europe and Canada. The birds then migrate halfway around the globe to Antarctica, in the southernmost part of the world, in order to find food and to avoid the cold northern hemisphere winter. The Arctic tern has the longest annual migration in the animal kingdom and can cover 90,000 km in one single year.

   a) Calculate the tern's average speed over this time. [2]

   b) The Arctic tern's migration brings it back to the same nesting grounds each year. Explain why the Arctic tern's average velocity is zero over this period of time. [2]

   c) An Arctic tern can live for 30 years, completing its migration every year. The distance to the Moon is 384,400 km. Calculate the distance that an Arctic tern can travel in its lifetime and express your answer in terms of the number of times that it might be able to travel to the Moon and back. [3]

2. A peregrine falcon is the fastest animal in the world. When it dives, it can accelerate to about $40\,\mathrm{m\,s^{-1}}$.

   a) Express this speed in $\mathrm{km\,h^{-1}}$. [2]

   b) The bird's acceleration is about $8\,\mathrm{m\,s^{-2}}$. Calculate the length of time the bird needs to get to its top speed from rest. [3]

   c) A graph of the vertical speed against time for one bird's dive is shown below. Calculate the distance the bird falls through during its dive. [3]

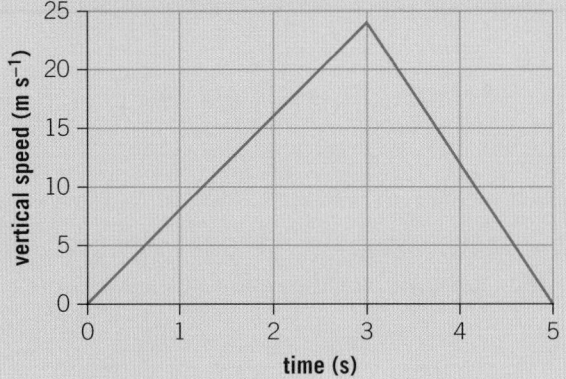

▲ Scientists believe that Arctic terns use the Earth's magnetic field to navigate effectively during their long migration

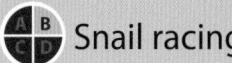

Snail racing

3. In snail racing, snails start at the center of a circle and the first snail to reach the outside of the circle wins. Usually, the ground is made wet so that the snails will want to move across it. Some snail racers think that a sugary solution or diluted beer makes the snails travel faster.

▲ In snail racing, the fastest and most athletic snails compete over a fixed distance

A student decides to design an experiment to test these ideas.

a) Formulate a hypothesis for this investigation. [2]

b) What should the student's independent variable be? [1]

c) Explain what the dependent variable is. How might it be measured? [3]

d) Suggest two suitable control variables for this experiment and explain how they could be kept constant. [4]

e) Formulate a hypothesis for this investigation. [2]

f) Explain what kind of graph the student should use to present the data. [3]

Measuring a horse's gallop

4. A horse rider wants to find out how fast his horse can gallop. He sets out wooden posts every 20 m and gallops the horse past the posts. When he passes a post, a friend uses a stopwatch to measure the time taken. The table of his data is shown below.

Distance (m)	Time (s)
0	0
20	2.83
40	4.04
60	4.96
80	5.89
100	7.10
120	8.17
140	11.08

a) Plot a graph of the data. Plot time on the x-axis. [4]

b) Using the data, determine the average speed over the first 20 m. [2]

c) Using your graph, determine the maximum speed of the horse from this graph. [3]

d) Comment on the reliability of this data. [2]

e) Suggest two improvements that the rider could make to this experiment in order to obtain a more reliable answer. [4]

Sensing magnetic fields

Scientists think that some animals are able to help themselves navigate by detecting the Earth's magnetic field. However, they are not certain about how animals are able to detect magnetic fields. In 2008, some Czech scientists analyzed images from Google Earth and found that cows and deer seemed to prefer to align themselves with the Earth's magnetic field.

The following text is from the introduction to a paper published in the *Proceedings of the National Academy of Sciences of the United States of America*, volume 105 on 9 September 2008. The paper was written by Sabine Begall, Jaroslav Červený, Julia Neef, Oldřich Vojtěch and Hynek Burda.

We demonstrate by means of simple, noninvasive methods (analysis of satellite images, field observations, and measuring "deer beds" in snow) that domestic cattle ($n = 8,510$ in 308 pastures) across the globe, and grazing and resting red and roe deer ($n = 2,974$ at 241 localities), align their body axes in roughly a north–south direction. Direct observations of roe deer revealed that animals orient their heads northward when grazing or resting. Amazingly, this [widespread] phenomenon does not seem to have been noticed by herdsmen, ranchers, or hunters. Because wind and light conditions could be excluded as a common denominator determining the body axis orientation, magnetic alignment is the most [convincing] explanation. [...]. This study reveals the magnetic alignment in large mammals based on statistically sufficient sample sizes. Our findings [...] are of potential significance for applied [ethics] (husbandry, animal welfare). They challenge neuroscientists and biophysics to explain the [underlying] mechanisms.

5. Write a bibliography reference for this paper. [1]

6. Discuss why non-invasive techniques are preferable when studying animal behavior. [3]

7. Imagine that you are one of the scientists involved in this research. Write a report suggesting why you should be given more funding to continue this research. Explain the potential benefits of understanding why cows and deer prefer to align themselves to the Earth's magnetic field. [5]

8. It is believed that some animals use magnetic fields to navigate while migrating. Suggest one other way that animals might navigate, and compare the advantages and disadvantages of this with sensing the Earth's magnetic field. [3]

9. It is clear that migrating must take a lot of energy so animals would not do this if they did not have to. Give three motivations for animal migration. [3]

5 Environment

The environment is the backdrop to all events; it is the history, geography and current climate that informs actions.

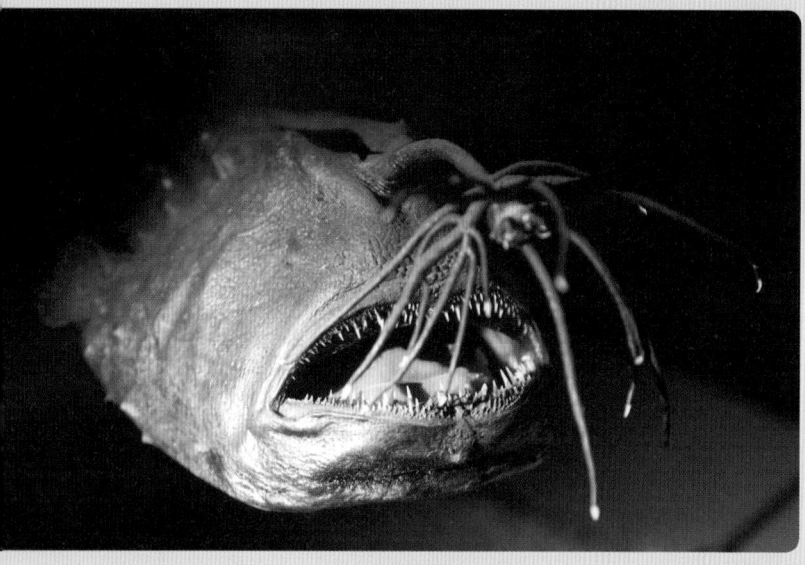

◄ Differences in environment cause animal species to evolve and adapt. This angler fish has adapted to its dark deep-sea environment by evolving a lantern-like organ which emits light from its tip to attract its prey. The production of light by an animal or plant is called bioluminescence, and in the case of the angler fish, it is created by symbiotic bacteria. How have other animals adapted to their environment?

◄ Tardigrades, sometimes called water bears, are small animals, normally about 0.5 mm long, that can survive extreme environments. They have been found to exist on every continent and live everywhere from deserts to the tops of mountains and the bottom of ocean trenches. They are known to have survived without food for 30 years; they can survive extreme low temperatures (below −200°C), extreme high temperatures (above 150°C), high doses of radiation and can even survive the environment of outer space for days. How do humans cope with extreme environments?

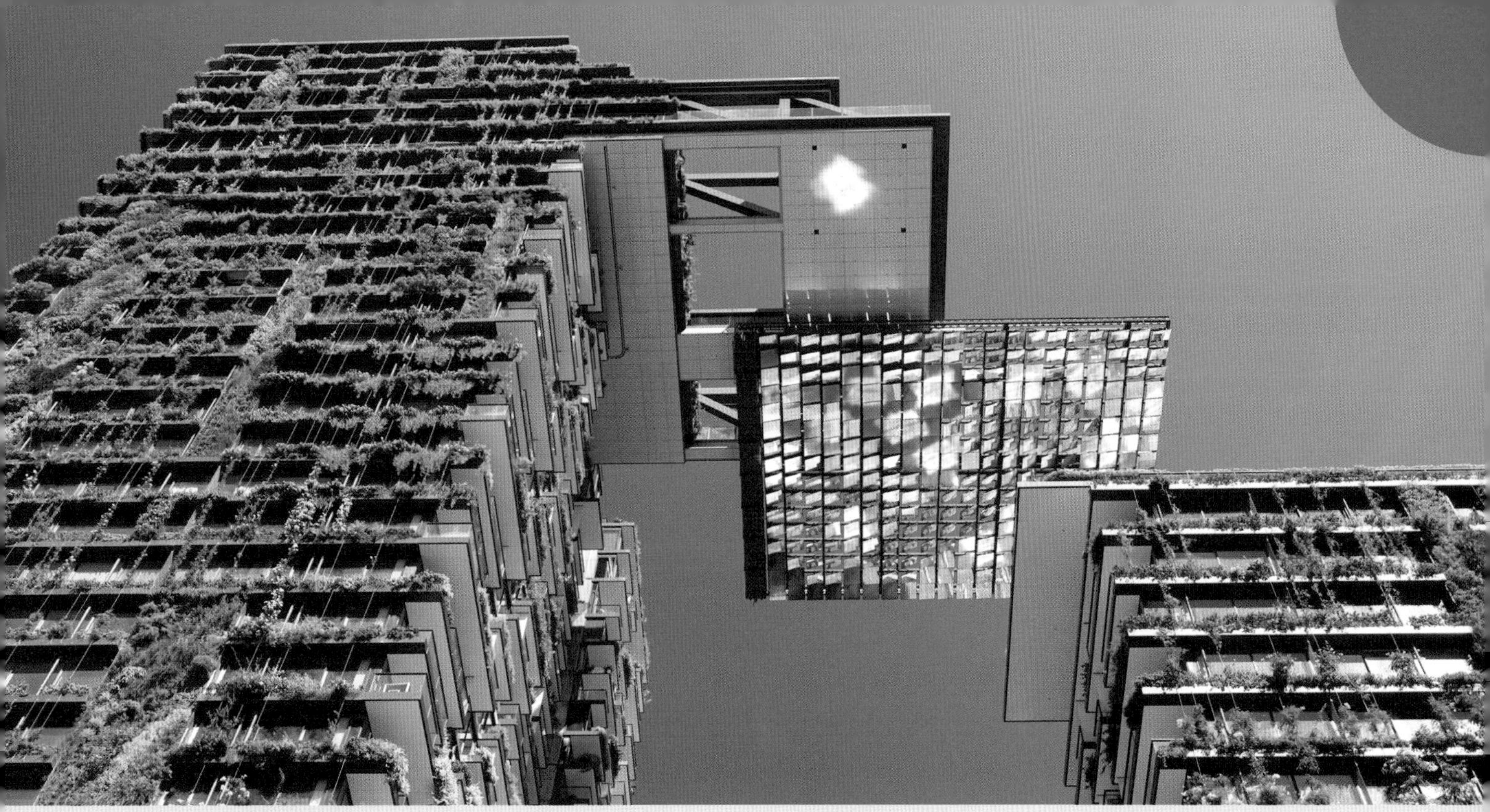

▲ Research has shown that as well as looking nice and supporting wildlife, urban gardens can moderate the temperatures in cities, prevent flooding, ease stress and promote well-being. How else can our environment affect our mental state?

▼ Cutting down trees for timber, paper, fuel or to clear land for agricultural use is known as deforestation. For about 200 years, the global rate of deforestation has closely followed the global increase in population, but this trend was reversed in the 1990s, when deforestation slowed down despite continued population growth. How do social and economic changes inform environmental considerations?

Introduction

Nothing is independent of its environment. The surrounding conditions such as temperature and air pressure do not only affect the weather and how comfortable we feel; they also affect the very nature of the substances around us.

Different parts of the Earth have different environments: near the equator, the intensity of the Sun's energy causes hotter weather than at the poles where it is colder. Oceans act to maintain a more constant temperature for their surroundings, creating different environments for islands and inland areas.

Each of these different environments is a finely balanced system. Factors such as the temperature and amount of rain interact to create unique environmental systems. For this reason, the key concept is systems.

Different seasons can affect the environmental system. In winter, temperatures drop and water turns to ice. In summer, as temperatures rise, the ice melts and the water is evaporated.

Key concept: Systems

Related concept: Environment

Global context: Globalization and sustainability

▼ The atmosphere and its temperature can change the state of matter of water. In winter, the lower temperature causes the water to freeze and sit as ice. As spring arrives, the increase in temperature causes the snow to melt in the mountains and these crocus flowers are quick to take advantage of the changing season

Statement of inquiry:

Changes in our environment require all living things to adapt in order to survive.

The global environment is also changing, and scientists are studying the reasons for these changes as well as the impacts that they may have on environmental systems. The complicated nature of these systems makes accurate predictions very difficult, but the study is of global significance. For this reason, the global context is globalization and sustainability.

One important system in the global environment are the ice caps. In this chapter we will see how the surrounding environment affects the state of matter of substances such as water. The density of water and other substances is also important as it determines which objects float and which sink. In this chapter we will look at what density is and how it is important to the environment.

▼ The density of oil is less than that of water. As a result, spilt oil will float on top of the water forming a slick. This can be devastating for shore-line wildlife and efforts are made not only to prevent spills, but also to clean up in the event that one occurs. What other examples of chemical releases can you think of which affect the environment?

▲ Changes in the temperature of our environment cause water to take different forms. This results in very different habitats and very different animals in different parts of the world

MATTER

How does matter behave?

Matter naturally occurs in three different states.

- Some matter has a fixed shape in which case we say that it is a solid.

- Other matter flows and spreads out without a container in which to hold it. It remains at the bottom of the container it is in, spreading out to take the shape of the container up to a certain level. We call this state liquid.

- A third type of matter has no surface at all. It spreads out to completely fill the container it is in. This is a gas.

Of course, not all matter in the same state behaves in exactly the same way. For some solids, like concrete, it is very hard to change its shape; these can be described as tough. Other materials are brittle and will break or shatter like glass when they are deformed. Some solids, such as metals, are malleable and ductile; they can be bent, stretched, twisted or hammered into different shapes without breaking. A malleable material deforms under compression; for example, aluminum can be rolled out into a foil. A ductile material can be stretched; for example, copper into a wire.

MATTER

Are there other states of matter?

Although matter on Earth falls into one of the three states, there is a fourth state of matter: plasma. A plasma is an ionized gas; this means that it is so hot that one or more of the electrons in an atom of the plasma are removed. The plasma is therefore like a gas of positively charged ions and negatively charged electrons.

The properties of a plasma are very different to that of a normal gas. Whereas most gases are transparent, plasmas are opaque. They also emit light because of their high temperature.

On Earth, plasmas can occur in electric sparks or lightning, but the most common occurrence in the solar system is the Sun which is essentially a giant ball of plasma. Given its large mass, this makes plasma the most abundant state of matter in the solar system.

Although the states of matter appear very different, the same substance can be transformed from one state to another. Water is a good example of this. When it is frozen, it can be a very tough solid. We have oceans of liquid water on Earth from which water evaporates as water vapor and rises up into the atmosphere.

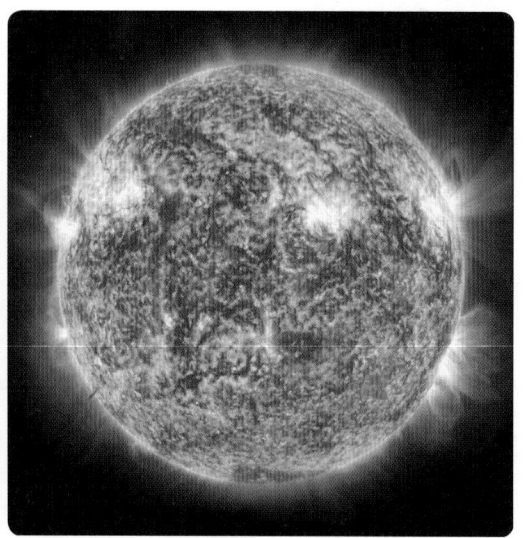
▲ The Sun is predominantly a plasma

▲ A glacier is a large body of ice that flows down a mountain under the force of gravity. Despite the ice being solid, the glacier behaves a bit like a liquid in that it flows. Its speed, however, is very slow, perhaps only a few centimeters per day

What causes states of matter to be different?

All matter is made up of atoms (see Chapter 1, Models). It is the behavior and interactions of these atoms that explains how solids, liquids and gases behave. Sometimes the atoms are chemically bonded together to form molecules. For instance, in water each particle of water is two hydrogen atoms and one oxygen atom. We shall use the word "particle" to mean the smallest bit of water, or any other substance, that we can have. These particles may be molecules or individual atoms.

The particles of a substance can exert forces upon each other. As a result, they interact and this affects the way they behave. The forces between particles only act over very small distances. When the particles are spread out, they do not exert forces on each other. When they are close together, they attract each other, but if they get too close they repel each other.

In a solid, the particles are tightly packed. They are in fixed positions, although they can vibrate back and forth about these fixed positions. Because the particles are already tightly packed together, it is hard to push them any closer since the forces between the particles would be repulsive. As a result, it is hard to compress a solid. It also requires a lot of energy to separate the particles because of the attractive forces between them. This is why it takes energy to break apart a solid, so solids maintain their shape with the particles in their fixed positions.

If a solid is heated, then the particles may gain enough energy to break out of their fixed positions, and the solid becomes a liquid. The particles can now move randomly around, but there are still attractive forces pulling them together. Because the particles are still close together, it is hard to compress a liquid.

If this liquid is heated up further, then the particles might gain enough energy to break free of the forces attracting them. The liquid turns into a gas. In a gas, the particles are spread apart and the forces between them are insignificant. They are free to move around so a gas will fill up the entire container it is in.

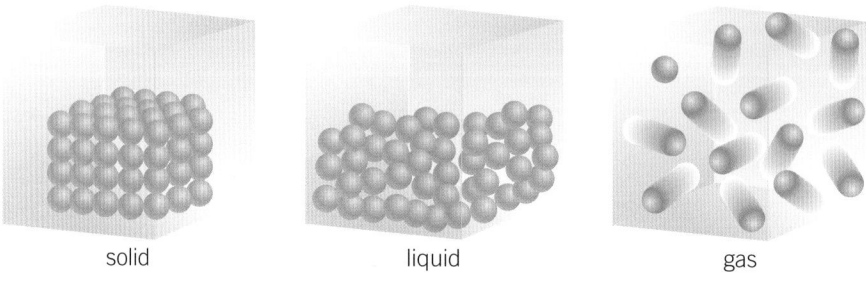

solid   liquid   gas

▲ The arrangement of atoms in a solid, liquid and a gas

Ⓐ Ⓑ Ⓒ Ⓓ Experiment

Cooling candle wax

The process of changing state can be monitored by measuring the temperature. In this experiment, candle wax turns from a liquid into a solid.

Method

- Using a hot water bath, melt some candle wax in a boiling tube.

- Once the wax is entirely melted, remove the boiling tube and place a thermometer in the wax.

- Keep stirring the wax with a thermometer to maintain an even temperature. Take a reading of the thermometer every 10 seconds as the wax cools.

Questions

1. Plot a graph of your data with time on the *x*-axis and temperature on the *y*-axis.

2. On your graph identify the temperature at which the wax changed from a liquid to a solid.

What is temperature?

The way in which the individual molecules in a substance move affects the state of the substance and its overall heat energy. If the molecules move or vibrate faster, they have more energy and the object is hotter.

A gas may be modeled as lots of atoms or molecules which are constantly moving and bouncing off each other and the walls of their container. This model is called kinetic theory. As the temperature of the gas increases, the gas particles move more quickly, colliding with each other more often and at higher speed.

The motion of the gas particles themselves is imperceptible, and some particles are moving faster than others. The average energy of the particles, on the other hand, is perceptible through their many collisions. If you put your hand into a container of hot gas, the particles hit your hand at high speed and transfer energy to your hand. You feel this transferred energy and perceive the gas to be hot. On the other hand, if you put your hand into a cold gas, the particles bounce off your hand slowly. They might pick up energy from the rapidly vibrating molecules on the surface of your skin and rebound off you faster. In this way the gas takes energy from your hand and you perceive the gas as being cold. The imperceptible motion of many molecules becomes temperature on a larger scale.

How can we demonstrate kinetic theory?

In 1827, a botanist named Robert Brown was looking at pollen grains in water through a microscope. He noticed that they moved around randomly, but he couldn't explain why. This effect also occurs with smoke particles in air and became known as Brownian motion.

The explanation of what was happening was supplied by Albert Einstein in 1905. He and Marian Smoluchowski showed that the particles of pollen or smoke were constantly colliding with the much smaller air or water molecules. The collisions occur very frequently ($10^{14} - 10^{16}$ times per second) and although these collisions are distributed around the smoke particle, they are random. This means that at any instant there may be a slight imbalance in the force that the air molecules are exerting on the smoke particle. This causes the smoke particle to experience a net force and accelerate in that direction. A small time later, the imbalance in the collisions may be different so the smoke particle accelerates in a different direction. The result is the larger particles of smoke or pollen appear to jitter about.

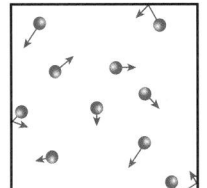
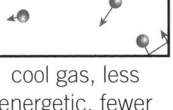
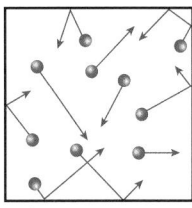

cool gas, less energetic, fewer collisions

hot gas, more energetic, more collisions

▲ The atoms or molecules in a gas are too small to be seen, however, their average energy may be detected as temperature. The gas particles move more slowly in a cold gas than in a hot gas and so they have fewer collisions and collide at slower speeds

MATTER

the smoke particle is much larger than the air molecules

the air molecules are constantly moving and colliding with the smoke particle

▲ An illustration of Einstein and Smoluchowski's explanation of Brownian motion

Experiment

Observing Brownian motion

- Place a tiny amount of milk on a clean microscope slide, using a needle.

- Dilute the milk with a drop of distilled water and place a coverslip on top.

- Using a microscope capable of about 400× magnification, first observe using the 10× objective and then with higher powers. Try to observe the tiny globules of fat suspended in the milky water. At first they may be all drifting in one direction, but when they settle down, you should be able to observe them jiggling around. This is Brownian motion caused by the collisions of the water molecules with the fat droplets.

MATTER

How can we change matter from one state to another?

If water is heated up to 100°C at normal room pressure, it boils. This is because 100°C is the boiling point of water. At this temperature, the average energy of the molecules is sufficient for them to break free of the surface of the liquid. As the liquid boils, water vapor rapidly forms bubbles in the liquid which rise up and escape once they reach the surface. Any molecule which gains enough energy escapes the water, so even if the water is heated continuously, the liquid cannot get above its boiling point.

If water is cooled to 0°C it starts to freeze. The molecules do not have enough energy to keep moving around and they start to take on a fixed position.

Data-based question: Changing state

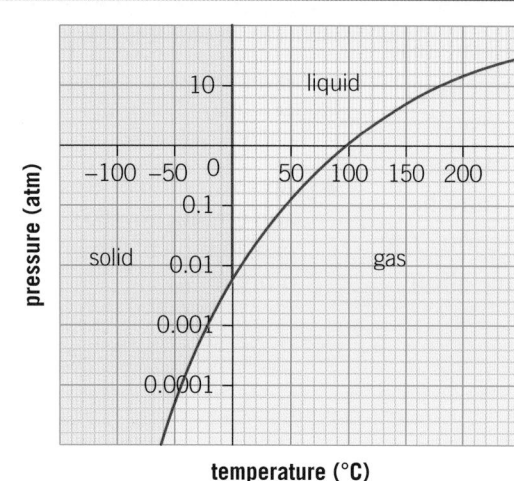

temperature (°C)

It is not just temperature that can change the state of a substance; pressure can too. A graph showing what state of matter a substance will exist in at different temperatures and pressures is known as a phase diagram.

Use the phase diagram for water to answer the questions that follow.

◀ Phase diagram of water. The units of pressure are atmospheres (atm); 1 atmosphere is the atmospheric pressure at sea level

1. The pressure at the top of Mount Everest is only 0.33 atm. What are the boiling and freezing points of water at this altitude?

2. To hard boil an egg it needs to be cooked at about 85°C. At what pressure will water boil at a high enough temperature to achieve this?

3. Using the graph of altitude against atmospheric pressure, find the maximum altitude at which you could hard boil an egg.

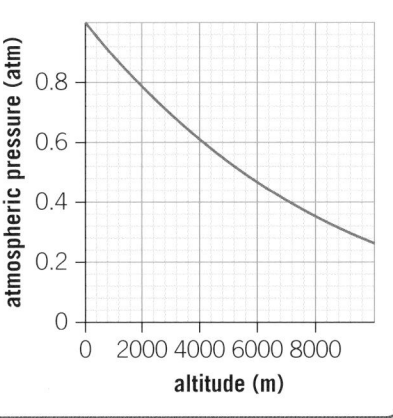

▶ Graph of altitude vs pressure

For a gas with the particles bouncing around in a sealed container, the speed at which they move is dependent on the temperature of the gas. If the gas is cooled, the particles slow and when they collide with the walls of the container or other particles, they spend longer in close proximity. It is when they are close together that these particles experience attractive forces and if they are moving sufficiently slowly the forces might hold the particles together. The gas is turning into a liquid – this is called condensation.

Higher up in the atmosphere, the temperature is cooler; this is why it is colder at the top of mountains than at sea level. Water vapor in the atmosphere cools down high up in the atmosphere and condenses. At first, it condenses into tiny droplets of liquid water and forms a cloud. Eventually, as more water condenses, the water droplets become bigger and fall as rain.

It is also possible to turn a gas into a liquid by squeezing it. If you can compress a gas so that the particles get close enough together to start attracting each other, the gas will turn into a liquid. It requires a pressure of about 10,000 atm (10,000 times atmospheric pressure) to liquefy air, however, other gases will liquefy at lower pressures. Propane and butane can be stored as liquids at pressures of 10 atm or less.

▲ Cooler temperatures higher up in the atmosphere cause water vapor to condense. This causes clouds to form and when there is enough water it falls as rain

Sublimation

The phase diagram on page 92 shows that at low pressures, the liquid state of water does not exist. Some substances do not have a liquid phase at atmospheric pressure, and so they change state straight from solid to gas. This process is called sublimation. Iodine is often used to show sublimation and solid carbon dioxide also sublimates.

1. Why are liquids not common in space?

2. Why would a planet have to have a reasonable size in order for liquids to exist on its surface?

3. Are liquids necessary for life to evolve?

▲ This solid carbon dioxide sublimates from a solid straight into a gas

▶ As comets get close to the Sun they heat up. In space the low pressure means that liquids do not easily exist, so substances such as methane and water in the comet sublimate from solid to gas. This gives the comet its distinctive tail

MATTER

What is evaporation?

The particles in a liquid are constantly colliding and moving past each other in close proximity. When two particles collide, energy transfers between them, and afterwards each particle may travel at a different speed. Some particles have a greater speed and some have less but the average speed of all the particles remains the same at a constant temperature. The very fastest particles might have enough energy to break free of the surface of the liquid and become a gas even though the temperature of the liquid is below the boiling point. This is evaporation. Because the particles that escape have an above average speed, the average speed of the remaining particles is lower, so evaporation cools a liquid.

1. Some water evaporates from the surface of a hot cup of coffee. Explain how this cools the coffee.

2. Evaporation and boiling both involve a liquid turning into a gas. Explain the difference between the evaporation from the surface of the cup of coffee and boiling.

3. When we exercise hard, our skin sweats. Explain how this cools us down.

Evaporation is an important process for the Earth's oceans. The Sun's heat falls on the vast surface area of the oceans, giving the water energy and heating it up. The water at the surface evaporates, cooling the oceans and counteracting the heating effect of the Sun.

Why is rain important?

The atmosphere of Venus is mainly carbon dioxide but it also contains nitrogen and water vapor as well as some noxious chemicals such as sulfur dioxide and sulfuric acid. These gases cause a large greenhouse effect heating the surface of Venus to more than 450°C.

It is thought that the early atmosphere of Earth consisted of similar substances to the current atmosphere of Venus. However, there was one important difference: on Earth it was cool enough for water to condense into a liquid. As a result it could rain. The rain water washed many of the acidic chemicals out of the atmosphere leaving an atmosphere of nitrogen and carbon dioxide. When primitive life evolved, photosynthesis resulted in carbon dioxide being converted to oxygen and the atmosphere started to become more like the current atmosphere on Earth.

Although the atmospheres on Earth and Venus were originally very similar, the final result has been vastly different environments. Scientists conclude that small changes in temperature have the potential for large-scale impacts on our atmosphere and for this reason, they are keen to monitor the changes in climate that occur (whether naturally or from human causes). However, it is controversial – since it is impossible to conduct controlled experiments on the climate of a planet, it is hard to produce definitive evidence as to the extent of the climate change that will occur as a result of human activity.

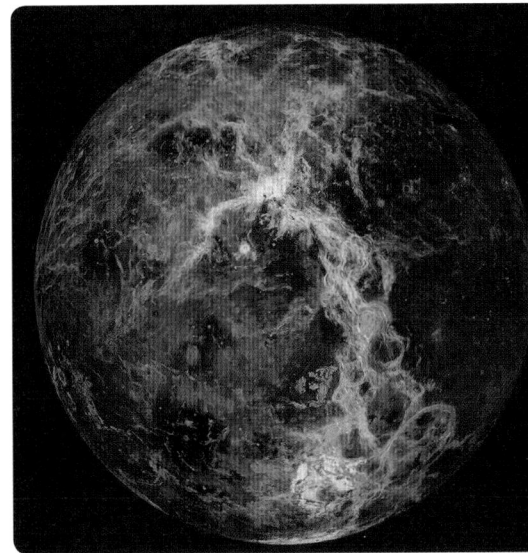

▲ The dense atmosphere of Venus blocks our view of its surface. This radar image shows a barren and probably volcanic surface to the planet. Although the atmospheres of Earth and Venus started in a similar way, the resulting environments on the planets have been very different

Water vapor is a greenhouse gas. This means that it allows the heat energy from the Sun to hit the Earth's surface, but absorbs the radiated heat from the Earth and reflects some of it back towards the Earth. This keeps the surface of the Earth at a hotter temperature than it would otherwise be. Other common greenhouse gases are carbon dioxide and methane. Scientists are concerned that our population's increased production of carbon dioxide (through burning fossil fuels) and methane (through farming) could increase the greenhouse effect and hence cause global temperature rises.

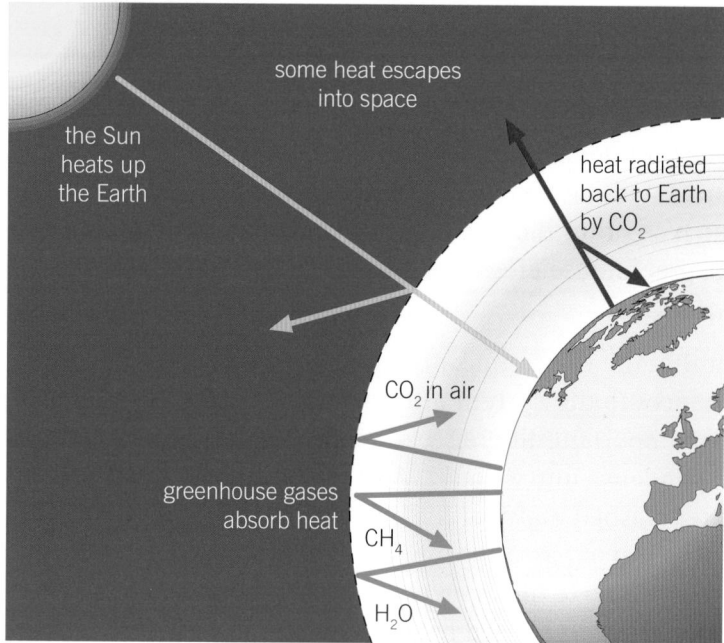

▲ Greenhouse gases such as water (H_2O), carbon dioxide (CO_2) and methane (CH_4) reflect some of the radiated heat from the Earth back towards the ground. This greenhouse effect causes the Earth's surface temperature to be warmer than it would be if there were no atmosphere

Warmer atmospheric temperatures mean that the ice at the North and South Poles starts to melt. Ice at the South Pole in Antarctica sits on top of land as does the ice in Greenland. If a substantial amount of this were to melt, it would flow off the land and into the oceans causing the sea level to rise. While some predictions suggest that sea levels will rise by less than a meter over the next century; other predictions suggest that this increase may be much larger.

Tracking your carbon emissions

Carbon dioxide is a greenhouse gas and many scientists are concerned by the amount that humans release into the atmosphere.

There are many websites which allow you to calculate the amount of carbon dioxide released from travel, energy use, food and waste. Find one of these calculators and then keep a diary for a week detailing your usage. At the end of the week estimate your carbon footprint.

Was any of your carbon footprint essential? Could any of it have been reduced?

What is density?

The mass of an object is not just defined by its volume; it also depends on its density. For example, $10\,cm^3$ of water will have a mass of $10\,g$. Because most metals are denser, $10\,g$ of metal will have a smaller volume. Brass has a density of $8,500\,kg\,m^{-3}$ which is 8.5 times greater than water and so only $1.2\,cm^3$ of brass is needed to make a $10\,g$ sample. A less dense material like balsa wood requires a larger volume to have a mass of $10\,g$; as the density of balsa wood is 6.25 times less than water, a volume of $62.5\,cm^3$ is required.

Density is the amount of mass per cubic meter and is calculated using the equation:

$$density = \frac{mass}{volume}$$

Since mass is measured in kilograms and volume in cubic meters, the unit of density is $kg\,m^{-3}$. Objects made of the same material will have the same density.

1. The density of air is about $1.2\,kg\,m^{-3}$. Estimate the mass of air in the room that you are in.

2. Iron has a density of $7,870\,kg\,m^{-3}$. Calculate the volume of iron which would have the same mass as your answer above.

3. The kilogram is defined by a cylinder of platinum iridium alloy called the international prototype kilogram kept in Paris. The cylinder has a density of $21,186\,kg\,m^{-3}$ and a height of $39.17\,mm$.

   a) Calculate the cross-sectional area of the cylinder.

   b) Calculate the diameter of the cylinder.

Units of volume and area

The normal unit of volume is cubic meters (m^3) but cubic centimeters (cm^3), cubic millimeters (mm^3) and cubic kilometers (km^3) are often used for small or big objects. Take care when converting between these units. For example, there are 100 centimeters in a meter but there are not $100\,cm^3$ in $1\,m^3$.

Consider the following diagram of a cube. Each side of this cube is $1\,m$ long (or $100\,cm$), and its volume is $1\,m^3$.

100 cm   1 m³   100 cm   100 cm

▲ Each of these objects has a mass of $10\,g$. The different sizes are caused by the materials having different densities. On the left, brass has a density of about $8,500\,kg\,m^{-3}$. Water has a density of $1,000\,kg\,m^{-3}$ and on the right, balsa wood has a density of $160\,kg\,m^{-3}$

▲ This worker is carrying three bricks. He knows that this is three times heavier than carrying one brick. He also knows that if the bricks were smaller, they would be lighter, or if they were made of a different material with a lower density they would also be lighter

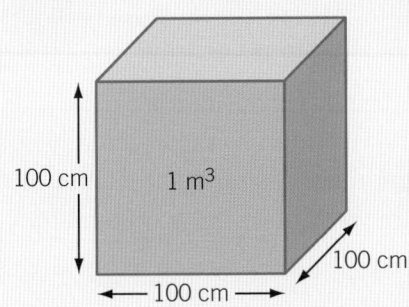

1. Calculate the volume of the cube in cm³. How many cm³ there are in 1 m³?

2. The area of one of the cube's faces is 1 m². Calculate the area in cm². Hence find how many cm² there are in 1 m².

3. Using a similar method, find the following:

   a) The number of square meters in 1 km²

   b) The number of cubic millimeters in 1 cm³

   c) The number of square meters in a square mile (1 mile = 1,608 m)

   d) The number of cubic meters in a cubic light year (1 light year = 9.46 × 10¹⁵ m).

FORCES

Why do objects float?

If an object is more dense than water, it will sink; similarly, an object which is less dense, will float. The reason for this lies in the mass of water the objects displace.

When a stone is put in water, the level of the water will rise because the stone displaces it. The weight of the water that is displaced pushes upwards on the stone. This force is called upthrust. As a result, the stone will be supported by the upthrust of the water, but because its own weight is greater it will still sink.

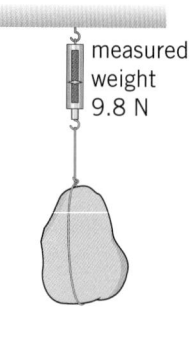
measured weight 9.8 N

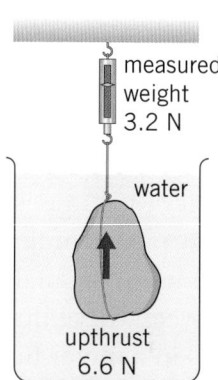
measured weight 3.2 N

water

upthrust 6.6 N

▲ The stone has a mass of 1 kg and so its weight is 9.8 N. It has a volume of 6.7 × 10⁻⁴ m³ and when it is submerged, it displaces this volume of water which weighs 6.6 N. As a result, the measured weight is only 3.2 N when it is submerged. What is the stone's density?

A wooden block, on the other hand, may have a density that is less than water. It will sink until it has displaced a weight of water that is equal to its own weight. At this point, the force of the upthrust from the water balances the weight of the wooden block so it floats.

◀ Whales can grow to be over 170,000 kg. This whale would be unable to support its huge weight on land; however, the force of upthrust from the water around it supports its bulk

Size, mass and density

Imagine the following objects:

- expanded polystyrene packaging
- tree
- bucket of water
- steel ball bearing
- person
- helium balloon.

Sort the objects in approximate order of size.

Now try to sort them in order of mass.

Finally, sort them in density order (Hint: think about which would float and which would sink).

How can you measure density?

MATTER

The first person to be credited with finding the density of an object was Archimedes, a Greek mathematician, scientist, and inventor who was born in about 287 BC. There is a story which says that the king of Syracuse, Hiero II, commissioned a golden crown as a gift to the gods. However, he suspected that the goldsmith had cheated him by mixing some cheaper silver into the crown. King Hiero asked Archimedes to determine whether the crown was pure gold, but Archimedes could not damage the crown in any way as it was a gift for the gods.

The story says that the answer came to Archimedes as he got into a full bath and caused it to overflow. He realized that by submerging the crown in water, he could compare its volume to that of the same mass of pure gold. He was so excited that he ran (naked) down the street shouting "Eureka", which means "I have found it".

The principle of displacement is known as Archimedes' principle. To find volume of an object by displacement, you can use a measuring cylinder. Put enough water in the measuring cylinder to submerge the object and record its volume. Add the object so that it is completely submerged and record the new volume. The difference in the two readings is the volume of the object.

An alternative method is to use an Archimedes can – a can with a spout. The can is filled up to the spout and any excess water drains out. When an object is put into the can it displaces water which pours down the spout and is collected in a beaker. The volume of the object is the same as the volume of water in the beaker, which can be measured with a measuring cylinder.

Archimedes found one method to find the volume of an object but sometimes, other methods are appropriate:

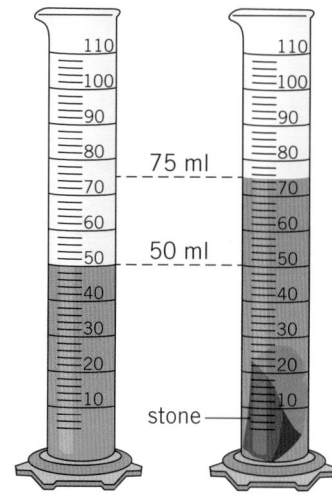

▲ When the stone is placed into the measuring cylinder, the volume increases by 25 cm³. This is equal to the stone's volume

- if the object is regular in shape, you can measure it and directly calculate its volume

- if the object is a liquid, you can use a measuring cylinder to measure its volume

- if the object is irregular in shape, then a displacement can be used to find its volume (as long as it doesn't float).

To measure the density of an object you also need to find its mass which can be measured on a balance. The density is then found by dividing the mass by the volume.

▶ An Archimedes can (or displacement can) can be used to measure the volume of an irregularly shaped solid. The volume of water displaced by the stone into the beaker is the same as the stone's volume. The volume of the water displaced can be measured with a measuring cylinder

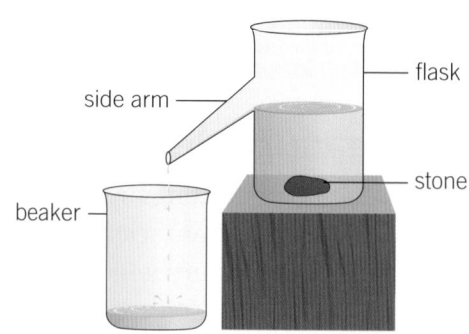

How to measure density

Describe how you would measure the density of the following objects:

● wooden block

● sugar cube

● solution of sugar in water

● stone.

ⒶⒷⒸⒹ Experiment

What happens when salt dissolves in water?

Some people say that when salt dissolves in water, the salt particles (ions) fit in between the water molecules. This would mean that the volume would not increase, but since extra mass is added, the density would increase. On the other hand, it might be that the volume does increase.

Design an experiment to investigate this. Formulate a hypothesis and carry out the experiment.

Measuring density

An empty measuring cylinder is placed on a balance and is found to have a mass of 90 g. 100 cm³ of liquid is added and the balance now reads 170 g. When a stone is dropped in so that it is fully submerged, the volume on the measuring cylinder reads 148 cm³ and the balance reads 290 g.

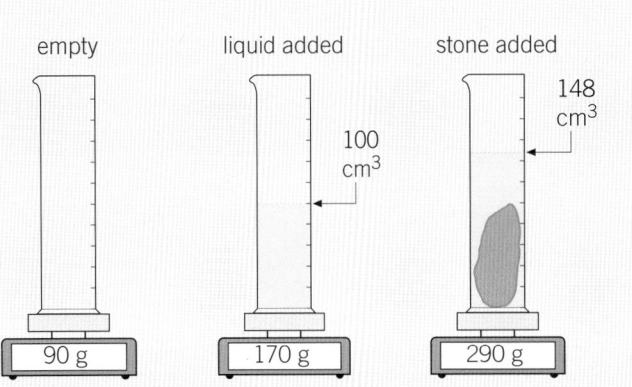

empty   liquid added   stone added

100 cm³   148 cm³

90 g   170 g   290 g

1. By finding the mass and the volume of the liquid, calculate the density of the liquid. Give your answer in g cm⁻³.

2. Calculate the density of the stone.

3. The stone is removed. The level of the liquid returns to 100 cm³ and the balance reads 170 g. Which of the following objects could have their densities calculated by placing them into the measuring cylinder? If the density cannot be measured in this way, explain why not.

   a) A thumb-sized piece of pumice stone which has an approximate density of 300 kg m⁻³.

   b) A piece of the same type of stone with a mass of 500 g

   c) A piece of copper pipe, 32 cm long, with an internal diameter of 2.5 cm and a wall thickness of 2 mm.

   d) 50 cm³ of sand.

   e) A block of rosewood that is approximately 2 cm × 2 cm × 3 cm and has a mass of 10.8 g.

What is so special about water?

In this chapter, we have often considered water as a good example of a liquid; however, in many ways water is very unusual. For a start, it is somewhat surprising that it is a liquid at all. Most simple molecules, other than metallic elements, are gases, such as carbon dioxide (CO_2), ammonia (NH_3) or methane (CH_4). Another unusual property of water is that its solid form, ice, is less dense than liquid water. This is why an iceberg floats. This property is very beneficial for fish in a pond as in cold weather the top of the pond freezes but the water remains liquid underneath.

Water has another unusual property: it takes a lot of energy to heat it up. To raise the temperature of 1 kg of water by 1°C requires about 4,200 J of energy – more than twice the amount of energy required to heat up 1 kg of oil by 1°C. As a result, large seas and oceans act as heat reservoirs. When the weather is hot, the sea absorbs heat energy but does not heat up very much. This keeps the surrounding land cooler. On the other hand, when the weather is cooler, the sea's heat energy warms the land around it. Ocean currents such as the Gulf Stream can significantly change the local environment by moving warm water around the seas.

▼ This fisherman is fishing through the ice. Unusually, ice is less dense than liquid water – most substances are denser as a solid than as a liquid. For water, this means that the lake freezes from the top and liquid water remains underneath

Summative assessment

Statement of inquiry:

Changes in our environment require all living things to adapt in order to survive.

Introduction

The Dead Sea is the lowest place on Earth below sea level. The water contains about ten times more salt than normal sea water and so, apart from some microscopic organisms, it contains no animals or plants – hence its name.

 ## The density of the Dead Sea

A tourist visiting the Dead Sea took a sample of the water and measured it. Its volume was 250 cm³ and its mass was 310 g.

1. Calculate the density of the water in the Dead Sea. Give your answer in:

   a) $g\,cm^{-3}$

   b) $kg\,m^{-3}$. [3]

2. The density of pure water is $1,000\,kg\,m^{-3}$. Explain why the density of the Dead Sea means that you float better in it than in ordinary water. [3]

The surface of the Dead Sea is 430 m below sea level which makes it the lowest place on the surface of the Earth. Water that flows into it evaporates and this concentrates the salt and other minerals.

3. Explain how the water from the Dead Sea evaporates, turning from a liquid into a gas, despite it not being near its boiling point. [3]

4. The Dead Sea has a volume of about 147 km³. Convert this volume into cubic meters. [2]

5. Using the density that you calculated in question 1b, calculate the mass of salty water in the Dead Sea. [2]

6. Explain why this large mass of water causes the local environment to have a more constant temperature. [2]

 ## Investigating evaporation

7. A student plans to investigate the effect of temperature on the rate of evaporation.

   a) Suggest a suitable hypothesis that the student might investigate. [3]

   b) The student has access to a water bath which can maintain a constant temperature. What other equipment does the student need to complete the experiment? [3]

c) Describe a suitable procedure that the student should follow. Detail the measurements that should be taken. [7]

d) Identify two control variables for this experiment. [2]

 Dead Sea water levels

The graph below shows how the depth of the Dead Sea has changed over a period of 15 years.

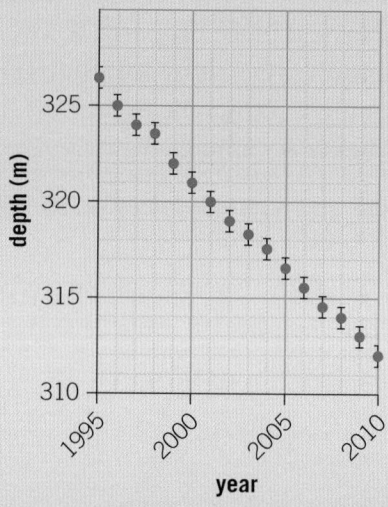

8. Add a line of best fit to a copy of the graph. [1]

9. Find the gradient of the graph. [2]

10. Comment on the reliability of this trend. [1]

11. Each data point has an error bar which indicates that the actual level of the Dead Sea lies somewhere within these bounds. Explain why it might not be possible to attribute an exact depth to the Dead Sea for any given year. You should consider more than one factor. [4]

12. Some people say that this graph might suggest that the Dead Sea might completely dry up one day. Using the graph and your value of the gradient, estimate the year in which it will dry up. [3]

13. How reliable is your estimate for the year at which the Dead Sea might dry up? You should evaluate two factors which might affect your estimate. [4]

 Protecting the Dead Sea

The Dead Sea is a unique environment which is fed by the River Jordan. The rapid loss of water threatens its existence. As a result, there are various proposals to protect the Dead Sea.

One scheme proposes that 2.05×10^{12} kg of water from the Red Sea is pumped into the Dead Sea every year. The water would have to be pumped along 140 km of pipes.

14. Discuss one advantage and one disadvantage of this scheme. You may wish to refer to a map. [4]

15. The density of the sea water is 1,025 kg m^{-3}. Calculate the volume of the water which would be pumped into the Dead Sea every year. [2]

16. The Dead Sea has a surface area of about 600 km^2. Convert this into m^2. [2]

17. Calculate the amount that the pumped water would raise the level of the Dead Sea by every year. Assume that there is no loss of sea level by any other means. [3]

18. Evaluate the effectiveness of this solution with reference to your calculations. [4]

6 Function

Function is the purpose and capability of things.

◀ The function of some things has been discovered by accident. Polytetrafluoroethylene is better known as Teflon, the non-stick heat-resistant coating on frying pans. It was discovered by accident by scientists looking to formulate new refrigerants. Since then, its high thermal stability and very low coefficient of friction have meant that it has been used in heat shields for spacecraft, lubricating oils, outdoor clothing and plumbing sealants. Can you think of any other things that were discovered by accident?

▼ Stonehenge is an ancient stone circle in the UK. It is believed to have been constructed between 3000 and 2000 BC. Apart from the uncertainties over how prehistoric people may have transported the stones and put them in place, there are uncertainties over its function. Some of the stones align with the rising sun on the morning of the summer solstice and the sunset on the winter solstice, so some people think that Stonehenge served an astronomical purpose. Others believe it was a religious site or a burial ground. Which other ancient monuments have mysteries surrounding their function?

The aye-aye is a nocturnal animal which lives in Madagascar. It has evolved an unusually long middle finger. It uses this to tap on tree bark then listens for a hollow sound which might indicate a grub is hiding there. It then uses this long finger to fish the grub out. Which other animals have evolved with specialised features adapted for specific functions?

▼ This bridge has a very particular function. In the first century AD the Romans wanted to supply the city of Nimes in France with water. To do this they built an aqueduct from a spring 50 km away to carry water to the city. To get the water over the Gardon River they built this bridge, the Pont du Gard. The top tier carries the aqueduct across the valley. Are there modern examples of impressive architecture being designed to serve a function?

Key concept: Systems

Related concept: Function

Global context: Fairness and development

Introduction

One of the defining characteristics of human beings is their use of complex tools or machines. While the use of tools has been observed in some other species (mainly primates, but also dolphins, elephants and some birds), only humans use and develop complicated machines.

The simplest early machines, such as levers, required a mechanical force to operate them. More complicated are clockwork machines; these store energy in a spring or a raised weight which is then used to deliver the required force. The function of the machine might be to move in some way or to exert some other force. In this way, a machine is simply a system which changes the nature of a force. In this chapter we will investigate the nature of forces and what they do.

▶ The difference engine was a machine invented by Charles Babbage in the 19th century. At that time, complex calculations had to be done by hand and would often include mistakes. The purpose of the difference engine was to improve the speed and accuracy of calculations. Although he never actually made a working prototype, a couple of machines have since been made following his designs. Today, calculators and computers can carry out complex calculations at speed

Statement of inquiry:

The development of machines and systems has changed the way in which human beings function.

Mechanical machines could be quite complex systems. Scientific progress in the 19th century and early 20th century enabled us to harness the power of electricity. Instead of needing such mechanical systems with complex moving parts, electrical components were used, although these could still form complex networks. This allowed machines to become smaller and instead of needing a mechanical input, they could be powered by electricity. In this chapter, we shall see how basic electrical circuits function and might be used in a machine.

Machines have changed the way in which society functions. While early humans were hunter-gatherers with every individual involved in sourcing enough food, machines such as the plow enabled farming to take place so that fewer individuals could grow more food. This gave other people time to do other useful tasks. Throughout history, machines have helped improve our productivity, enabling one person to do more than before. This changes the systems we use and the way in which we work. The key concept of the chapter is systems.

Some people think that technological advances will enable society to operate with people working fewer hours per week and having more time for leisure. Other people are worried that their jobs will become unnecessary as they might be replaced by machines in the future. It is clear that our working habits will have to adapt and we will need to develop new systems of employment. Because of this, the global context of this chapter is fairness and development.

▲ These Neolithic age arrowheads date to about 4000 BC. The earliest evidence of use of tools in humans dates to about 3 million years ago

▼ Modern machines can carry out complex tasks in all sorts of environments. The Mars Rover Curiosity is searching Mars for evidence of water and the building blocks of microbial life

What types of force are there?

A force can be described as a push or a pull on an object. There are many ways in which an object could receive a force. Here are some common forces.

- **Weight (gravitational force):** The Earth's gravitational field pulls all objects downwards. This force is called weight (see Chapter 2, Interaction).

- **Reaction:** Although objects are pulled toward the center of the Earth, they rest on the ground or some other surface. The Earth's surface exerts a force which counteracts an object's weight and keeps it from falling further downwards. This force, due to the contact between two objects, is called a normal reaction. It stops us falling through floors and enables us to sit on chairs without falling through them.

- **Friction:** When two objects slide over each other, friction acts against their motion. This force can be reduced by making the two objects smoother or by lubricating the contact with a substance such as oil, but it cannot be eliminated without removing all contact between the objects.

- **Air resistance:** Another type of friction is air resistance. This occurs when an object moves through air. The resulting "wind" acts against the motion of the object.

- **Electrostatic force:** This force acts between two charges (see Chapter 2, Interaction). It can be attractive or repulsive.

- **Magnetic force:** This is the force of attraction between two opposite magnetic poles or the repulsion between two like magnetic poles (see Chapter 4, Movement).

- **Tension and compression:** Tension is a force that occurs when something like an elastic band or a rope is stretched. The force of tension pulls objects. The opposite is compression where an object exerts a force by being squashed, such as a spring.

- **Upthrust:** Objects which are submerged in water or floating on the surface are supported by the buoyancy of the water (see Chapter 5, Environment). This force is called upthrust. It is also felt by objects in the air, but is not normally noticeable unless the object has a low density such as a helium balloon.

- **Lift:** Wings on a plane generate an upwards force that help it to fly. This is called lift.

▲ What are the forces acting on a bungee jumper when she has just jumped off the platform? What about when she reached the bottom of the jump and is about to bounce back up?

▲ What are the forces acting on a helicopter hovering above the ground?

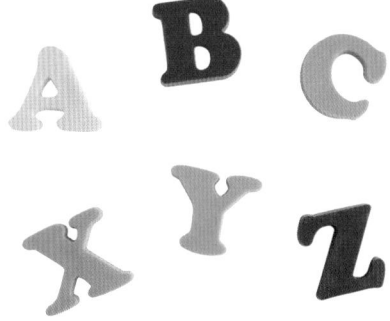

▲ What are the forces acting on a magnet stuck to the side of a fridge?

How do we measure forces?

FORCES

It is common to measure weight using a balance. As we saw in Chapter 2, Interaction, a balance gives a result in grams or kilograms (units of mass), but it is really measuring the weight of the object which is a force. The force F can be found using the formula:

$F = m g$ where m is the mass of the object and g is the gravitational field strength (9.8 N kg^{-1} on Earth).

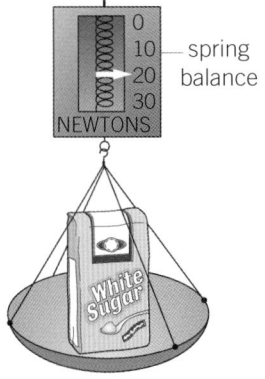

◀ A spring balance and a set of scales both measure the weight of an object. The scales convert their result into a mass according to the equation $F = mg$. As a result, the reading is 2.00 kg. The spring balance shows the weight of the bag of sugar which is 19.6 N

Another way of measuring an object's weight is to use a spring balance. This consists of a spring which stretches when the object is hung on it. The greater the weight of the object, the more the spring stretches. A spring balance does not have to be used vertically to measure weight; it could be used to measure other forces as well.

The unit of force is a newton which is abbreviated to N. As a result, a device which measures force is sometimes called a newton-meter.

How can we represent forces?

Forces are vector quantities (see Chapter 4, Movement). This means that the direction as well as the size of the force is important. Often there is more than one type of force acting on an object with the same magnitude but in different directions. These forces cancel each other out and the sum of the forces, called the resultant force, is zero. In this instance, the object is said to be in equilibrium and the forces are balanced. An object in equilibrium is either stationary or moving at a constant speed.

To represent the forces that act on an object, we often draw a free-body diagram. This is a simplified diagram which represents the forces with arrows. The direction of the force is represented by the direction of the arrow and the magnitude of the force is represented by the length of the arrow. To keep things simple, the object itself is normally represented by a simple shape such as a rectangle.

As an example, consider the forces that act on a child sliding down a slide. The child's weight acts downwards. Because the weight acts through the center of mass, it is usual to draw the weight from the

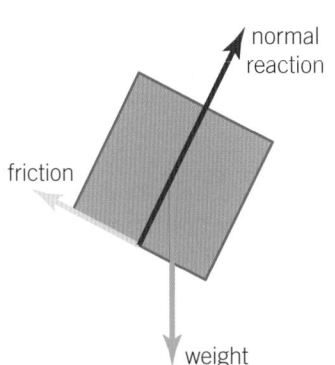

▲ What are the forces that act on the child sliding down the slide?

▲ Free-body diagram of the child on a slide

Worked example: Balanced forces

Question

An ice skater has a weight of 600 N. She glides along the surface of the ice at a constant speed. Draw a free-body diagram to show the direction and the magnitude of the forces that act on her.

Answer

The ice skater's weight acts downwards (600 N). Since the ice skater is not accelerating into the ice (or jumping off it) there must be a force which balances the weight. This is the normal reaction which acts upwards with a force of 600 N.

As she is skating along at a constant speed, there must be no net horizontal force since a constant speed indicates equilibrium. There is no force pushing her along and, in this case, the friction is negligible.

The free-body diagram looks like this:

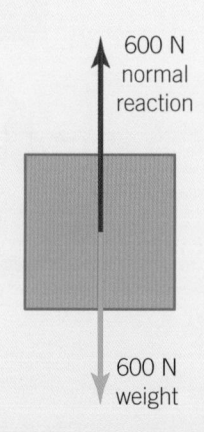

600 N normal reaction

600 N weight

center of the rectangle. The child is in contact with the slide and so the slide exerts a normal reaction force. This acts at right angles to the slide. There is also some friction which acts against the motion of the child hence it acts up the slide.

1. A skydiver is in freefall. His weight is 800 N and he is falling at a constant speed (terminal velocity).

    a) What can be said about the total force acting on the skydiver?

    b) Other than the skydiver's weight, what other force acts and how big is it?

    c) Draw the free-body diagram for the sky diver.

2. What happens when the skydiver opens his parachute?

How do machines use forces?

FORCES

As mechanical machines apply forces, many do work. In physics, work is the process of transferring energy to an object. This might be achieved by:

- lifting it – this is doing work against gravity

- moving it against another force; for example, doing work against friction by dragging an object along the ground

- deforming an object.

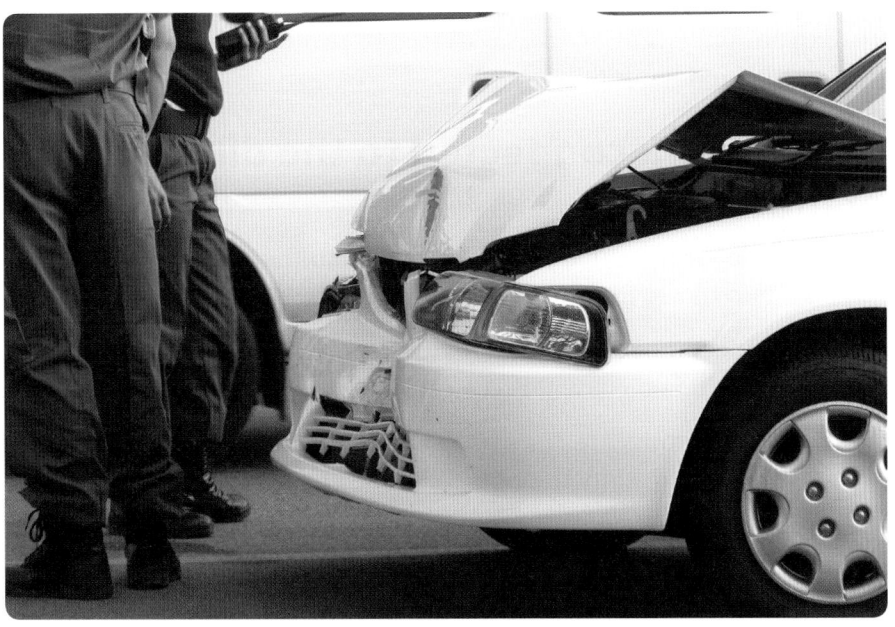

◀ If a car crashes, work has to be done to transfer the kinetic energy of the car's motion into another form. The work is done by deforming the front of the car. Crumple zones are included in the design of cars so that work is done deforming the car. What would happen to the forces on the car and its passengers if the crumple zone was designed to crumple over a larger or smaller distance?

Because work is the transfer of energy, the unit of work is the joule (J). The work done against a force may be calculated using the equation:

$$\text{work done} = \text{force} \times \text{distance}$$

This may be written using symbols as:

$$W = F\,d$$

Worked example: Work done by a weightlifter

Question

A weightlifter lifts a 200 kg mass through a height of 1.8 m. How much work is done? (The value of g is 9.8 N kg^{-1}.)

Answer

$$\text{work} = \text{force} \times \text{distance}$$

The force is the weight of the 200 kg mass:

$$\text{weight} = 200 \times 9.8 = 1{,}960\,\text{N}$$

So

$$\text{work} = 1960 \times 1.8 = 3{,}528\,\text{J}$$

1. A train traveling at a constant speed requires a driving force of 15,000 N to counteract friction. How much work must it do to travel 10 km?
2. A 60 g tennis ball is dropped from a height of 3 m.
   a) What is its weight?
   b) What work is done by gravity on the tennis ball?
3. Explain why more work is required to run 100 m up a hill than to run 100 m downhill.

FORCES

▲ The orbits of the Moon around the Earth and the Earth around the Sun are nearly circular. Since the gravitational force acts at right angles to the motion, no work is done

How is work connected to the direction of motion?

The distance in the equation $W = F\,d$ refers to the distance moved in the direction of the force.

- If the object moves in the same direction as the force then work is done and the object will accelerate and hence gain kinetic energy.
- If the object moves in the opposite direction to the force, then the force acts to slow the object down. We say that work is done against the force and the kinetic energy of the object's motion is transferred away to a different type of energy.

In some instances, the object moves at right angles to the force. In this case the object does not move in the direction of the force at all. This is the case in circular motion, for example, the Earth orbiting the Sun. The force of gravity acts to pull the Earth closer to the Sun, but the distance between the Sun and the Earth remains almost constant. As a result, the distance in the equation $W = F\,d$ is zero and so no work is done. This is why the Earth maintains a constant speed as it orbits the Sun and all other planetary orbits are able to maintain their speed rather than spiraling into the Sun or accelerating away into space.

How can machines do work?

A crowbar can be used to pull a nail out of wood. This is a good example of a simple machine which takes an input force and uses it to do work. Work needs to be done to remove the nail and although the crowbar does not do the work itself, it makes the task much easier by giving a mechanical advantage. This means that the user exerts a smaller force and the crowbar converts this to a larger force at the other end. For this to happen, the user has to exert their force over a larger distance, so the work done is the same. This is an example of a class 1 lever.

A lever has a bar and a pivot. On one side of a class 1 lever there is a load, which might be a heavy object to lift, and on the other a force is applied. This force is called the effort.

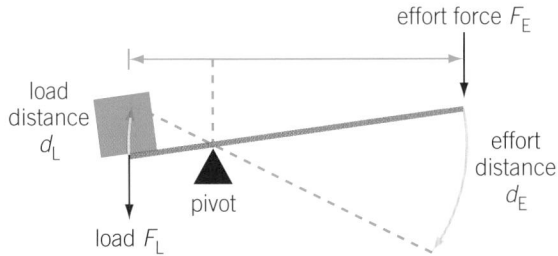

▲ Lever consisting of a bar and a pivot

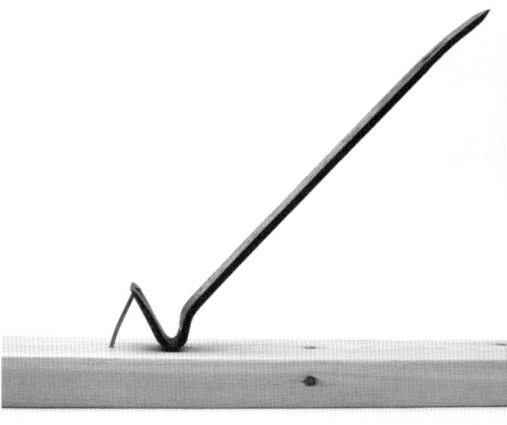

▲ A crowbar makes removing a nail much easier

The work done W by applying the effort F_E is given by the work equation:

$$W = F_E \, d_E$$

where d_E is the distance over which the effort is applied. As long as there is very little friction, we can assume that the work done by the effort will all be applied to the load. Therefore:

$$F_L \, d_L = F_E \, d_E$$

◄ Archimedes is reputed to have said, "Give me a lever long enough and I shall move the Earth."

The distance for which the effort force is applied is greater than the distance that the load is moved. Rearranging the equation gives:

$$\frac{F_L}{F_E} = \frac{d_E}{d_L}$$

The ratio $\frac{F_L}{F_E}$ is the mechanical advantage, the factor by which the load force is greater than the effort. As a result, if d_E is greater than d_L, the mechanical advantage is greater than one. When the mechanical advantage is greater than one, the effort force is less than the load. As a result the lever acts to make the applied force bigger and makes the task easier.

1. A lever is used to operate a water pump.

   a) A force of 15 N is applied to the handle and it is lifted 75 cm. Calculate the work done by the force.

   b) The work done by the applied force will be the same as the work done on the water pump on the other side of the lever. The piston of the pump only moves 15 cm. Calculate the force applied to the piston.

   c) Explain why in reality the work done on the piston is a bit less than the work applied to the lever.

There are three types of lever:

A first-class lever has the load on one side of the pivot and the effort force on the other side. The mechanical advantage of a first-class leaver will be directly correlated with the distance between the effort and the pivot. When the effort force is further away from the pivot, the lever can support a larger load, and so the mechanical advantage > 1; otherwise, when the effort force is close to the pivot, the mechanical advantage is <1. Scissors are an example of a first-class lever.	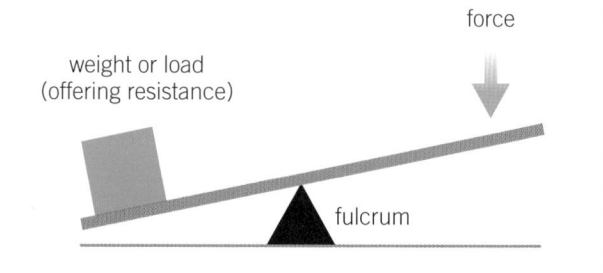
A second-class lever has the effort and the load on the same side. In a second-class lever, the effort force is further from the pivot than the load, so the mechanical advantage > 1. A bottle opener is an example of a second-class lever.	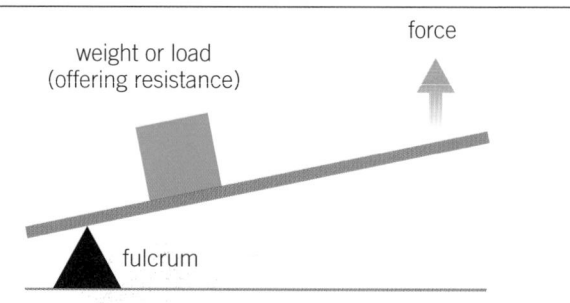
Similarly to a second-class lever, the effort and the load in a third-class lever are on the same side of the pivot. The difference is that the effort is closer to the pivot than the load, and so the mechanical advantage of this leaver is <1. A fishing rod is an example of a third-class lever.	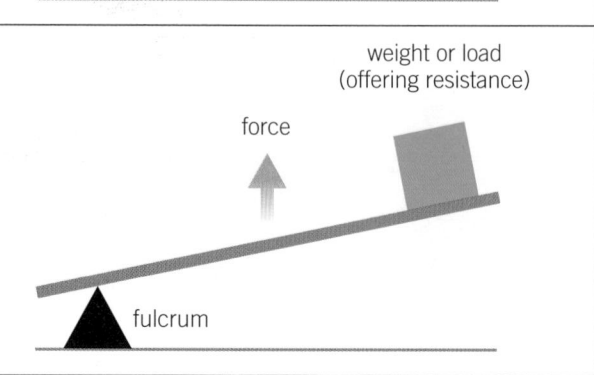

Which type of lever?

Draw the force diagrams and identify which type of lever is in use in the following pictures.

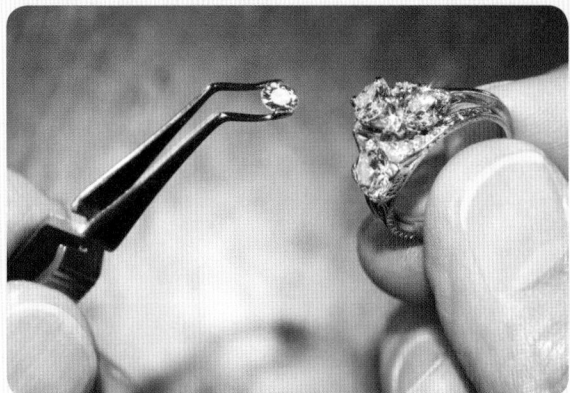

Other simple machines

Archimedes and other Greek philosophers defined five simple machines: the lever, the pulley, the wheel and axle, the screw, and the wedge. Later, Renaissance scientists and engineers added the inclined plane to this list. Like the lever, all these machines change the nature of a force.

Explain how each of the following objects uses a simple machine to change the nature of the force applied in order to do work.

▲ A G-clamp is used to hold parts in place

▲ This ramp enables wheelchair access

▲ An axe uses its shape to drive apart a log

▲ This device helps to lift heavy rigging on a ship

▲ This winch converts a rotational force into a linear force

▲ An auger is used to drill through the ice

FORCES

How do forces influence motion?

One of the greatest thinkers of Antiquity was Aristotle, who lived in Greece in the 4th century BC and wrote about many subjects, from philosophy and logic, to poetry and music. He also wrote about physics, although what Aristotle thought of as physics was a broader topic than nowadays as it also covered the philosophy and science of nature.

One of Aristotle's ideas was that heavier objects would fall faster than light objects. This seemed correct at the time, but without the scientifically defined concepts of acceleration or velocity, he was not able to carry out actual experiments. It was not until Galileo carried out experiments at the end of the 16th century that Aristotle's ideas were discovered to be incorrect. Through these experiments, Galileo found that an object that experienced no resultant force would continue to move as it was, or, if it were stationary, would remain stationary. In other words, forces cause a change in motion – acceleration – and heavier objects and light objects accelerate at the same rate.

◀ In 1971, David Scott, an *Apollo 15* astronaut, carried out a version of Galileo's experiment on the Moon, in which he dropped a hammer and a feather. Because of the Moon's negligible atmosphere, there was almost no air resistance, so the hammer and the feather hit the ground at the same time

How do forces cause acceleration?

If a force generates a motion, a double force will generate double the motion [...] And this motion [...], if the body moved before, is added to or subtracted from the former motion [...] so as to produce a new motion compounded from the determination of both.

Isaac Newton

ATL Communication skills

Using subject-specific terminology

Because the language of his time did not have scientifically defined words such as "acceleration", in order to report his observations, Newton relied on describing what he saw. Nowadays, to communicate their findings, scientists rely on many words with precise definitions. This enables them to communicate concepts to other scientists without having to define and redefine their terms.

Just like Newton, the scientists who first investigated energy had no word for it – they called it *vis viva* (meaning living force). The first scientist to use the word energy in the way physicists use it today was Thomas Young (who also demonstrated that light was a wave – see Chapter 9, Development).

In a similar way, languages develop words to describe color. English had no word for orange until the 13th century. Some languages only have two terms which describe color: one for black and one for white.

When Isaac Newton formulated his laws of gravity to explain planetary motion (see Chapter 2, Interaction), he used some of Galileo's ideas about forces. This led him to present three laws which are now known as Newton's laws of motion.

- **Newton's first law:** An object remains at rest or continues to move at a constant velocity unless acted on by an external force.

  This is a rewording of Galileo's ideas about forces and means that an object cannot change velocity without a force acting on it. Because velocity is a vector quantity, a change in direction is also a change in velocity. An example of this is any object going around in a circle, such as a planet orbiting the Sun. As the Earth goes around the Sun, it maintains a constant speed but because it is constantly changing direction, its velocity is not constant – it is accelerating. Since it is accelerating, this requires a force, which in this case is the force of gravity between the Earth and the Sun. Without the interaction of gravity, the Earth would continue moving in a straight line and move out of the solar system.

- **Newton's second law:** The sum of all the forces F on an object is equal to the mass of the object m, multiplied by the resulting acceleration of the object. This can be written as:

$$F = m\,a$$

  This law describes the effect of forces and allows us to calculate the acceleration that they cause. Newton also observed that the acceleration would be in the same direction as the force.

- **Newton's third law:** When one object exerts a force on another, the second object exerts a force of the same size back on the first in the opposite direction.

  This law essentially says that forces come in pairs. Newton used the example of a horse dragging a stone on a rope. The force which drags the stone along has the same magnitude as the force which pulls on the horse and slows it down, but these two forces act in the opposite direction.

▲ How do Newton's laws of motion apply to this motorcycle and its rider?

Identifying Newton pair forces

Take care when identifying the pairs of forces in Newton's third law. The forces are always of the same type and have the same magnitude, but act in opposite directions.

For example, consider a book on a table. The forces on the book are its weight acting downwards and the normal reaction acting upwards. These forces balance each other and so the book remains in equilibrium; however, they are not a pair of forces according to Newton's third law as they are of different types.

- The paired force of the normal reaction pushing on the book is another normal reaction force, this time from the book pushing downwards on the table.

- The weight of the book is caused by the gravitational pull of the Earth. The Newton pair of this force is an upwards pull on the Earth due to the gravitational field of the book. This force has the same magnitude as the weight of the book but because the Earth is so large, it has no observable effect.

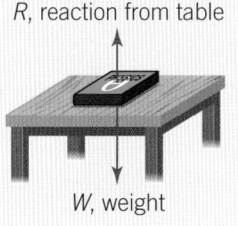

R, reaction from table

W, weight

These two forces are *not* third law pairs. There must be another force (on a different object) that pairs with each one:

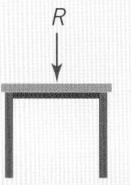

R

If the table pushes upwards on the book with force *R*, then the book must push down on the table with force *R*.

W

EARTH

If the Earth pulls the book down with force *W*, then the book must pull the Earth up with force *W*.

Identify the Newton pairs of these forces:

- the normal reaction of a tennis racket hitting a tennis ball and making it accelerate

- the air resistance acting on a skydiver's parachute

- the frictional force between a runner's shoes and the ground which stop them slipping at the start of a race

- the weight of an airplane.

Worked example: Hitting a tennis ball

Question

In a tennis serve, a tennis ball of 60 g is accelerated from rest to a speed of 40 m s^{-1}. The tennis racket exerts a force on the ball for 5 ms.

a) Calculate the acceleration of the tennis ball.

b) Calculate the force that the racket exerts on the ball.

c) What force is exerted on the racket by the ball?

Answer

a) $\text{acceleration} = \dfrac{\text{change in speed}}{\text{time taken}} = \dfrac{40}{0.005} = 8,000 \text{ m s}^{-2}$

b) $F = ma = 0.06 \times 8000 = 480 \text{ N}$

c) Because of Newton's third law, the tennis ball exerts an identically sized force (480 N) back on the tennis racket.

▲ In medieval warfare, catapults were used in sieges to hurl rocks at castle walls

1. The catapult fires a 10 kg rock. The arm which fires it exerts a force over 5 m and provides 5,000 J of work.

   a) Calculate the force on the rock.

   b) Calculate the acceleration of the rock.

   c) The work is done by a large mass which falls through a distance of 2 m. Calculate the minimum mass required.

   d) Explain why in practice a larger mass is required.

   e) Explain why the catapult recoils backwards when the rock is fired.

   f) Explain why the recoil of the catapult is much slower than the launch speed of the rock.

ATL **Thinking in context**

What happens to the Earth when you jump up in the air?

Newton's third law means that the Newton paired force of your weight is the equal force that you exert upwards on the Earth. It may seem strange to think that you can exert a force on the Earth. If you jump off a 1 m high table, you accelerate towards the ground and the Earth accelerates towards you!

Newton's second law, $F = ma$ tells us that the force you exert on the Earth is the same as your weight. The Earth's mass is approximately 10^{23} times heavier, and so its acceleration is 10^{23} times less. As a result, it moves 10^{23} times less distance than you; that is, it only moves 10^{-23} m (a tiny amount).

So, what if the entire human population were to jump 1 m in the air – could we get the Earth to move? Even if we assume that all the people on Earth are able to get to the same location and jump at the same time, the total mass of humans is still only about 4×10^{11} kg which is still significantly less than the Earth's mass. If everyone jumped 1 m in the air, the Earth would only recoil by 6.7×10^{-14} m which is only a little bigger than an atom's nucleus. Even if the entire biomass of the Earth were to

jump 1 m (which is hard for many plants!), the Earth would only recoil by the size of an atom.

The Earth's vast size can lead people to believe that their actions have a negligible impact on it. However, scientists are increasingly realizing that humans are affecting the planet in many different ways such as intensive agriculture, pollution and climate change. As our developments in technology allow the human population to grow, it is important that our resources are able to support that population and that they have the same access to the resources that we might currently enjoy.

What is an electric current?

When charge flows from one place to another, an electric current is produced. Often this current is electrons moving through a metal conductor.

In metal atoms the outer electrons are so loosely held in place that they can move freely within the metal. This means that it is easy for electrons to flow through metals. We say that they are good conductors of electricity. Materials such as plastics on the other hand do not allow electrons to flow very much at all. These materials are called insulators.

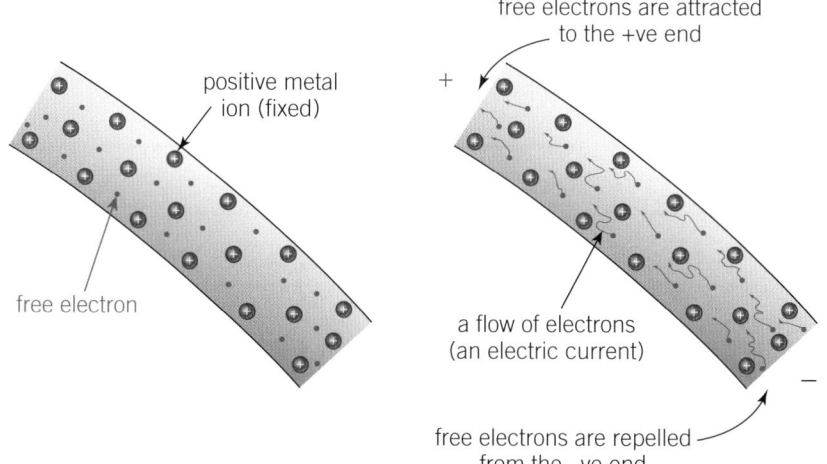

◀ In a metal there are free electrons which are able to move out of their atoms. The atoms are left without an electron so they are positively charged. When you make one side of the wire positively charged and the other negatively charged, for example, by connecting a battery, the electrons are able to move along the wire. This flow of electrons is called an electric current

Often a battery is used to generate a current. Chemical reactions inside the battery cause one side to have an excess of positive charge (that is, fewer electrons to balance out the positively charged nuclei) while the other side of the battery has a negative charge (more electrons). Electrons in the wire are repelled from the negative side of the battery and attracted to the positive side of the battery. Since all the electrons

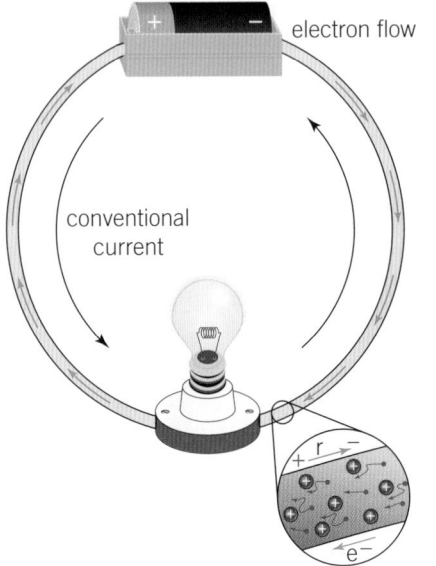

electron flow

conventional current

▲ Electron flow is in the opposite direction – "conventional current"

repel each other, they do not clump together or leave gaps but instead try to distribute themselves evenly throughout the metal. As a result, the electrons flow from the negative side of the battery to the positive side.

Since the electrons are negatively charged, when they arrive at the positive side of the battery, they lower its charge and when they leave the negative side of the battery they increase its charge. In other words, the positive side of the battery loses charge and the negative side gains charge. We say that charge has flowed from the positive side to the negative and call this "conventional current" even though what has actually happened is that electrons have flowed in the opposite direction.

Current may be calculated using the equation:

$$Q = I\,t$$

where I is the current and Q is the amount of charge that passes a point in time t. The unit of current is an ampere which is normally abbreviated to an amp or A.

ELECTRICITY

How can we draw a circuit?

A circuit diagram is a good way of representing a circuit. The wires are represented by lines and they are usually drawn as straight horizontal or vertical lines.

Each component has a circuit symbol. Some of the more common ones are listed below.

Component	Symbol	Component	Symbol
Cell		Battery	
Lamp		Motor	
Resistor		Variable resistor	
Ammeter		Voltmeter	
Thermistor		Light dependent resistor (LDR)	

What are series and parallel circuits?

If a circuit has only one loop, there is only one path that the current can take. We call this a series circuit. When current flows around a series circuit, the current is the same in any part of the circuit.

If a circuit has multiple paths to take, we call this a parallel circuit. In a parallel circuit the current splits or recombines at a junction. The total current flowing into any point still adds up to the total current flowing out. As a result, the current flowing out of the battery splits into smaller currents through different branches of the circuit, but it all recombines at the end to flow back to the battery with the same current.

1. A battery has a rating of 2,500 mA h which means that it can supply a current of 1 mA for 2,500 hours.

    a) What charge flows in this time?

    b) If this battery needs to keep a machine running for a year, what is the maximum current that the machine could take?

2. A current of 0.25 A flows through lamp A in the circuit below.

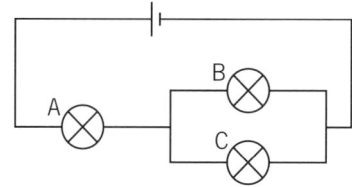

    a) How much charge flows through the circuit in 10 minutes?

    b) If the current through lamp B is 0.15 A, what current must flow through lamp C?

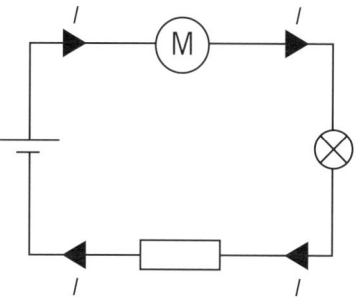

▲ Series circuit

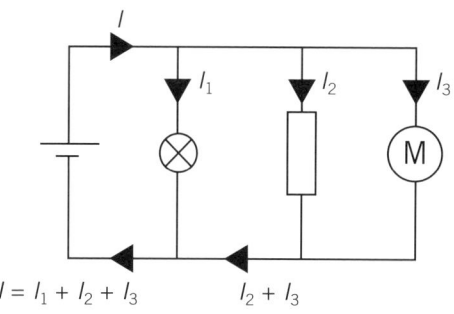

$I = I_1 + I_2 + I_3$ $I_2 + I_3$

▲ Parallel circuit

What causes an electric current?

Electrons don't flow around a circuit unless they receive some sort of force to push them around. The electron flow is caused by the battery which has one negative side that repels the electrons while the other side is positively charged and attracts them. The arrival of negatively charged electrons at the battery's positive side soon brings the overall charge to zero; however, the battery keeps pushing electrons off its positive side onto its negative side. The result is that the battery has an electromotive force or e.m.f. which causes electrons to move. This is also called the potential difference or voltage across the battery.

Potential is a measure of the energy that the electrons have at a given point in the circuit. The positive side of the battery has a positive potential and the other side has a negative potential. The charge flows around the circuit because of the resultant difference in energy, much as a ball rolls down a hill because of the difference in height. Of course, the absolute height of a ball on a slope does not affect its acceleration down the slope, but the tilt of the slope does. In the same way, the actual potential is not important, what matters is the difference in potential between one part of a circuit and another. This is called the potential difference or voltage.

ATL Creative thinking skills

Proposing metaphors and analogies

Physicists often need to communicate complex ideas that are not easily understood. Electricity is a good example of this as it is impossible to see the electrons moving through a circuit or perceive how much energy they have.

To help people use their imagination in a useful way, physicists often use analogies to help explain what is going on. A good analogy (see Chapter 1, Models) should be more intuitive than the abstract idea that you are trying to communicate, but it should also provide a good model of what is happening and help make predictions about what will happen in certain situations.

A common analogy for electrical circuits is that of water. A pump pushes water around a series of pipes. Sometimes the pipes split into two paths and the water flow divides at this point. A big pipe with a large internal diameter can carry a large flow of water, whereas a thinner pipe reduces the flow of water through it. The pressure from the pump pushes the water through the pipes and the water always flows from high pressure to low pressure. The pressure drop across a certain pipe determines the flow of water through it.

1. In this analogy, what do the following represent?
   - Pump
   - Pipe
   - Flow of water
   - Water pressure

2. In this analogy, what could represent an electric motor? Can you think of a way in which this model does not work?

3. Can you think of a different analogy to help explain electricity? What could represent the different components in a circuit?

ATL Thinking in context

How can we use electricity to drive machines?

Mechanical machines normally require a force to be applied so that work can be done. Machines can be human powered, but large machines used to be driven by horses, wind or water. The Industrial Revolution saw the invention of the steam engine to power machines (see Chapter 10, Transformation). Nowadays machines are often powered by electricity.

Electricity has many advantages when powering machines. It is easy to turn on and off and by controlling the current, it is possible to control the amount of work done by the machine. Sophisticated computer controls enable very subtle adjustments to its operation. Electric machines are often quieter and more efficient than their mechanical counterparts; however, they require a source of electricity or, if a battery is to be used, one that can store enough energy.

As technology has developed, the cost of machines has fallen. As a result, we now have machines in our homes that most people never had 100 years ago. Cars, washing machines, lawnmowers and food mixers are all examples of appliances in our homes which can be powered by electricity.

▲ Machines have been powered by humans, horses, petrol and electricity at different times. Each has advantages and disadvantages. What are they?

How can we measure the properties of an electrical circuit?

Current is measured with an ammeter. An ammeter is placed in a circuit and the current flows through it. Its reading gives the current through the circuit at that point. In a series circuit, the current is the same everywhere since there is no other branch for it to flow into, so it doesn't matter where the ammeter is placed.

Voltage is measured with a voltmeter and the units of voltage are volts. Because voltage is the difference in potential between two points, the voltmeter has two wires which are placed at different points in the circuit to measure the potential difference between them. As a result, a voltmeter is often placed in parallel to a component in the circuit and the reading is referred to as the voltage across that component.

◀ Measuring current and voltage

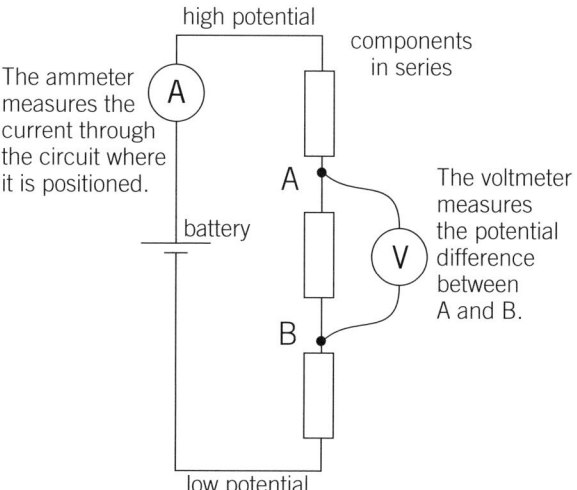

high potential

The ammeter measures the current through the circuit where it is positioned.

components in series

The voltmeter measures the potential difference between A and B.

battery

low potential

How can we control the current in a circuit?

Some things are easy for an electrical current to flow through and others are harder. A thick wire has plenty of "free" electrons in it which can move, but a thin wire has fewer "free" electrons so these electrons have to move faster to achieve the same flow of current.

The electrons traveling through a wire often collide with the atoms in the wire. If the electrons are moving slowly they are unlikely to lose much energy, but the faster they are moving along the wire, the more energy they lose in these collisions.

The result is that it is easier for a current to flow through a thick wire than a thin wire. We say that the thin wire has a greater resistance. Resistance can be calculated using the equation:

$$V = I\,R$$

where V is the voltage across a particular component (measured in volts), I is the current through that component (measured in amps) and R is the resistance of that component. This equation is called Ohm's law and the unit of electrical resistance is the ohm (Ω).

▶ In a thin wire, there are fewer electrons in any given length than in a thick wire. For a given current the electrons in the thin wire have to move faster. This results in them having more collisions with the ions and losing more energy. The thin wire therefore has a higher resistance

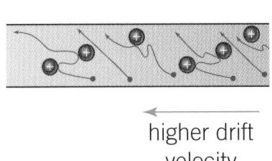
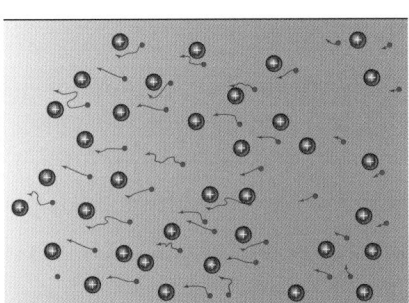

higher drift velocity

lower drift velocity

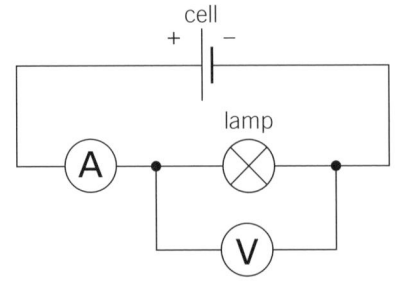

Experiment

Measuring resistance

To measure the resistance of a component, you need to measure the voltage across it and the current which passes through it. The diagram shows a circuit that can be used to measure the resistance of a lamp.

Make this circuit using a 12 V lamp. Instead of the cell, use a power pack with an adjustable voltage. Vary the voltage from 1–12 V

▲ Circuit to measure the resistance of a lamp

and record the voltage and current on the voltmeter and ammeter. Use Ohm's law to calculate the resistance at each voltage. What happens?

As the current through the bulb increases, the filament heats up and so the atoms inside it vibrate more. They cause more of an obstruction to the flow of current so the resistance of the lamp increases.

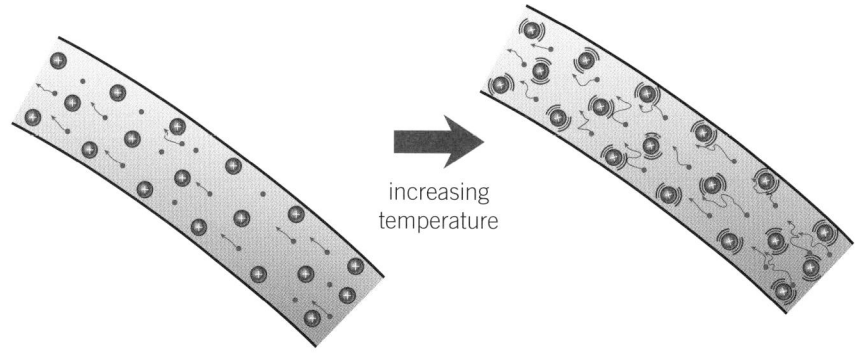

increasing temperature

Experiment

The length of a wire also affects its resistance. Write a hypothesis for how you think the resistance of a wire will change with length.

Method

- Assemble a suitable circuit to pass a current through a length of wire. Use a thin bare metal wire – 1 m is a suitable length. Include an ammeter and a voltmeter in your circuit to measure the current through the wire and the voltage across it. Use a power pack set to 1–2 V to power your circuit or a single 1.5 V battery. Include a variable resistance or a fixed resistance of about 10 Ω.

- Connect the wire into the circuit with two crocodile clips and measure the length of wire between these two connections.

- Vary the length of wire between the crocodile clips and measure and record the voltage across the wire and the current through the wire. Record your results in a suitable table.

Questions

1. Using Ohm's law ($V = I R$) add another column to your table for the resistance of the wire.

2. Plot a graph of your results. Do your results agree with your hypothesis?

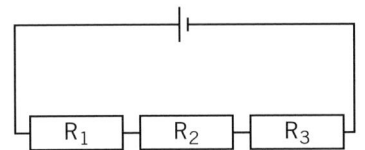

▲ In a series circuit the total resistance is given by
$R_{total} = R_1 + R_2 + R_3$

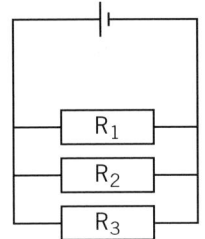

▲ In a parallel circuit the total resistance is given by
$$\frac{1}{R_{total}} = \frac{1}{R_1} + \frac{1}{R_2} + \frac{1}{R_3}$$

What happens to multiple resistances in a circuit?

If there are several resistances in series, their combined effect is added together. This is because the current must flow through each one. The total resistance is given by:

$$R_{total} = R_1 + R_2 + \ldots$$

If resistances are in parallel, the current splits so each resistor has a smaller current. This smaller current means that the electrons do not have to travel as fast so they lose less energy as they flow through the resistors. As a result, the combined resistance is less than the individual resistances. The combined resistance can be calculated using the formula:

$$\frac{1}{R_{total}} = \frac{1}{R_1} + \frac{1}{R_2} + \ldots$$

Worked example: Combining resistors

Question

Calculate the total resistance of the resistors below. Then deduce the reading on the ammeter.

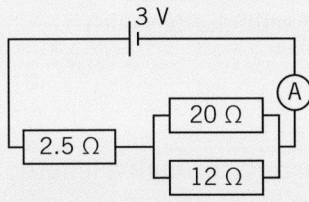

Answer

The $20\,\Omega$ and $12\,\Omega$ resistors are in parallel. Their combined resistance can be found using:

$$\frac{1}{R_{combined}} = \frac{1}{20\,\Omega} + \frac{1}{12\,\Omega} = \frac{2}{15\,\Omega}$$

Therefore, $R_{combined} = 7.5\,\Omega$. So

$$R_{total} = 7.5\,\Omega + 2.5\,\Omega = 10\,\Omega$$

The reading on the ammeter is given by:

$$I = \frac{V}{R_{total}} = \frac{3\,V}{10\,\Omega} = 0.3\,A$$

Combining resistors

If you are given four resistors each of $4\,\Omega$, can you find a way of combining them to make a total resistance of any whole number up to $10\,\Omega$?

How can resistance be used to control a circuit?

Some components have a fixed resistance but others have a resistance that changes. A variable resistor has a resistance that changes as you turn a knob or slide a slider. These could be used for anything that requires manual adjustment such as dimmer switches on lights and volume controls on audio equipment.

Other devices change their resistance according to their surroundings. A thermistor changes its resistance at different temperatures. As it gets hotter, the resistance of the thermistor decreases. This allows the current in a circuit to be adjusted according to changes in temperature, perhaps to monitor the temperature in an air conditioning system, or to provide a protection mechanism if something overheats.

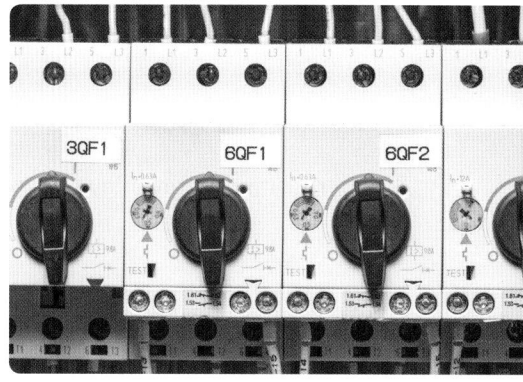

▲ A sliding rheostat is often used in a school laboratory to provide a variable resistance. In more complex electrical circuits, a rotating adjustment is often easier. A variable resistor can provide delicate adjustment for complex machines

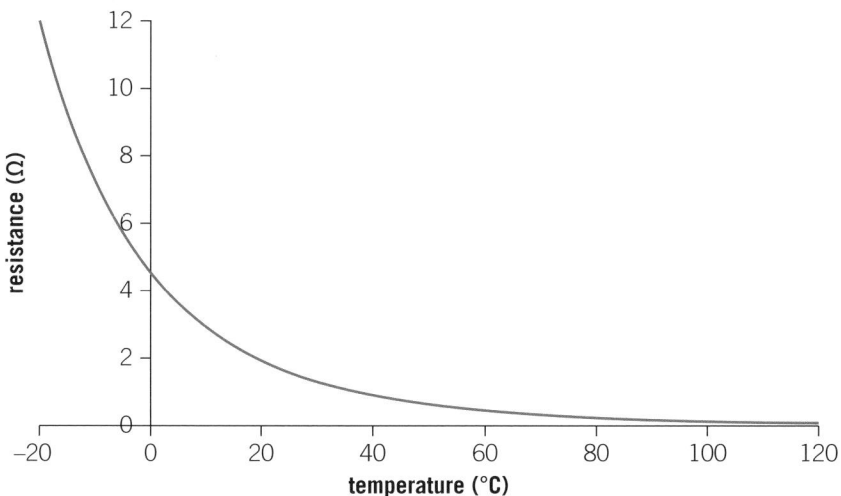

◄ The resistance of a thermistor decreases as temperature increases

A light dependent resistor (LDR) changes its resistance according to the ambient light level. With more light, the resistance of the LDR becomes less. An LDR can be used to turn on lights at night or it might detect the shadow of something nearby and be used as a proximity sensor.

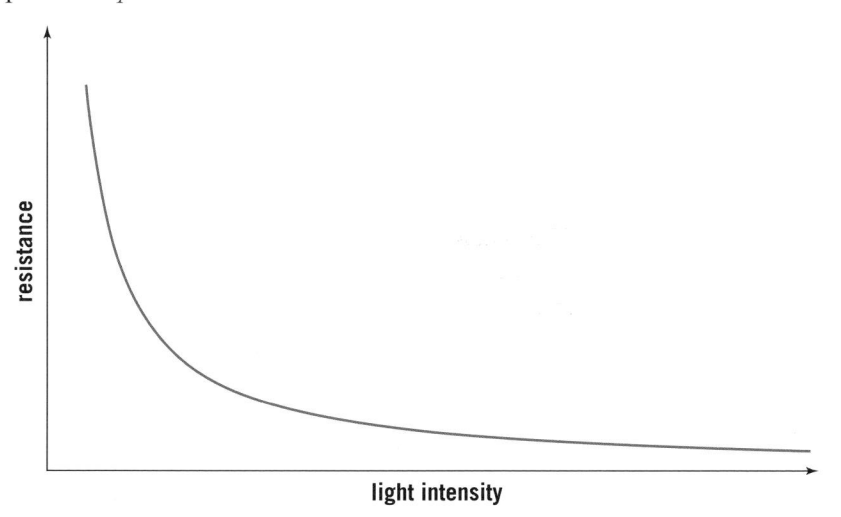

◄ The resistance of a light dependent resistor decreases with light intensity

Summative assessment

Statement of inquiry:

The development of machines and systems has changed the way in which human beings function.

Introduction

This assessment is about the use of robotic machinery in industry.

 Robotic circuits

1. An engineer is testing one part of a robotic circuit. The circuit being tested has a 3 V battery and two 100 Ω resistors in series. An ammeter and a voltmeter are added to the circuit to measure the current and the voltage across one of the resistors.

   a) Draw a circuit diagram for this circuit. [3]

   b) Explain why it does not matter where the ammeter is placed. [1]

   c) Determine the values that you would expect on the voltmeter and ammeter. [4]

2. The circuit is used to work a robotic arm that moves parcels in a warehouse. The arm picks up a parcel with a mass of 5 kg, moves it 2 m to the left and puts it down 0.75 m higher than it started.

   a) Explain why moving the parcel to the left does not require any work to be done. [2]

   b) How much work is done in lifting the parcel? [2]

   c) Lifting a heavy object can be done with a lever. Explain how a lever might be used to change the force required to lift the parcel. [3]

 Testing an electric motor

To test an electric motor, a student devises the apparatus shown in the diagram.

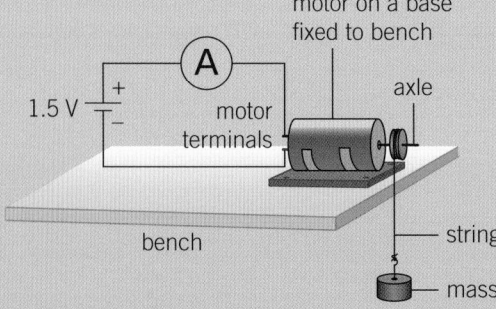

The student proposes changing the mass that the motor tries to lift and timing how long it takes for the mass to be lifted 1 m.

3. Why is it important to keep the distance that the mass is lifted the same each time? [2]

4. Suggest one other experimental factor which should be kept constant throughout the experiment. [1]

5. When the motor is loaded with a mass of 100 g, the motor lifts it in 11 s, 200 g takes 12.4 s, 300 g takes 14.2 s, 400 g takes 16.4 s and 500 g takes 19.6 s. Put these results into a suitable table. [3]

6. Plot a graph of the data and add a line of best fit. [4]

7. Calculate the weight of the 500 g mass. [1]

8. The weight of the 500 g mass is caused by the gravitational pull of the Earth. According to Newton's third law, there must be an equally sized force acting in the opposite direction. Describe what this force is and which object the force acts on. [2]

9. When the motor is switched on, the 500 g mass accelerates upwards. The acceleration lasts for 0.1 s.

   a) Use the experimental data to show that the speed of the 500 g mass was about 0.05 m s^{-1}. Assume that the distance traveled while the mass is accelerating is negligible. [2]

   b) Calculate the acceleration of the mass. [2]

   c) From your answer to part b, determine the size of the unbalanced force. [2]

   d) What is the tension in the string during this acceleration? [2]

10. After the first 0.1 s, the mass travels upwards at a constant speed. Explain why this shows that the tension must have the same magnitude as the weight of the 500 g mass. [2]

11. Calculate the work done in lifting the 500 g mass through 1 m. [2]

12. The current through the motor when lifting the 500 g mass is 0.17 A. Calculate the resistance of the motor when lifting this mass. [2]

13. The student notices that as the mass is increased, the current in the circuit also increases. Explain why the current increases. [3]

 ## The use of robots to replace a human workforce

Many industrial processes now use automated robots to carry out various tasks. Some manufacturers are increasing the number of robots they use on production lines.

14. Describe the advantages of using robots in industry. [5]

15. Some manufacturers are removing some robots in their factories and employing people to do these jobs instead. Explain what advantages there might be to employing a human workforce rather than using robots. [5]

16. For centuries machines have been used to make certain tasks easier. Pick one machine, describe what it does and explain how it makes that task easier. Try to use simple scientific terms effectively. [5]

▲ Robotic arms carry out the assembly of cars on a production line

7 Form

Form is the outward appearance of objects.

▼ The Cattedrale di Santa Maria del Fiore in Florence was designed to have a huge dome without any external support that was bigger than any previous dome (with the possible exception of the Pantheon in Rome). Work began in 1296 but a century later nobody knew how to construct the dome. The architect Filippo Brunelleschi won a competition to design the dome. To be self-supporting, the arches are in the form of a catenary curve (the shape a chain makes when it hangs between two supports). Where else does aesthetic form have to compete with engineering limitations?

▲ The regular hexagonal structure of these amethyst crystals is due to the arrangement of the silicon and oxygen atoms in the crystal. The color is caused by small amounts of iron in the crystal. How else can the invisible atomic structure of materials influence the overall form that they take?

▲ Form can be misleading. On the left is an orchid mantis. This is an insect pretending to be a flower. On the right is a bee orchid – a flower pretending to be an insect. What advantages are there to imitating another form?

◀ These fossilized ammonites are remnants of a species of animals that became extinct 65 million years ago. Their shape can be described mathematically as a logarithmic spiral as the radius of the spiral follows a specific mathematical equation. Where else in nature can form be described mathematically?

Introduction

The shape of an object is sometimes one of its most easily observed characteristics; for example, it can be used to identify plants and animals. As a result, the global context for this chapter is identities and relationships.

Understanding the shape and structure of something is often the first step to deducing how it works. We saw in Chapter 1, Models, how the nature of atoms was discovered from understanding their structure. Once their form was understood, the way the system behaved could be explained. Because of this link between systems and form, the key concept is systems.

Although the form, shape and appearance of a system might be one of its most basic characteristics, it might not be easy to observe. The structure of the atom was hard to observe because of its tiny size. In this chapter, we will look at how scientists have grappled with the problems of determining the form of objects too large to see.

▼ The Cassini–Huygens mission, launched in 1997, set out to study the form of Saturn, its rings and its moons. This picture shows the moon Enceladus and its ice volcanos. On 15 September 2017 Cassini was deliberately crashed into Saturn to end its mission. By destroying the probe in this way, scientists made sure that it did not contaminate any of the moons which were thought to be potential places to find life in the solar system

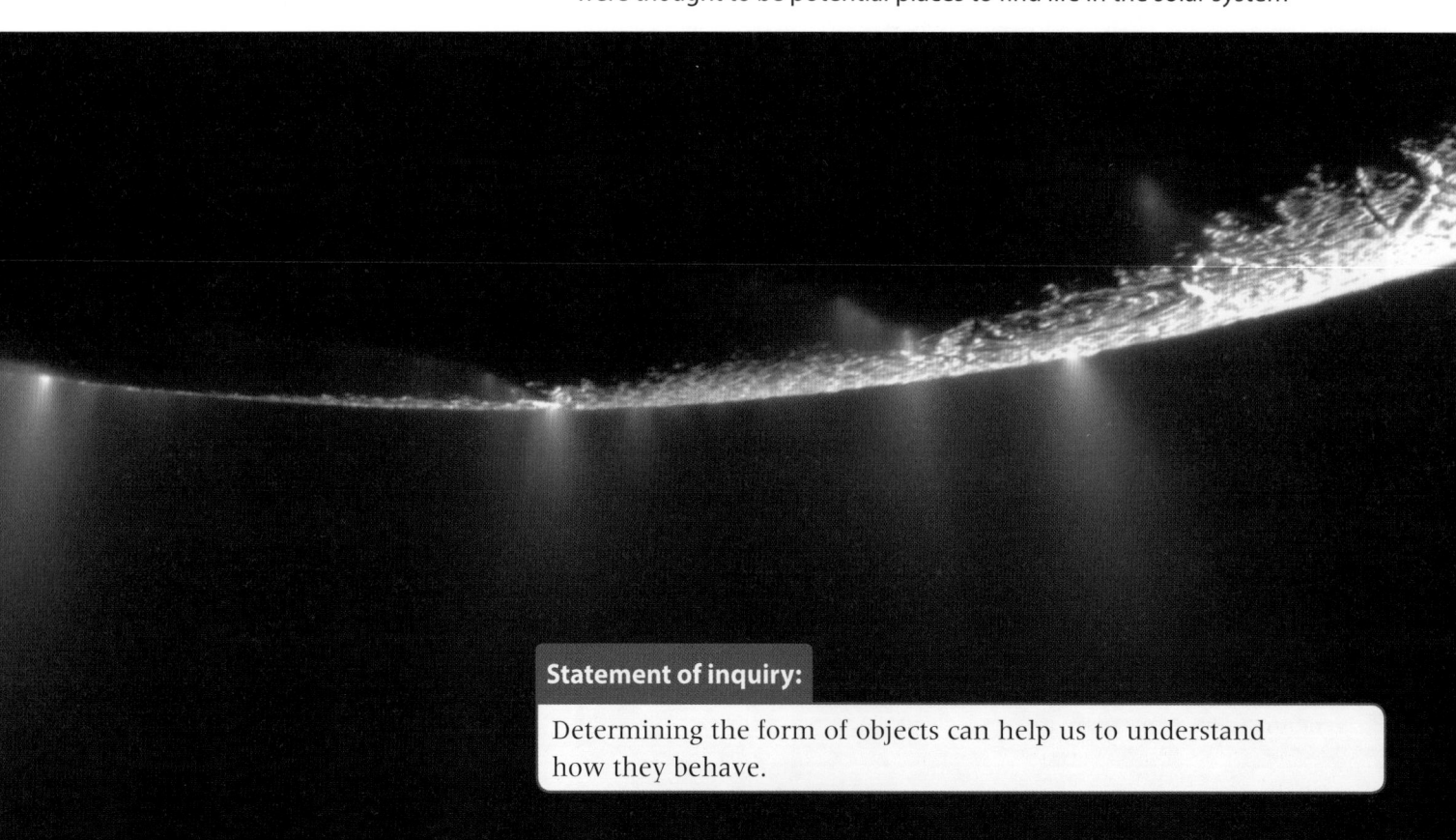

Statement of inquiry:

Determining the form of objects can help us to understand how they behave.

Early thinkers debated whether the Earth was flat or spherical. Although experiments were able to answer this question, seeing its true shape was only made possible by the developments in technology that led to space exploration. In this chapter we will see how it was possible to determine the Earth's form. In a similar way, scientists debated the form of the solar system and the Earth's place in it. We will look at how our knowledge of the solar system has developed and what there still is to discover.

We will also see how modern astronomy uses observations to establish our place in space and determine the form of the very largest objects, galaxies, superclusters, and even what the form of the universe might be.

◀ In 1967, Jocelyn Bell Burnell observed regular pulses of radio waves coming from a point in space. This was the first observation of what is now known as a pulsar. There was no visible star or galaxy and astronomers considered many explanations for them – even extra-terrestrial communication. Once the form of the object was established, astronomers could explain these pulsars as rapidly rotating neutron stars

▶ Maps are a way of expressing the form of the Earth's surface. As explorers discovered the shape of the land and the shape of the Earth, maps had to be redrawn. This map shows a 15th century reprint of a representation of the Earth according to Isidore of Seville in the 7th century. This type of map is often called a T and O map because of the T shape formed between the three continents of Asia, Europe and Africa inside the O of the ocean. How do modern maps sacrifice accuracy to achieve simplicity?

What is the form of the Earth?

The Earth is so large that we cannot see all of it. This means that it is not easy to see what its shape is. Many early civilizations believed that the Earth was flat, although the ancient Greek philosophers Pythagoras (in about the 6th century BC) and Aristotle (in about the 4th century BC) appreciated that it was spherical.

In the 3rd century BC, Eratosthenes calculated the circumference of the Earth to a high degree of accuracy. Evidence for its spherical shape can also be seen when the shadow of the Earth passes across the moon during a lunar eclipse – the shape of the shadow is curved.

The Earth is not actually a perfect sphere. As it rotates, the equator bulges outwards slightly giving it a slightly flattened shape. This is sometimes described as an oblate spheroid.

Space exploration has allowed us to see pictures of the Earth from a distance, showing its form clearly. Despite this, some people throughout history have argued against the round Earth. The Flat Earth Society still exists today.

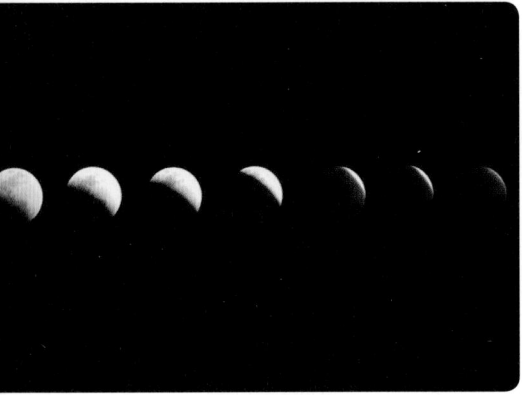

▲ During a lunar eclipse, the Earth's shadow passes over the moon. The shape of the shadow is curved because the Earth is spherical

How spherical is the Earth?

The radius of the Earth is 6,371 km. Mount Everest is the highest point above sea level at 8,848 m.

1. If the Earth were shrunk to the size of a football with a radius of 11 cm, how high would Mount Everest be?

The Earth's radius is slightly different if it is measured to the poles or to the equator. The distance from the center of the Earth to the poles, the polar radius, is 6,356.8 km whereas the distance to the equator, the equatorial radius, is slightly larger at 6,378.1 km.

2. If the Earth were shrunk to a polar radius of 11 cm, by how much would the equatorial radius be larger?

▶ This picture, often called Earthrise, was taken by William Anders on the *Apollo 8* mission which orbited the moon in 1968. With direct observation, it is easy to see the Earth's true form, although the curvature of the moon cannot be seen

Understanding and using units

Christopher Columbus was an Italian explorer who proposed the idea of sailing from Spain to Southeast Asia (the East Indies as they were known) by sailing westward around the globe.

It is often supposed that Christopher Columbus struggled to get backing for his voyage because people thought that the Earth was flat, and that he would therefore fall off the edge. In fact, educated people of the time were very used to the idea of a spherical Earth.

However, Columbus did mistake the distance that he was proposing to sail. Because of some confusion between an Arabic mile (about 1,900 m) and a Roman mile (about 1,450 m) Columbus believed that the circumference of the Earth was much smaller than it actually was!

As a result, when he landed in the Bahamas, he thought that he had traveled far further around the Earth than he actually had.

Christopher Columbus is not the only person to have made a miscalculation over units. The Mars climate orbiter (a NASA mission), launched in 1998, was supposed to orbit Mars but instead went too low in the atmosphere and disintegrated. The reason for this was that one part of the system used a unit of pounds as a force rather than the SI unit of newtons.

Another consideration with units is their reproducibility. In other words, can the quantity be defined so that it could be easily replicated? For example, Eratosthenes used units of stadia. A Greek stade is 600 podes but this is not useful unless a pode is defined. There are also different definitions of a stade which can range from 160 m to over 200 m.

The Roman mile was defined as one thousand paces, but it was not until the Emperor Agrippa defined the foot as being the length of his own foot and one pace as being five feet, that these units were consistently the same.

The original definition of the meter was that it was a ten millionth of the distance from the North Pole to the equator, passing through Paris. Now, it is defined as the distance that light travels in a vacuum in 1/299,792,458 of a second.

Try to find out other original definitions of the units that are used today and what the current precise definitions of them are. Why is it important to define these units to such a high degree of precision?

Measuring the circumference of the Earth

The first person to measure the circumference of the Earth was a Greek astronomer called Eratosthenes who lived in Alexandria, Egypt. He knew that in a place called Syene, the Sun was directly overhead at noon on the summer solstice because the Sun shone straight down a deep well. This is because Syene is on the equator.

Eratosthenes measured the angle of a shadow cast by the Sun on the same day and time but in Alexandria. He found that the angle was about 7°. Using this and the distance between Syene and Alexandria, which was 5,000 stadia (the unit of distance at the time, equivalent to the length of a stadium), he was able to calculate the circumference of the Earth.

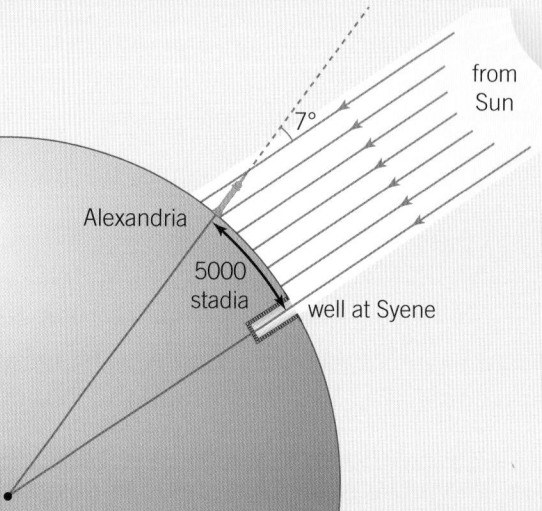

1. Show that 7° is about $\frac{1}{50}$ of the circumference of a circle.

2. Eratosthenes calculated that the distance between Syene and Alexandria, 5,000 stadia, represented the same fraction, $\frac{1}{50}$, of the Earth's circumference. Use your answer above to calculate Eratosthenes's circumference of the Earth (giving your answer in stadia).

3. If one stade is 160 m, calculate the circumference of the Earth in meters.

4. Compare this answer to the value that is currently accepted.

What is in the sky?

Humans have always wanted to explain what is around them. This is where our scientific interest comes from. Early civilizations saw the changing sky and wanted to explain these changes. The most important change was the Sun rising in the morning, bringing heat and light to the day. Probably because of its power, many early civilizations associated the Sun with a god traveling across the sky.

At night, the Moon and stars appeared. In ancient traditions, the Moon was often depicted as a goddess who was sometimes reunited with the Sun god. The stars, however, form fixed patterns which move across the sky in the same way each night, and ancient civilizations joined these stars into shapes and invented stories to explain what they represented. These patterns of stars are called constellations. Different cultures have traditions which associate different stories to the patterns of the stars.

Some "stars" appeared differently; they were bright and easily visible, but they moved against the backdrop of the fixed stars every night. They were called wandering stars – *planetastra* in Greek. It is from this word that our term planet derives.

What are constellations?

The stars form fixed patterns in the sky which have not changed for millennia. Although these stars appear to be in the same pattern in the same part of the sky, this is not representative of their true form. The stars are often large distances from each other and only appear close to each other from the viewpoint of Earth. For example, the three stars across the middle of the picture to the right appear close together. In reality, the star on the left is about 820 light years away while the central star is almost 2,000 light years away. Today, astronomers use 88 patterns called constellations to describe regions of the sky; these are mostly named following the Roman tradition.

The constellation of Orion is one of the most distinctive. The Roman tradition describes Orion as a hunter whose success at hunting was so great that Mother Earth dispatched a giant scorpion (depicted in the constellation Scorpio) to kill him.

The three stars across the middle are described as Orion's belt, but in some aboriginal cultures, the three stars represent fishermen. A nearby cluster of stars (the Pleiades, which are not shown in this picture) represent their wives on the shore.

In Egyptian mythology, the constellation represents the god Sah. In Arabic traditions, Orion is a giant and the three stars of his belt are a string of pearls. The Navajo Indians called Orion the First Slim One. Its position in the sky was a useful sign for when to plant crops.

▲ Constellation of Orion

How have our identities been shaped by the stars?

The stars and constellations were an important part of the cultural identity of many early civilizations. The various forms and patterns in the sky were linked to stories and events of the past. These tales helped the people to explain how the world came to be as it was.

The stars were also useful signals of the changing seasons and although we no longer use these signs, there are still many traditions which are based around these – for example, Christmas day falls very close to the winter solstice.

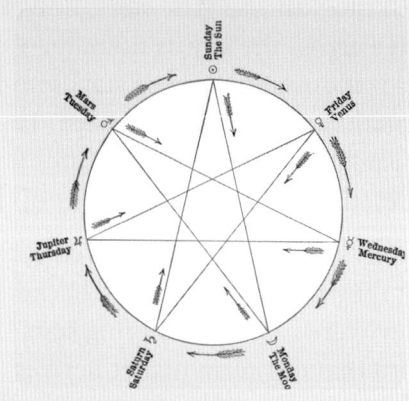

The days of the week are named after the planets. In the geocentric model, the order of the celestial objects from the outer orbits inwards is Saturn, Jupiter, Mars, Sun, Venus, Mercury and Moon. One ancient principle of astrology was that a different planet was associated with each hour of the day. If midnight on Monday was associated with the Moon, then the next hour would be Saturn, and then Jupiter and so on round the cycle. Seven o'clock in the morning would be associated with the Moon again and the cycle would continue until midnight. The next day is Mars (three places later in the sequence of planets). As a result, the sequence of celestial objects when associated to days is the Moon, Mars, Mercury, Jupiter, Venus, Saturn and the Sun.

Many astronomers of the past were also astrologers who used their observations of the motion of the planets to assign certain identities to people according to what was in the sky at the time they were born. Some people still believe in horoscopes today.

ASTROPHYSICS

Where is the Earth in the solar system?

Once the spherical form of the Earth had been accepted, a model of the solar system with the Earth at its center and the Sun, Moon, planets and stars orbiting around it developed. Such a model is called the geocentric model (meaning Earth centered). It is often referred to as the Ptolemaic model after the Greek astronomer Ptolemy.

In the geocentric model, the Moon was considered to be the closest object to the Earth because it was able to sweep through the whole of the sky in the shortest time. Mercury and Venus were next, followed by the Sun. Beyond this were Mars, Jupiter and finally Saturn. (The outermost planets of the solar system such as Uranus and Neptune were yet to be discovered.) Each planet was thought to exist on a dome or orb, which rotated around the Earth. Outside the orbits of the planets was the firmament. This was the most distant orb, rotating the slowest and carrying the stars. Often the model included heaven beyond the firmament, sometimes with the different levels of heaven.

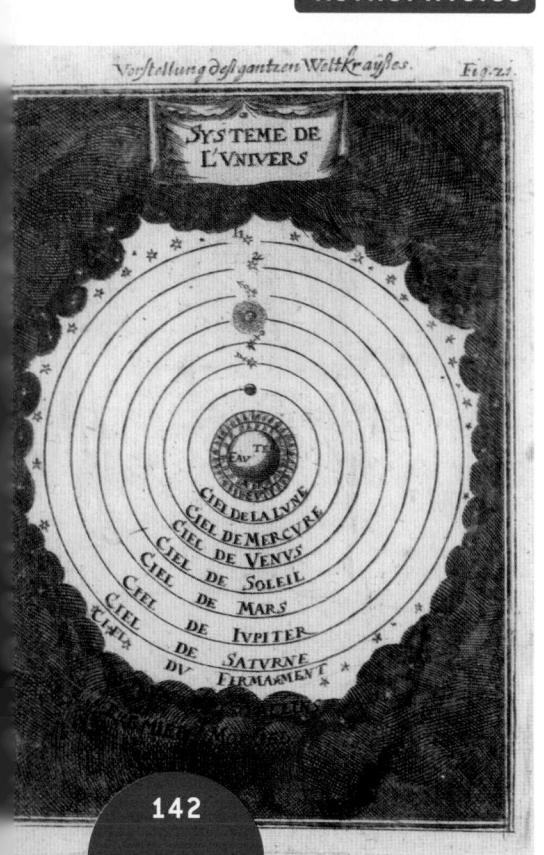

◀ In this picture from 1719, the planets (as well as the Moon and the Sun) are shown in circular orbits around the Earth. This is the geocentric model of the solar system

What is wrong with the geocentric model?

Sometimes a planet appeared to reverse its direction of travel against the background stars and move in the opposite direction for a time. This is called retrograde motion but circular orbits of planets around the Earth could not explain this.

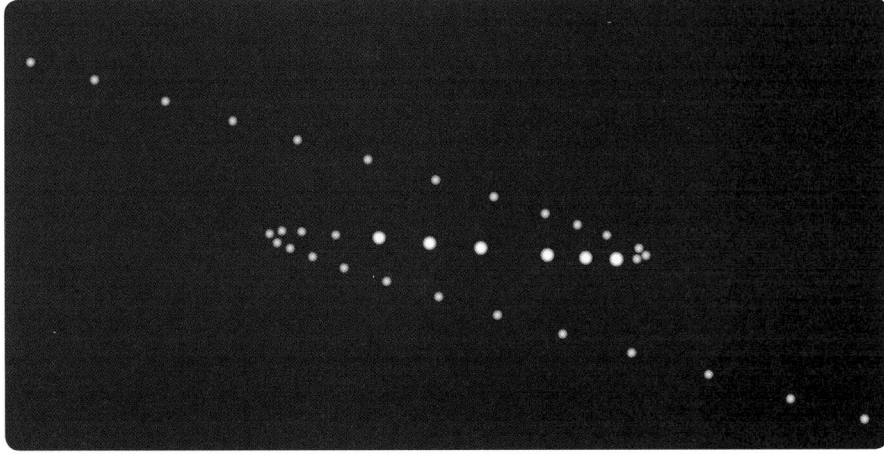

◄ The path of Mars across the sky sometimes appears to go backwards. This is called retrograde motion and was not easily explained by the geocentric model of the solar system

Astronomers adapted the geocentric model so that the planets went round in circles about points which themselves orbited the Earth. These were called epicycles and they made the model much more accurate but also more complicated. Some astronomers started to doubt that the geocentric model represented the true form of the solar system.

In 1543, Nicolaus Copernicus published a new model of the solar system, the heliocentric model, with the Sun at the center. This enabled astronomers to explain retrograde motion as they found

DE MOTIB. STELLÆ MARTIS

▲ This diagram appeared in Kepler's Astronomia Nova. It shows the retrograde motion of Mars as viewed from Earth between the years 1580 and 1596. Kepler was able to explain the observed orbits of the planets by showing that they followed elliptical orbits

▲ Nicolaus Copernicus, who proposed the heliocentric model of the solar system

What happens when science challenges our identity?

Nicolaus Copernicus died soon after the publication of his ideas about the Sun being the center of the solar system. When Galileo Galilei published a book in 1610 which supported these ideas, the Catholic Church objected as they believed that it contradicted the Bible. They pronounced the ideas to be false and ordered Galileo to stop teaching them.

In 1623, Galileo published another book which was considered to ridicule the geocentric views of the Church. He was suspected of heresy and sentenced to house arrest, where he remained until his death in 1642. The Catholic Church did not formally accept Galileo's work until 1992.

Often individuals and groups can find it hard to accept views which seem to challenge their own personal or cultural identity. When alternative views are dismissed without debate, this can cause conflict. Can you think of other issues (in the past or the present) which are caused by one group holding views which challenge another group's identity?

that it occurs when a planet overtakes another planet with a larger orbit. As astronomers became better able to test this model with observations, they realised that the heliocentric model is a good representation of the form of the solar system.

ASTROPHYSICS

What is a planet?

The planets Mercury, Venus, Earth, Mars, Jupiter and Saturn have been known for many centuries. In 1781, William Herschel discovered a new planet – Uranus – bringing the total number of planets to seven. Since then, new discoveries of planets and planet-like objects have caused astronomers to question what to define as a planet.

Around the time of Herschel's discovery of Uranus, it was suggested that there was a gap in the distribution of planets between the orbits of Mars and Jupiter. Astronomers suspected that there might be a missing planet so they searched for it. In 1801, a Catholic priest named Giuseppe Piazzi discovered an object that seemed to fit this description; he had discovered Ceres, which is now known to be the largest of the asteroids in the asteroid belt.

The next year another object, named Pallas, was discovered, and soon after, Juno and Vesta. They all had orbits between Mars and Jupiter. This now brought the total number of planets to 11. Many further objects with orbits between Mars and Jupiter were discovered, and it became clear that they were different from normal planets in that they were smaller and many had very similar orbits. In 1846, Neptune was discovered. It was much larger than the many objects between Mars and Jupiter so these objects were classified as asteroids and Neptune became the eighth planet.

In 1930, the ninth planet Pluto was discovered. Pluto was always slightly different to the other planets. It was the only rocky outer planet and its orbit was more elliptical and tilted. In 2003 another distant object in the solar system was discovered – Sedna. In 2005, Eris was discovered. Eris is larger than Pluto and has a larger orbit. Some astronomers named this the tenth planet, however, many believed that Pluto, Sedna and Eris belonged to a different classification.

Creating a scale model of the solar system

The following table gives the sizes of the planets and their distances from the Sun.

Planet/ object	Distance from the Sun (million km)	Radius (km)
Sun	–	695,700
Mercury	57.91	2,440
Venus	108.2	6,052
Earth	149.6	6,371
Mars	227.9	3,390
Jupiter	778.5	69,911
Saturn	1,429	58,232
Uranus	2,877	25,362
Neptune	4,498	24,622

Consider the following questions.

1. Why is the Sun not drawn to scale in the picture above? Measure one planet and calculate how many times smaller it has been drawn. By applying the same scale factor, how big would the Sun have to be at that scale? How far away would it have to be?

2. Measure the size of the Sun in the picture and work out how far away the Earth would be on that scale. How far away would Neptune be? How big would the Earth be on this scale?

Your answers to the questions above should show you that making a scale model of the solar system is difficult. Either the distances are vast or the planets end up being tiny.

By finding some suitable objects try to make your own scale model of the solar system. You might choose to only calculate the distances from the Sun or the sizes of the planets.

In 2006, the International Astronomical Union (IAU) set out an official definition of a planet:

- it is not so massive that it starts fusion (this is the process by which the Sun generates energy – if a planet were big enough to start fusion, it would become a star)

- it orbits around the Sun

- it is sufficiently massive that it becomes round in shape

- it clears the neighborhood around its orbit.

This means that large objects which have a large enough gravitational field that they are pulled into a round shape and are able to dominate their orbits can be classed as a planet. The IAU introduced a new category of dwarf planet which was for planets which failed to satisfy the last criterion. Both Ceres and Pluto are large enough to have pulled themselves into a round shape; however, they have not cleared their orbits. Ceres shares its orbit with the other asteroids and Pluto is just one object among many in a region of asteroids called the Kuiper Belt.

Another solar system

Planets that orbit other stars are being discovered frequently. Suppose you were to discover another solar system. A drawing of it is shown to the right. Identify which of these objects is most likely to be:

- a star

- a planet

- a dwarf planet

- a moon

- an asteroid.

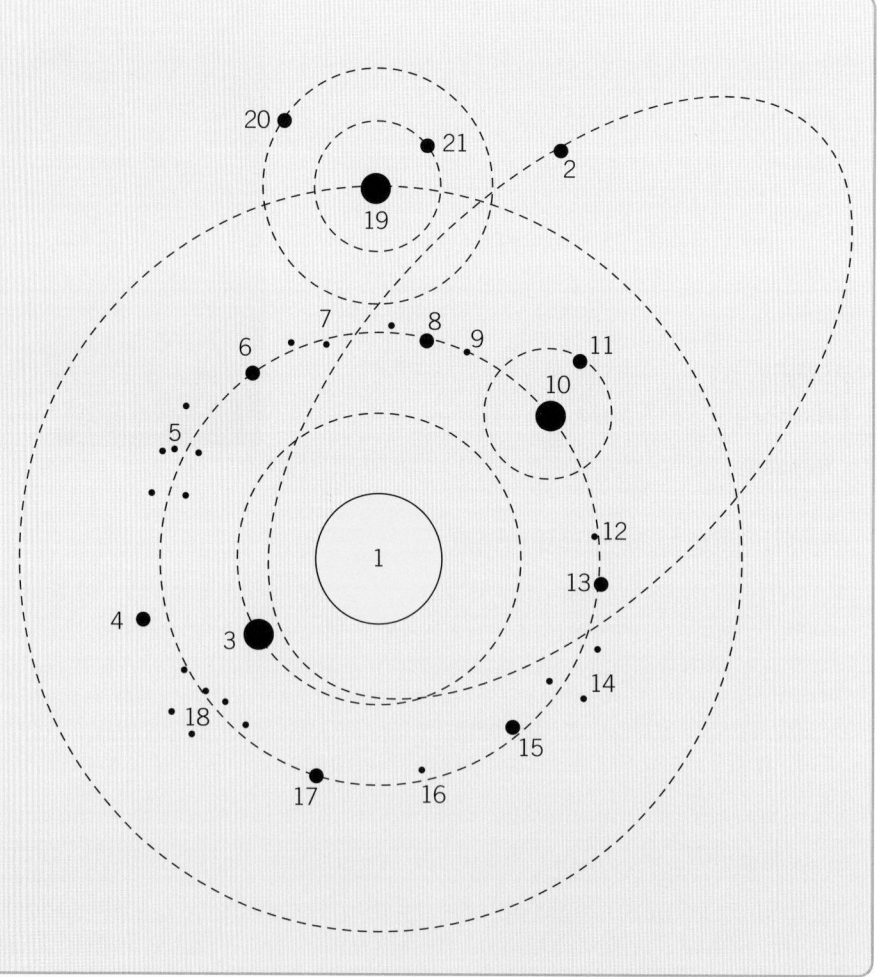

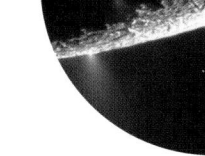

What is a galaxy?

At the turn of the 20th century, astronomers thought that the most distant objects in the universe were only tens of thousands of light years away. Although this seemed like a vast distance to them, and indeed it still is a vast distance, it meant that they thought that all objects were in what we now know as our galaxy.

In 1923, Edwin Hubble showed that the distance to Andromeda was in fact millions of light years. Previously it had been thought that it was a nebula – a cloudlike structure – but if it was millions of years away, Hubble reasoned that it must be exceptionally bright to still be visible. He had shown that this nebula was in fact another galaxy. Within a couple of years, Hubble and other astronomers had classified many other galaxies.

A galaxy is a collection of hundreds of billions of stars held together by their own gravity. Our own solar system lies in a galaxy called the Milky Way. Many galaxies, including our own, have a supermassive black hole at the center. It is believed that there might be hundreds of billions of galaxies in the universe.

▲ The Andromeda galaxy is one of the closest galaxies to the Milky Way

Black holes

A black hole is an object with such a large density that the gravitational field near it is so big not even light can escape. They are among the strangest objects in the universe. At the center lies a singularity which is a point containing all the black hole's mass and yet its volume is zero. This results in an infinite density. Unsurprisingly, the laws of physics struggle to describe this singularity.

Around the black hole lies an imaginary boundary called the event horizon. It is impossible for anything inside the event horizon to leave the black hole; instead, all paths through space and time lead to the singularity.

Black holes can be formed from the death of the largest stars in a supernova. These stellar black holes can have a mass which is about 10 times the mass of the Sun. They can also be much larger with masses of millions or even billions of times the mass of the Sun. These are called supermassive black holes and it is believed that there is a supermassive black hole at the center of our galaxy and indeed almost every galaxy.

The radius of the event horizon R can be calculated using the equation:

$$R = \frac{2GM}{c^2}$$

where the gravitational constant $G = 6.67 \times 10^{-11} \, \mathrm{m^3 \, kg^{-1} \, s^{-2}}$, the speed of light $c = 3 \times 10^8 \, \mathrm{m \, s^{-1}}$ and M is the mass of the black hole (in kg). Use this equation to answer the following questions.

1. If the Sun ($M = 2 \times 10^{30} \, \mathrm{kg}$) were to be compressed into a black hole, what would the radius of the event horizon be?

2. The supermassive black hole at the center of our galaxy is believed to have a mass of $8.2 \times 10^{36} \, \mathrm{kg}$. Calculate the radius of its event horizon.

3. The largest supermassive black hole discovered so far is believed to have an event horizon that has a radius of $1.18 \times 10^{14} \, \mathrm{m}$. Calculate the mass of this black hole. How many times heavier than the Sun is it?

Data-based question: Where is the center of our galaxy?

Because dust obscures our view of the center of our galaxy, we cannot see exactly where it is, so it is hard to work out how far we are away from it. One way of estimating this is to use globular clusters. Globular clusters are groups of stars that orbit outside the plane of the galaxy. They are distributed symmetrically about our galaxy, so by measuring their positions, we can work out where the center of the galaxy is.

The following is a table of the positions of some globular clusters. X and Z are the positions of the clusters relative to Earth in light years. X is in the direction along the plane of the galaxy towards the center; Z is the direction at right angles to the plane of the galaxy.

Name	X (light years)	Z (light years)	Name	X (light years)	Z (light years)
M2	18,256	−21,842	M54	83,456	−21,190
M4	6,846	1,956	M62	21,842	2,934
M5	16,626	17,930	M68	13,366	19,560
M9	25,102	4,890	M69	28,036	−5,216
M10	12,714	5,542	M70	28,688	−6,520
M12	13,692	6,846	M71	7,172	−978
M14	27,058	7,824	M72	38,142	−29,992
M15	12,714	−15,648	M75	57,376	−29,666
M19	28,362	4,564	M79	−25,102	−20,538
M22	10,432	−1,304	M80	30,644	10,758
M28	17,604	−1,630	M92	8,150	15,322
M30	15,974	−19,234	M107	19,234	8,150

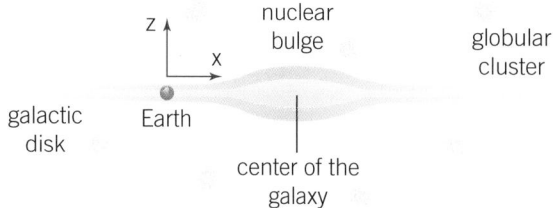

▲ Most of the stars in the Milky Way exist in the galactic disk and the nuclear bulge. Dust obscures our view of the galactic center but globular clusters can help us to locate the center of the galaxy

1. By taking an average of the X and Z coordinates, estimate the coordinate for the center of the galaxy.

A graph showing the coordinates of the globular clusters is shown below.

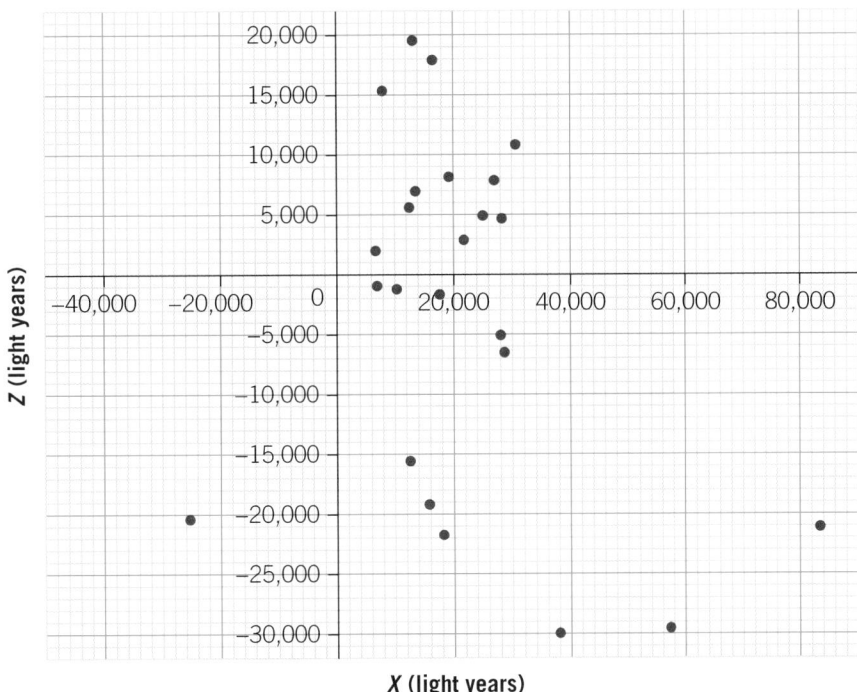

X (light years)

2. Plot the location of the galactic center on a copy of this graph.

There are various factors which might affect the reliability of this estimate:

- all these globular clusters were observed from France by Charles Messier in the 18th century (this is why their names all begin with M)

- distant globular clusters are fainter and harder to observe.

3 Which of these factors might best explain why there are no clusters plotted in the top left quadrant of the graph (negative X values, positive Z values)?

4 How might these limitations of the data affect the value you obtained for the location of the center of the galaxy?

What is the form of galaxies in the universe?

ASTROPHYSICS

Galaxies are not spread throughout the universe in a uniform way. Instead they are found in small clusters. The nearest galaxies to the Milky Way, including Andromeda, form the Local Group.

Groups of galaxies themselves tend to form larger groups; these are called superclusters. The Local Group is part of the Virgo Supercluster of galaxies which contains over a million galaxies and is more than 100 million light years across. Some studies show that the Virgo Supercluster is part of the even bigger Laniakea Supercluster.

▶ The Virgo Supercluster of galaxies

These superclusters of galaxies form long strings and sheets called filaments, the largest known structures in the universe. The gaps between them are called voids.

ASTROPHYSICS

What is the form of space–time?

Just as in the past scientists wondered about the shape of the Earth and the shape of the solar system, modern scientists are contemplating the shape of the universe. According to Einstein's theory of general relativity, mass can warp space and time. This can cause all sorts of strange effects. For example, the path of light can be bent by the gravitational field of a large mass (see Chapter 9, Models). The light continues in what it thinks is a straight line, but because the space it travels through is bent, we see the path of the light bend. This causes effects such as the Einstein cross.

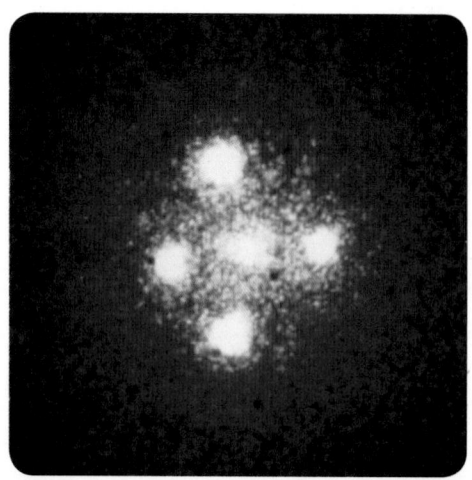

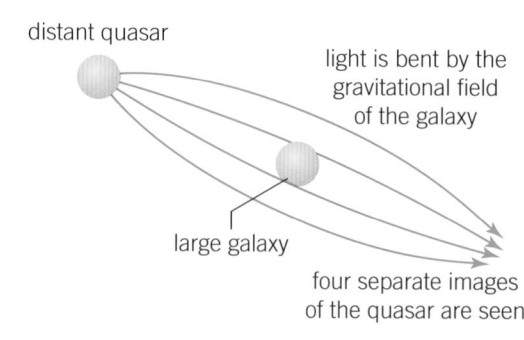

distant quasar

light is bent by the gravitational field of the galaxy

large galaxy

four separate images of the quasar are seen

▲ This is the Einstein cross. The central object is a galaxy about 400 million light years away. Behind it is a distant quasar, an early galaxy, which is 8 billion light years away. The nearer galaxy bends space–time so that the light from the distant quasar takes a curved path. The result is that we see four images of the quasar, one on each side of the galaxy. If the galaxies were perfectly aligned and were symmetric, then a complete ring would be seen

Einstein's theory also predicts that time will pass more slowly in a gravitational field. As a result, time on Earth flows a little bit more slowly than it would in space away from all gravitational fields, including the Earth's. On Earth, the effect is so tiny that it only accounts for a couple of seconds in a century.

Because the effect of large masses is to bend space and slow time, physicists often consider space and time together in a concept they call space–time. Since mass can change the shape of space–time, then the total mass of the universe must act to change the overall shape of the universe's space–time. The universe's form will also determine the ultimate fate of the universe.

- **Flat universe:** In the past many astronomers believed that the universe was flat. Such a universe continues expanding indefinitely. As it expands, it cools. Gradually, the stars burn out and the eventual fate of this universe is called the Big Freeze as the universe slowly cools towards absolute zero.

- **Spherical universe:** The mass of the universe acts to bend space–time into a sphere. If the universe is spherical in shape, then the gravitational interaction between all the galaxies is enough to start attracting them back together and the universe will end in what is sometimes called the Big Crunch. The extent to which this happens has been made all the more complicated by the discovery of dark matter. Astronomers now believe that the universe has about five times more dark matter than normal matter, yet we cannot see it.

- **Warped universe:** Recent studies of the expansion of the universe show that the universe is not just expanding, but that the expansion is getting faster. Such a universe requires something that acts in the opposite way to gravity, pushing everything apart. We call this dark energy. Astronomers believe that dark energy accounts for 70% of the universe, but it is not yet understood what it is. The effect of dark energy is to warp the form of the universe into a different shape. The accelerating universe would also end in the Big Freeze, although some models predict a Big Rip where the universe expands so quickly that atoms and even the protons and neutrons in the nuclei of atoms are ripped apart.

▲ The three possible forms of space–time in the universe. If the universe is flat then the universe will continue expanding. If there is enough mass in the universe, the shape will become spherical and the universe will eventually collapse in on itself. If, however, there is enough dark energy, the universe will be warped in a different way and its acceleration will increase

Summative assessment

Statement of inquiry:

Determining the form of objects can help us to understand how they behave.

Introduction

For a long time astronomers suspected that distant stars might be similar to the Sun in that planets orbited around them. However, because of the vast distances involved, detecting such extra-solar planets, or exoplanets, was difficult, so confirmation of their discovery did not happen until the 1990s. In 2009, NASA launched the Kepler mission with the aim of detecting more exoplanets. Since its launch, the mission has discovered thousands of exoplanets.

 Exoplanets

1. Give one difference between an exoplanet and the star that it orbits. Hence, explain why it is so difficult to observe exoplanets. [3]

An exoplanet should fit the definition of a planet in our own solar system, with the only difference being that it orbits a different star.

2. Give the definition of a planet in our solar system. [3]

In 1995, the first exoplanet in orbit around a star like our Sun was confirmed. The mass of the planet was about half the mass of Jupiter, but it orbited very close to its parent star so that it completed one orbit every four days.

3. Which of the definitions of a planet can this exoplanet demonstrate? Why is it reasonable to assume that it fits the description of a planet? [4]

Astronomers are particularly interested in planets which lie in the habitable zone, which is defined as the range of orbits where water could be present on a planet in its liquid state.

4. Explain why a planet might not be in the habitable zone if its orbit is too close or too far away from its parent star. [3]

5. Explain how the range of the habitable zone would change around a star much smaller than our Sun. [2]

Discovering exoplanets

The Kepler telescope monitors about 150,000 stars and can detect the change in their light if a planet passes in front of the star. As of 2017, about 3,500 exoplanets had been confirmed orbiting 2,600 stars.

6. Using the information above, calculate:

    a) the fraction of stars which have planets [2]

    b) the average number of planets per star. [2]

7. Explain why, in reality, both these numbers are likely to be larger. [2]

8. A graph of the observed brightness of a star is shown below.

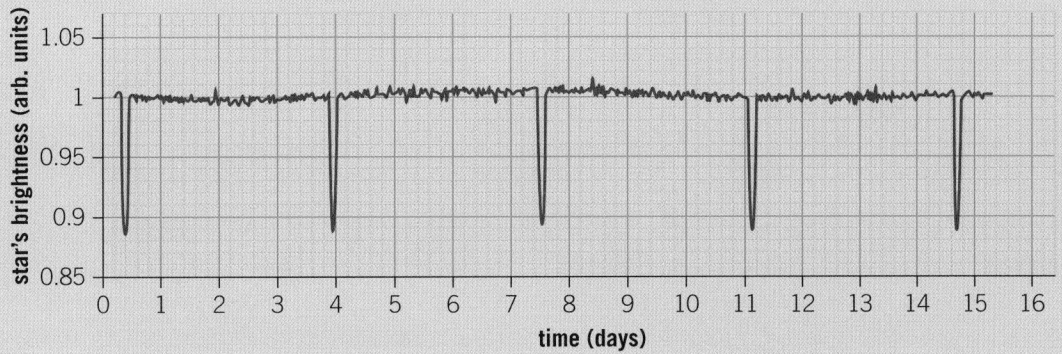

    a) Use the graph to find the orbital period of the planet. [2]

    b) How might the graph appear different if the planet was larger? [3]

    c) Some exoplanet systems have many planets. Explain why many planets might make interpretation of the data more difficult. [4]

 An exoplanet system

The star Kepler-296 is interesting to astronomers because it has five confirmed exoplanets in orbit around it. The table below shows some of the properties of these exoplanets. The units of orbital radius are astronomical units (AU) which is the average distance from the Earth to the Sun.

Planet	Orbital radius (AU)	Orbital period (days)
Kepler-296c	0.0521	5.84
Kepler-296b	0.079	10.86
Kepler-296d	0.118	
Kepler-296e	0.169	34.14
Kepler-296f	0.255	63.34

A graph of the data is shown below.

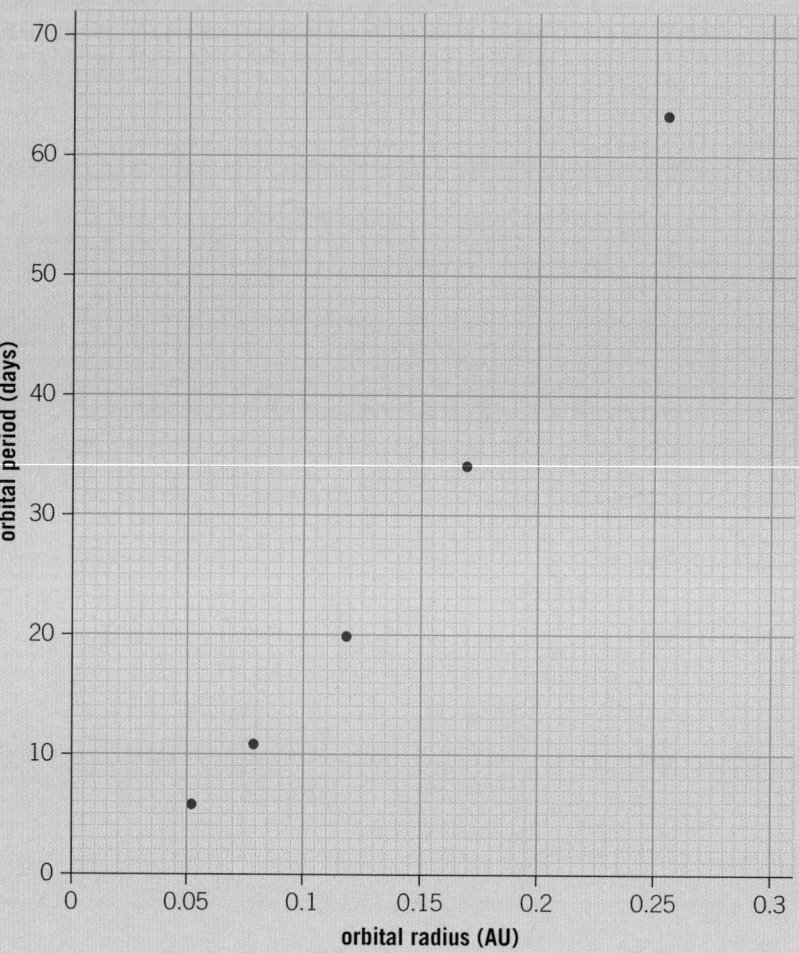

9. On a copy of this graph:

   a) add a line of best fit [1]

   b) determine the orbital period for Kepler 296-d. [1]

10. Given that 1 AU = 1.5×10^{11} m, calculate the circumference of the orbit of Kepler-296c and hence calculate its orbital speed. Give your answer in km h⁻¹. [5]

11. Most of the exoplanets that the Kepler telescope has found are large and have short time periods. Explain why this does not necessarily mean that these types of planets are the most common. [4]

Although there are thousands of exoplanets that the Kepler mission has confirmed, many more thousands of potential observations have not been confirmed. To confirm the presence of an exoplanet, there must be multiple observations.

12. Explain why is it important to have multiple observations before confirming an exoplanet's existence. [2]

The search for extra-terrestrial life

The search for exoplanets has found many planets which share similarities with Earth. This raises the question of whether they might also have life on them. The following table contains data for some of these planets.

Planet name	Orbital radius (AU)	Orbital period (days)	Planet mass (Earth masses)	Planet radius (Earth radii)	Planet temperature (K)	Host star mass (Solar masses)	Host star temperature (K)
Earth	1	365.25	1	1	287	1	5,730
HD 38283b	1.02	363.2	108	?	?	1.08	5,998
Kepler-952b	0.5	130.4	?	7.6	347	0.99	5,730
HD 142245b	2.77	1,299	604	?	288	1.69	4,878
Trappist-1d	0.02	4.05	0.41	0.772	288	0.08	2,559

13. Explain why astronomers are interested in investigating whether other planets have life. [4]

14. Assuming that alien life is very much like life on Earth, describe the advantages and disadvantages of the environments of these planets for supporting life. [8]

15. Suppose that a long time in the future, the Earth becomes uninhabitable and the human race has to travel to a new planet. Which of these planets do you think would be most suitable? Explain your reasons. [3]

Encouraging others to contribute

The Kepler mission generates so much data that it has to be processed by computer. However, the human brain is better at pattern spotting than computers. In order to find exoplanets that the computer programs miss, scientists are using the power of citizen science.

Citizen science is a term used for a collaborative project where many amateur volunteers (often non-scientists) contribute a little bit of time to a project. When enough people are involved, the total of their output can be significant and meaningful. Examples of this are wildlife surveys where lots of small-scale contributions (such as counting birds or butterflies for an hour) can gather enough data to create a large-scale survey.

The Planet Hunters project (www.planethunters.org) gets volunteers to look at light curves from the Kepler mission in order to look for evidence of exoplanets that the computers have missed. Several exoplanets have already been discovered. Visit the website and see if you can identify any exoplanets.

8 Consequences

Consequences are the results of earlier actions.

◄ Japanese knotweed is a plant that was introduced into Europe in the mid-19th century. It was used in gardens due to its attractive flowers and because it would grow almost anywhere. It is, however, highly invasive and very hard to remove. As a result, its sale is now banned in many countries. What other examples are there of animals or plants which have been too successful in the habitats they were introduced to?

▼ In normal economic theory, the consequence of high prices is that demand goes down. Some luxury items, however, show the opposite effect: increased prices make the goods more exclusive and increases demand for them. Can you think of other examples where the consequences are opposite to what you would normally expect?

▲ Sometimes consequences are impossible to predict. Edward Lorenz was an American mathematician who studied meteorology – the science of forecasting weather patterns. In 1961 he noticed that running the computer simulations with tiny variations in the initial starting conditions led to vastly different results. Today, the study of such systems where small changes at the start can lead to wildly differing situations later on is called chaos theory. Lorenz is often quoted as saying, "Does the flap of a butterfly's wings in Brazil set off a tornado in Texas?" This refers to the possibility that a small cause can have an unpredictable and large effect. Can you think of other situations where the consequences are unpredictable?

▶ On 2 July 1505, Martin Luther was caught in a thunderstorm. When lightning struck very near him he prayed to be saved, saying that he would become a monk in the Catholic Church. Luther kept his promise, but later came to dislike some of the corrupt practices of the church. He rebelled against the church and published his *95 Theses*, which was widely read due to the recent invention of the printing press. This period of history is called the Reformation. Luther translated the Bible from Latin so that more people could read it. As a result, literacy and education improved in Europe as people were encouraged to read the Bible. Which other single events in history have had far-reaching consequences?

Key concept: Change

Related concept: Consequences

Global context: Personal and cultural expression

Introduction

Physics is full of consequences. The laws of physics predict the outcomes of a situation and explain the nature of the consequences. In fact, it is impossible to do or change anything without there being some kind of consequence. The key concept of this chapter is therefore change.

Physicists try to find laws of nature that explain as much as possible. Rather than have many rules that explain what happens in certain specific situations, physicists prefer to have fewer, more general rules which apply universally.

In Chapter 6, Function, we investigate many different types of force. Physics has already established that many of these forces are aspects of just four fundamental interactions: electromagnetism, gravity, the strong force and the weak force. (The strong and weak interactions only occur on a tiny scale: smaller than the nucleus of an atom.) Physicists would like to be able to explain how all these forces are linked and hence devise a theory which unifies them all. This is sometimes known as the theory of everything, although it remains a distant prospect.

▼ One law of physics is the second law of thermodynamics. It states that the amount of disorder in a system must always increase. The consequence of this is that when you mix paint together, the different colors will merge together more and more as the system moves from the ordered arrangement of two separate colors into a disordered mixture. It is impossible to stir the paint and for the two colors to become separate again

Statement of inquiry:

The consequences of actions are predicted by the laws of physics.

One of the first unification theories was that of James Clerk Maxwell, a British physicist, who devised a theory which linked the electrostatic interaction of charges (see Chapter 2, Interaction) and magnetism (see Chapter 4, Movement). In this chapter, we will see how a current of moving charges has a magnetic field around it and how a changing magnetic field can generate a current. One of the applications of this is the generation of sound by a loudspeaker. We will see how sound can be produced and how we perceive it. The global context is personal and cultural expression.

▶ James Clerk Maxwell devised the theory of electromagnetism which unified electrostatic and magnetic interactions

▼ These musicians rely on the application of electromagnetism in the microphones and loudspeakers that they use. Without these, their voices and instruments would not be heard as clearly

How do electricity and magnetism relate?

While giving a lecture in 1820, Hans Christian Ørsted, a Danish physicist, noticed that a compass needle was deflected when a nearby electric current was switched on. This showed that the current flowing through the wire must have had a magnetic field which interacted with the magnetic field of the compass needle.

When a current flows, a magnetic field is created around it. This is in a circular shape around the wire – this means that there is no north or south pole. If the current is flowing towards you, the magnetic field is in an anticlockwise direction. You can use the right-hand grip rule to remember which way the magnetic field goes around the wire. If you point the thumb of your right hand in the direction of the conventional current (remembering that the electrons actually travel in the opposite direction), your fingers will bend in the direction of the magnetic field.

▶ This illustration shows the shape of the magnetic field around a current-carrying wire. You can use the right-hand grip rule to remember which way the magnetic field goes. If you point the thumb of your right hand in the direction of the current, your fingers will curl in the direction of the magnetic field

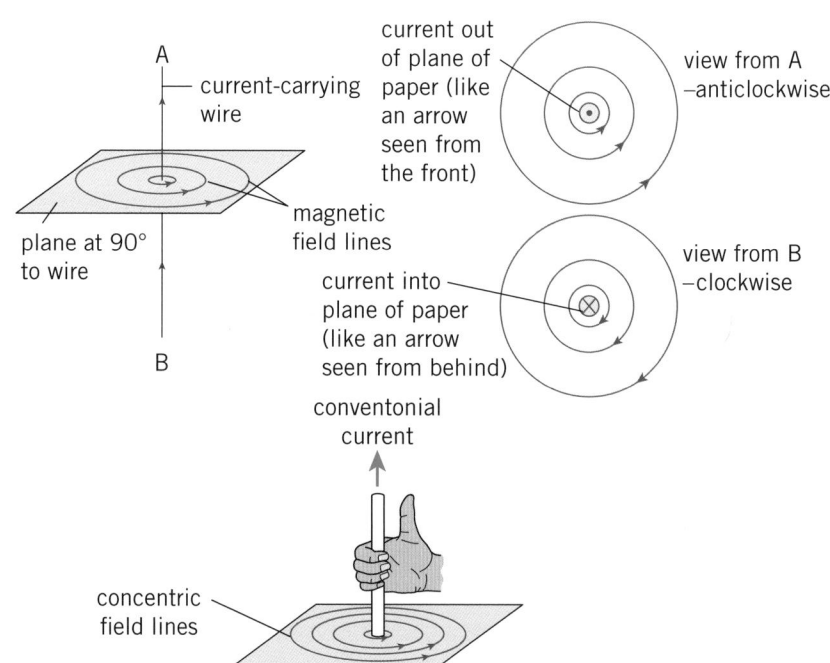

Observing the magnetic effects of an electric current

You can repeat Ørsted's observations of the electric effect of magnetic fields. You will need a compass, a power pack or battery and a wire. Place the wire across the compass and touch each end to the battery. You should see the compass needle move. You may need a reasonably large current to make this work.

Alternatively, you can use the magnetometer that is present in many smartphones by downloading a free app that allows you to use the sensor to measure magnetic fields. Place the wire near the phone's magnetic sensor. (You can find this by using a weak magnet, for instance, a magnetized paperclip, and moving it over the phone to find the highest reading.) Connect the ends of the wire to a battery and you will be able to detect the magnetic field due to the current in the wire. See Chapter 4, Movement, for the units of magnetic field strength.

How can we create electromagnets?

The magnetic field of a current-carrying wire can be used to make an electromagnet. If the wire is wound into a long coil, the shape of which is called a solenoid, then the shape of the magnetic field will be the same as the field from a bar magnet.

The strength of the electromagnet can be increased by increasing the current flowing through the coil of wire or by using more turns of wire. Using an iron core also increases the strength of an electromagnet significantly. The magnetic domains (see Chapter 4, Movement) in the iron align when the electromagnet is switched on and the resulting magnetic field can be about a hundred times stronger than that produced without the iron core.

As the strength of electromagnets is easily adjusted by varying the current and they can be switched on and off, they can be used to pick up certain metal objects and can also release them easily.

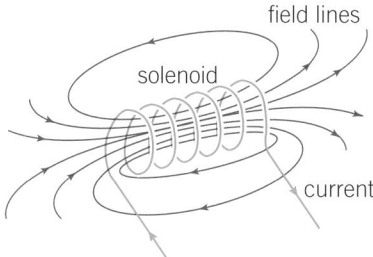

▲ Magnetic field from a coil of wire

Experiment

Investigating the strength of an electromagnet

You can make a simple electromagnet with an iron rod or a large iron nail, some insulated wire and a power supply. Wrap the wire around the rod or nail (you may need to secure it with some tape) and connect it to the power supply (on a d.c. setting).

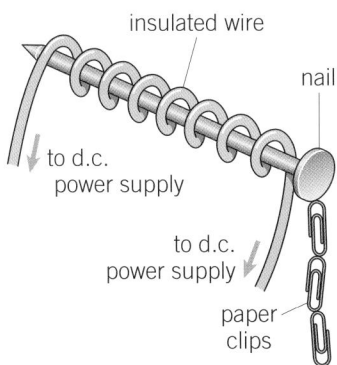

insulated wire

nail

to d.c. power supply

to d.c. power supply

paper clips

You can assess the strength of the electromagnet by:

- seeing how many paperclips or staples it can hold

- using a smartphone app to record the magnetic field, holding the electromagnet a fixed distance away

- placing a piece of iron on a balance and clamping the electromagnet a small distance above it. When the electromagnet is on, the iron will be attracted to the magnet and the reading on the balance will be lower. The force of the electromagnet on the iron can be found using the equation $F = mg$ where m is the change in mass reading of the balance.

▲ Electromagnets can be used to lift scrap metal. By turning them off and on, the metal can be dropped or picked up. Why would this only be useful for scrap iron, cobalt and nickel?

Questions

1. List the factors that affect the strength of an electromagnet.

2. Choose one of these as your independent variable.

3. Decide the best way to measure the strength of your electromagnet.

4. Write an experimental method for your investigation.

5. Write a hypothesis for your investigation.

6. Carry out your experiment and record your data in a suitable table.

7. Plot your data in a suitable graph.

8. Add a line of best fit to your data. What is the trend of your data? Does this support or contradict your hypothesis?

9. Suggest an improvement that you could make to your investigation.

ELECTROMAGNETISM

How can we use the force of electromagnetism?

Because a wire carrying an electric current has a magnetic field around it, it experiences a force in the presence of another magnetic field.

The direction of the force on the wire is at a right angle to the direction of the current and at a right angle to the direction of the magnetic field. A useful way to remember the direction in which the force acts is Fleming's left-hand rule. If you point your first finger in the direction of the magnetic field (north to south) and your second finger in the direction of the current in the wire, then your thumb will point in the direction of the force on the wire.

▼ Fleming's left-hand rule helps find the direction of the force. The first finger points in the direction of the magnetic field and the second finger is pointed in the direction of the current in the wire. The thumb will then point in the direction of the force on the wire

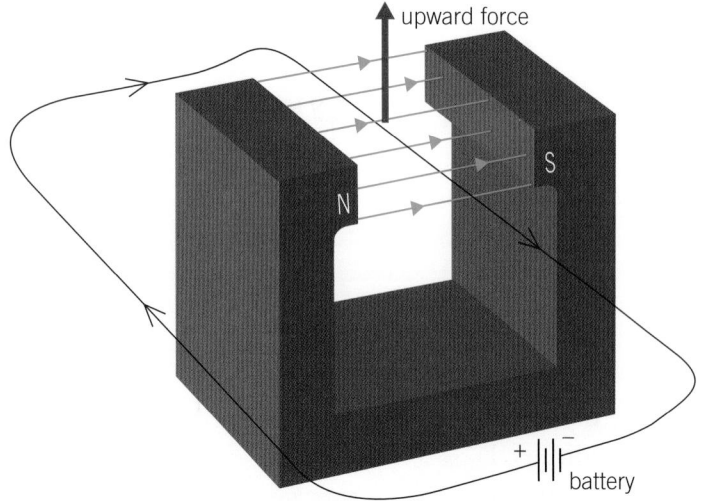

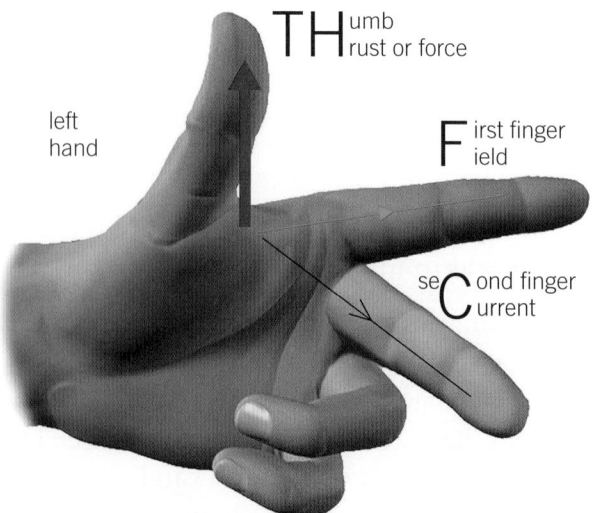

Investigating the force on a current-carrying wire in a magnetic field

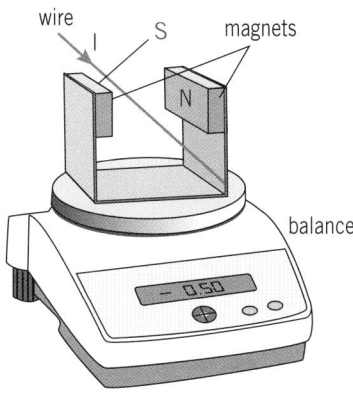

wire I S magnets
N
balance
0.50

Method

- Position two ceramic magnets on a U-shaped holder. Place this on a balance that is precise enough to measure masses of 0.1 g or less.

- Clamp a wire so that it passes between the magnets parallel to them (at right angles to the magnetic field). Connect the wire in series with a power pack (set to about 4 V d.c.), an ammeter and a variable resistor.

- With the power pack off, zero the balance.

- Switch on the power pack, and record the current through the wire and the reading on the balance.

- Change the current by adjusting the variable resistor and record the new readings of current and mass in a table.

Although the balance shows mass in grams, it is really detecting a change in the overall force on the magnets. If the wire is being pushed up by the magnetic field, then there is an equal force on the magnets acting downwards. This increases the reading on the balance.

Use the equation $F = mg$ to convert the mass reading on the balance into a force. To do this, convert the mass readings into kilograms and then multiply by g (9.8 N kg^{-1}). This will give you the force acting on the wire. Record these values in a new column of your table (don't forget to include the unit).

Draw a graph of your results.

One very useful application of the force on a current-carrying wire is the electric motor. An electric motor has a coil of wire with a current passing through it. The coil is placed in a magnetic field. Opposite sides of the coil of wire have current flowing in opposite directions so the forces on them also act in the opposite direction. This creates a turning force where one side of the coil is pushed upwards while the other side is pushed downwards.

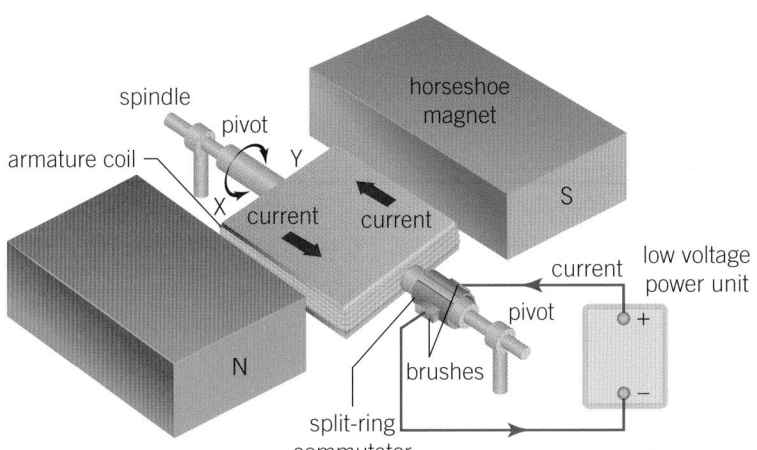

spindle
pivot
armature coil
Y
X
current current
horseshoe magnet
S
N
split-ring commutator
brushes
pivot
current
low voltage power unit
+
−

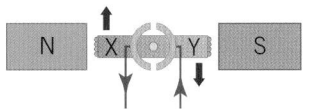

N X Y S

Initially, current is up side X and down side Y. Therefore the coil turns clockwise

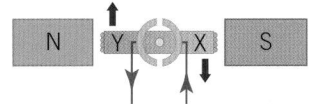

N Y X S

After half a turn, current is up Y and down side X. Therefore the coil continues to turn clockwise

▲ Simple electric motor

An important component of an electric motor is the commutator. A common type is called the split-ring commutator because it is shaped as a ring that is split into two halves. The commutator has a sliding contact (called a brush) so that current can flow in and out of the coil as it spins. The commutator also reverses the current in the coil every half turn. If this were not the case, the side of the coil with the upward force would be pushed upwards until it reached the top. As it rotated slightly past the vertical, it would again be pushed upwards. This would stop the motor making a full turn. The commutator reverses the current so that as the top part of the coil rotates past the vertical, it is pushed downwards causing the whole coil to make another half rotation. As a result, the motor keeps spinning.

ELECTROMAGNETISM

How can we generate electricity?

Generating electricity is important for supplying electrical power to homes, businesses and industries.

In the motor effect, a magnetic field with a current flowing through it causes a wire to move. To generate electricity, we need the reverse of this process: for motion and a magnetic field to cause a current to be induced. This is called electromagnetic induction.

When a wire, or any conductor, passes through a magnetic field at right angles, it cuts through the field lines, and the electrons in the wire experience a small force which causes them to move. This causes an induced voltage. If the wire is connected to a circuit, these electrons can flow causing a current. The more field lines that the wire cuts through every second, the greater the force on the electrons in the wire. As a result, the induced voltage is larger and so is the induced current. This can be achieved by:

- moving the wire faster

- using a stronger magnetic field so that the field lines are closer together

- looping the wire around multiple times in a coil so that more of it passes through the magnetic field.

If a wire is held stationary in a magnetic field, there is no induced voltage as the wire does not cut through any field lines. However, if the magnetic field is changed or removed, then the changing field lines cut through the wire and a voltage is induced. This is also true for a coil of wire.

▼ If the wire is moved upwards through the magnetic field lines, the ammeter registers a current. If the wire is moved downwards or the direction of the magnetic field is reversed, the direction of the current is reversed

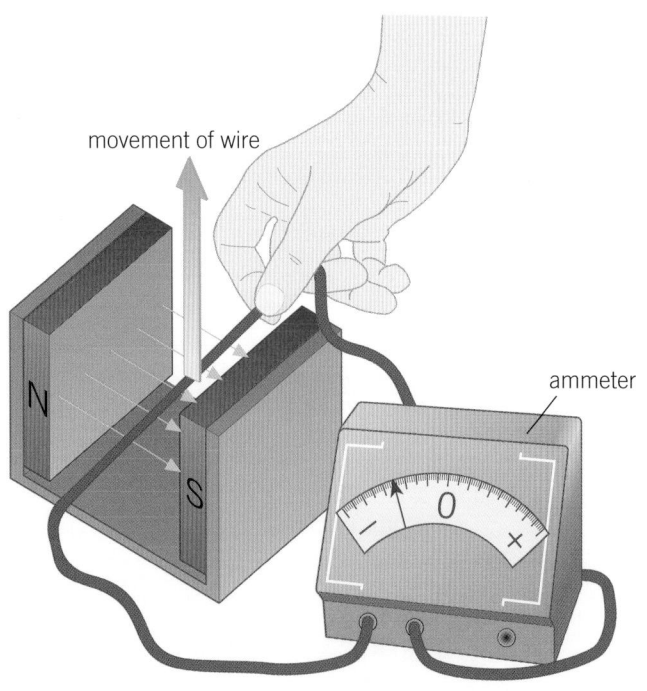

movement of wire

ammeter

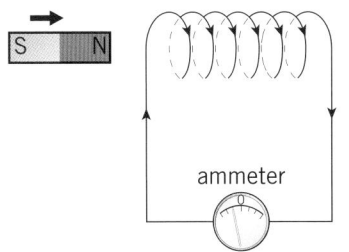

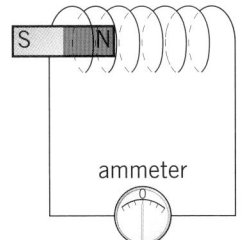

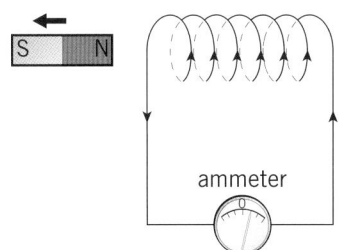

When a magnet is brought towards a coil of wire, the magnetic field through the coil of wire increases and this changing magnetic field induces a voltage in the coil. The ammeter registers a current.

If the magnet is stationary in the coil then there is no change in magnetic field, and so no induced voltage or current.

When the magnet is brought out again, there is a change in the magnetic field and the induced voltage is the reverse of what it was before.

▲ Electromagnetic induction means that a coil of wire that experiences a changing magnetic field will have a current induced in it

The diagram below shows an iron rod with two coils of wire around it. Coil X is connected to a battery and a switch; coil Y is connected to an ammeter. When the switch is closed, coil X acts like an electromagnet. Coil Y experiences a change in the magnetic field and has a current induced in it which causes the ammeter to jump to the right. The ammeter then returns to zero.

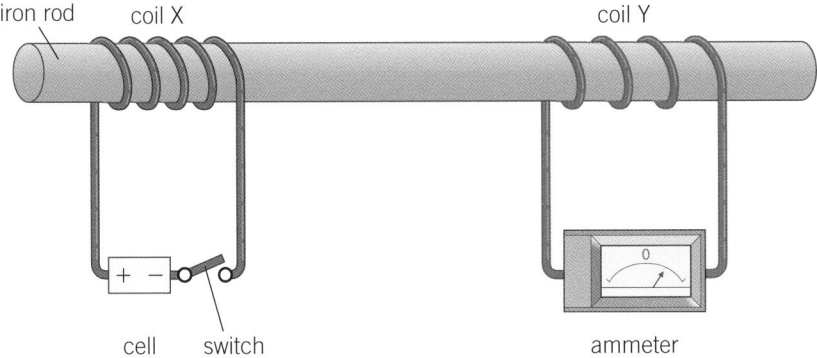

1. Explain why the ammeter registers a current when the switch is first closed, but after a short time, the current reading returns to zero.

2. Describe the reading on the ammeter when the switch is opened again.

3. The iron rod is replaced with a wooden one. Explain what the difference in the induced current would be.

4. The number of turns in the wire in coil X is doubled. Explain why the ammeter reading is greater when the switch is closed.

5. Give one other way in which the ammeter reading could be increased.

How does an electric generator work?

If a motor is operated in reverse, it essentially becomes an electric generator. A force is used to turn the motor round, so a voltage is induced across the coil. This is because the coils of the motor cut through the magnetic field lines. The turning force might be generated by a steam turbine, a windmill or a waterwheel – see Chapter 11, Energy, for the different ways in which energy is generated and Chapter 10, Transformation, for how a steam turbine works.

There are other ways in which a generator can operate. The coil of wire does not have to move; it could be the magnets that move relative to the coil of wire. A simple dynamo can be constructed by having a magnet spinning in a coil of wire. Other generators use a spinning disk of magnets to create a changing magnetic field near the coils.

▲ This dynamo in this illustration from 1895 was used to power Chicago's overhead railway. At the time, it was the largest dynamo in the world

What is the difference between a.c. and d.c. voltages?

When a battery is used to power a simple circuit, the flow of current is constant. This is because the battery provides a constant voltage. We call this direct current, d.c. for short.

Electricity that is provided from a generator, however, is different. As the generator in a power station turns and generates electricity, the wires in the coil of the generator move through a magnetic field. Since the coil rotates, a wire might sometimes be moving upwards through the magnetic field and half a turn later, be moving downwards. As a result, the direction of the current is always changing. This is called alternating current, a.c. for short.

Measuring voltage

The two graphs show the voltage output from a mains power supply (left) and from a battery (right).

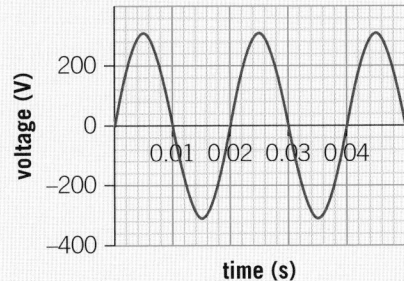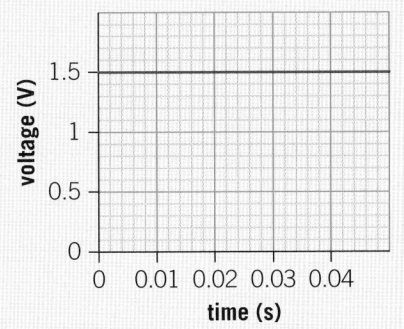

1. What is the peak voltage from the mains supply?

2. Use the graph to calculate the frequency of the mains voltage.

3. Explain which of these electricity supplies is the more dangerous.

How can electromagnetism be used to transform voltages?

Electromagnetic induction can be used to change voltages in a circuit using a device called a transformer. A transformer has a coil of wire around an iron core connected to an a.c. voltage. This acts like an electromagnet and generates a magnetic field. Because the current in the coil is always changing, the magnetic field also changes.

The iron core is bent round to form a loop. On the other side of the iron core is another coil of wire, the secondary coil. Because it experiences a changing magnetic field, it has a voltage induced across it.

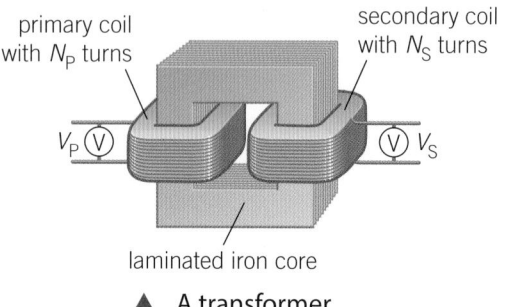

primary coil
with N_P turns

secondary coil
with N_S turns

V_P ⓥ   ⓥ V_S

laminated iron core

▲ A transformer

Transformers are useful because they can change the output voltage of a circuit.

- If the number of turns on the secondary coil is greater than the number of turns on the primary coil, the induced voltage in the secondary coil is larger than the voltage supplied to the primary coil. This is called a step-up transformer as the voltage is increased from the primary to the secondary. Although the voltage increases, the current decreases by the same factor.

- If the number of turns on the secondary coil is less than the number of turns on the primary coil then the induced voltage is less. This is a step-down transformer. Although the voltage is decreased, the current in the secondary coil is larger.

The number of turns on the primary and secondary coils are related to the voltages across those coils by the transformer equation:

$$\frac{N_P}{N_S} = \frac{V_P}{V_S}$$

where N_P and N_S are the number of turns on the primary and secondary coils and V_P and V_S are the voltages across those coils. The fraction N_P/N_S is sometimes called the turns ratio. It gives the ratio by which the voltage is decreased and the current is increased.

1. A transformer has 20 turns on its secondary coil and a primary coil of 100 turns that is connected to a voltage of 30 V.

   a) Is this a step-up or step-down transformer?

   b) Calculate the voltage of the secondary coil.

2. In an experiment, a student wants to use a transformer to convert a primary voltage of 3 V a.c. to a secondary voltage of 10 V a.c. They have coils with 100, 150, 200, 500, 1,000, 1,500 and 2,000 turns available to make into the transformer.

   a) Which coils should they use?

   b) What is the largest and smallest voltage they could generate with these coils?

   c) Why would this not work with a d.c. voltage?

Transformers are useful when distributing electrical power from power stations. As we saw in Chapter 6, Function, larger currents result in larger energy losses, so when distributing electrical power through power cables, a small current is desirable. To achieve enough power distribution, however, a large voltage is required. To meet this requirement, the electrical output from a power station is put into a step-up transformer. This gives the higher voltage and lower current required to reduce power losses in the cables.

Overhead power lines can carry voltages over 200,000 V but this would be very dangerous in the home. A step-down transformer is

used to reduce the voltage supplied to buildings. In fact a series of transformers is used. A large transformer may reduce the voltage to supply a whole town with subsequent smaller transformers stepping the voltage down for streets of houses. A final transformer will step the voltage down to the correct level for connecting a building.

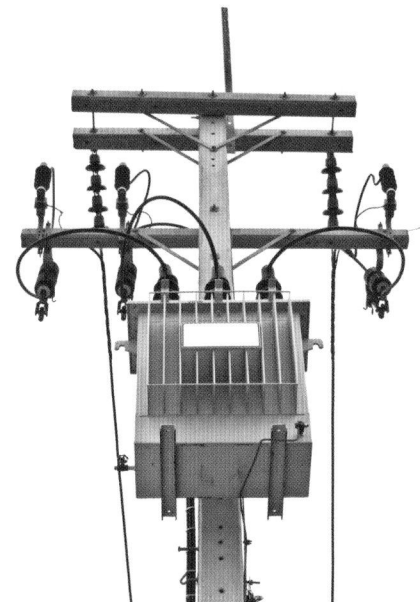

▲ Transformers are used in electricity distribution. A large transformer is required in an electricity sub-station that might supply a whole town. Smaller transformers are mounted on the poles that carry overhead cables to step the voltage down to a suitable level to connect to a house

How does sound travel?

WAVES

Electromagnetism and electromagnetic induction are important in the production and recording of sound. In Chapter 1, Models, we saw that sound is a longitudinal wave. The air molecules vibrate backwards and forwards, and collisions between them send compression waves through the air.

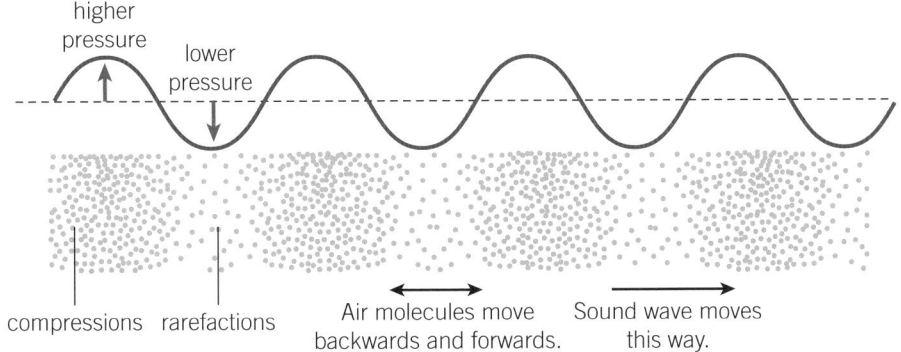

▲ Sound is a longitudinal wave which means that the air molecules move in a parallel direction to the direction of the wave's travel

▲ This jar is connected to a vacuum pump. The pump removes the air from the jar. As the air is removed, the sound from the bell heard outside the jar gets quieter. This is because the sound needs a medium to travel through

Sound needs a medium to travel through. As well as traveling through air it can travel through liquids and solids. Without a medium to travel through, however, sound cannot be heard. As a result, sound does not travel through space.

The speed of sound waves depends on the medium through which they travel. In air, the speed is about 330 to 340 m s^{-1}, but this depends on the temperature (and to a lesser extent the humidity and pressure) conditions.

Experiment

Measuring the speed of sound

To measure the speed of sound, you need a method of generating a loud sound that also provides a visual indication of when the sound is made. One method is to use two pieces of wood hinged together to make a clapper.

Method

Working with at least one other student, find a large, open space and stand as far as part as possible. One of you makes the sound with a visual indication at the same time. The other starts a stop clock when they see the sound being made and stops timing when they hear the sound. Measure the distance between the observer and the source of the sound, then calculate the speed.

Measuring the time between making a sound and hearing its echo from a large flat wall is another way of measuring the speed of sound.

Questions

1. Carry out the experiment and obtain a value for the speed of sound.

2. How accurate do you think your measurement is?

3. Suggest how you could improve your measurement.

WAVES

What sounds can we hear?

There is a limited range of frequencies that the human ear can detect. We can detect anything between about 20 Hz and 20 kHz, although the top range of frequencies that we are able to hear declines with age.

Sound with a wavelength above 20 kHz is called ultrasound because it is beyond the range of our hearing. Although humans cannot hear these high frequencies, there are many animals that can. Dogs and some other mammals can hear frequencies up to 40 or 50 kHz. Dolphins and bats use ultrasound at frequencies in excess of 100 kHz for echolocation.

Sound volume

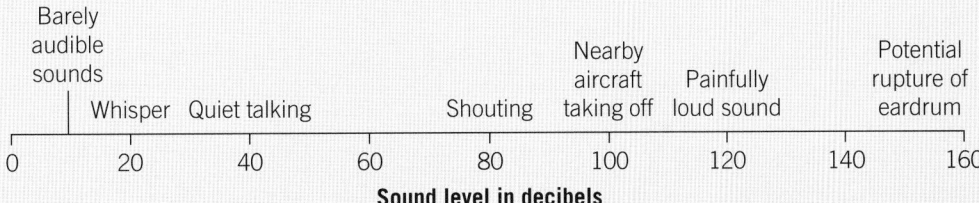

Sound volume is often measured in decibels. What we perceive as silence might be 10–20 dB, average background noise might be 40–50 dB and 110–120 dB is painfully loud and potentially damaging to your hearing.

Many smartphones have apps that use the phone's microphone to measure the sound level in decibels. Measure the background sound level in various places during your day and mark them on a chart similar to the one above.

Try to measure the background sound levels of:

- your physics class
- your nearest road
- your bedroom as you go to sleep
- the place where you have lunch.

Where is the loudest place you go in the day? Where is the quietest place you can find?

Data-based question: Hearing infrasound

Some animals are capable of hearing sound well below the range of human hearing. Such sound is called infrasound. For example, pigeons have been shown to perceive frequencies as low as 0.05 Hz.

The following data is from a paper entitled "Audiogram of the chicken (*Gallus gallus domesticus*) from 2 Hz to 9 kHz" by E. M. Hill, G. Koay, R. S. Heffner and H. E. Heffner. It was published in the *Journal of Comparative Physiology A* in 2014 on pages 863–870. The graph compares the chicken's ability to hear different frequencies of sound with that of pigeons and humans. The graph shows the volume of sound required for it to be detected.

▲ *Gallus gallus domesticus*

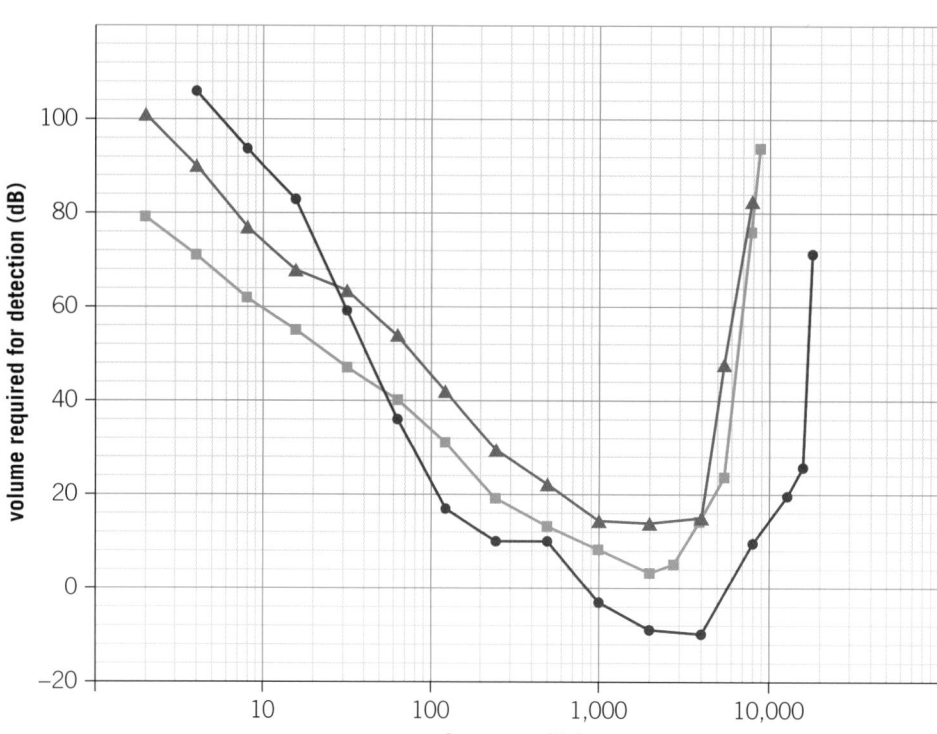

1. Which animal is best able to hear sounds at:

   a) 10 Hz

   b) 1 kHz?

2. The frequency range of hearing is usually taken to be the range of frequencies that can be heard below a volume of 60 dB. Find the hearing ranges of:

   a) a chicken

   b) a pigeon

   c) a human.

3. Which animal seems to exhibit:

   a) the most sensitive hearing

   b) the most sensitivity to low frequency sounds

   c) the most sensitivity to high frequency sounds?

4. The paper presents data on the hearing ranges of chickens. To produce this graph, the authors needed to use data from other studies so they could compare chickens to pigeons and humans. They referenced their sources of data in a bibliography.

   a) Explain why it is important for the authors to reference their sources.

   b) Write a suitable bibliography reference for this paper.

Data-based question: Ultrasound imaging

Ultrasound imaging is a useful, non-invasive way of seeing inside the body. For example, to monitor a pregnancy using ultrasound imaging, a transducer is placed against the mother's abdomen. This emits ultrasound waves and detects the echo as they bounce off the fetus. The ultrasound has a frequency of about 2.5 MHz and the waves travel at about 1,500 m s^{-1}.

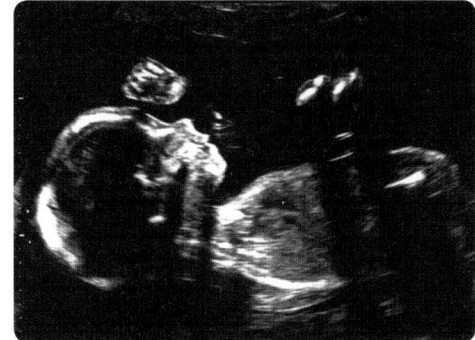

▲ An ultrasound is a way of monitoring the development of babies in the womb

1. Calculate the wavelength of the ultrasound.

2. The image is built up by sending ultrasound waves and measuring the time between the emission of the waves and the detected echo. If the waves bounce off an object that is 3 cm away from the transducer, what is the time delay between the ultrasound wave being emitted and the echo being received?

3 Discuss the advantages and disadvantages of invasive and non-invasive techniques for monitoring unborn babies.

The use of sound in films

Sound is a highly emotive sense; film-makers use it to amplify emotion in scenes.

Various studies have shown that low pitched sounds with low frequencies can sometimes be associated with boredom or sadness, while high pitched sounds might convey fear or surprise. There are even studies that show that infrasound (sound below the range of human hearing) can cause feelings of unease, even though the sound itself cannot be heard, and some films have used low sounds to heighten a sense of fear.

Find a film scene and listen to see if the frequency and pitch of the music affects the emotion of the scene. Are there any other non-verbal ways in which the mood is communicated?

ELECTROMAGNETISM

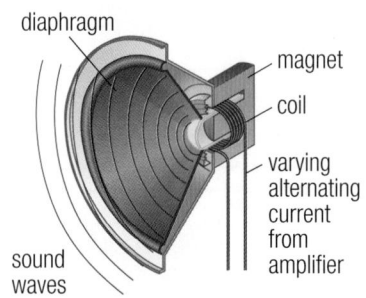

diaphragm

magnet

coil

varying
alternating
current
from
amplifier

sound
waves

▲ A diagram of a loudspeaker

How does a loudspeaker work?

Sounds can be generated by loudspeakers. To make a sound, a loudspeaker needs to move the surrounding air in order to send compression waves (longitudinal waves) through it. The speaker cone, or diaphragm, is a structure made from a thin paper-like material. It is able to oscillate and move enough air to create different frequencies of sound at an audible volume.

The speaker cone is attached to a coil through which an alternating current flows. The coil itself sits in the field of a magnet and so it experiences a force when the current is flowing. When the current reverses direction, the force on the speaker cone also reverses, causing the cone to vibrate backwards and forwards at the same frequency as the alternating current. In this way, an electrical signal can be converted into sound.

ELECTROMAGNETISM

How does a microphone work?

The principles behind the operation of a loudspeaker can also be used to make a microphone. Like a speaker, a microphone has a diaphragm which can move. Sound waves cause it to vibrate. The diaphragm is attached to a coil which is held in a magnetic field. The diaphragm moves the coil backwards and forwards in the magnetic field so that it experiences a changing magnetic field. As a result, an alternating voltage is induced in the coil.

ATL Thinking in context

What are the consequences of personal expression?

The invention of the loudspeaker and the microphone quickly enabled the invention of the telephone which was first patented in 1876 by Alexander Graham Bell. Later, improvements in technology enabled the microphones and speakers to become smaller and mobile phones were developed.

The opportunities of mobile electronic devices have led to a rapid development in other means of communication via social media. This enables people to express themselves in a number of different ways.

However, the consequences of mobile phones and social media are still largely unknown. It is thought that increased use of social media can lead to increased anxiety and mental health issues.

Summative assessment

Introduction

The electric car is an increasingly popular alternative to petrol- or diesel-powered vehicles. This assessment investigates the use of electric cars and the use of electromagnetism in their design.

 ## Uses of electromagnetism in car design

Electromagnetic induction can be used in the braking system of cars. By using the motor as a generator, the energy of the moving car can be used to drive the generator and the current that is produced can charge a battery or be used in other ways by the car. Such a system is called regenerative braking.

1. Describe the way an electric motor works. [4]

2. Explain why operating a motor in reverse can generate an electric current. [4]

The velocity–time graph of a car braking is shown here.

3. Use the graph to determine:

   a) the deceleration of the car [2]

   b) the distance traveled in this time. [2]

4. If the car has a mass of 1,000 kg, calculate the braking force applied to the car. [2]

5. Calculate the work done by the brakes on the car. [3]

 ## Using regenerative brakes

Engineers designing a braking system for an electric car want to test the current that the system generates. They drive a car which is fitted with this braking system at different speeds, brake, then measure the voltage generated.

6. Identify the independent and dependent variables in this experiment. [2]

7. As an improvement to the experiment, the engineers realize that when they brake they can monitor the speed of the car as it slows down and the voltage generated by the braking system at the same time. Describe one advantage of using this method. [2]

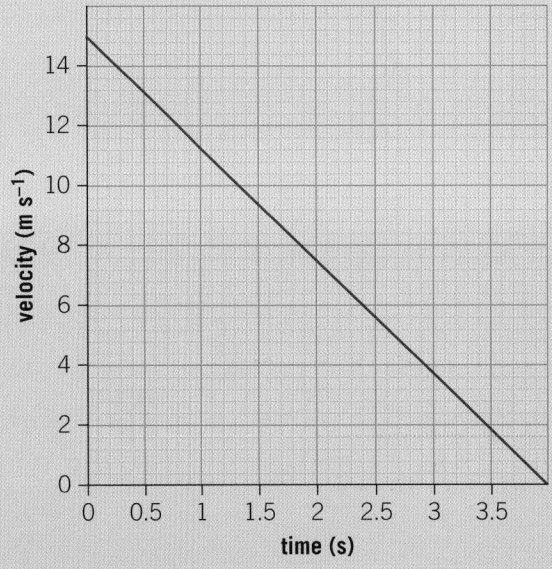

Two graphs of their results are shown below.

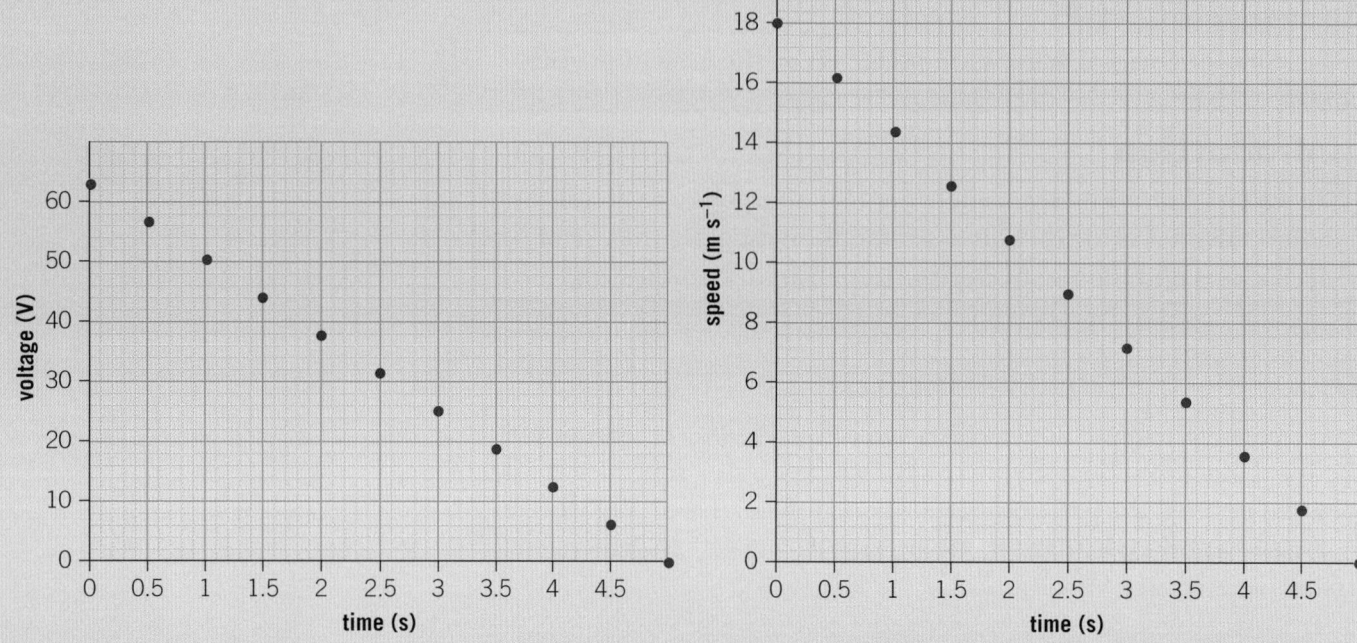

8. Using the graphs, deduce what voltage would be generated at a speed of $30\,km\,h^{-1}$. [4]

9. The maximum voltage that the braking system could deliver without damaging the battery is 60 V. What is the maximum speed at which this braking system could be used? [2]

10. The engineers who conducted this experiment formulated a hypothesis that the voltage generated by the braking system would be directly proportional to the speed at which the car is traveling. Determine whether their hypothesis was correct or not. [3]

11. The engineers used data-logging equipment to simultaneously measure the speed of the car and the voltage from the braking system. Explain why the measurements needed to be simultaneous. [2]

Testing electric cars

12. When testing an electric car, engineers drive it at different speeds and measure the current that the motor draws from the battery at that speed. Their results are shown on the next page.

   a) Draw a line of best fit on a copy of the graph. [1]

   b) Describe the trend of the data. [2]

c) Suppose the engineers had tested the car on a slight uphill slope. Draw a line on the copy of the graph to show how their results would have differed. Explain your answer. [4]

d) If the maximum current that the battery can deliver is 300 A, determine the fastest speed that the car can go on a flat road. Give your answer in kilometers per hour. [3]

13. A team of engineers is going to test electric cars made by three competing companies and they intend to publish their results. The car companies believe that it is important that the results of the tests are reliable and fair. Explain what the engineers should do to ensure that their results are reliable and fair. [5]

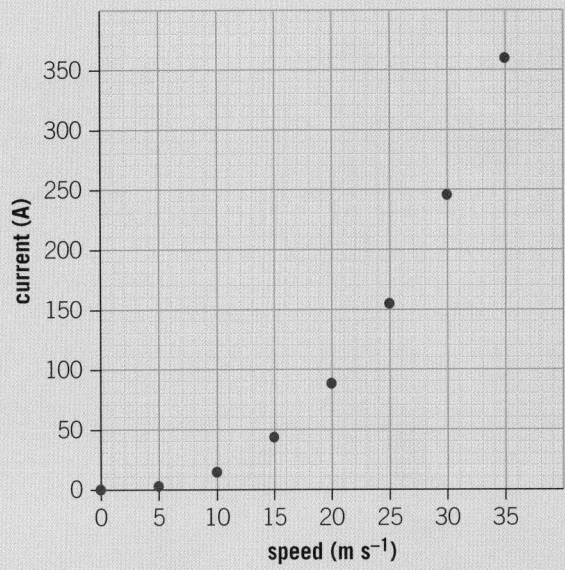

 ## The future of electric cars

Electric cars are an alternative method of transport to petrol- and diesel-powered cars.

14. One disadvantage of electric cars is that they are so quiet they are not easily heard. It is argued that this makes them more dangerous to pedestrians. One solution is to connect a loudspeaker to the battery so that the car makes more noise. A scientist on the design team for an electric car points out that the battery is a d.c. supply, so the loudspeaker would not be able to generate a sound. Instead the scientist proposes that a circuit which generates an alternating current at a certain frequency should be used. Write an explanation that the scientist might use to persuade the rest of the design team that a.c. current should be used and suggest a suitable frequency. Try to use simple scientific terms effectively. [4]

15. Apart from the noise issue, describe one advantage and one disadvantage of electric cars over petrol and diesel cars. [3]

16. Electric cars are a solution to the problem of how to get from one place to another.

a) Give one alternative method of getting from one place to another and describe an advantage and a disadvantage compared to a car. [4]

b) People travel more today than they did 100 years ago. Discuss whether modern society and technology require people to travel more or not. [4]

9 Development

Development is the process of growth and change.

◀ Axolotls are an endangered amphibian native to Mexico. Most amphibians start their life in the water (like a tadpole) and then metamorphose into adults who live on land, but axolotls have evolved to develop in a different way. Instead, they keep their gills and stay in the water all their lives. They do this because their bodies do not generate the hormones required to undergo metamorphosis. If they are given these hormones, they develop into creatures that are similar to salamanders, although they would never do this in the wild. How do chemicals and hormones affect our development?

▼ Charles Darwin first suggested that species develop through evolution – a series of small changes over millions of years. This is the skeleton of Lucy who was a member of the early species *Australopithecus afarensis*, which lived more than 3 million years ago. How might humans appear millions of years from now?

The development of written language was an important milestone in human evolution. This writing is one of few samples of a language called Linear A which was used in ancient Greece as early as 2500BC. It is one of only a couple of known languages that has never been deciphered. How has science and technology benefited from the development of writing?

Drums were first used for communication tens of thousands of years ago and became the basis of primitive music. From the beginning of the 20th century, the development of different musical forms, in particular jazz, resulted in drums being used differently. This required the development of drums from orchestral instruments and those used in marching bands into modern drum kits. How has modern technology influenced the development of music and of drums?

Key concept: Systems

Related concept: Development

Global context: Fairness and development

Introduction

Scientific theories are not static, unchanging beliefs. As our scientific knowledge increases and technology enables us to build more sensitive equipment to test these theories, we can refine and improve the theories we use to explain the universe. These developments in our understanding of how the universe works leads to an improved ability to manipulate our surroundings and change how things operate. In this chapter we will look at how science has developed a systematic way of examining and testing ideas and theories through experiment. As a result, the key concept of the chapter is systems.

Improvements in our technological abilities can help us to tackle problems such as disease and famine. To solve problems such as climate change or pollution that result from our use of fossil fuels also requires the application of science to develop new technologies. Because of this, the global context of the chapter is fairness and development.

▶ This photo of X-rays diffracting off DNA was taken in 1953 by Rosalind Franklin. It confirmed the double helix structure of DNA. Today, the development of technologies such as genetic modification and engineering offers us possible solutions to the problems of disease and famine

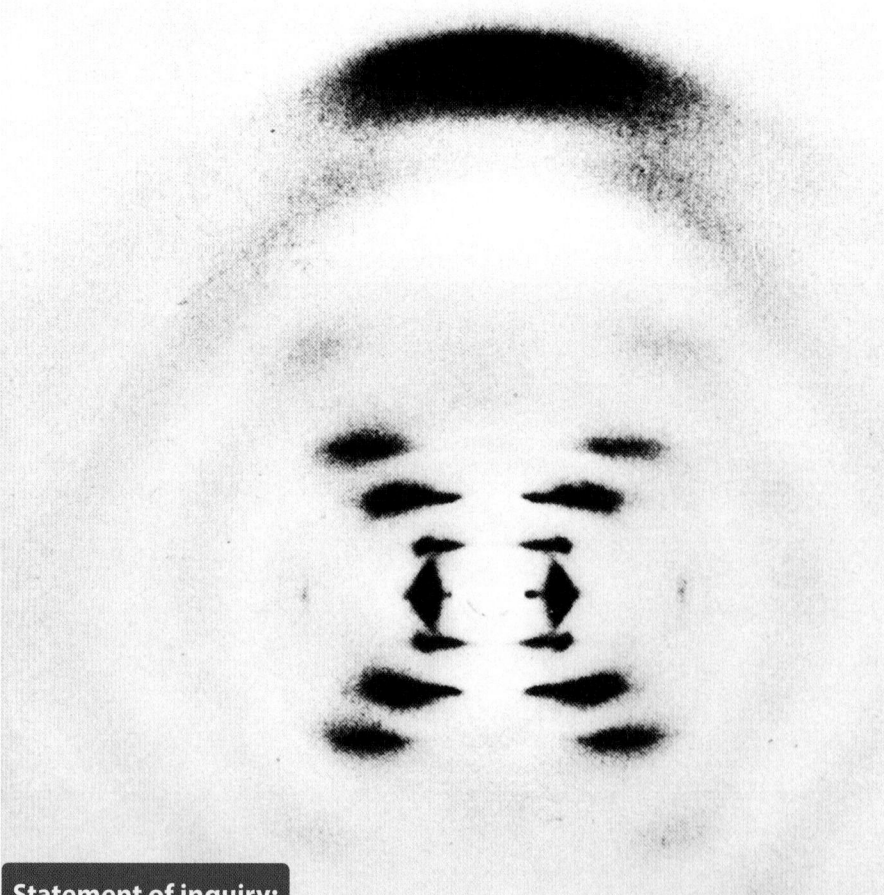

Statement of inquiry:

The development of science and technology gives us the possibility of changing the world for the better.

An important area of investigation throughout the history of physics has been the nature of light. At the end of the first millennium, philosophers were considering how we see. In the 18th and 19th centuries, scientists were investigating whether light was a wave or a particle. In the 20th century, Albert Einstein used the nature of light to understand the way that space and time are linked. In this chapter we will see how our theories of what light is have developed and in doing so, have inspired new theories and systems to explain the universe.

Einstein's theory of general relativity was a significant development in the theories that underpin our understanding of the universe. One prediction of this theory was the existence of gravitational waves. This illustration is a representation of gravitational waves being formed by two neutron stars spiraling closer and closer together. Gravitational waves were finally observed in 2016 by the LIGO experiment in Louisiana, USA

Without our knowledge of the nature of light, we wouldn't have been able to develop technology like these solar cells on the International Space Station. Such improved technology can help us to find solutions to problems like finding sustainable energy resources. It can also help develop scientific theories and new tools to test our scientific understanding

How does science progress?

Many scientists in the past have appreciated the importance of experimentation as a test of their theories. One of the earliest scientific thinkers to understand the importance of this approach was Ibn al-Haytham who was born in Basra, Iraq in about 965AD. He devised an experimental method and used the results of his experiments to provide evidence for his theories. Through his experiments, he showed that we are able to see as a result of light entering the eye rather than from vision leaving the eye and extending to an observed object. Later, scientists in the 15th to 17th centuries developed Ibn al-Haytham's experimental methods into what is now called the scientific method in which hypotheses are tested by experiment.

Ibn al-Haytham believed in the importance of developing a hypothesis and then testing it with an experiment. The results of the experiment might support the hypothesis, they might lead to the hypothesis being refined or they might result in the abandonment of the hypothesis if they contradict it. If the results of the experiment support the hypothesis, then the results can be published and other scientists can check to see if their experiments agree. If the scientific community accepts the results, then the hypothesis might become accepted scientific theory.

◀ A diagram of the eye from Ibn Al-Haytham's *Book of Optics* in which he used experimental methods to develop a theory for vision

```
┌─────────────────────────┐
│ Ideas and initial observations are │
│ gathered on a chosen topic │
└─────────────────────────┘
            │
            ▼
┌─────────────────────────┐        ┌─────────────────────────┐
│ A testable hypothesis is formed │        │   Hypothesis is adapted   │
└─────────────────────────┘        └─────────────────────────┘
            │
            ▼
┌─────────────────────────┐
│ Experiments are carried out to │
│     test the hypothesis     │
└─────────────────────────┘
            │  Hypothesis is
            │  confirmed
            ▼
┌─────────────────────────┐
│ The results are published and │
│ other scientists can check if │
│ their own experiments agree │
└─────────────────────────┘
            │  Hypothesis is confirmed by
            │  scientific community
            ▼
┌─────────────────────────┐
│    The hypothesis becomes    │
│  accepted scientific theory  │
└─────────────────────────┘
```

Hypothesis is disproved

Hypothesis is disproved by scientific community

◀ The process of the scientific method

What makes a good hypothesis?

MEASUREMENT

A hypothesis is a prediction of the outcome of an experiment, although sometimes the technology required to carry out an experiment is not developed until long after the hypothesis is made. Since the scientific method relates the experimental outcomes to the hypothesis, it must be sufficiently detailed so as to inform the analysis of the experiment. A good hypothesis must:

● be testable

● make predictions about how changes in the independent variable will affect another factor – the dependent variable

● relate the predictions to scientific theory.

If a hypothesis is not testable, then it is either not specific enough or not scientific.

Developing a hypothesis

The owners of a café want more customers. They think that changing the café's name will gain more customers.

1. Is this a good hypothesis?

2. How could the hypothesis be improved?

3. How could the hypothesis be tested?

▲ A cartoon from 1874 showing Charles Darwin as one of the apes he suggested that we are descended from

Considering ideas from multiple perspectives

There is sometimes a conflict between science and religion. For example, the creationist belief that the Earth was created only a few thousand years ago disagrees with Darwin's theory of evolution (also see Chapter 7, Form, for how Galileo's model of the solar system angered the Roman Catholic Church).

The difference between the two arises from the scientific method. Science uses testable hypotheses to examine whether theories work. Religion, on the other hand, uses different approaches to knowledge – for example, faith. As a result, religious views do not provide scientific, testable hypotheses.

Many scientists hold religious views and see no conflict, and there are religious organizations that look to promote harmony between the two disciplines.

1 Discuss which has made the greater contribution to human progress: science or religion.

MEASUREMENT

Do all experiments have to have a hypothesis?

The scientific method uses the idea of a hypothesis, but sometimes an experiment can seem not to have one. Often the hypothesis exists even though it does not form part of the original experiment.

Some experiments have the simple aim of measuring a quantity, for example, the charge of an electron. It might appear that such an experiment does not have a hypothesis; however, there is an accepted value for the charge of an electron, $-1.6 \times 10^{-19}\,\text{C}$, and this essentially serves as the hypothesis. Although the new measurement might be more precise, it will either agree with, or improve, an existing value, or suggest that previous measurements were wrong.

Sometimes an experiment might consist of an observation that cannot be fully explained with current theories. For example, in 1859 Le Verrier noticed that Mercury's orbit rotated gradually by about 0.0016° per year. Most of this could be explained by Mercury's interaction with the Sun and by gravitational interactions with other planets. However,

Le Verrier's measurements showed that Mercury's orbit was rotating a little bit faster than could be explained. In other words, the theories of gravity and motion, mainly according to Newton, hypothesized a rotation of 0.00148° per year whereas the measured value of the rotation of Mercury's orbit was 0.00159° per year. This is not a large discrepancy, but the measurements were very precise so experimental uncertainty could not account for this difference.

When Einstein published his theory of general relativity in 1915, it accounted for this extra rotation and Mercury's orbit was one of the first tests of the theory. An important step in the scientific method is publishing theories and letting other scientists test them.

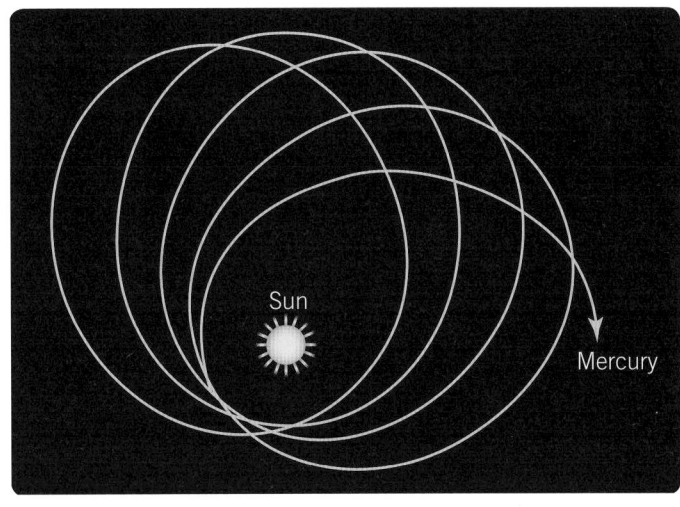

▲ Mercury's orbit rotates slightly. This diagram is exaggerated as each successive orbit of Mercury is only rotated by about 0.0004°

ATL Information literacy skills

Publishing a scientific paper

Publishing a scientific paper is different to many other forms of publishing in that most scientific journals put the paper through a process of peer review before publishing it. This means that the paper is examined by one or more researchers in the field who judge whether the paper is worth publishing or not. To be published, a paper should report new experimental data or new theoretical work.

The idea of peer review is that scientists in the same field are best placed to judge whether the paper draws valid conclusions. They are also able to judge whether or not the work is original – in rare cases the work that is presented might be plagiarized (this means that the authors are claiming credit for work that was carried out by someone else).

Almost all scientific papers build on the work of others. It is important that this work is correctly referenced so that the authors acknowledge this work. The reviewers of a paper ensure that such work is correctly referenced so that there can be no accusations of plagiarism.

One of the predictions of general relativity is that large masses bend the path of light. To test this, Arthur Eddington organized an expedition to Brazil and Africa to observe the total eclipse on 29 May 1919. His aim was to photograph the eclipse and measure the position of the background stars which would normally be obscured by the Sun's brightness. Before he went he took a photograph of the stars from Oxford to use as a comparison. Since this photograph was

taken at night, the light from the stars did not pass near the Sun, so the stars' positions in the sky would be unaffected. When he examined the positions of the stars as seen in the backdrop of the solar eclipse, he found that their position had been moved by the same amount that Einstein's theory had predicted.

Since then the predictions made by the general theory of relativity have been upheld by experimental evidence, although sometimes the experiments are tricky to perform. The theory predicts the existence of black holes: extremely dense objects from which even light cannot escape (see Chapter 7, Form). This makes them difficult to directly observe; however, the motion of stars near the center of our galaxy suggests that there is a supermassive black hole there. General relativity also hypothesized the existence of gravitational waves. This is a good hypothesis as it is specific and testable, although it is very difficult to build a detector sensitive enough to detect these waves. Nevertheless, in 2016 the LIGO experiment detected the gravitational waves for the first time as a result of the merging of two distant black holes.

▲ Albert Einstein and Sir Arthur Eddington. Eddington's observations of the position of stars near the Sun during the 1919 eclipse provided experimental verification of Einstein's theory of general relativity

▼ The Laser Interferometer Gravitational-Wave Observatory (LIGO) is one of the most sensitive pieces of equipment ever built. There are two detectors which are 3,000 km apart. Each has two arms that are 4 km long. At the end of each arm is a mirror; laser beams bounce up and down each arm in order to detect tiny changes in the length of one of the arms. In September 2015, LIGO detected a change of about 10^{-18} m in both of its detectors. This was due to two black holes merging about one billion light years away. The detection of these gravitational waves earned Rainer Weiss, Kip Thorne and Barry Barish the 2017 Nobel Prize in physics

▲ This is one of the pictures taken by Sir Arthur Eddington's expedition to observe the total eclipse of 1919. Analysis of the positions of the background stars supported Einstein's general theory of relativity

What makes a good experiment?

For an experiment to test scientific theories, then it must be well designed so that other scientists can trust and replicate the results. One of the first stages of designing an experiment is to identify the variables that are to be investigated. In an experiment a variable is something that could be changed to affect the outcome. There are three important types.

- **Dependent variables:** This is the property that is measured or tested that will determine the outcome of the experiment. It might be directly measured or it could be calculated from the experimental measurements.

- **Independent variables:** This is the property that is changed in the experiment in order to cause a change in the dependent variable.

- **Control variables:** There may be other factors that could cause a change in the outcome of the experiment. It is important to keep these factors constant so that the results of the experiment can be attributed to the changes in the independent variable. Such variables are called control variables.

Plotting graphs

A graph is a useful visual representation of the data. It is much easier to see a trend on a graph than from a table of data.

It is usual to plot the independent variable on the *x*-axis and the dependent variable on the *y*-axis. The exception to this is some experiments in which time is the dependent variable, as it sometimes makes more sense to plot this on the *x*-axis.

It is also important to choose a sensible scale when plotting a graph. The scales on the axes should be chosen so that the plotted data extend across the axes. Sensible increments are also important. The scale should go up in units of one, two or five times a factor of ten (so it is perfectly acceptable to go up in units of 0.5, 20 or 5,000).

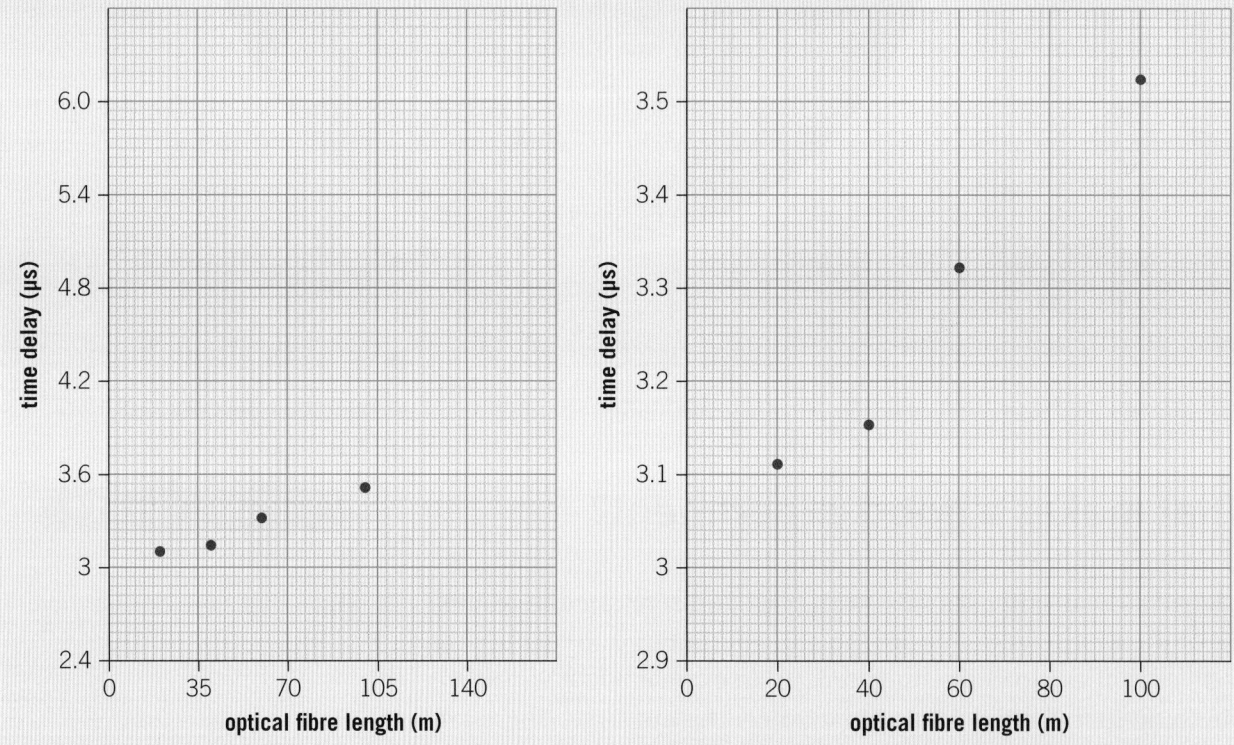

▲ These two graphs show the same data. In the left graph, the data points are bunched in the bottom left-hand corner of the graph; there is no need for the *x*-axis scale to go above 120 or for the *y*-axis scale to go above 4. Moreover, the *y*-axis goes up in increments of 0.6 and the *x*-axis has increments of 35. Try reading a value off the graph: how easy is it? By comparison, the graph on the right is much clearer

WAVES

What did Al-Haytham's experiments show?

Ibn al-Haytham set out to determine how we see light. Some Greek philosophers thought that vision came from the eye and extended outwards, whereas others believed that light entered the eye. Al-Haytham did an experiment with two lamps which he placed on one side of a wall. The light shone through a small hole in the wall into a darkened room. Al-Haytham saw two spots of light in the room, one from each lamp. He observed that blocking one lamp caused one of the spots to disappear. This showed that the spot of light was caused by light from the lamp traveling in a straight line and not from the eye's vision extending to the spot.

Al-Haytham's experiments with light also demonstrated reflection and refraction. It was these properties of light that led scientists to debate its nature for many centuries afterwards. Some scientists thought that light behaved as a stream of particles since light traveled in straight lines and reflected in the same way that objects bounced off other surfaces. Other scientists thought of light as a wave and could show that if light traveled at different speeds, the path of the light would bend. Without experimental evidence, the theory of the nature of light could not develop.

It was not until 1801 that Thomas Young conducted an experiment that determined whether light consisted of waves or particles. He used the light from the Sun shining through a small hole in a window blind, and focused the beam using mirrors. He then placed a thin card in the beam of light which split the light beam into two. Young examined what happens when the two beams of light overlapped again and saw alternate light and dark patches.

- The particle theory of light suggests that where the beams overlapped, the particles of light would add to give more particles and hence a brighter patch of light, but it could not account for the dark patches.

- On the other hand, waves can add together to give a larger wave or cancel each other out. The patches of light and dark could only be explained by the wave theory of light, so he had shown that light was a wave.

▲ This picture shows reflection and refraction of light. Light bounces off the mirrored table so a reflected image can be seen. As the stem goes into the water, it appears bent because the water refracts the light and changes its direction

▼ In this modern version of Thomas Young's experiment, a laser beam is shone through two narrow slits. The resulting pattern has alternating light and dark regions. The wave theory of light can explain the dark patches as regions where the light waves cancel each other out. As this cannot happen with particles, the experiment shows that light is a wave

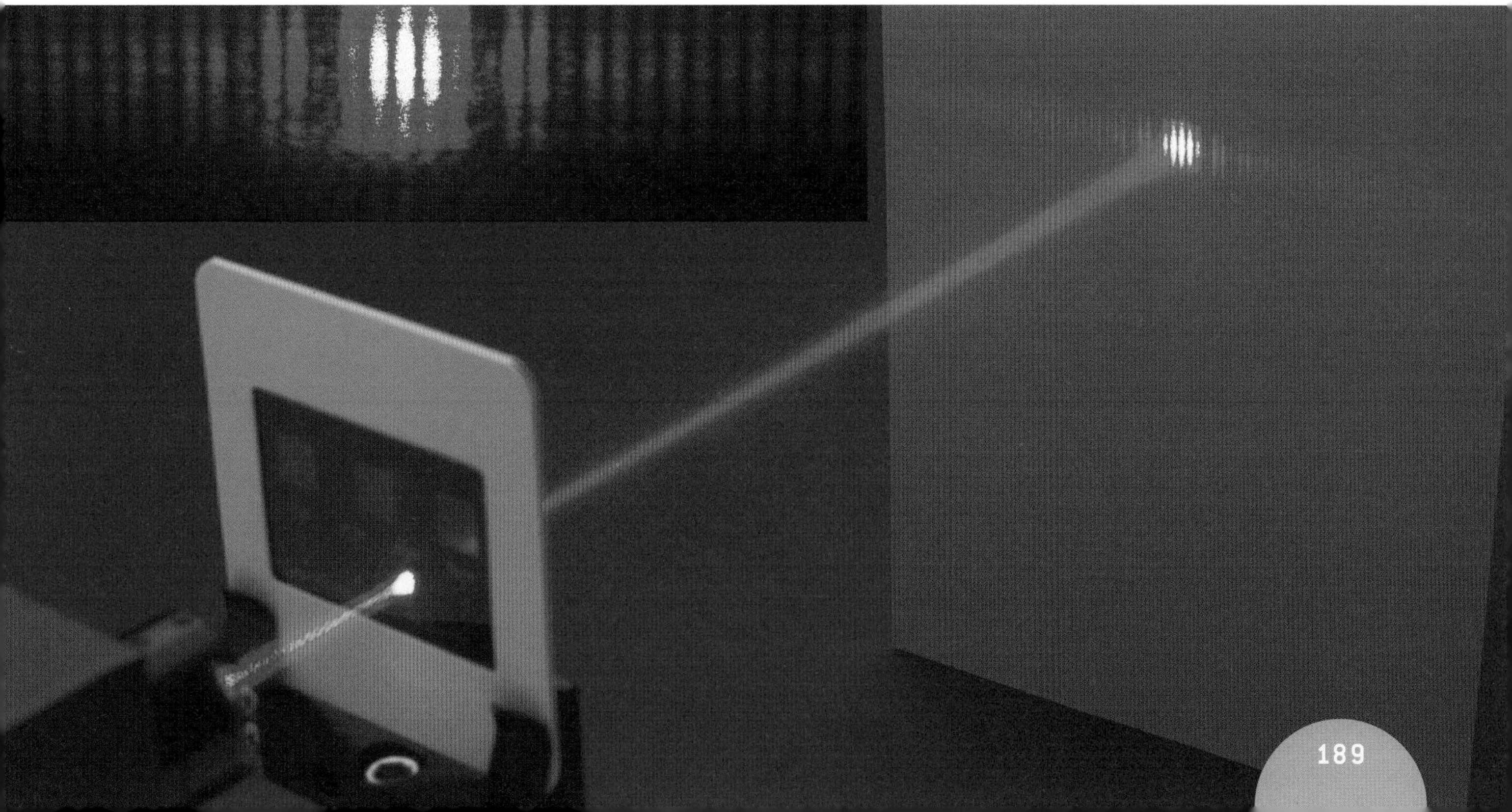

WAVES

How can waves cancel each other?

In Chapter 1, Models, we saw how waves can transfer energy and information without transferring matter itself. The properties of waves that can be measured are their wavelength λ and their frequency f which are both related to the speed of the wave by the equation:

$$v = f\lambda$$

An important property of waves is their ability to add together in different ways. We call this effect interference.

- When two waves add together to create a larger wave, this is constructive interference. The peaks of both waves overlap and add together to give a higher peak and the troughs add together to give a lower trough. In this way, the amplitude of the wave increases.

- When the peak of one wave overlaps with the trough of another, the waves cancel each other out. This is called destructive interference and the amplitude of the wave is reduced.

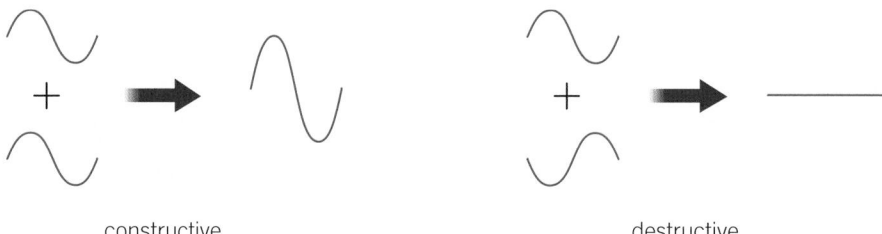

constructive   destructive

▲ When two peaks or two troughs of waves overlap, they add together to give a larger wave, but when the peak of one wave overlaps with the trough of another wave, the two waves cancel each other out to give a smaller wave

Interference can only occur when the two waves are of the same type and of the same (or nearly the same) wavelength and frequency. This means that sound cannot cancel out light, and a high-pitched sound cannot cancel out a low-pitched sound.

▶ When a drum is hit, waves travel across the surface of the drum skin and reflect off the sides. When these waves meet they can add constructively to give a larger amplitude wave or they can add destructively and cancel each other out. If sand is placed on the drum and it is hit, the sand settles on the places where destructive interference occurs because the drum skin moves less at these points

Noise cancellation

Destructive interference can be used to reduce background noise. Noise cancelation can be used to reduce the volume of sound from the engine in a car or airplane cockpit. Noise-canceling headphones detect ambient sounds outside the headphones and produce an opposite wave inside the headphones, which destructively interferes and reduces the amount of outside noise that is heard.

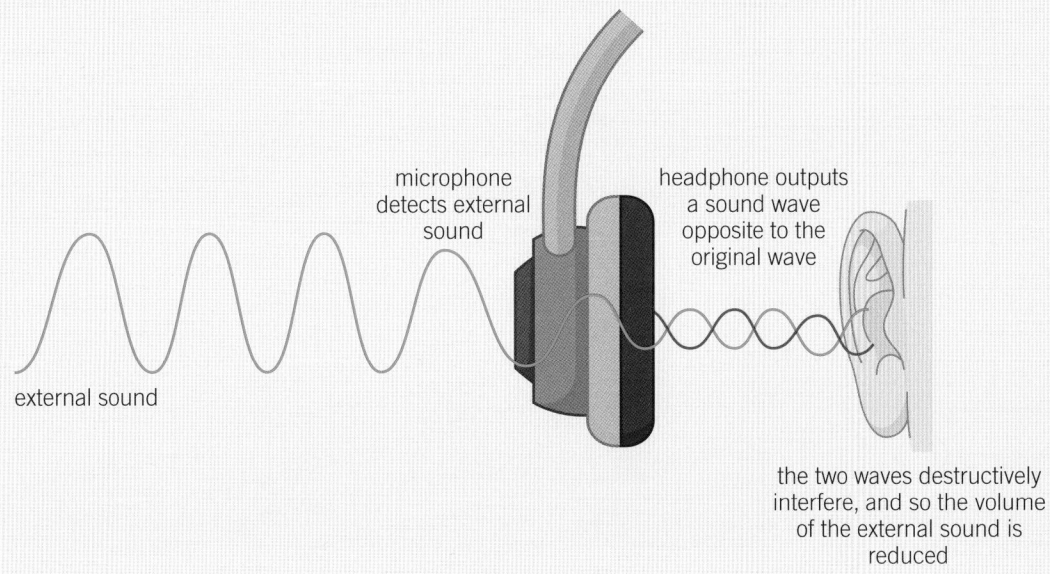

microphone detects external sound

headphone outputs a sound wave opposite to the original wave

external sound

the two waves destructively interfere, and so the volume of the external sound is reduced

1. Suggest one benefit and one disadvantage of noise-canceling headphones.

2. Other than in headphones, suggest one use of noise-canceling technology.

As well as interference, waves exhibit three other properties:

- diffraction
- reflection
- refraction.

How do waves diffract?

WAVES

When waves pass through a small gap, they spread out on the other side. This is called diffraction.

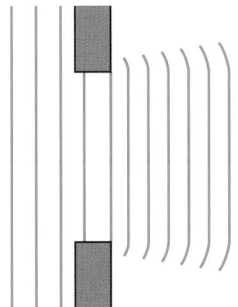 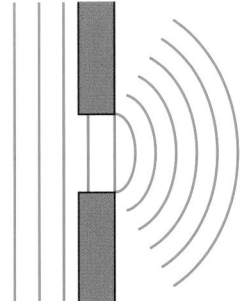

◀ When a wave passes through a gap, it diffracts

The effect is more pronounced as the gap gets smaller. When the gap is the same size as the wavelength of the wave, the diffraction effect is greatest and the wave spreads out completely on the other side.

▲ As these waves pass through the gap in the barrier, they spread out

Sound waves have a wavelength of about a meter, and so are often diffracted by apertures such as doorways. This makes it easy to hear sounds even if there is no direct line of sight. Because light waves have such small wavelengths, around 5×10^{-7} m, it is harder to see them diffract.

WAVES

How do waves reflect?

All waves can be reflected. Reflection is a process in which a wave bounces off an object. We see reflection occurring when light bounces off a mirror, and we hear the reflection of sound waves as echoes.

When waves bounce off a smooth surface they reflect at the same angle as the angle at which they hit the surface. We say that the angle of incidence is equal to the angle of reflection. We measure these angles to the normal – this is an imaginary line at right angles to the surface. An incident angle of 0° is therefore a wave that is traveling directly at the surface.

Not all surfaces are smooth. Waves still bounce off rough surfaces and they obey the law of reflection, but as the normal to the surface varies due to the varying angle of the surface, the waves reflect in lots of different directions. This is called a diffuse reflection. If light hits a shiny surface, then all the light rays are reflected in the same way. This is a specular reflection.

reflected ray

mirrored surface

normal   angle of reflection

angle of incidence

incident ray

▲ Light hitting a mirrored surface undergoes reflection. The angle of reflection is equal to the angle of incidence

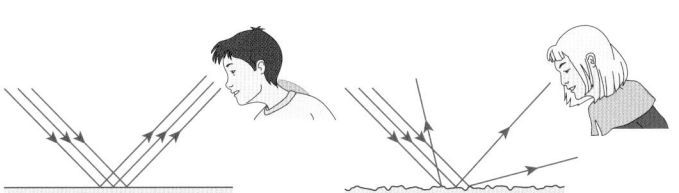

A shiny surface is smooth and causes a specular reflection. The light rays remain parallel to each other so a reflected image can be seen. Rough surfaces scatter the light in different directions causing a diffuse reflection with no image

1. The reflection of sound is often heard as an echo. If a person claps her hands and hears an echo off a wall 0.25 s later, how far away is the wall? The speed of sound is 330 m s^{-1}.

2. Light can be reflected off the Moon. The Apollo astronauts put some reflectors on the Moon which enable a laser beam to be reflected back to Earth. The moon is 384,400 km away and light travels at 3×10^8 m s^{-1}. How long does it take the light to travel from the Earth to the Moon and back?

3. At a certain time of day, the Sun is 20° above the horizon. The Sun's light hits the surface of a calm lake and is reflected.

   a) What is the angle of incidence?

   b) What is the angle of reflection?

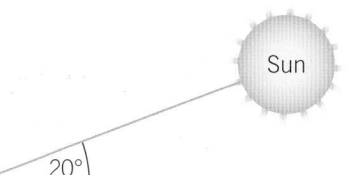

Light from the mountain can reach your eyes either in a direct line, or by bouncing off the reflective surface of the water. Because the light from these paths arrives at different angles, you see two different images of the mountains

How do waves refract?

When waves enter a different medium, they change speed. Sound travels at about $330\,\text{m}\,\text{s}^{-1}$ in air, but speeds up to about $1{,}500\,\text{m}\,\text{s}^{-1}$ in water. Light, on the other hand, travels at about $300{,}000\,\text{km}\,\text{s}^{-1}$ in air but slows down to about $230{,}000\,\text{km}\,\text{s}^{-1}$ in water. When waves pass from one material to another and change speed, their path also bends. This process is called refraction.

▶ These fish appear closer to the surface of the water than they are. This is because the light refracts as it leaves the water

The speed of light in a vacuum c is $2.9979 \times 10^8\,\text{m}\,\text{s}^{-1}$. When it enters a different material, it slows down. The factor by which it slows down is called the refractive index. The refractive index n is related to the speed v at which the light travels through the material by:

$$v = \frac{c}{n}$$

As with reflection, we measure the angles at which the waves travel relative to the normal. When waves slow down, they bend towards the normal. When they speed up, they bend away from the normal.

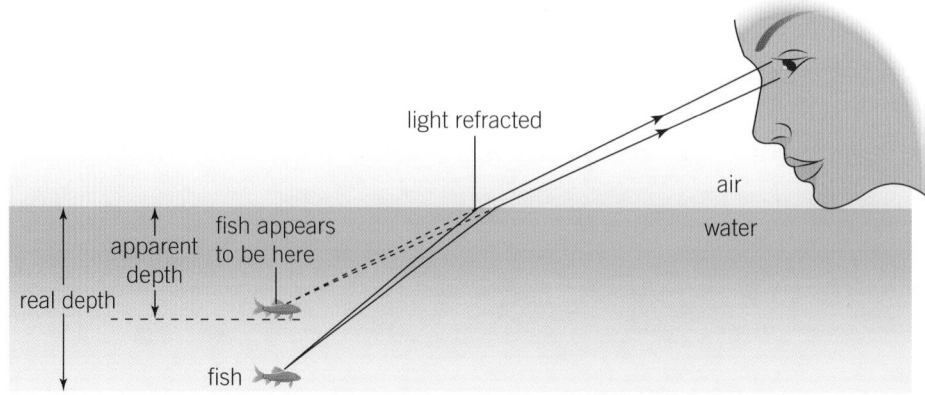

light refracted

apparent depth

fish appears to be here

real depth

air

water

fish

▲ Your eye assumes that the light has traveled in a straight line so it sees the fish at a shallower depth

The way in which light bends can be calculated using Snell's law:

$$n_1 \sin(\theta_i) = n_2 \sin(\theta_r)$$

where n_1 and θ_i refer to the refractive index of the first material and angle of the light ray to the normal in that material (the angle of incidence) and n_2 and θ_r refer to the second material's refractive index and the angle of refraction.

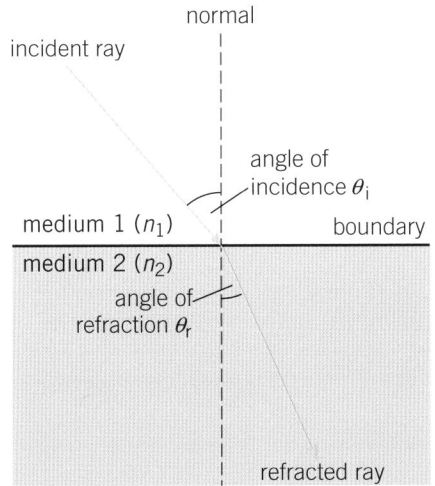

Worked example: Using Snell's law

Question

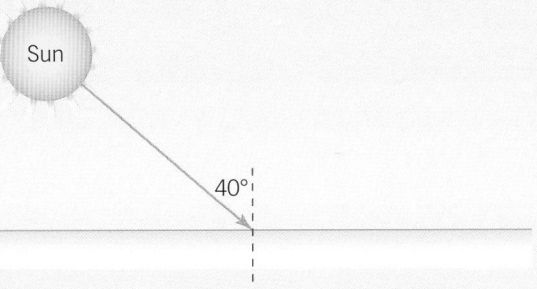

Light from the Sun hits the surface of a lake at 40° to the normal. The water in the lake has a refractive index of 1.33. Calculate the angle of refraction for the Sun's light in the lake. The refractive index of the air is 1.

Answer

From Snell's law:

$$n_1 \sin(\theta_i) = n_2 \sin(\theta_r)$$

In this case, $n_1 = 1$, $\theta_i = 40°$ and $n_2 = 1.33$, so

$$1 \times \sin 40 = 1.33 \sin \theta_r$$
$$\sin \theta_r = \frac{0.643}{1.33}$$
$$= 0.483$$

And so

$$\theta_r = \sin^{-1}(0.483) = 28.9°$$

Refraction of sound

Refraction is most commonly seen in light rays, but sound can also refract.

In the American Civil War, the Battle of Gettysburg resulted in the most casualties. On the second day, two of the Confederate generals, Ewell and Longstreet, were to attack the Union forces from opposite sides. The instructions were that Ewell should attack when he heard Longstreet's artillery, but Ewell did not hear the artillery so he did not attack at the right time. As a result, the Union forces repelled the attacks.

This battle is considered one of the turning points in the American Civil War. But why did Ewell not hear the artillery? The Union forces were on higher ground and it is possible that these hills shielded the sound. However, this does not explain why the battle was heard in Pittsburgh, 150 miles away, but was not heard 12 miles away. It is thought that the hot weather on the ground caused the speed of the sound waves to be increased. When waves change speed, they change direction and bend. This effect would have bent the sound waves from the artillery upwards so that Ewell did not hear them. The sound could then have been bent again higher up in the atmosphere, enabling the people in Pittsburgh to hear the battle.

1. If the sound waves speed up, will they bend toward the normal or away from it?

2. On a copy of the diagram, continue the lines showing the direction of the sound waves.

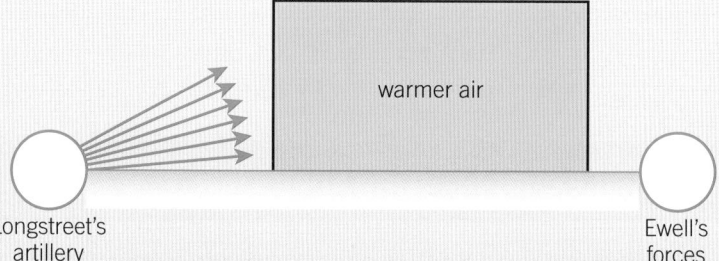

warmer air

Longstreet's artillery

Ewell's forces

Ⓐ Ⓑ Ⓒ Ⓓ Experiment

To investigate Snell's law, you will need a ray box or a lamp and a slit, a glass or acrylic glass block, a protractor, a pencil and some paper.

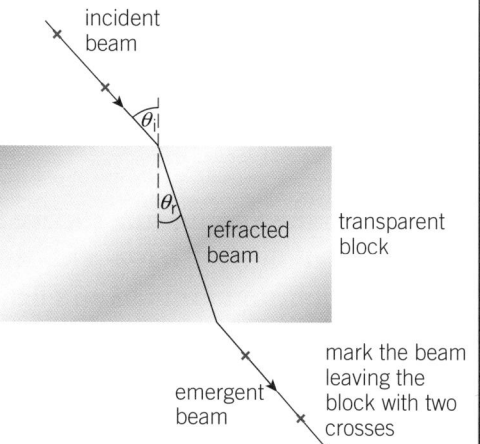

incident beam

θ_i

θ_r

refracted beam

transparent block

emergent beam

mark the beam leaving the block with two crosses

Method

● Place the glass block on the paper and aim the light ray through it.

● Draw around the glass block and mark the direction of the light rays that enter and exit the block. You can do this by drawing a couple of crosses along the line of the light ray.

● Remove the glass block and, using your markings on the paper, measure the angle of incidence and the angle of refraction. You may not have been able to see the light ray inside the glass block but you can retrace its path since you know where the ray entered the block and where it left again.

● Repeat the experiment for different values of the incident angle and record your values of the angle of incidence (θ_i) and angle of refraction (θ_r) in a table.

Question

1. Plot a graph of sin θ_i against sin θ_r. How can you find the refractive index of the glass block from your graph?

1. The refractive index of glass is 1.5.

   a) Calculate the speed of light in the glass.

   b) If light is incident on the glass at 45° from the air ($n = 1$), calculate the angle of refraction in the glass.

2. Light passes from the glass into water which has a refractive index of 1.33.

   a) Does the light speed up or slow down?

   b) Would you expect the light to refract towards or away from the normal?

What happens when waves speed up?

When light passes from water into air it speeds up. As a result, the rays of light refract away from the normal. At a certain angle, however, the light rays bend away from the normal so much that the angle on the other side of the boundary is 90° and they skim along the surface.

It is not possible for light to be refracted any more than this as the angle of refraction is as large as is possible while the ray of light still leaves the original medium. If the angle of incidence is any larger than this, the light will reflect from the boundary instead. This is called total internal reflection.

The angle at which refraction stops and total internal reflection starts is called the critical angle θ_c. It occurs when the angle of refraction reaches 90°, so at the critical angle, $\theta_i = \theta_c$, $\theta_r = 90°$, and in most cases of total internal reflection, light is exiting a material into air and so $n_2 = 1$. So, using Snell's law:

$$n_1 \sin(\theta_c) = 1 \times \sin(90)$$

as $\sin(90) = 1$:

$$\sin(\theta_c) = \frac{1}{n}$$

▲ A laser beam hits the boundary between water and air. Because the angle of incidence is greater than the critical angle, the beam is totally internally reflected

1. Glass has a refractive index of 1.5. Calculate the critical angle for this material.

2. What would the refractive index of a material have to be in order to have a critical angle of 30°?

3. Why doesn't total internal reflection occur when light travels from air into water?

4. Sound waves speed up when they enter water. In air, the speed of sound is about $330\,\text{m s}^{-1}$, but in water the sound waves travel at about $1,500\,\text{m s}^{-1}$. Explain whether total internal reflection will occur when sound travels from air into water or from water into air. Explain how this affects how well you can hear sounds above the surface of the water if you are under the surface (it may help to calculate the refractive index and the critical angle).

Worked example: Total internal reflection

Question

A diver is underneath the surface of the sea. The water has a refractive index of 1.33. When the diver looks straight up at the surface, he sees the bright light of the sunny day above him. At an angle, however, he sees a reflection of the darker water.

Explain why the diver can see out of the water above him but not at an angle.

Calculate the angle at which the diver will see a reflection of the water rather than the daylight above.

Answer

When the light from above the surface enters the water, it slows down and refracts towards the normal. Light leaving the water speeds up and refracts away from the normal. At the critical angle to the normal, light is at an angle of 90° to the normal on the air side of the boundary. This is the maximum angle possible. At angles greater than the critical angle, light reaches the diver through total internal reflection.

The critical angle is found using:

$$\sin(\theta_c) = \frac{1}{n}$$

Here $n = 1.33$ so:

$$\sin(\theta_c) = \frac{1}{1.33} = 0.752, \text{ and so } \theta_c = \sin^{-1}(0.752) = 48.8°$$

light from above surface of the water is refracted and appears to come more directly from above

light skimming the surface of the water at 90° to the normal will refract at the critical angle

light from underwater that is incident at an angle greater than the critical angle will be totally internally reflected

▲ Light from above the diver has come from above the surface of the water. Beyond the critical angle, the diver will see light that is totally internally reflected from below the surface of the water. This appears much darker

WAVES

What is light after all?

The development of the theory of light is a long story that spans many centuries of scientific progress. Early scientists debated if light was a wave or a particle. Newton was convinced that light was a particle and because of his status, many scientists followed his beliefs. It was not until about 75 years after Newton's death that Thomas Young demonstrated that light was a wave.

However, experiments near the end of the 19th century showed that light waves have some strange properties. Heinrich Hertz was experimenting with sparks crossing a small gap. The spark gap generated radio waves and Hertz showed that the waves were reflected

and refracted in the same way as light. Through these experiments, he proved that radio waves travel at the speed of light and that they are part of the electromagnetic spectrum (see Chapter 12, Patterns).

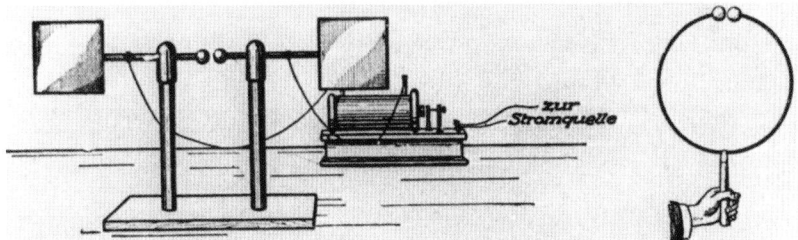

He also discovered that his sparks could travel much further when ultraviolet light was shone on the spark gap than when there was no light. Later, physicists carried out further experiments on this effect. They discovered that the particle which jumped across the spark gap was an electron and that the frequency of the light, not the intensity, was the factor responsible for giving the electrons the extra energy to jump across the gap.

These discoveries were a puzzle to physicists. The wave theory of light would suggest that the intensity of light would be the factor that gave increased energy to the electrons.

This effect was called the photoelectric effect. In 1905 Albert Einstein came up with an explanation for which he later won the Nobel Prize. He suggested that light could behave like a particle after all and that the energy of these light particles is related to the frequency of the light. We now call the particles of light photons and the energy of a photon is given by the equation:

$$E = hf$$

where E is the energy of the photon, f is the frequency and h is the Planck constant ($h = 6.626 \times 10^{-36}\,\text{J}\,\text{s}$).

This creates a paradox: light can behave as a particle, but the particle's energy is related to the frequency which is a property of a wave. The answer to this is that light can behave as both a particle and a wave. This is called wave–particle duality. Later experiments showed that particles such as electrons can also behave as particles and waves, and that the wavelength of a particle can be calculated using the equation:

$$\lambda = \frac{h}{mv}$$

where λ is the wavelength of the particle, m is its mass, v is its speed and h is the Planck constant.

1. A tennis player can serve a tennis ball at $45\,\text{m}\,\text{s}^{-1}$. The tennis ball has a mass of $0.06\,\text{kg}$. Using the equation $\lambda = \dfrac{h}{mv}$ where $h = 6.626 \times 10^{-36}\,\text{J}\,\text{s}$, calculate the wavelength of the tennis ball.

    How does the tennis ball's wavelength compare to the size of the tennis ball?

2. Why do we think of the tennis ball as behaving like a particle rather than a wave?

Heinrich Hertz's detector is shown in the diagram on the left. When radio waves were present a small spark would travel across the gap. He observed that when ultraviolet light shone on the spark gap, the sparks formed more readily but he could not explain how this happened. Albert Einstein later explained this effect by using the idea of particles of light called photons. This showed that light was both a wave and a particle

Summative assessment

Introduction

Signals can travel through optical fibers at high speeds. One impact of this is the possibility of fast internet connections to houses and businesses. This assessment looks at how optical fibers work.

 Optical fibers

1. Light enters an optical fiber at an angle of incidence of 15°.

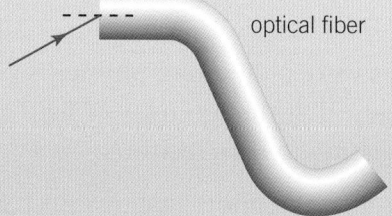

optical fiber

   a) On a copy of this drawing, draw a line to show how the path of the light continues down the fiber. [3]

   b) The refractive index of the fiber is 1.4. Calculate the angle of refraction of the light beam shown entering the fiber. [3]

   c) Calculate the critical angle for this optical fiber. [3]

   d) Calculate the speed of the light in the fiber. [2]

   e) Some of the light is reflected off the surface instead of being refracted and entering the fiber. The amount of reflected light can be found from the equation:

   $$R = \left(\frac{n-1}{n+1}\right)^2$$

   where R is the fraction of light that is reflected and n is the refractive index of the material. Using this equation, show that most of the light is refracted into the fiber. [4]

 Investigating the refractive index of water

When designing an optical fiber, scientists need to consider the effects of temperature on the refractive index. As an initial experiment, they measure the refractive index of water at different temperatures.

2. Suggest what the independent and dependent variables for their experiment should be. [2]

The scientists use a laser pen and a rectangular tank of water. They take a photograph of the tank from above:

3. Give the names of two pieces of measuring equipment that the scientists will need. [2]

4. Outline how the refractive index may be found from this picture. [3]

5. Outline the method they should follow to obtain suitable data. [4]

The scientists think that as the water is heated up, it will expand slightly and therefore be less dense. As a result, they think that the hotter water will not slow the light down by the same amount, and so light will be able to travel through hotter water at a slightly faster speed.

6. Write a hypothesis for this experiment based on these ideas. [4]

 Measuring the speed of light through an optical fiber

An experiment was conducted to determine the speed of light through a fiber optic cable. An electrical signal was sent to an LED. The light from the LED was transmitted down the optical fiber and a pulse was detected at the other end. An oscilloscope was used to measure the time delay between the initial electrical pulse and the detected signal. A diagram of the apparatus is shown below.

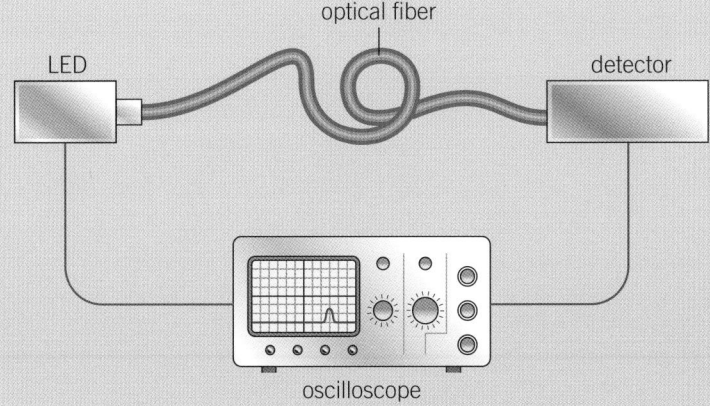

▲ LEDs (light emitting diodes) are efficient sources of light meaning that they do not generate much waste heat. They can also change brightness very quickly and so are useful in communications with optical fibers

When the length of optical fiber is 80 m, the signal on the oscilloscope appears like this.

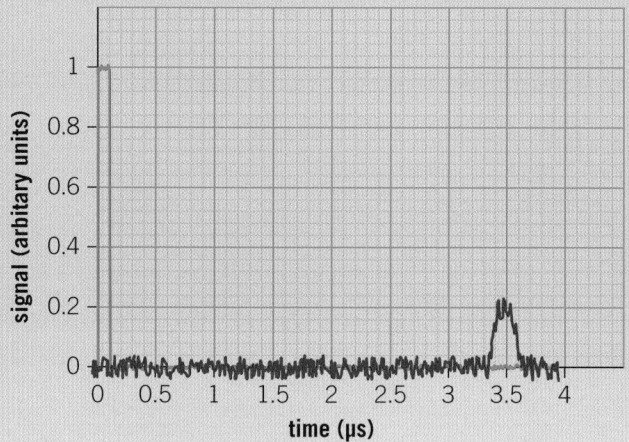

7. Measure the time delay between the initial signal and the detected signal. [2]

The length of the optical fiber is varied and the delay between the signals is measured. A graph of the results is shown below.

8. On a copy of the graph, add the result from when the optical fiber was 80 m long. [2]

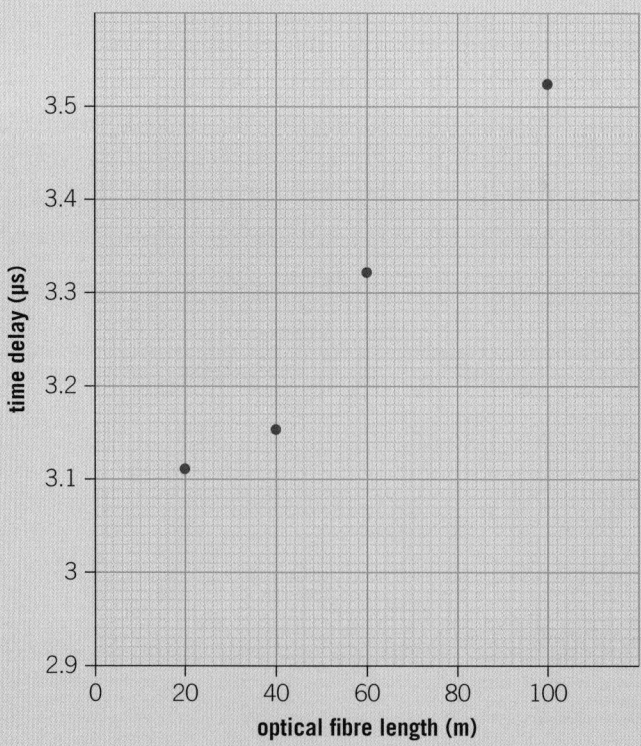

9. Add a line of best fit to your copy of the graph. [1]

10. Find the gradient of your line of best fit. [2]

11. Using your value for the gradient, calculate the speed of the light through the fiber giving your answer in m s^{-1}. [4]

12. Explain why you would expect your answer above to be less than 300,000 km s^{-1}. [2]

13. Even without the optical fiber, there was a delay between the initial electrical signal being sent and the detection of a signal from the detector. Use your graph to find this time delay. [2]

Uses of optical fibers

Imagine that you work for a company that manufactures optical fibers. You need to convince the local government to spend money on replacing their existing telecommunications wire cables with optical fibers.

14. Write a brief for the local authority outlining how optical fibers work and how they can be used to transmit information. You should use simple scientific terms in a way that is understandable to non-scientists. [6]

15. Describe the advantages and disadvantages of optical fibers over traditional wire cables for transmitting information. [4]

16. Rural communities sometimes have slow internet speeds available to them. Telecommunications companies often say that it is too expensive to provide faster optical fiber links. Outline a counterargument to this. [5]

▲ Information can be transmitted by light traveling through optical fibers. Changes in the light's brightness carry the signal through the fiber and allow communication or access to the internet

10 Transformation

Transformation is a significant change in the nature of something.

▲ Some animals undergo a complete transformation during their lives. This caterpillar will develop into a mullein moth and these tadpoles will develop into frogs. Which other animals complete a transformation in their lifetimes?

▼ In April 2017, residents of Kampung Pelangi, a small village in Indonesia, painted all the houses in a rainbow color scheme. The effect was to transform a village that was previously considered a slum into a tourist attraction. How else can urban spaces be transformed?

W
SOT

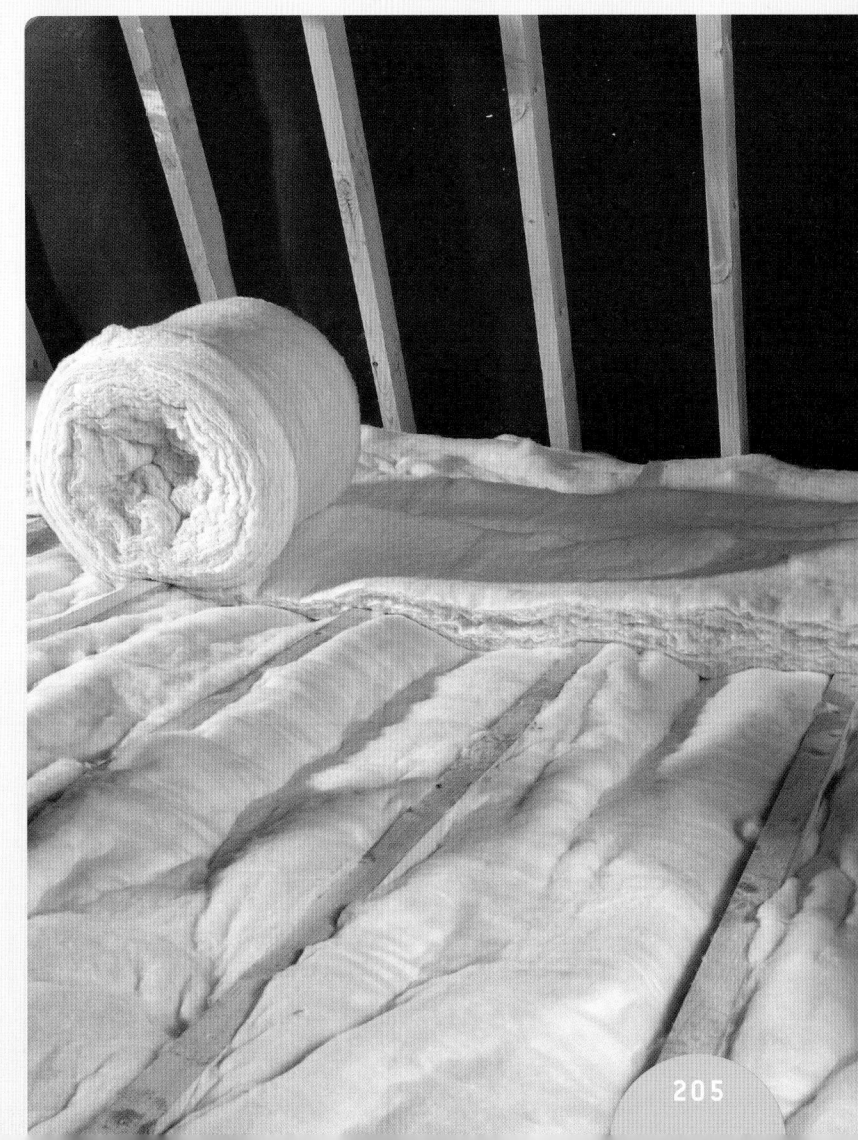

▲ This is the cooling lake of the nuclear power plant in Chernobyl. On 26 April 1986, during a safety test, the nuclear reactor suffered an explosion, and radioactive material was ejected into the atmosphere which then fell across Europe and Russia. It is considered the worst nuclear accident in history. A large exclusion zone was established around the scene of the accident and still remains today. Although the contamination had a negative effect on the ecosystem at first, animals and plants have recovered well. The exclusion zone has transformed the area into a nature reserve where the ecosystem is undisturbed. Where else have spaces been transformed following disasters?

▶ Waste materials can be transformed through recycling. Here recycled material from plastic bottles and plastic bags has been transformed into insulating material. How else can waste materials be transformed and used for other functions?

Introduction

The Industrial Revolution transformed the way we live. For 80 years from the mid-18th century, technological innovation allowed people to invent machines that replaced human labor and fundamentally changed manufacturing processes.

One of the most important inventions of this period was the steam engine. By converting thermal energy released from the burning of fuel into mechanical work, steam engines could drive machines which made manufacture and agriculture more efficient. Later, the steam train revolutionized transport.

In this chapter we will see how steam engines use pressure to exert a force and hence create motion. We will also investigate the thermal physics that allow these energy transformations to occur.

Not only did the steam train change the way in which we live our lives, the fundamental physics of its operation evolved into a whole new branch of physics called thermodynamics. Because thermodynamics is the study of how heat energy changes a system, the key concept of this chapter is change. The inventions of the Industrial Revolution transformed our lives so the global context is scientific and technical innovation.

Key concept: Change

Related concept: Transformation

Global context: Scientific and technical innovation

▼ Developments in our understanding of heat and pressure enabled us to harness steam power. Railways used steam engines to power trains. This improved our ability to transport goods and created the first efficient, long-distance public transport

Statement of inquiry:

Scientific innovation can transform our human existence.

The development of the steam engine allowed fuel to be burned in order to produce mechanical work. This early steam engine was used to pump water out of a mine shaft

Much of the physics of gases and atmospheric pressure came from the development of hot air balloons. These Chinese lanterns operate in the same way. The air is heated by the flame and expands. This causes the density of air inside the lantern to be less than the density outside so the lantern floats

FORCES

What is pressure?

Anyone who has stepped on a sharp object knows that it hurts. The reason for this is not due to an increased force, as your weight which is pushing you down onto the object remains the same; it hurts because all your weight is acting through a small area. What has increased, and is causing the pain, is pressure.

Pressure is the measure of how much force acts per unit area (e.g. per square meter). It can be calculated using the equation:

$$P = \frac{F}{A}$$

where P is the pressure, F is the force and A is the area over which the force is applied. There are many different units of pressure, but the SI unit is the Pascal (Pa) which is one newton per square meter ($1\,Nm^{-2}$).

▼ Walking barefoot along a shingle beach hurts your feet much more than walking across sand. The contact area between your feet and the sharp stones is less than the area between your feet and the sand and so the pressure is greater on the stones. Why does a small child find it easier to walk across a stony beach than an adult?

Worked example: Calculating pressure

Question

A drawing pin is pushed with a force of 10 N. The blunt end of the drawing pin has a diameter of 0.9 cm and the sharp end has a diameter of 0.25 mm. Calculate the pressure at each end of the drawing pin.

Answer

First find the area of each end using the equation for the area of a circle:

$$A = \pi r^2.$$

The radius is half of the diameter so the radii are 4.5×10^{-3} m and 1.25×10^{-4} m. (Note that centimeters and millimeters have been converted into meters.) Hence the areas are 6.36×10^{-5} m² and 4.91×10^{-8} m².

The force is 10 N, so the pressure can then be calculated using the equation:

$$P = \frac{F}{A}$$

This gives pressures of 1.57×10^5 and 2.04×10^8 Pa or 157 kPa and 204 MPa.

Experiment

Measuring the pressure you exert on the ground

You will need some weighing scales and some squared paper.

To calculate the pressure that you exert on the ground, you need to find the force you exert and the area over which you exert it.

Place one foot on the squared paper and draw round it. By counting the squares, find the area of your foot. Convert this area into square meters ($1\,m^2 = 10{,}000\,cm^2$) then double it to account for both feet.

Weigh yourself on the scales. Convert your mass into weight using the equation $F = mg$.

Now find the pressure you exert on the ground using the equation:

$$P = \frac{F}{A}$$

Data-based question: The Eiffel Tower

The total mass of the Eiffel Tower is about 10,000 tonnes. The base of the tower consists of four feet, each of which is a square of side 25 m. The tower is very efficient in its use of materials – if all the metal in the tower were melted down and placed on one of the bases, it would only be about 1.5 m high. As a result of its light weight and large area of its footprint, it exerts a low pressure on the ground and so does not require deep foundations.

1. Calculate the weight of the Eiffel Tower.

2. Calculate the total area of the base.

3. Calculate the pressure that the Eiffel Tower exerts on the ground.

▷ The Eiffel Tower opened in 1889 and was the tallest building in the world for over 40 years. It has come to symbolize the Industrial Revolution in France

The Great Pyramid of Giza is estimated to have a mass of about 6 million tonnes and its square base has a side of 230 m. The air pressure on the ground is about 101,000 Pa.

4. Compare the pressure exerted on the ground by the Eiffel Tower and the Great Pyramid of Giza to the air pressure.

▲ The pyramids at Giza. The Great Pyramid of Giza (far right) was the tallest manmade structure for over 3,800 years. The Pyramid of Khafre in the middle appears taller because it is on higher ground

▼ The large surface area of skis and snowboards reduces the pressure on the snow so that the skier or snowboarder doesn't sink in

1. A hammer hits a nail with a force of 10,000 N. The head of the nail has a diameter of 8.5 mm. Calculate the pressure on the head of the nail.

2. The same force is exerted at the point of the nail which has a surface area of 8×10^{-7} m². Calculate the pressure exerted at the point of the nail.

The size limit on animals

Pressure plays a part in the physiology of large animals. The large dinosaurs in the picture to the right (Argentinosaurus) were possibly the largest land creatures to have ever walked the Earth. It is thought that they had a mass of about 80,000 kg.

1. Calculate the weight of an Argentinosaurus.

2. An Argentinosaurus's thigh bone had a cross-sectional area of 0.1 m². Calculate the pressure in the thigh bone. (Don't forget that Argentinosaurus walked on four legs.)

The smaller dinosaurs in the picture are half the size of the large dinosaurs or smaller. They are half the size in all dimensions, their length, width and height are all half that of the large dinosaurs. Their volume (approximately the length × width × height) will therefore be eight times smaller than that of the large dinosaurs and as a result their mass will also be eight times less.

3. Calculate the mass of the smaller dinosaur.

4. Calculate the area of the smaller dinosaur's thigh bone. You may assume that the cross-section of the thigh bone is circular and that the radius of the smaller dinosaur's thigh bone is half that of Argentinosaurus.

5. Calculate the pressure in the smaller dinosaur's thigh bone.

6. How does this pressure compare to the Argentinosaurus?

This explains the difference in physiology between the giant dinosaurs and smaller animals. The Argentinosaurus needed thick legs to support its weight whereas the smaller dinosaurs in the picture have much thinner legs relative to the size of their bodies and could support their weight on only two legs.

What is the pressure around us?

FORCES

The weight of the air above us exerts a pressure on us; this is called atmospheric or air pressure. The average atmospheric pressure is about 101 kPa which means that a force of 101,000 N acts on every square meter of ground. This is equivalent to the weight caused by over 10 tonnes of mass on every square meter. Sometimes a unit of 1 atmosphere (1 atm) is used to describe pressure where 1 atm is 101.325 kPa. Units of atmospheres are often used in deep-sea diving.

Sometimes, pressure is reported in units of a bar. 1 bar is 100 kPa which makes it very similar to the atmosphere. 1 millibar (0.001 bar) is 100 Pa or 1 hectopascal (hPa). As a result hectopascals are sometimes used as units of pressure. Often weather forecasting pressure maps use units of bars, millibars or hectopascals.

Units of pressure

Pressure can be measured with a barometer. A traditional barometer used a column of mercury in a glass tube with a vacuum at the top. Atmospheric pressure pushes the mercury up the tube to a height of about 760 mm, at which point the pressure of the mercury (calculated using the equation $P = h \rho g$) is equal to the atmospheric pressure. As a result, millimeters of mercury (mmHg) is sometimes still used as a measure of pressure.

In the picture, the pressure is 747 mmHg.

1. Using the equation $P = h \rho g$, calculate the pressure at the bottom of the column of mercury. The density of mercury ρ is 13,560 kg m⁻³.

2. Express this pressure in units of:

   a) atmospheres   b) bars.

3. Why do you think that millimeters of mercury are less common as a unit than they were a century ago?

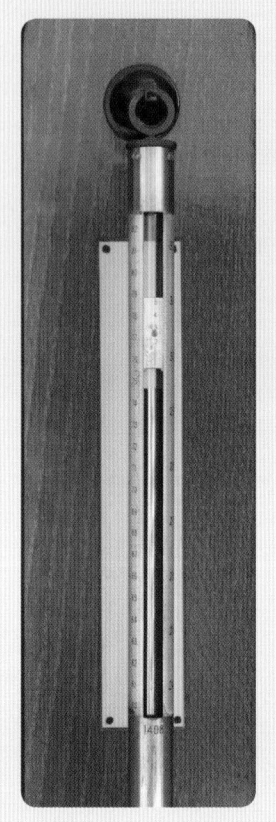

▶ This barometer has a column of mercury, the height of which is proportional to the atmospheric pressure

We don't notice the air pressure around us because it exerts its force in all directions. As a result, there is no net force; instead it squashes us inwards. When the pressure changes, however, we notice the difference. Flying in an airplane or going up a mountain causes our ears to pop. This sensation is caused by the fact that there is less air above us at higher altitudes, so the air pressure is less. The popping sensation comes as our ears equalize the pressure on either side of the ear drum.

The pressure of air above us is given by the equation:

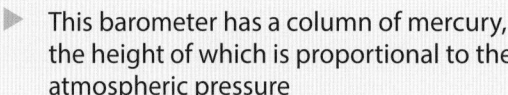

$$P = h \rho g$$

where h is the height of air above you, ρ is the density of the air and g is the acceleration due to gravity.

The pressure around you increases significantly if you are underwater. The additional pressure can be found using the same equation, $P = h \rho g$, but because the density of water is so much larger (1,000 kg m⁻³) than that of air, the pressure increase is much greater. If you swam to a depth of 10 m, the pressure would increase by about 100,000 Pa which is about atmospheric pressure. As a result, the pressure around you increases by 1 atmosphere for every 10 m underwater that you descend.

Worked example: Free diving

Question

In 2002, Tanya Streeter, a free diver, swam to a depth of 160 m. At the time it was not only the women's record, it was also deeper than the men's record.

Calculate the additional pressure at this depth under the water. The density of sea water is 1,025 kg m⁻³. Express your answer in atmospheres (1 atm = 101.325 kPa).

Answer

$$P = h \rho g$$

$$= 160 \times 1,025 \times 9.8 = 1,607,200 \text{ Pa} = 1,607.2 \text{ kPa}$$

1 atm = 101.325 kPa so the pressure in atmospheres is 15.9 atm.

Experiment

Measuring atmospheric pressure to calculate the density of air

Many modern smartphones have a barometer sensor that measures air pressure. You can download a free app which will allow you to use this sensor to measure the atmospheric pressure. (Some sensors use unusual units such as hPa where 1 hPa = 100 Pa.)

Using this sensor measure the atmospheric pressure at different heights. A stairwell is an excellent place to do this, although it can be done within just an ordinary room.

Record your data in a table, and plot a graph of your results with the height on the x-axis and pressure in pascals on the y-axis. Because your values of pressure should all be around 100,000 Pa, your y-axis should not start at zero.

Find the gradient of your graph. Because the gradient is the change in pressure for every meter change in the height:

$$\text{gradient} = \frac{\Delta P}{\Delta h}$$

As $P = h\rho g$,

$$\Delta P = \Delta h \rho g \qquad \text{giving} \qquad \frac{\Delta P}{\Delta h} = \rho g$$

or

$$\text{density} = \frac{\text{gradient}}{g}$$

The density of air is often reported as 1.2 kg m⁻³. How close is your value to this?

Evaluate your experiment and suggest an improvement to the method.

Deep-sea creatures have to cope with huge pressures. This deep-sea rockling can live more than a kilometer under the sea near hydrothermal vents. This far down the pressure can be 100 atm or more

1. If the atmospheric pressure is 101,000 Pa and the density of air is 1.2 kg m⁻³, calculate the height of the atmosphere above you.

2. Why is it likely that the height of the atmosphere is larger than your result in the previous question?

3. On Venus, the atmosphere is much denser than on Earth. As a result, the surface pressure is about 9.2 MPa. 870 m above the surface, the pressure drops to 8.7 MPa. The density of the atmosphere is 65 kg m⁻³. By calculating the difference in pressure, calculate the gravitational field strength g on Venus.

FORCES

How can the pressure of a gas be changed?

The molecules of a gas are constantly moving around and bouncing off the walls of their container (see Chapter 5, Environment). When they rebound, they exert a force which is responsible for the gas pressure.

When a gas is compressed, the particles occupy a smaller volume. They still travel at the same speed, but now collide with the walls more often. This increases the pressure that the gas exerts.

Boyle's law describes the way in which pressure and volume are related. For a fixed mass of gas, pressure P is inversely proportional to volume V. This means that, as long as no gas escapes, compressing a gas into half its original volume doubles its pressure. Boyle's law may be written as:

$$P \propto \frac{1}{V}$$

or more often:

$$P \times V = \text{constant}$$

The constant depends on the mass of gas in the container and its temperature.

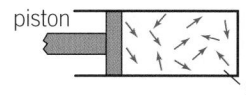

Worked example: Boyle's law

Question

A gas syringe contains 9 cm³ of gas at a pressure of 101 kPa. The syringe is sealed and compressed so that the volume is 4 cm³. What is the new pressure in the syringe?

Answer

From Boyle's law, PV = constant.

Initially, P = 101 kPa and V = 9 cm³ so:

$$\text{constant} = 101 \times 9 = 909$$

After compression, the volume is 4 cm³ so:

$$P \times 4 = 909$$

Hence,

$$P = \frac{909}{4} = 227 \text{ kPa}$$

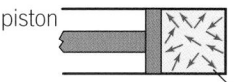

gas before compression

gas after compression

⚠ Boyle's law states that the pressure of a gas is inversely proportional to the volume it occupies. As the gas is compressed, the pressure increases because the particles collide with the walls of the container more frequently

1. A sealed piston has a volume of 25 cm³ and the gas inside it is at a pressure of 141.4 kPa. The piston expands until the gas reaches air pressure (101 kPa). What is the new volume of the gas inside the piston?

2. A gas syringe holds 12 cm³ of gas at 101 kPa. If it is sealed and compressed to 8 cm³, what is the new pressure of the gas inside?

3. A bubble forms at the bottom of the sea 100 m below the surface. It has a volume of 0.1 cm³. The density of seawater is 1,030 kg m⁻³. Normal air pressure is 101 kPa.

   a) Calculate the additional pressure due to being 100 m beneath the surface of the sea.

   b) Calculate the volume of the bubble when it reaches the surface of the sea. Assume that none of the gas in the bubble dissolves in the sea and that the temperature of the bubble remains constant.

How does temperature affect the pressure of a gas?

FORCES

The pressure of a gas can also be affected by its temperature. When a gas is heated, the molecules gain energy and move faster. As a result, they collide with the walls of the container at a higher speed and more frequently. These factors increase the pressure that the gas exerts.

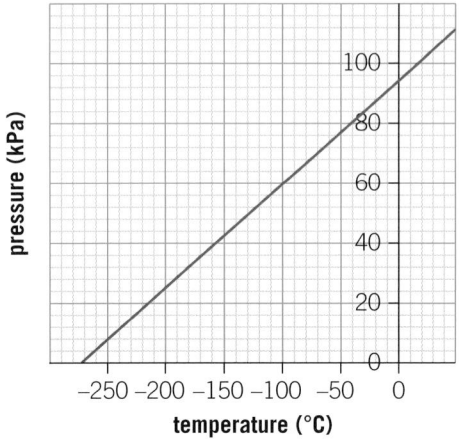

This graph shows how the pressure of a gas varies if its temperature is lowered. Initially, the gas is at 20°C and its pressure is 100 kPa. The pressure reaches zero at a temperature of −273°C. This is absolute zero

Cooling a gas has the opposite effect – the pressure drops. At 0°C, the pressure is not zero and the gas can be cooled further, below 0°C. However, at some point the molecules in the gas will be slowed down so much that they are no longer moving and the temperature cannot be reduced any further. Only at this point does the pressure reach zero since there would be no collisions with the walls of the container. This temperature is called absolute zero and is the lowest possible temperature. Absolute zero is −273.15°C; nothing can have a colder temperature.

The discovery of the zero point of temperature led scientists to devise a new scale. This absolute scale starts at absolute zero and each increment is the same as 1°C. The unit of this scale of temperature is the kelvin. To convert from degrees Celsius to kelvin:

$$\text{temperature (K)} = \text{temperature (°C)} + 273$$

so 0 K (−273°C) is absolute zero and 273 K is 0°C.

With this new temperature scale, the relationship between pressure and temperature is directly proportional so that:

$$P \propto T \quad \text{or} \quad P = kT$$

where k is a constant, which depends on the mass of the gas and the volume of the container. This is called the pressure law.

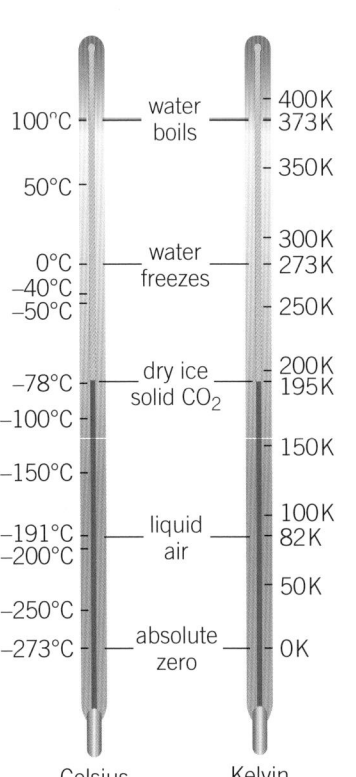

Comparing the temperature scales of degrees Celsius and kelvin

Worked example: The pressure law

Question

A sealed vessel contains 100 cm³ of gas at a pressure of 101 kPa at 18°C. The gas is heated to 115°C. What is the new pressure of the gas?

Answer

Use the equation $P = k \times T$, where T is the temperature in kelvin.

The initial conditions are that $P = 101$ and $T = 18$°C, which in kelvin is $18 + 273 = 291$ K. So, the constant k is given by:

$$k = \frac{P}{T} = \frac{101}{291} = 0.347$$

The final pressure can be found using this value of k and the new temperature which is $115 + 273 = 388$ K. So:

$$P = 0.347 \times 388 = 135 \,\text{kPa}$$

1. The melting point of copper is 1,358 K. Express this temperature in degrees Celsius.

2. The surface temperature of Venus is 462°C. Express this temperature in kelvin.

3. A balloon contains 4,000 cm³ of air at a pressure of 99 kPa. The weather changes and the pressure increases to 102 kPa. What is the new volume of the balloon? Given that the volume of a sphere is $\frac{4}{3}\pi r^3$, by how much has the balloon's radius changed?

4. A glass bottle is filled with air at 20°C and at a pressure of 100 kPa. It is then heated until the temperature is 80°C. What is the new pressure inside the bottle?

Data-based question: Atmospheric pressure

The pressure and density of air decrease with height above sea level.

A mountaineer seals a gas syringe at an altitude of 4,000 m and descends to sea level. The initial volume of gas is 40 cm³.

1. Using Boyle's law, show that the volume of gas in the syringe at sea level should be about 25 cm³.

When the mountaineer gets to sea level, she finds that the volume of gas is 27.4 cm³. She realizes that this is because it is warmer at sea level.

2. Explain why an increase in temperature will increase the volume of the gas.

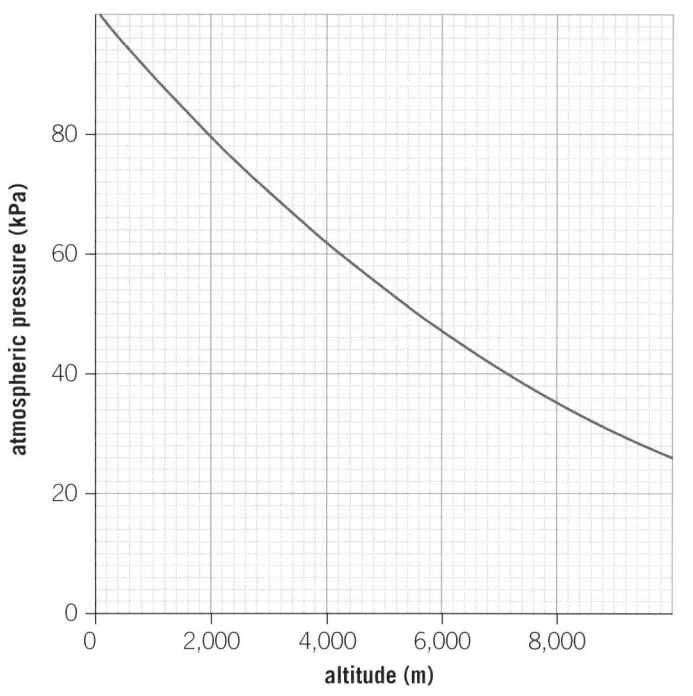

▲ Atmospheric pressure at different altitudes

The change in atmospheric pressure can be determined using the equation $P = h\,\rho\,g$ where h is the height of the air above you. The gradient of the graph is change in pressure per meter of altitude gained and is given by $-\rho\,g$. Because the density of the air changes at altitude, the gradient is not constant.

3. Use the graph above to estimate the gradient at altitudes of 0, 2,000, 4,000, …, 10,000 m and record your gradients in a suitable table.

4. Add another column to your table to calculate the density of the air at each altitude. The density of air can be calculated by taking the positive value of the gradient and multiplying by 1,000 in order to convert from kPa into Pa. Then, divide your value by g (9.8 N kg⁻¹) to obtain the density of the air.

5. Plot a graph of the density of the air against altitude.

FORCES

What happens at low pressure?

If all the atoms and molecules were to be removed from a container, the pressure would be zero as there would be no particles to collide with the walls of a container. This would be a perfect vacuum.

The possibility of a perfect vacuum has been controversial in the past. Ancient Greek scientists who proposed that matter was made of atoms were criticized by those who did not like the idea of the vacuum that must exist between these atoms. Aristotle is often quoted as saying, "Nature abhors a vacuum".

In reality, it is impossible to remove all the particles from a container and create a perfect vacuum. At normal air pressure and temperatures, there are about 10^{25} air molecules in a cubic meter. A simple pump is able to reduce this by about ten times (to about

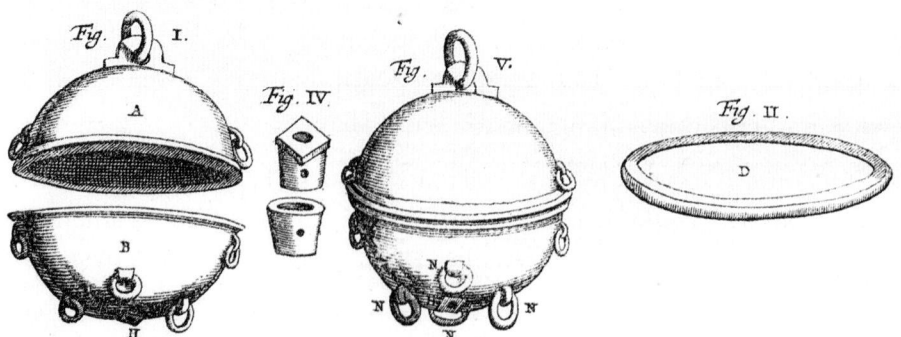

In 1654, Otto von Guericke demonstrated the power of his new vacuum pump. He placed two hemispheres together and pumped the air out from inside. As a result, there was very little pressure from air inside the hemispheres acting outward. The air pressure from outside the hemispheres was unaffected and held the spheres together. He then attempted to pull the hemispheres apart using two teams of horses but the force from the atmospheric pressure was too great. Although the picture shows eight horses, he carried out the demonstration with up to 30 horses

10^{24} molecules per cubic meter) and a simple vacuum pump may reduce it by a thousand times. Some sophisticated experiments require high vacuums which reduce the number of particles to below 10^{12} per cubic meter but it becomes increasingly expensive and difficult to attain such a high vacuum.

The highest vacuums are found in intergalactic space. Far away from other galaxies, there may be only a couple of hydrogen atoms in any given cubic meter. This is a pressure of about 10^{-21} Pa and is far lower than can be achieved in a laboratory but is still not a perfect vacuum.

How do we feel heat?

ENERGY

The human body is able to sense fairly small changes in temperature. The differences between a hot day and a cold day may be less than 10°C, but it affects our decisions regarding the clothes we wear to stay comfortable. Outside the narrow band of comfortable temperatures, our experience of hot or cold temperatures can easily cause pain.

Despite our ability to sense small changes in temperature, we are not good at sensing the actual value of the temperature of objects. The reason for this is that we tend to sense whether something is hotter or colder than we are. This can be tested in a simple experiment, using three bowls of water: one with cold water, one with warm water and the other with hot water. Place one hand in the cold water and the other in the hot water. Wait for about a minute. Now put both hands into the warm bowl of water. The hand that has been in the cold water feels the new water temperature to be warm, whereas the hand that was in the hot water finds the new temperature cold. This shows that although we think we are sensing temperature, our perception is closer to that of heat transfer. When we lose heat to the surroundings we feel cold and when an object transfers heat to us, we feel warm.

How does heat energy transfer?

ENERGY

Heat energy can move from one object to another and in doing so, things can get hotter or colder. Heat energy always transfers from the object with higher temperature to the object with a lower temperature and it can be transferred in three ways:

- conduction
- convection
- radiation.

Conduction

Conduction is the transfer of heat energy between two objects that are in contact. The atoms and molecules (or electrons in the case of metals) of the two different objects are able to collide because they are in contact. The fast motion of the molecules in the hotter object passes energy on to the slower molecules in the cold object. When these molecules collide, the molecules of the hotter object are left at a slower speed, hence a colder temperature, and the colder object is heated up.

Conduction is also responsible for transferring energy from one side of an object to another. Heat energy is transferred quickly through some materials and slowly through others. Materials such as metals transfer heat energy through them quickly and are called good conductors. Other materials such as wood or plastic do not conduct heat energy through them quickly and are called insulators.

In Chapter 6, Function, we saw that metals were the best conductors of electricity because they had lots of free electrons. The free electrons also make metals good conductors of heat energy. The best electrical conductor is silver, followed by copper and then gold. These three metals also have the highest thermal conductivities among metals. Metals such as titanium which are not as good at conducting electricity are also not so good as thermal conductors.

◀ This relationship between thermal conductivity and electrical conductivity does not hold for non-metals. Diamond has the highest thermal conductivity of any naturally occurring substance but it is a poor conductor of electricity

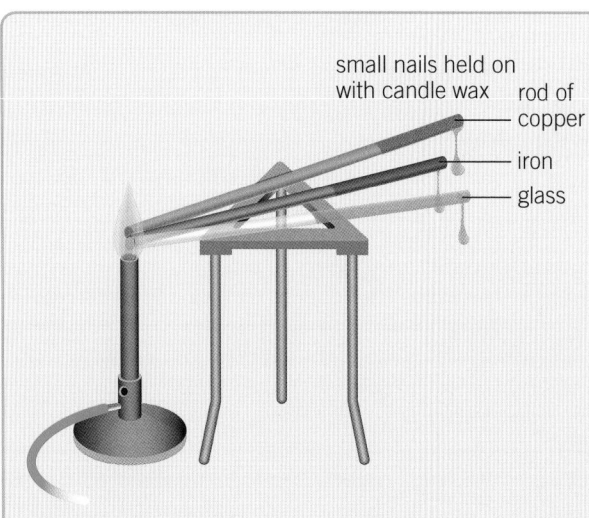

small nails held on with candle wax

rod of copper
iron
glass

Demonstrating conduction

A simple demonstration of conduction can be achieved with a Bunsen burner and some rods of different materials (copper, iron and glass are good materials to try).

Melt some candle wax and dip the end of each rod into it; use the melted wax to stick a small nail or a pin to the end of each rod. Put the rods on a tripod and place the ends without candle wax into a Bunsen burner flame. The nail on the end of the best conductor will fall off first. In which order do you expect the nails to fall?

▲ ▶ The African elephant has a very different need to control its body heat to the arctic fox. The elephant lives in a hot climate and has adapted ears with a large surface area. This allows for more heat to be lost to keep it cool. Air is a poor conductor, and the air around the elephant's ears could heat up. This would reduce the temperature difference between the elephant's ears and the surrounding air, therefore reducing the rate at which the heat is lost. Flapping its ears causes the air to move, increasing the temperature difference and as a result the rate of heat loss. The arctic fox has much smaller ears to reduce heat loss. It also uses the poor conductivity of air in a different way. Its thick fur coat traps air, reducing the rate of heat loss

The rate at which thermal energy is conducted through a material is proportional to the temperature difference between the different sides of the material and the cross-sectional area of the material. It is inversely proportional to the thickness of the material. This means that to reduce heat loss through conduction, you should have thick walls which are made of a good insulator. These walls should also have a small surface area.

Convection

Convection is a process of heat transfer which occurs in liquids and gases. If the gas at the bottom of a container is heated up, the particles move faster and the pressure increases. As the pressure increases, the gas expands and takes up a larger volume. This gives it a lower density than the cold gas so the hot gas will rise and float on top of the cold gas. In this way the hot material rises and the heat energy is transferred upwards.

Convection currents in the atmosphere

As the Sun is higher in the sky at the equator than at the poles, more of the Sun's energy hits the land at the equator, so the temperatures are higher. Air near the ground at the equator is heated and convection causes it to rise. At the poles, the air cools and sinks again. This causes large-scale convection currents in the Earth's atmosphere. The Earth's rotation breaks up the convection currents into smaller currents; these are called Hadley cells.

1 Jupiter also has Hadley cells in its atmosphere but there are many more cells than in Earth's atmosphere. What differences between Jupiter and Earth might account for this?

2 Venus is a little smaller than the Earth, but it rotates much more slowly – a day on Venus is 225 Earth days. How would this affect the convection in Venus's atmosphere?

▲ Similar convection currents to the Hadley cells cause the bands of Jupiter

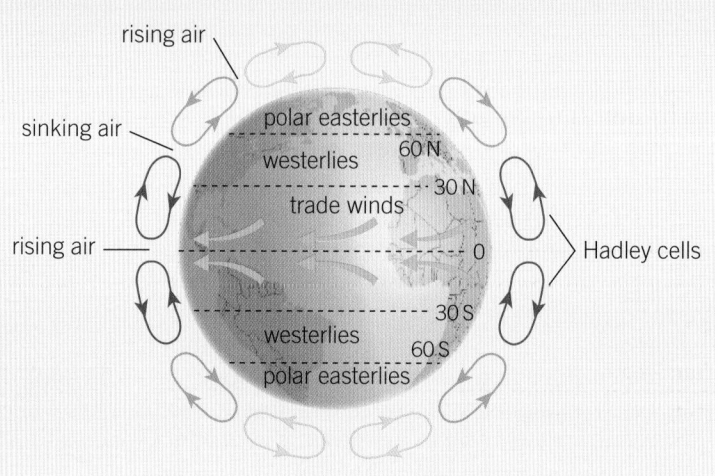

Radiation

Hot objects can also transfer heat energy by emitting thermal radiation in the form of electromagnetic waves. The wavelength of the radiation depends on the temperature of the object. Most objects emit infrared radiation; however, if the object is really hot, around 1,000 K, some of the radiation will be in the form of visible light and the object will glow a dull red color. If the object is hotter still, the light may be orange or yellow.

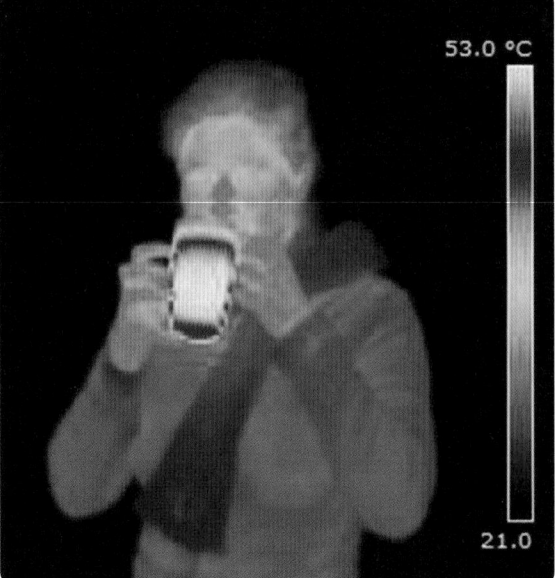

◄ This image has been taken using an infrared camera. The bare skin on the face and hands radiates the most as it is at a higher temperature than the surrounding clothes. The hot drink is emitting much more infrared radiation

Organising and depicting information logically

A graph is a good way of presenting data so that it can be easily visualized. Sometimes the scales on the axes have to be adjusted in order that the data can be properly seen.

A logarithmic scale can be used to display data that has a large range. An example of a logarithmic scale is shown below. Instead of the scale increasing in equal increments (1, 2, 3, 4, … or 0.05, 0.1, 0.15, 0.2 …) the scale increases in equal multiples (1, 10, 100, 1,000 … or 2, 4, 8, 16 …).

.1   0.2   0.3   0.5   0.7   1   2   3   5   7   10   20   30   50   70   100

The smaller divisions on a logarithmic scale are not equally spaced because the scale is not linear. The scale above shows a large gap from 0.1 to 0.2. The same gap then takes you up to 0.4 and then 0.8 because these are the same multiples. Once you get to 1, the increments are no longer in tenths but in units, and so the scale continues with 1 and then 2 and so on. When you get to 10, the same thing happens and the scale increases in tens.

To see how a logarithmic scale can be useful, consider the data in the following table.

Animal	Length (m)	Mass (kg)
Leafcutter ant	0.003	0.00001
Glass frog	0.05	0.02
Golden lion tamarin	0.25	0.6
Three-toed sloth	0.45	3.5
Capybara	1.2	50
Jaguar	1.5	75
Tapir	2	225

◀ A three-toed sloth
Bradypus tridactylus

Plot a graph of the data on normal graph paper. Which data points are hard to plot?

Plot the same data on a copy of the grid below. How does the logarithmic scale help?

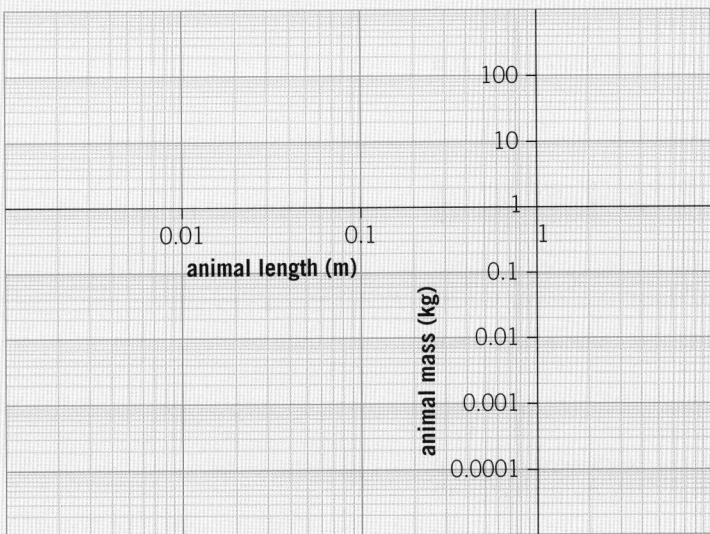

223

Data-based question: Measuring the temperature of the Sun

Objects at different temperatures emit different wavelengths of radiation. This enables us to measure the temperature of the Sun and other more distant stars without the need to travel the vast distances required to get there.

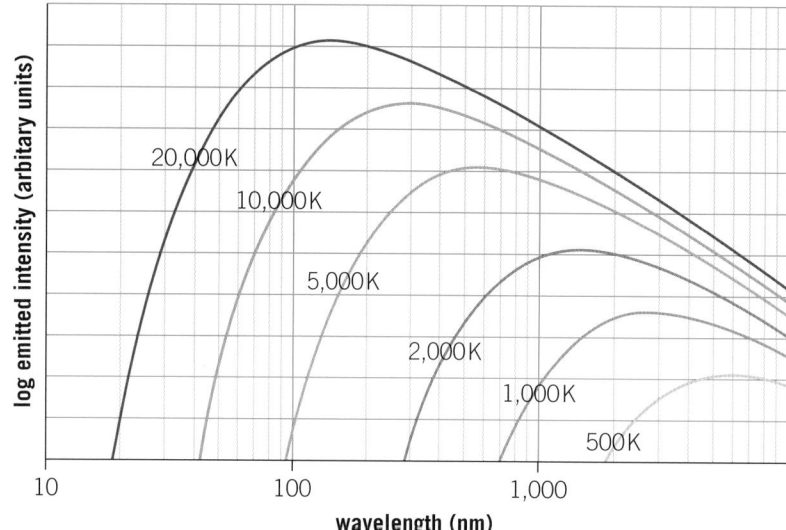

The graph above shows the intensity of radiation that is emitted at different frequencies for objects of different temperatures. Note that the scales are logarithmic.

1. Using the graph, find the wavelength that has the peak intensity for each temperature. Record your results in a table.

2. Plot a graph of the data in your table.

3. The detected radiation from the Sun at different wavelengths is measured and a graph of the results is shown below.

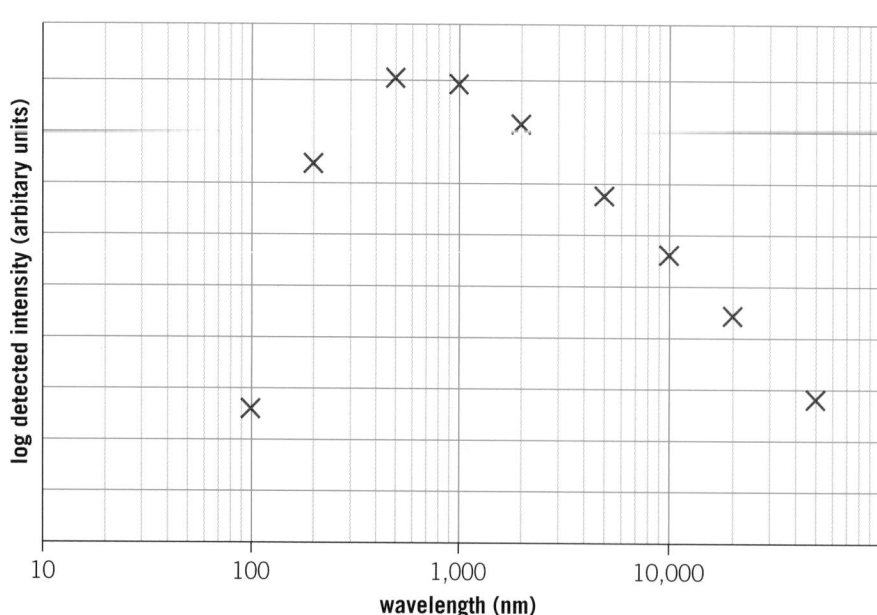

4. Add a line of best fit to a copy of this graph then estimate the wavelength of peak intensity.

5. Using this value and the graph you have drawn, find the temperature of the surface of the Sun.

The amount of radiation emitted by an object doesn't just depend on its temperature; it also depends on the color. White or shiny objects reflect more light, but also emit less thermal radiation. Black objects absorb light that hits them, and they also emit more thermal radiation.

▷ This villa is in a hot climate. Why are the walls painted in a light color?

▽ This house is in a colder climate. Why are the windows so small? Would having small windows be an advantage to a house in a hot climate?

How does a steam engine work?

A steam engine uses heat transfer to create changing pressure in a piston. This causes the piston to move and as a result do work.

The first steam engine that could be used industrially was invented by Thomas Newcomen in the 18th century. It was used for pumping water out of coal and tin mines. A fire was used to boil water, and this created steam which increased the pressure in the container. The steam was allowed to escape into a piston and the pressure pushed the piston outwards. A valve then closed the piston off and a small amount of cold water was sprayed into the piston. The steam in the piston condensed and the pressure dropped. The outside atmospheric pressure pushed the piston back in and the cycle started again.

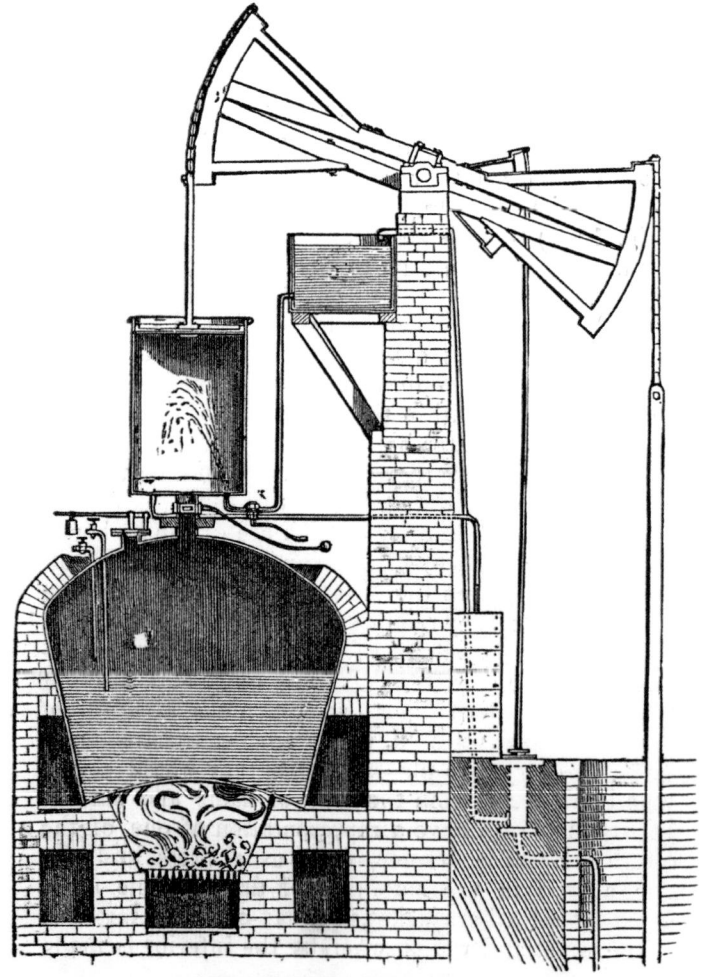

1360.—Newcomen's Steam-engine

▲ The Newcomen engine

Newcomen's engine converted thermal energy into mechanical work, but it was not very efficient. About 50 years later, James Watt, a British inventor, made significant improvements to the efficiency of the steam engine. As a result, they could be used to power

factories, and they became powerful enough to make steam trains possible. The result was the Industrial Revolution. Over the next 80 years, people's lives were transformed by the developments in transport and the changes in factories and the way in which people worked.

Today, steam engines are rarely used; however, we still rely on extracting mechanical work from sources of thermal energy. Many power stations burn coal or other fuels and use the heat to drive steam turbines. Just like the steam engines of the Industrial Revolution, a steam turbine uses the high pressure caused by hot steam and the pressure difference that is created when it cools.

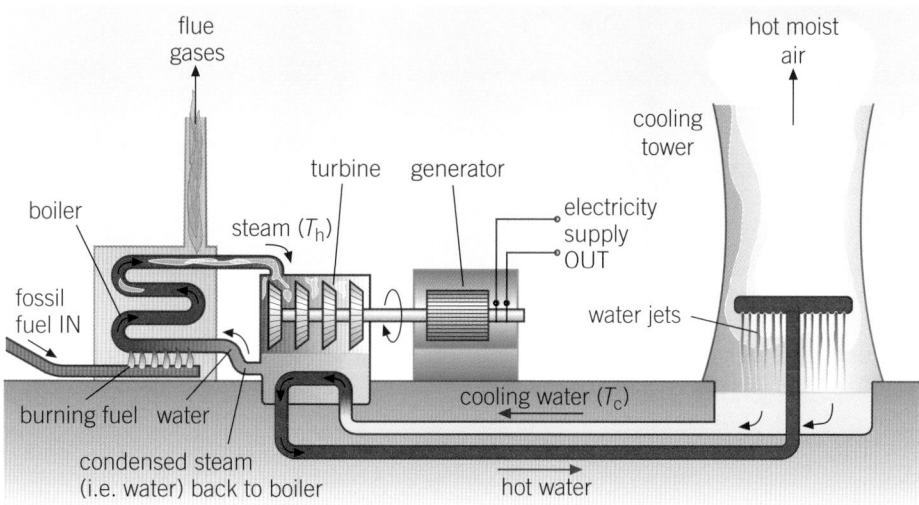

▲ The workings of a power station. The efficiency is determined by the temperatures of the steam (T_h) and the cooling water (T_c). The large cooling towers help to improve the efficiency by keeping T_c as low as possible

Steam engines and steam turbines have a limitation on their efficiency. The maximum possible efficiency is given by:

$$\text{efficiency} = \left(1 - \frac{T_c}{T_h}\right) \times 100\%$$

where T_h is the hot temperature of the steam (which depends on the temperature of the fire) and T_c is the cold temperature of the steam. Both these temperatures are in kelvin. This means that a power station that generates steam at 400°C (673 K) and allows it to condense at 100°C (373 K) cannot have an efficiency greater than 45%. Since this is a theoretical maximum, in practice the efficiency is much lower due to other energy losses. Using lower pressures, the steam can be made to condense at lower temperatures which improves the efficiency, although the cold temperature of the steam cannot be lower than the outside temperature without using energy to cool it down.

▲ These cooling towers ensure that the power station removes excess heat, so the cold temperature (T_c) is kept low. This improves the efficiency of the power station. Why is the efficiency of a power station greater in winter than in summer?

ATL Critical thinking

Formulating counterarguments

Steam turbines are used in coal-fired power stations as well as other fossil fuel power stations. Although fossil fuels are still used to generate the majority of the world's energy, there are concerns that burning fossil fuels causes pollution, contributes to the manmade greenhouse effect and therefore contributes to global warming. There are also concerns that fossil fuels will run out.

In response to these concerns, other methods of generating heat have been developed. Nuclear power uses nuclear processes to generate heat, although the way in which this heat drives a turbine is very similar to fossil fuel power stations. The temperature at which the nuclear power plant operates is also limited for safety. This reduces the efficiency of nuclear power plants. In addition, although nuclear power plants generate a small volume of waste, it is highly radioactive and needs careful disposal.

Consider the following arguments:

- Increasing the temperature at which nuclear power plants operate would increase their efficiency. This would make them cheaper and as a result they would be more economically viable. More nuclear power stations would be built and there would be a reduction in the use of fossil fuels to supply the world's energy.

- Improving the efficiency of coal-fired power stations would reduce the amount of coal required. This would reduce the amount of greenhouse gas emissions.

Using suitable research to supplement your own knowledge, formulate a counterargument to these statements.

Summative assessment

Introduction

Steam engines use the physics of how gases behave at different temperatures and pressures to convert thermal energy into mechanical energy. Although they are not used for driving industrial machines or for transport any more, similar technology is used in many power stations where steam power is used to drive a generator.

This assessment is based on the physics of steam engines and the efficiency of steam turbines.

 The pressure in a piston

A steam engine operates using steam in a piston. The steam is at a high temperature and exerts a high pressure on the walls of the piston.

1. Explain how the motion of the water molecules causes higher temperatures to exert higher pressures. [4]

2. When the piston has a volume of $2 \times 10^{-4} \, m^3$, the gas in the piston is at a pressure of 150 kPa.

    The area of the end of the piston is 0.00133 m². Calculate the force that the gas exerts on the end of the piston. [2]

3. The pressure of the air outside the piston is 100 kPa and this pushes inwards on the end of the piston. Calculate the net force pushing out on the piston. [3]

4. If the mass of gas in the piston remains the same, what is the pressure of the gas if the volume is reduced to $1.5 \times 10^{-4} \, m^3$? [3]

5. The piston operates at a temperature of 300°C. Express this temperature in kelvin. [1]

6. Which method of heat transfer (conduction, convection or radiation) is most likely to be responsible for:

    a) heat flowing from the gas inside of the piston to the outside of the piston? [1]

    b) heat energy leaving the outside of the piston? [1]

Investigating how gas pressure depends on temperature

In an experiment to determine how the pressure of a gas depends on the temperature, a group of students use the apparatus shown in the diagram to the left.

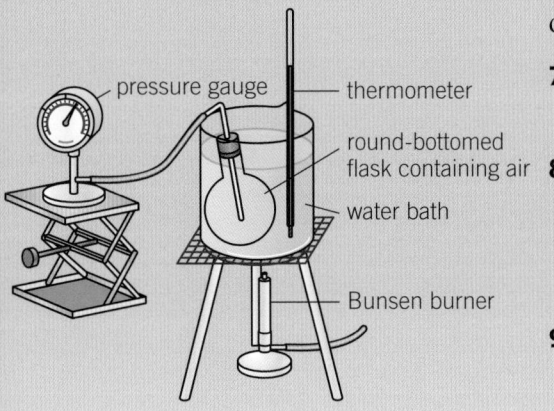

pressure gauge

thermometer

round-bottomed flask containing air

water bath

Bunsen burner

7. Identify the independent and dependent variables for this experiment. [2]

8. The flask containing the air is made of glass, so it does not change shape when the pressure inside is greater or smaller than the pressure outside the flask. Explain why it is important that the flask does not change shape. [2]

9. The students know that the flask starts with air at room temperature, which is about 20°C, and room pressure, which is about 100 kPa. The maximum temperature of the water is 100°C. They are concerned that heating water from 20°C to 100°C is an increase of five times. They know that pressure is proportional to temperature and fear that 500 kPa would be enough to shatter the glass flask. Explain why they do not need to be concerned and calculate the maximum pressure that could be attained in the flask. [6]

10. As an improvement to the experiment, a student suggests using a flask made of copper rather than glass. What properties of copper make it suitable for this experiment and how would this improve the experiment? [3]

11. Identify one safety consideration when carrying out this experiment. [2]

The efficiency of a steam engine

The efficiency of a steam engine depends on the temperature to which the steam is heated. A steam engine is tested to determine its efficiency at different steam temperatures and the results are shown below.

Steam temperature (°C)	Efficiency (%)
244	11.2
248	15.4
251	16.3
261	16.5
287	17.5
304	18.2
342	19.1
400	19.6

12. Plot a graph of the data in the table. [4]

13. Add a line of best fit to your graph. [1]

14. At low temperatures, the water did not boil and create enough steam pressure to drive the steam engine (the water is under pressure and so boils at a higher temperature than 100°C). Estimate the temperature at which the water boils sufficiently to drive the engine. [2]

15. The engine is unlikely to be able to pull a carriage unless it reaches 19% efficiency. Use your graph to estimate the temperature of the steam required to achieve this. [2]

16. In theory, higher efficiencies could be achieved by using much higher temperatures. In reality, heat loss from the boiler and cost are two factors which mean that very high temperatures are not used in steam engines.

   a) Explain why high temperatures would result in increased heat loss. [3]

   b) Explain why high temperatures would be more expensive to maintain. [3]

 ## Using steam power in coal-fired power stations

Most of the world's electricity is produced with a steam turbine. Steam turbines are similar to steam engines in that they use changes in the pressure and temperature of steam to generate mechanical work.

Use the following facts to answer the questions that follow:

- A typical coal-fired steam turbine operates at about 33% efficiency.

- About 40% of the world's power is generated by burning coal in order to drive steam turbines.

- The total world power generation is about 1.5×10^{13} J every second.

- 1 tonne of coal typically costs $100.

- 1 tonne of coal produces about 3×10^{10} J of thermal energy.

17. How much useful energy is generated by 1 tonne of coal? [2]

18. How much energy in the world is generated using coal-fired steam turbines? [2]

19. Estimate the mass of coal that is burned every second in order to generate energy. [2]

20. How much energy is wasted by steam turbines? [3]

21. Increasing the efficiency of a turbine would reduce the costs of electricity. Describe two other advantages of increasing the efficiency of steam turbines in coal-fired power stations. [6]

11 Energy

Energy enables the process of change to take place.

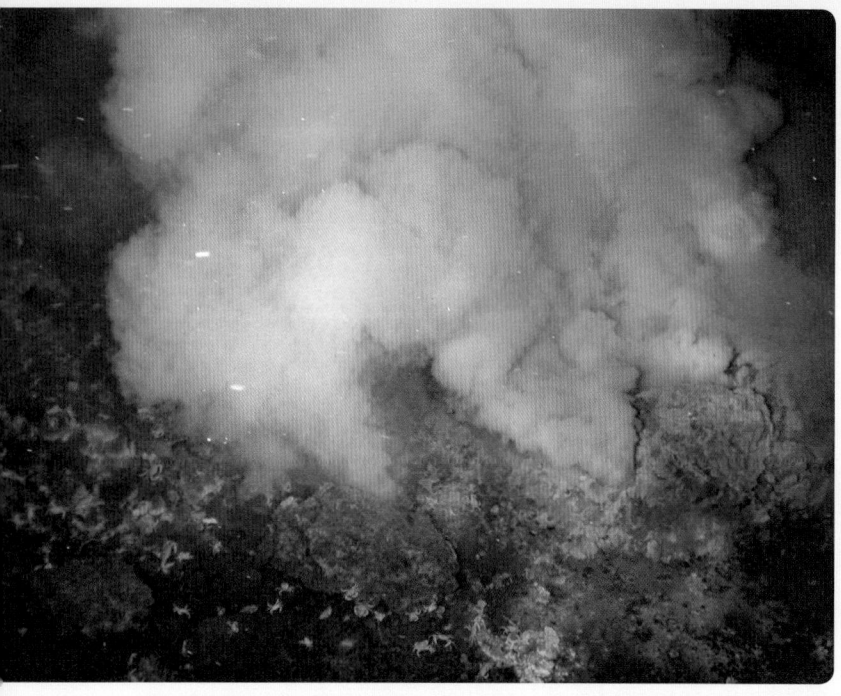

Most life on Earth depends on the Sun's energy, but deep under the ocean where there is no light, small ecosystems exist around hydrothermal vents. Here seawater that has permeated into the Earth's crust and has been heated by the hot rocks underneath bursts out of cracks in the rocks. In this vent, which is 1.5 km below the surface, photosynthesis is not possible as there is no sunlight, but bacteria that live here can break down hydrogen sulfide in a process called chemosynthesis. This provides food for many other creatures near these vents, such as the small crabs in the picture. Similar vents are thought to exist on Europa, a moon of Jupiter, and Enceladus, a moon of Saturn. What does this say about the prospect of finding extraterrestrial life?

One of the most energetic events in human history was the eruption of Krakatoa in Indonesia. This picture shows the island in May 1883. Three months later the island's volcano exploded in an event which destroyed most of the island. It is estimated that the eruption released about 10^{18} J of energy. The tsunamis caused by the explosion killed about 36,000 people and are estimated to have been more than 30 m high. The shock wave from the explosion traveled around the globe three and a half times. The sound of the explosion was clearly heard in Australia (3,000 km away) and in Mauritius (4,800 km away). Which other natural events in Earth's history have involved such huge energies?

▲ The Crab Nebula is the remnant of a supernova explosion which was observed in 1054. Supernovae are some of the most energetic events in the universe. When a large star reaches the end of its life and runs out of fuel, its core collapses and forms a neutron star or even a black hole. The energy released in these events can be about 10^{44} J – similar to the amount of energy that the Sun will release in its entire lifetime. For a short time, the supernova is brighter than the rest of its galaxy. How could a nearby supernova affect life on Earth?

▶ Sloths have a reputation for being lazy but because they eat leaves which are hard to digest and do not give them much energy, they need to be as efficient as possible. They sleep for 15 to 20 hours a day and have a very low metabolic rate. Whereas most mammals maintain a body temperature of about 37°C, sloths let their body temperatures drop to below 33°C in order to save energy. How can humans save energy by changing the way they behave?

Key concept: Change

Related concept: Energy

Global context: Globalization and sustainability

Introduction

Energy is a commonly used word. We often talk of having enough energy to carry out tasks and sometimes refer to mental or emotional energy to represent whether or not our brain has the resources to cope with a task or situation. Although physics has a specific definition of the word energy, the colloquial uses of the word are right to associate energy with a resource that can be used to do work and, as with any resource, you can run out of. In this chapter we will investigate what physicists mean by the word energy and the resources that society uses for its energy.

Energy is a valuable resource. With energy, buildings and homes can be lit and heated or air conditioned, factories can operate and transport systems can function. However, with such a valuable resource comes the need to guarantee its source. With an ever-increasing demand for energy from growing populations, scientists are looking at ways to ensure that even remote communities can harness the energy resources around them. Because of this the global context of this chapter is globalization and sustainability.

▼ These solar panels transfer energy from the Sun into electrical energy to power our homes

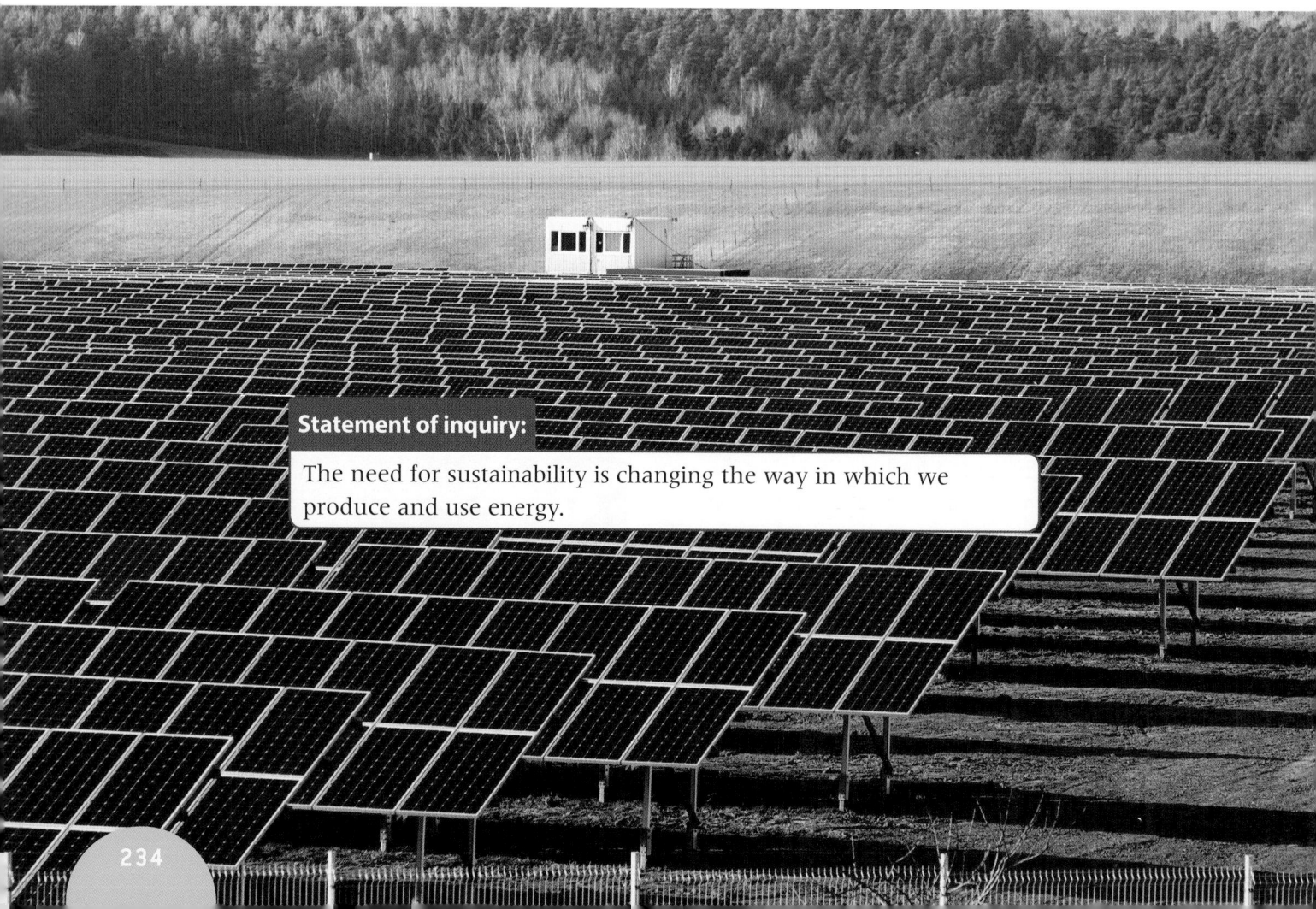

Statement of inquiry:

The need for sustainability is changing the way in which we produce and use energy.

The demand for energy also comes with environmental concerns about the resources that we use and the impacts that they have. Scientists are not just concerned with changing the way in which we source our energy, but also in changing the way in which we use energy in our lives, ensuring that it is used efficiently. The key concept for this chapter is change.

▲ Changes in technology allow us to use our energy resources more efficiently

▶ In athletics events, energy transfers are very important. In the pole vault, this athlete transfers kinetic energy from her run-up into elastic potential energy caused by bending the pole. This stored energy is then returned to the athlete propelling her upwards. The pole improves the efficiency of the energy transfer and is the reason why the female pole vault world record is just over 5 m, whereas the high jump record is just over 2 m

What is energy?

Because energy is a common word in our language, we are usually able to identify things that have a lot of energy: they are hot, bright, loud or they might be moving fast. Although this is not the definition of energy that a physicist would use, the properties of such objects do reflect the amount of energy that they have.

Physicists define energy as the capacity of an object to do work. Work is defined as (see Chapter 6, Function)

work = force exerted × distance over which it is exerted
$$W = F\,d$$

This is the mechanical description of work, but work can also be done in heating an object up. The unit of energy is the same as the unit of work and is the joule (J).

What forms does energy take?

Energy can exist in many different forms. Some important forms of energy are:

- **Kinetic energy**: This is the energy of something that is moving. The kinetic energy of an object can be calculated using the equation:

$$E = \frac{1}{2}mv^2$$

where E is the kinetic energy, m is the mass of an object and v is the speed at which it is traveling.

- **Thermal energy**: This is the energy gained by something when it is heated. The amount of energy required to heat a substance can be calculated using the equation:

$$E = m\,c\,\Delta T$$

where E is the thermal energy gained, m is the mass of an object and ΔT is the increase in temperature. The quantity c is the specific heat capacity which is a measure of how much energy is required to heat up any given substance. The specific heat capacity is a useful quantity because for any given substance, it has the same value. For example, water has a specific heat capacity of 4,200 J kg^{-1} °C^{-1} which means that it takes 4,200 J of energy to heat up 1 kg of water by 1°C, whereas aluminum has a specific heat capacity of 900 J kg^{-1} °C^{-1}.

- **Gravitational potential energy**: Potential energy is a stored form of energy. If you lift an object into the air, you do work against gravity. Work is calculated with the equation $W = F\,d$. The gravitational force (weight) is given by the equation $F = m\,g$ and the distance in the work equation is the height through which the object is lifted, h. As a result, the gravitational potential energy, E, gained by an object is:

$$E = m\,g\,h$$

- **Electrical energy**: A flowing electric current transfers energy. It is one of the easiest ways to transmit energy over long distances and in a controlled way. As a result, a large proportion of a household's energy use is from electrical energy, and the majority of household appliances are electrical. The amount of energy transferred is calculated from the equation:

$$E = I V t$$

where I is the current (measured in amps), V is the voltage drop across the appliance or the component which is transferring the energy (measured in volts) and t is the time for which the current flows (measured in seconds).

1. A runner covers 3,000 m in 13 minutes. If she has a mass of 55 kg, calculate her kinetic energy.

2. A man of mass 75 kg climbs up the stairs to the top of a 180 m high tower block. What is his increase in gravitational potential energy?

3. A light bulb has a current of 0.12 A passing through it, and a voltage of 120 V across it. How much electrical energy will it use in one minute?

4. The specific heat capacity of copper is 385 J kg^{-1} °C^{-1}. How much energy does it take to heat 0.5 kg of copper from 20°C to 40°C?

How much energy?

For each of these pictures:

1. Identify the type of energy shown.

2. Calculate the amount of energy.

Which situation shows the most energy and which shows the least?

▲ A cyclist in a velodrome travels at a speed of 20 m s^{-1}. The mass of the cyclist and bicycle is 100 kg

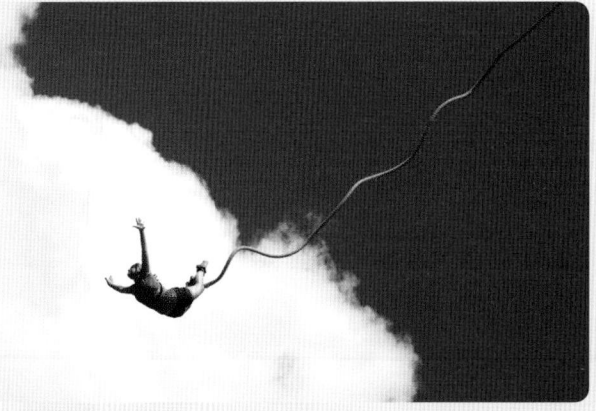

▲ A bungee jumper jumps from a height of 25 m. She has a mass of 60 kg

A cup of coffee contains 0.2 kg of water at 90°C. The specific heat capacity of water is 4,200 J kg^{-1}°C^{-1} and the coffee cools down to 20°C

This battery can supply a current of 4.2 A for 1 hour at a voltage of 1.5 V

In addition to the four types of energy discussed before, there are many other forms that energy can take, such as light energy and sound energy. Because waves transfer this energy, these forms of energy are often regarded as part of an energy transfer. Light energy is normally emitted by objects with so much thermal energy that they glow and sound energy is generally created by moving things, particularly when they collide. As a result, the amount of energy released in the form of light or sound is often insignificant when compared to the overall energy in the situation which caused the light or sound.

When the mallet hits the drum, kinetic energy is lost. Most of this energy is transferred to thermal energy, but some is carried away in the form of sound

These lumps of steel have so much thermal energy that they are glowing. The radiated light carries energy away from the metal

There are also other types of potential energy. Any stored energy that can be released is a form of potential energy, and each type involves work being done against a force to store the energy. For example, energy can be stored by stretching an elastic band or compressing a spring. The work done against the tension force stores energy as elastic potential energy.

On an atomic level, the different forces that bind atoms together into molecules mean that some molecules store energy in the bonds between the atoms. In certain chemical reactions, these bonds may be broken and energy released, usually in the form of thermal energy. The form of the stored energy is chemical potential energy.

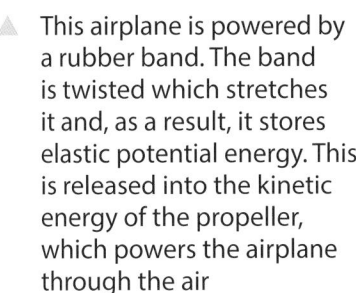

△ This airplane is powered by a rubber band. The band is twisted which stretches it and, as a result, it stores elastic potential energy. This is released into the kinetic energy of the propeller, which powers the airplane through the air

◁ Miners use explosives to blast into rock. The explosives store energy in the form of chemical potential energy. In the explosion this is released, and the energy is transferred into doing work by breaking the rock apart, as well as the kinetic energy of the rock fragments. Some energy is lost as thermal energy and a small fraction is lost as sound

Some atomic nuclei are unstable and may decay (see Chapter 12, Patterns). Energy stored by the short-range forces in the nucleus is nuclear potential energy. Such energy is rarely accessed; however, the amount of energy can be vast.

◁ The enormous amounts of energy that are stored in the nuclei of atoms are hard to release. This is why nuclear weapons are so destructive

How does energy transfer?

One of the most fundamental and important laws of physics is the conservation of energy. It states that energy can be transferred between objects and can be converted from one form to another, but that it cannot be created or destroyed. As a result, the total amount of energy remains the same overall.

ATL **Communication skills**

Interpreting discipline-specific terms

Science uses laws and theories to provide explanations of how the universe works.

A scientific law is something that always applies in given circumstances. In the case of the law of the conservation of energy, this always applies, but other laws are more restricted in their application. For example, Ohm's law (see Chapter 6, Function) only applies when the resistance of the component does not change. Laws of physics do not have exceptions. A law of physics is so fundamental that if any exceptions are found, they would represent a major discovery. This happened when Einstein suggested his theory of relativity as an explanation for some observations that did not follow Newton's laws of motion.

A scientific theory, on the other hand, is an explanation of the way things work. Theories are devised to explain experimental observations and set out to answer the question of why things are as they are. Scientific theories such as the Big Bang theory explain the start of the universe and why distant galaxies are moving away from us. A theory is valid while experimental observations support it, but a theory may be disproved by contradictory evidence and it would become invalid.

Worked example: Falling objects

Question

Two ball bearings of mass 10 g and 100 g are lifted to a height of 2 m above the ground and released.

1. Calculate the gravitational potential energy given to each ball bearing.

2. After they are dropped, what is the kinetic energy of each ball bearing just before they hit the ground.

3. Show that the ball bearings hit the ground at the same time.

Answer

1. Using gravitational potential energy $E_p = mgh$:
   first ball bearing: $m = 0.01$ kg
                        gravitational potential energy
                        $= 0.01 \times 9.8 \times 2 = 0.196$ J.

second ball bearing: m is 10 times larger (0.1 kg)

gravitational potential energy is also 10 times larger, that is 1.96 J.

2. Using the conservation of energy, all the gravitational potential energy is transferred to kinetic energy as the balls fall. Therefore, the kinetic energy of the ball bearings is 0.196 and 1.96 J.

3. Kinetic energy $E_k = \frac{1}{2}mv^2$:

This can be rearranged to $\qquad v = \sqrt{\dfrac{2E_k}{m}}$

So for the 10 g ball bearing: $\qquad v = \sqrt{\dfrac{2 \times 0.196}{0.01}} = \sqrt{39.2} = 6.26 \text{ m s}^{-1}$

For the 100 g ball bearing: $\qquad v = \sqrt{\dfrac{2 \times 1.96}{0.1}} = \sqrt{39.2} = 6.26 \text{ m s}^{-1}$

That is, they have the same speed. Furthermore, both balls have the same speed as each other at any time in their fall and so land at the same time.

A simple example of an energy transfer is a ball rolling down a slope. At the top of the slope, the ball has gravitational potential energy. As it rolls down the slope, this energy is converted to kinetic energy, and when the ball reaches the bottom of the slope, all the gravitational potential energy has been transferred into kinetic energy. This assumes that no energy is lost via air resistance or friction with the slope.

1. A skier has a mass of 80 kg. He starts from rest and skis down a slope which drops 50 m in height.

   a) Calculate the amount of gravitational potential energy the skier loses skiing down the slope.

   b) What kinetic energy does he have at the bottom of the slope?

   c) How fast is the traveling skier at the bottom?

Identifying energy transfers

Many devices transfer energy from one form into another, for example, a motor transfers electrical energy into kinetic energy. Identify the energy transfers which take place in these devices:

- loudspeaker
- solar cell (photovoltaic cell)
- light bulb
- microphone
- plant leaf photosynthesizing.

▶ Photovoltaic cells supply power to a light and loudspeakers. What are the energy transfers in these devices?

Experiment

The aim of this experiment is to investigate how the kinetic energy of an object varies with its speed. To do this, you will drop a ball bearing (or similar object) from varying heights.

There are many different ways to measure the final speed of the ball bearing. Here are a few suggestions; you could use one of these or a combination, or you may have a different idea.

Method 1: Use a data-logger with light gates to measure the speed of the ball.

Method 2: Place a meter rule and a stop clock just behind where the ball lands and film it. By using a slow-motion setting or pausing the video at two points just before the ball lands, you can work out the final speed of the ball.

Method 3: The speed–time graph of the ball's fall is a straight line (see below and Chapter 4, Movement). If you use the equation:

$$v = \frac{d}{t}$$

where d is the height from which the ball falls and t is the time it takes to fall, the calculated speed is the average speed for the duration of the ball's fall. If you double this speed, you obtain the final velocity.

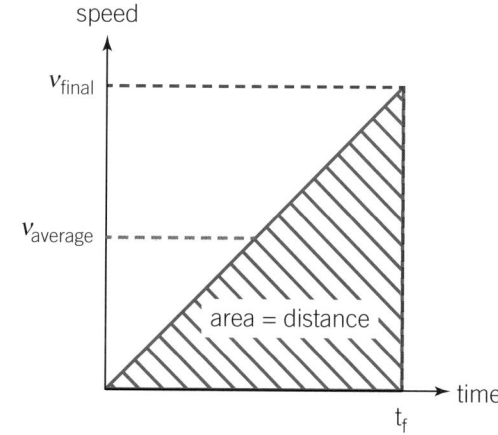

Method

- Measure the mass of the ball bearing and record its value.

- Lift the ball bearing to a height of 50 cm above the desk or floor. Measure the height from the surface of the desk to the bottom of the ball bearing. Drop the ball bearing and measure its speed just before it lands (using one of the methods described above).

- Repeat the experiment for different heights. Record your data in a table.

Questions

1. Add a column to your table for the energy of the ball bearing. This can be found by using the equation $E = mgh$.

2. Plot a graph of the energy on the x-axis and final speed on the y-axis. Describe the trend of your data.

3. If the equation for kinetic energy is $\frac{1}{2}mv^2$, then we can hypothesize that $E \propto v^2$. Plot another graph with E on the x-axis and v^2 on the y-axis to verify this hypothesis.

How can energy be lost?

When two objects slide over each other, friction acts. Because friction is a force and the objects are moving, work is done. This work converts some kinetic energy into thermal energy. The thermal energy is not normally useful and generally cannot be recovered; it is transferred to the surroundings. In moving systems, frictional losses are usually minimized by lubricating moving parts.

Friction also occurs when objects move through air or water. Air resistance (or water resistance) slows down any object moving through it. A more streamlined shape can help reduce energy losses.

▲ The falcon (on the left) can adopt a streamlined shape and hence reduce air resistance. This enables it to fly much faster than the peafowl (right) which is less aerodynamic

A raindrop of mass 4.2×10^{-6} kg falls from a raincloud 1.5 km in the air. When the raindrop hits the ground, it is traveling at 6.5 m s^{-1}.

1. Calculate the initial gravitational potential energy of the raindrop.

2. Calculate the final kinetic energy of the raindrop.

3. Hence find the energy that the raindrop loses though friction.

4. If all this lost energy is transferred to thermal energy in the raindrop, calculate the temperature rise of the raindrop during its fall. The specific heat capacity of water is 4,200 J kg^{-1} °C^{-1}.

5. In reality, the raindrops do not increase their temperature by this amount. Using the ideas of energy transfers, explain why the temperature increase may be less.

Data-based question: James Joule and the waterfall at Sallanches

▲ The Cascade de l'Arpenaz in Sallanches, close to the Mont Blanc massif

In 1847, while on his honeymoon, James Joule went to the waterfall at Sallanches in France. He tried to measure the temperature of the water at the top and at the bottom.

The water going over the falls drops 270 m.

1. Calculate the gravitational potential energy of 1 kg of water at the top of the waterfall.

2. What kinetic energy will 1 kg of water have at the bottom of the falls (assuming that none is lost to friction)?

3. The specific heat capacity of water is 4,200 J kg^{-1} °C^{-1}. Assuming that when the water lands in the pool at the bottom of the waterfall, all the energy is converted to thermal energy in the water, how much warmer should the water at the bottom be than at the top?

4. Explain why the temperature difference is in fact much less than your calculated value.

5. What would the theoretical temperature difference be for the Angel Falls, the highest waterfall in the world, which drops 807 m in its longest drop?

Watt is power!

As well as considering the amount of energy transferred, it is often important to know the time in which the transfer takes place. There is a difference between a bright flash of light that lasts for a fraction of a second and a dim light that is emitted for a few hours, even though the amount of light energy emitted could be the same.

An important quantity in this case is power, which is the amount of energy transferred in one second. The unit of power is a watt (W) and power P can be calculated using the equation:

$$P = \frac{E}{t}$$

where E is the energy transferred and t is the time taken to transfer the energy.

1. A man runs up a flight of stairs which goes up 12 m. His mass is 80 kg and it takes him 5 s. Calculate the power he transfers.

2. A car has a mass of 500 kg and accelerates from rest to $25\,\mathrm{m\,s^{-1}}$ in 7.5 s. Calculate the power of the car.

For electrical circuits, the power transferred can be calculated using the equation:

$$P = IV$$

where V is the voltage across a component and I is the current flowing through it.

3. The electrical power use of a home is about 500 W. If the voltage of the supply is 120 V, what is the average current supplied?

4. A microwave oven delivers a power of 1,000 W. How long does it take to heat 0.2 kg of water from 20°C to 80°C assuming all the power is delivered to the water? The specific heat capacity of water is $4,200\,\mathrm{J\,kg^{-1}\,°C^{-1}}$.

Finding the power output of waterfalls

1. Using the data in the table, describe the energy transfers which take place in a waterfall.

Waterfall	Height (m)	Flow rate (kg s⁻¹)
Angel Falls	807	14,000
Niagara Falls	51	2,407,000
Victoria Falls	108	1,088,000

2. Consider 1 kg of water falling down the waterfall. What kinetic energy has the water gained at the bottom of each waterfall?

3. Using the values for the flow rate, calculate the energy transferred by each waterfall in one second.

4. Which is the most powerful waterfall?

How do we measure efficiency?

Many machines and devices convert energy from one form to another. However, they invariably release energy in other forms as well. For example, a light bulb is designed to convert electrical energy into visible light. However, it also gets hot and radiates thermal energy. Because of the conservation of energy, if it radiates thermal energy, it cannot be converting all the electrical energy into light.

A process which converts most of the energy into the desired form can be described as efficient, whereas one which wastes a lot of energy by converting it to other forms can be described as inefficient. Efficiency is expressed as the percentage of energy which is successfully transferred into the desired form. It can be calculated using the equation:

$$\text{efficiency} = \frac{\text{useful output energy}}{\text{total input energy}} \times 100\%$$

The efficiency can also be calculated using power:

$$\text{efficiency} = \frac{\text{useful output power}}{\text{total input power}} \times 100\%$$

Most wasted energy is in the form of thermal energy. Any mechanical process is likely to suffer energy losses from friction which converts kinetic energy into thermal energy. Any electrical process experiences some resistance which also causes heating.

1. A laser pointer produces a beam with a power of 0.6 mW. It is powered from a 1.5 V battery that supplies a current of 1.6 mA. Calculate the efficiency of the laser.

2. A lift uses 47 kJ to raise 800 kg (the lift and people in it) through a height of 10 m. What is its efficiency?

3. An electric kettle heats 0.5 kg of water from 20°C to 100°C in 2 minutes. The specific heat capacity of the water is 4,200 J kg^{-1}°C^{-1}.

   a) Calculate the thermal power heating the water.

   b) The voltage supply to the kettle is 120 V, and it draws a current of 12 A. Calculate the electrical power supplied to the kettle.

   c) Calculate the efficiency of the kettle.

   d) In Europe, where the voltage supply is about 220 V, electric kettles are common. In the USA, where the voltage supply is 120 V, electric kettles are rare (stove-top kettles are more common). Why might this be?

Data-based question: Light bulb efficiency

Filament light bulbs, also called incandescent bulbs, operate by passing an electrical current through a thin wire (filament) which gets very hot and glows. As well as emitting visible light, 95% of the energy is emitted in the form of thermal energy which is considered wasted.

1. State the efficiency of a filament light bulb.

2. A typical incandescent light bulb uses 60 W of electrical power. Calculate the power given off by the light bulb in:

   a) wasted thermal power

   b) useful light energy.

Alternative light bulb designs are compact fluorescent bulbs, which use a glass tube which coils tightly, or LED bulbs. The efficiency of compact fluorescent light bulbs is about 75% and the efficiency of LED bulbs can be as high as 90%.

3. Calculate the electrical power that a compact fluorescent and an LED bulb would require in order to produce the same light power as a 60 W filament light bulb.

The table below shows some properties of the three different light bulbs.

The cost of electricity is about $1.40 to supply 1 W of electrical power for a year.

Light bulb type	Efficiency	Life time (hours)	Cost ($)
Filament	5%	1,000	0.65
Compact fluorescent	80%	8,000	4.5
LED	85%	15,000	6.5

4. Assuming that a light bulb is operated continuously, evaluate the relative costs of running a light bulb for:

   a) half a year

   b) five years.

Where do we get our energy from?

ENERGY

Modern society uses a lot of energy. Some of this energy is taken from fossil fuels directly, such as petrol in cars or gas for heating homes. Although gas and petroleum account for the majority of our energy usage, another way in which we get energy to its point of use is in the form of electricity. Electricity lights our homes and powers many of the devices that we use. Power lines transmit the energy from power stations to where it is needed in our homes and in industry.

The conservation of energy means that the energy we use must come from somewhere. The source of the Earth's energy is the Sun, which has been radiating its heat and light on the Earth for billions of years. Some of this energy is reflected back into space, but the rest is absorbed by the Earth, warming the planet.

Coal is formed from dead plant matter which has been compressed under the surface of the Earth. When we burn coal or other fossil fuels, we are releasing the energy that plants absorbed from the Sun and that has been stored for millions of years

Some of the Sun's light is absorbed by the leaves of plants, allowing photosynthesis to occur. The plants convert the energy into chemical energy and store it. When we burn wood, we are releasing energy that originally came from the Sun years before.

When plants and animals reach the end of their lives, they die and either sink to the bottom of the ocean or end up buried on land. The surrounding conditions affect how the organic material decays. Bacteria can convert some of the matter to gas which can become trapped under the Earth's surface as natural gas. Other material is compressed by increasing layers on top of it. The increased temperature and pressure cause the chemicals to change, and oil and coal are formed over millions of years. Coal, oil and natural gas are called fossil fuels. Burning fossil fuels releases energy that originally came from the Sun, but has been trapped for millions of years.

The heat and light from the Sun also hits the oceans and evaporates water. When this water falls as rain, it sometimes lands on higher ground. It has gained gravitational potential energy from the Sun, and as rivers run back to the sea, the energy is converted to kinetic energy.

ENERGY

How do we generate energy?

Most of the world's electricity is generated by burning coal, oil or natural gas.

In a coal-burning power station, the thermal energy from burning this fuel can be used to create steam, which in turn drives a turbine. This converts the thermal energy into kinetic energy. The turbine turns a generator which converts the kinetic energy into electrical energy. The electrical energy is then distributed through wires to homes, businesses and industries.

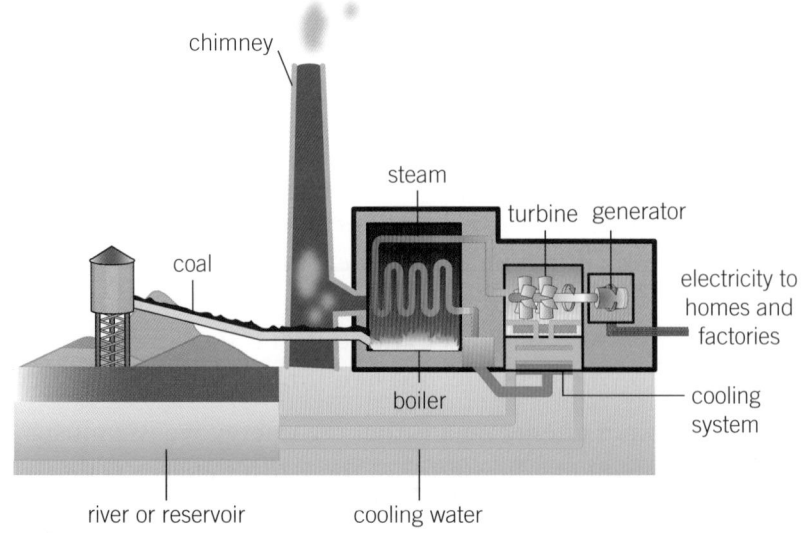

A typical coal-fired power station. Many other types of power station work in a similar way but generate heat from another source

1. A coal-fired power station generates 3 GW of electricity. It has an efficiency of 30%. Calculate the input power that the power station requires.

2. 1 tonne of coal produces 30 GJ of energy when it is burned. Calculate the amount of coal that the power station requires. Give your answer in tonnes per day.

How we can store energy?

ENERGY

Electricity demand changes according to the time of day and year. For example, in winter more electricity is used for heating and lighting than in summer, and homes use more electricity at weekends and in the evenings on weekdays.

Power stations try to respond to the amount of energy that is required. However, any excess electricity that is generated is often wasted. It is not easy to store electricity, but finding ways of storing the excess electricity is becoming more important. Two of these methods include:

- **Pumped hydroelectricity**: Excess electricity can be used to pump water to a reservoir at the top of a hydroelectric power station. This water can be allowed to flow though the generator and generate electricity when it is needed.

- **Compressed air energy storage (CAES)**: Surplus electricity is used to pump air into an underground cavern or a large vessel deep under the sea. This high pressure gas can then be used to drive a turbine when electricity is required.

What are the problems with burning fossil fuels?

ENERGY

Burning fossil fuels creates pollution and releases carbon dioxide (CO_2) into the atmosphere. As CO_2 is a greenhouse gas, scientists and environmentalists are concerned about the long-term effects that this might have on the Earth's climate. As a result, scientists are looking for other ways to generate electricity.

Data-based question: How long will our supply of coal last?

1. The world's energy production is about 5.5×10^{20} J per year. Express this value in watts.

2. 1 tonne of coal produces about 3×10^{10} J. If all the world's energy needs were to be met by coal-fired power stations, how many tonnes of coal would be required per year?

3. It is thought that there are about 1.4×10^{12} tonnes of coal reserves that could be mined. How long will this supply last at the current rate of consumption?

4. In fact, coal only accounts for 28% of energy production, but it is only 33% efficient. How does this affect your estimate of the length of time the world's coal supplies will last?

Some of these alternative methods rely on using an alternative source of fuel to generate the thermal energy required to drive the steam turbine.

What do we mean by renewable?

Fossil fuels take millions of years to form, but the rate at which we are using them suggests that they will be exhausted within a couple of centuries. This could result in an end to fossil fuels as a means to generate our energy. An energy resource which will run out over a short period of time (approximately 500 to 1,000 years) is called non-renewable.

Some power stations can run on biofuels. These are fuels produced from plants in a short timescale. They include biogas which is methane generated from rotting waste in landfill sites and ethanol made from fermenting plant matter. Other renewable sources of biomass are managed woodland or farms where the crop is entirely devoted to providing energy. As these sources of energy are replanted as they are used, they are considered renewable.

▶ These sugar beets are a useful source of biofuels. Fermenting them creates bioethanol which can be used as fuel

Another source of fuel is nuclear power (see Chapter 12, Patterns). Controlled nuclear fission reactions, where a nucleus is split into two smaller fragments, release an enormous amount of energy. One kilogram of coal can produce 3×10^7 J of energy, but 1 kg of uranium-235 can produce more than 8×10^{13} J. When other radioactive elements are taken into account, it is possible that there are hundreds of years' worth of supply; although nuclear power accounts for less than 5% of the world's energy production. As a result, nuclear power is not considered to be a renewable resource since when it runs out, it cannot be replaced. One problem with nuclear power is the dangerous waste that is created which needs careful disposal; another is the risk of accidents with the potential to be very dangerous and have long-term consequences.

A nuclear power station looks similar to a conventional coal-fired power station. The large towers are cooling towers which cool water in order to power the turbines. It is steam, not smoke, that is coming from the tower

Data-based question: Could nuclear power provide the world's energy?

It is thought that there is at least 4×10^7 kg of uranium-235 that could be mined. The energy available from 1 kg of uranium-235 is about 8×10^{13} J.

1. Calculate the amount of energy that the world's uranium-235 supply could generate.

2. The world's energy needs are about 5.5×10^{20} J per year. If all this energy were to be generated with nuclear power, how much uranium-235 would be needed per year?

3. How long would the current resources of uranium-235 be able to supply the world's energy?

4. Nuclear power only accounts for about 4.5% of energy generated. If we continue to use uranium-235 at current rates, how long will supplies last?

Further inside the Earth, deeper than any mine could reach, it is thought that there is much more uranium and other radioactive isotopes. These radioactive elements decay, releasing energy which keeps the inside of the Earth hot. As a result, the mantle underneath the Earth's crust consists of molten rock. The Earth's crust is also heated as this energy conducts to the surface.

Volcanoes are a good example of the energy that is stored inside the earth. Volcanoes are most usually found on the boundaries between tectonic plates, but they can also be seen in hot spots where convection currents in the mantle cause hotter material to rise closer to the crust. Examples of these are found in Hawaii and Iceland.

Iceland is on a hot spot on the Earth's crust. There are many volcanoes, geysers and these boiling mudpots

The thermal energy can also be seen in the form of hot springs and geysers. This resource of thermal energy is called geothermal energy. By drilling into the Earth, water can be sent to the hotter rocks below. If it is hot enough, the water will turn to steam and can be used to drive a turbine. If the rocks are not hot enough to generate steam, then the returning water might be hot enough to provide heating for buildings. This energy resource is most useful where the hot rocks are more easily accessible. Iceland, for example, generates about a quarter of its electricity from geothermal sources, and most houses are heated from this resource. Since geothermal energy is a resource that will not run out in the immediate future, it is classed as renewable.

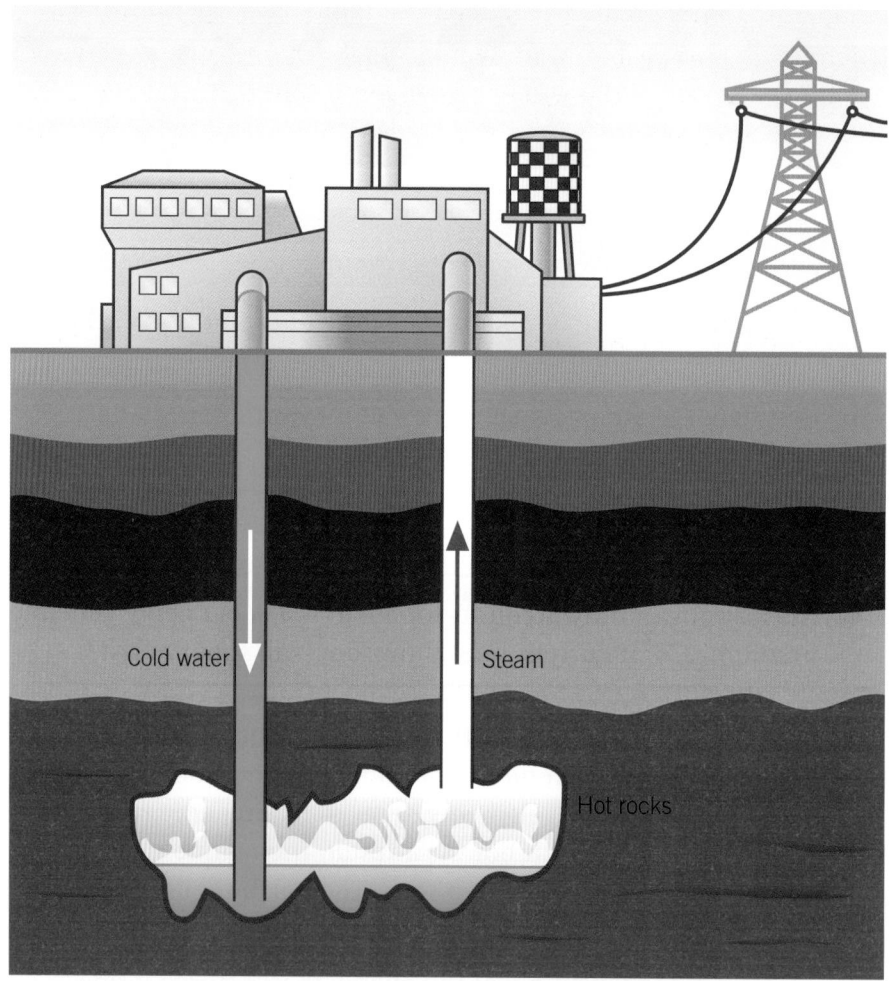

Cold water   Steam   Hot rocks

Geothermal power stations use the thermal energy of the Earth's interior to generate electricity

There are other sources of power that are classed as renewable. Hydroelectricity relies on water falling as rain onto high ground. This water then flows into rivers and these flow towards the sea. Whenever a river has a large drop, it is possible to use it to drive a turbine and generate electricity. Because the rainfall is created by the Sun's energy evaporating water from the oceans, this is a renewable source of energy.

The Sun's energy can be harnessed directly using photovoltaic cells which convert it into electrical energy. This is also a renewable source of energy. Although it is expensive to set up and can require a large area of land, it is very dependable in environments where sunshine is reliable. It is a fast-growing resource but still accounts for a small proportion of the world's energy generation.

Another way in which the Sun's energy can be used is in wind power. The Sun's intensity is stronger near the equator than at the poles as the Sun's rays hit the Earth from overhead rather than obliquely. This causes the air above the equator to be hotter than at the poles and a convection current is caused. The Earth's rotation also affects the flow of air so that instead of moving in a north–south direction, prevailing winds form in patterns called Hadley cells (see Chapter 10, Transformation). In addition, fluctuations in the weather, differences between the land and sea, as well as obstacles such as mountains all contribute to the winds in different locations. In places where there is a reliable wind, wind turbines can be used to harness the kinetic energy of the wind and convert it into electrical energy. Since the kinetic energy of the wind originates from the Sun and the rotational energy of the Earth, this is a renewable source of energy.

Another source of renewable energy is tidal power. Tides are caused by the gravitational pull of the Moon which causes the ocean level to rise and fall as the Earth spins. Although the tides are less than a meter in height on average, they are amplified by continents and the changing depth of the ocean and can be over 5 m in some places. This large mass of rising and falling water carries a large amount of energy. If the water at high tide can be trapped in a tidal lagoon, then it can be allowed to flow out at low tide and drive a turbine.

ATL Media literacy skills

Seeking a range of perspectives from multiple sources

The way in which renewable energy is portrayed in the media and online often differs hugely depending on the opinions of the writer and the intended audience.

Many people agree that the pollution caused by burning fossil fuels should be reduced, and the scientific consensus is that fossil fuels are contributing to global warming. On the other hand, there are many people who dispute the impact of fossil fuels or say that the scientists are wrong. There are also times when people want to avoid burning fossil fuels for energy, but object to the alternatives and do not want a renewable alternative installed near where they live.

Look for media articles giving examples of each of these. If possible, start by looking for articles relating to a new energy resource in your local area. It might be one that has been built or it might be just a proposal. Try to identify any flaws in the arguments that are presented or any bias of the writer.

Summative assessment

Introduction

Hydroelectric power is a renewable source of electricity. Micro-hydroelectric systems typically generate between 5 kW and 100 kW, enough for a small village.

 The energy changes in a micro-hydroelectric system

A small waterfall has a drop of 10 m.

1. Describe the energy transfers that take place as water flows over the waterfall. [2]

2. One kilogram of water drops over the waterfall. Calculate the speed at which it lands in the pool at the bottom. [4]

3. Explain why, in reality, the water will land at a slightly lower speed. [2]

4. A micro-hydroelectric generator is used to supply power to the local community. Describe the energy transfers which take place in a hydroelectric generator. [3]

5. The micro-hydroelectric generator generates 10 kW of power. If this is supplied to the community at a voltage of 480 V, what is the maximum current that could be supplied? [4]

A micro-hydro system can supply remote locations

Testing a micro-hydroelectric generator

Engineers who install micro-hydroelectric generators want to test the electric current that they generate. They design an experiment where water is pumped through a generator at varying speeds and the current generated is measured.

6. State the independent variable in this experiment. [1]

7. What instrument should be used to measure the dependent variable? [1]

8. Suggest two control variables for the experiment. [2]

When the engineers carried out the experiment, they used flow speeds of 0, 1, 2, 3, 4 and 5 m s^{-1}. The currents that they measured were 0, 0.1, 0.3, 0.8, 1.3 and 2.1 A.

9. Present their results in a table. [2]

10. Plot a graph of the data. [4]

11. The engineers' hypothesis was that the current would be directly proportional to the speed of the water. Explain why their results do not support this hypothesis. [2]

12. Use scientific reasoning to explain the trend of their results. [3]

Using a micro-hydroelectric system to supply a village

Micro-hydroelectric generators can be installed anywhere that there is a flow of water with a reasonable drop in height. The graph below is used to estimate the amount of power that could be generated with a micro-hydroelectric power station in a particular geographical situation. The amount of water that flows down the river is plotted on the x-axis and the vertical drop that the river falls by is shown on the y-axis. By measuring these properties of the river and plotting their values on the graph, the amount of power that could be generated can be found.

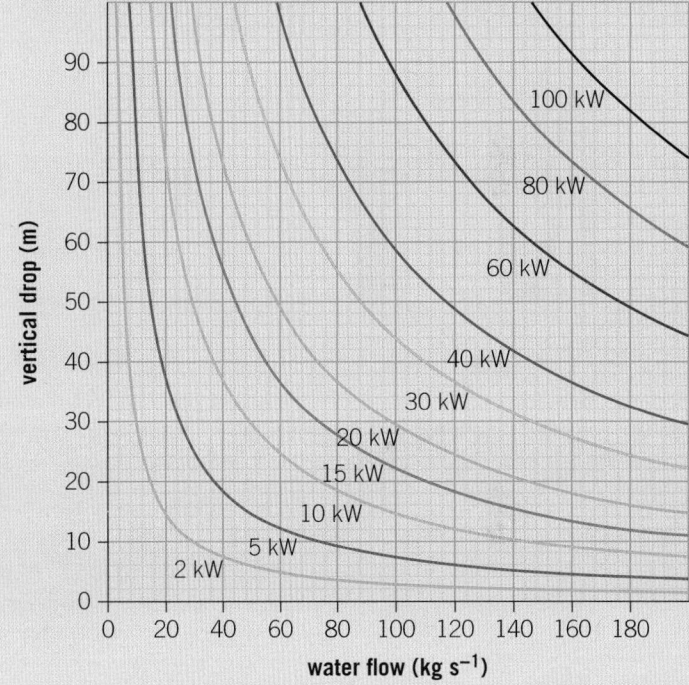

13. A village is near a river which drops 30 m in height. The average flow rate of the river is about 100 kg s^{-1}. How much power could be generated from this site? [2]

14. In the wettest season the flow rate of the river can be double its average and in dry season the flow can be halved. In these seasons, what power could be generated from the river? [4]

15. To generate 50 kW of power from a river with a drop of 80 m, what flow rate is required? [4]

16. By taking a value from the graph, calculate the efficiency of a micro-hydroelectric generator. [5]

Can hydroelectricity solve the world's energy problems?

17. The Earth's average rainfall is about 1 m per year. The surface area of the Earth is about 5×10^{14} m^2. Given that the density of water is 1,000 kg m^{-3}, show that the total mass of water that falls as rain is 5×10^{17} kg. [2]

18. The total world consumption of energy in one year is about 5×10^{20} J. Calculate the vertical drop that the Earth's annual rainfall would require in order to supply this energy. [3]

19. Comment on the following statement: Hydroelectricity cannot solve the world's energy problems. [4]

20. Imagine that you are encouraging a remote community on a mountainside to install a micro-hydroelectric generator. Write a brief article explaining how the hydroelectric plant works and why it is worth investing in. Try to use simple scientific terms correctly. [6]

12 Patterns

Patterns are regular, rhythmic, repeating or predictable sequences.

▲ The patterns on these animals have different purposes. Can you identify what they are?

Snowflakes form in many different patterns, although they are usually hexagonal. The patterns that are formed depend on the temperature and humidity of the atmosphere at the point where they form. How else can the conditions of the atmosphere and weather create patterns?

The patterns in this rock are called banded iron formations. The rock contains layers of iron compounds which were formed when early bacteria (called cyanobacteria) that could photosynthesize first evolved. As these bacteria released oxygen into the oceans, it reacted with iron to form insoluble iron oxides which were deposited as layers in this rock. What other patterns can tell us about the past?

Key concept: Relationships

Related concept: Patterns

Global context: Identities and relationships

Introduction

People are good at spotting patterns. It enables us to identify cause and effect, and to predict the outcomes of situations based on past experiences. Pattern recognition is likely to have evolved as a survival mechanism; for example, learning which plants are good to eat and which creatures are dangerous is something that almost all animals need to learn for survival.

Patterns underpin scientific observation. Scientists carry out experiments to see if changing one variable causes a predictable outcome in another. When they discover a pattern, scientists look to develop a theory to explain the relationship and then test that theory with further experiments. Sometimes we think we see patterns where there isn't any underlying relationship. This is the basis of superstitious beliefs and conspiracy theories. Science provides a structure for testing these patterns with experiments to determine which are real. The key concept of this chapter is relationships and the global context is identities and relationships.

Some processes in physics, such as the radioactive decay of atomic nuclei, are random. In this case this means that there is no way of predicting when any nucleus will decay. However, using statistics, we can still describe the pattern of their decay. In this chapter we look at how patterns can be found in radioactive decay.

▼ By analysing the X-ray diffraction pattern of iridium metal, scientists can deduce the arrangement and size of the iridium atoms

Statement of inquiry:

Patterns can demonstrate relationships between events and shed light on how they are caused.

The feathers of these macaws reflect different wavelengths of light and hence appear as different colors to us

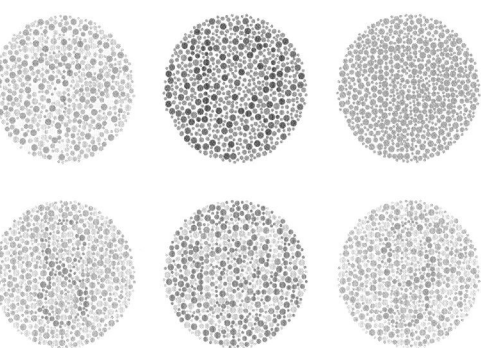

Many patterns use different colors, however, some individuals cannot distinguish the full range of colors that most people can. Color blindness is rare in women, but affects about 8% of men. These patterns are used to test for color blindness. People with normal color vision see numbers in the patterns, but people with color blindness may not

Sometimes patterns are appealing or pretty. Humans have good color vision and we are able to see the world in many colors. In this chapter we see how different colors form a spectrum and how there are other frequencies of light that are beyond our vision.

Rainbows

This girl is watering the garden. The water from the hose creates a rainbow. Rainbows are formed in the sky when rain water reflects the Sun's light. For this to occur there must be a patch of sky with rainclouds, but also a clear part of the sky so that the Sun is unobscured by clouds. The Sun's light refracts in the water droplets and bounces off the back surface through total internal reflection (see Chapter 9, Development). Because different wavelengths of light refract through slightly different angles, the light is split into a rainbow.

1. Can you think of any other situations where light is split into a spectrum?

2. What shape is a rainbow?

What is visible light?

The Sun emits a lot of light – about 10^{45} photons every second. These have different wavelengths and frequencies, and they are emitted in different directions. Although these waves have differing wavelengths and frequencies, they all travel at the same speed: $3 \times 10^8\,\mathrm{m\,s^{-1}}$, the speed of light. About 10^{36} photons hit the Earth's atmosphere every second. The different properties of these photons affect the way in which they interact with matter and hence whether they pass through the atmosphere. Although lots of photons are absorbed, there is a small band of wavelengths – from about 300 nm to about 1,000 nm – where the photons pass through the atmosphere. Most animals on the planet have evolved to be able to detect these photons. The range of wavelengths visible to humans, from 400 to 700 nm, is called visible light.

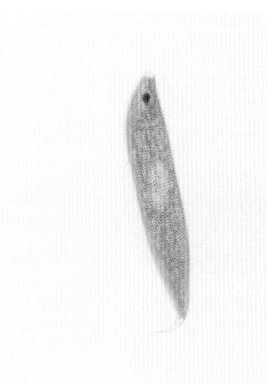 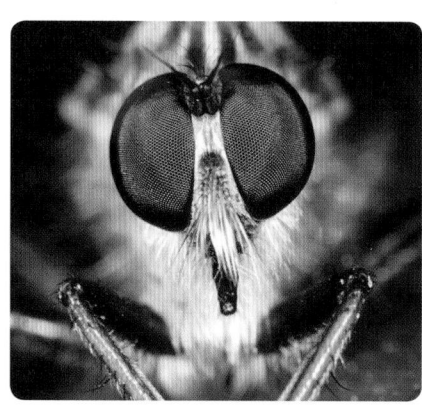 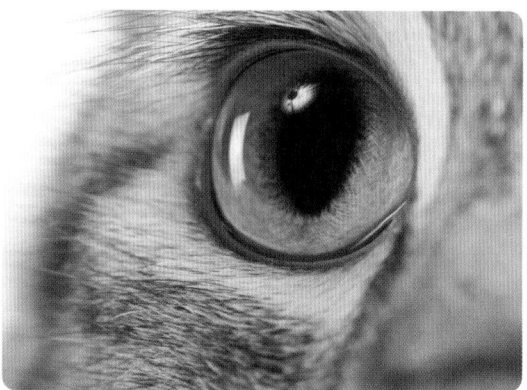

▲ The ability to detect light has evolved in many different organisms. The single-celled organism euglena (left) has an eyespot, a small area that is sensitive to light and allows it to move towards the light. It is unable to detect shapes or color. Insects (center) have compound eyes allowing them to detect more detail and even different colors. Mammals (right) have complex eyes with lenses which allow for focusing detailed images

How do we see?

The eye works by using a lens to focus an image onto the back of the eye. Muscles in the eye stretch the lens into different shapes in order to focus objects that are at different distances from the eye. At the back of the eye there is the retina, an area of light-sensitive detectors. These are connected to the optic nerve which transmits the signal to the brain.

The retina has two types of detectors: rods and cones. Rod cells are very sensitive to low levels of light. They are spread around the retina and so they are not good for detailed vision and they are also unable to detect color. This is why you can see in a dark room, but you cannot read or make out the color of objects.

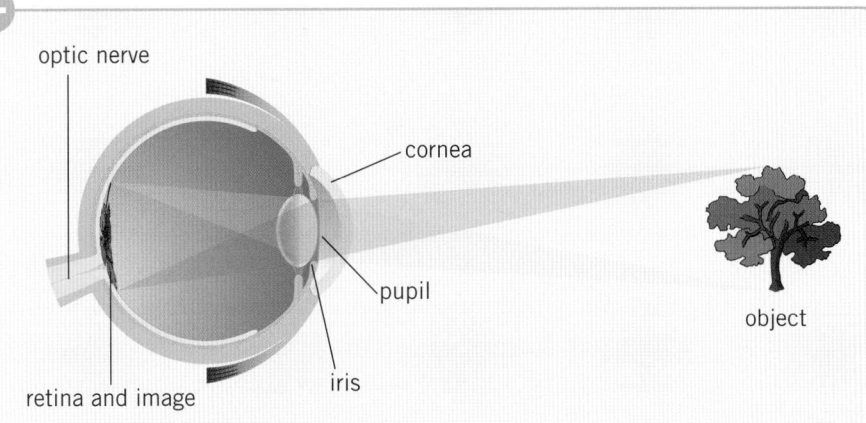

optic nerve
cornea
pupil
object
iris
retina and image

In the center of the retina is the fovea, an area of cone cells. The cone cells are less sensitive to light, but they are tightly packed, so they enable detailed vision. This is why you are able to read, but only if the writing is directly in front of you. The cones come in three types which are able to detect three different colors. One type is most sensitive to green–yellow light at about 560 nm, another is most sensitive to green light at about 530 nm and the third type is most sensitive to blue light at about 420 nm. Our brain can detect the relative amounts of these colors so it can interpret the color.

1. Focus on the picture of the oil film at the bottom of this page. Can you still read this question?

2. Dim the lights in a room until you cannot read these words. Look at the picture of the oil film in the dim light. Can you make out the different colors?

3. Can you explain your observations above?

What is color?

WAVES

When light shines on a surface, some of it might be reflected and some might be absorbed. Different surfaces absorb or reflect different wavelengths of light and this gives them color. A black surface absorbs all the light that hits it and none is reflected; this is why it appears dark. On the other hand, a white surface reflects most of the light; this combination of all colors appears white.

◀ When a thin film of oil forms on water, small variations in its thickness cause it to absorb or reflect different wavelengths of light. This causes it to appear different colors

261

When white light which contains visible light of many different wavelengths is split up to show its component colors, we see a spectrum or a rainbow. The visible light with the longest wavelengths, around 700 nm, is red. Blue–violet light has the shortest wavelength, about 400 nm.

In between red and violet, there is a continuous spectrum of color. The colors appear in the order red, orange, yellow, green, blue, indigo and violet, although the color indigo is sometimes omitted. There are also gradual variations in between each of these so that red gradually merges into orange and then yellow rather than there being distinct transitions.

1. Red light has a wavelength around 650 nm, the wavelength of yellow is about 570 nm and blue is about 475 nm. A certain color of light has a frequency of 5.66×10^{14} Hz. What color is this light?

▲ The refractive index of glass varies slightly with different wavelengths. As a result, the different colors of light are refracted by slightly different amounts and so this prism splits white light into a spectrum

Information literacy skills

Using mnemonics to remember sequences

There are many ways to remember the order of the colors of the rainbow. Often people use mnemonics to remember the order. This is where the first letter of each word is used to construct a new sentence.

Try to create your own mnemonic using the letters R O Y G B I V in that order. You could also try to create a mnemonic for the order of the components of the electromagnetic spectrum discussed later in this chapter.

Thinking in context

Color and identity

Different colors can invoke different moods. For example, red is often associated with anger or passion while blue is a thought to be more calming. Interior designers use this when deciding what mood to try to create in different rooms, and people's clothes can sometimes express their mood or their identity.

Two colors, pink and blue, are particularly linked to identity in that pink often has feminine associations and blue, masculine associations. Despite these associations being widespread throughout Europe and America, the trend was the opposite only 100 years ago in America with pink being thought of as for boys and blue for girls.

What lies beyond the visible spectrum?

The visible spectrum is a continual range of wavelengths from 400 to 700 nm, but just because we don't see wavelengths outside this range does not mean that they do not exist or are not useful to us.

The wavelength of light can vary considerably outside the visible range. Some photons of light have tiny wavelengths of 10^{-11} m or less, and other light can have wavelengths which are a kilometer or longer.

This continuum of waves is called the electromagnetic spectrum. Just like the spectrum of visible light, the electromagnetic spectrum is continuous; however, we divide it into seven different parts. Starting with the longest wavelengths, the electromagnetic spectrum consists of radio waves, microwaves, infrared, visible light, ultraviolet, X-rays and gamma rays.

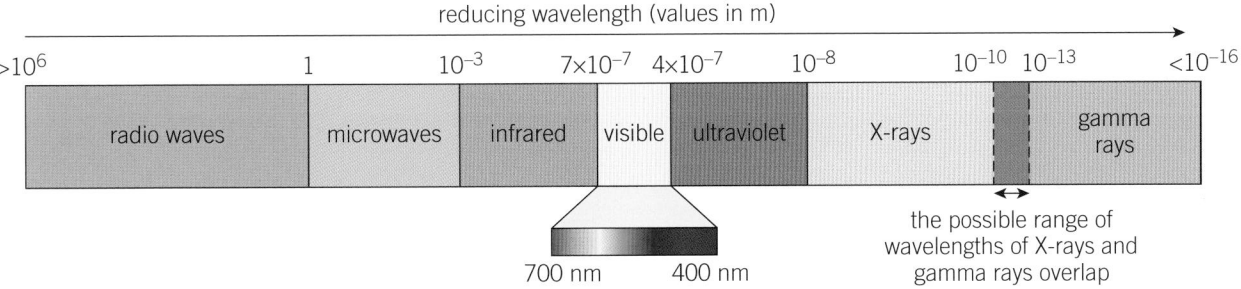

▲ The electromagnetic spectrum is divided into seven regions: radio waves, microwaves, infrared, visible light, ultraviolet, X-rays and gamma rays

These waves have different wavelengths and frequencies and, as a result, they behave in different ways. They are also often emitted from different types of objects which leads to them being classed as different parts of the electromagnetic spectrum. However, these different waves all have many properties in common. They all travel at the same speed, the speed of light (3×10^8 m s^{-1} in a vacuum). Also, they are all transverse waves (see Chapter 1, Models).

1. A remote control uses light at 940 nm.

    a) In which part of the electromagnetic spectrum does this lie?

    b) Calculate the frequency of the light.

2. Photons of light emitted from a nucleus of $^{60}_{28}$Ni have a frequency of 3.2×10^{20} Hz.

    a) In which region of the electromagnetic spectrum is this radiation classed?

    b) Calculate the wavelength of these photons.

What's so special about the speed of light?

In the 17th century, it was believed that light traveled so fast that it didn't have a speed, but that it traveled instantaneously from its source to its destination. However, studies later in the 17th century started to show that it had a finite speed.

In the mid-18th century, James Clerk Maxwell showed that the speed of an electromagnetic wave, a wave consisting of a magnetic and electric field at right angles, was very close to the speed of light. As a result, he deduced that this was what a light wave was.

Maxwell's results also showed that the speed of these waves could not be any faster and that the speed of light represented a maximum possible speed.

▶ A light wave is a combination of oscillating magnetic and electric fields

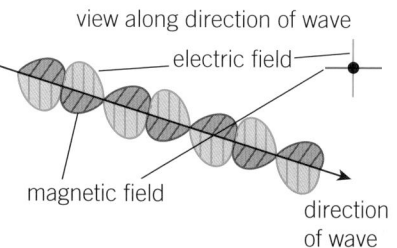

view along direction of wave

electric field

magnetic field

direction of wave

In 1905, Einstein published his theory of special relativity which suggested that light always travels at the same speed. This has some strange results. If a stationary car shines its headlights at you, the light travels at 299,792,458 m s^{-1}. If the car is driving towards you at 50 m s^{-1}, the light still leaves the car at 299,792,458 m s^{-1} relative to the car and you might expect the light to hit you at 299,792,508 m s^{-1}; however, it still hits you at 299,792,458 m s^{-1}!

How does this happen? Since the speed of light doesn't change, the perceived time taken must be different. As the car approaches you, it experiences time at a slower rate than you. This is why, although the light appears to be moving more slowly than it should from your viewpoint, the passengers in the car do not notice because their time progresses more slowly and so they see the light travel at the same speed.

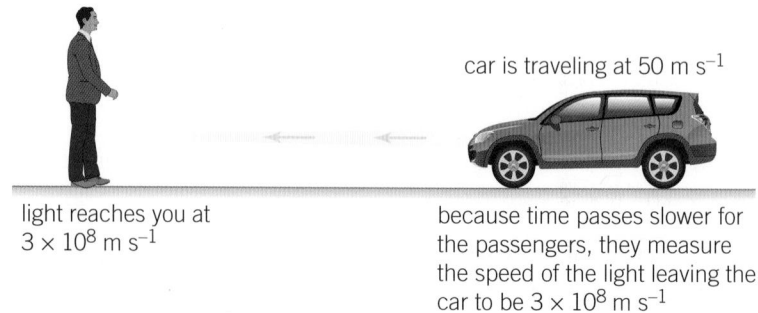

car is traveling at 50 m s^{-1}

light reaches you at 3 × 10^8 m s^{-1}

because time passes slower for the passengers, they measure the speed of the light leaving the car to be 3 × 10^8 m s^{-1}

Although the idea that moving objects experience time to be slower seems strange, it has been tested with experiments and shown to be true. However, large effects only occur when objects travel very close to the speed of light.

What happens at long wavelengths?

As the wavelength of light increases beyond 700 nm, out of the visible range, the light becomes invisible; however, it still behaves in a similar way to visible light. This light is called infrared light (*infra* means below).

> ### Observing near-infrared light
>
> Remote controls use light that is only just outside the range of human vision, but a digital camera such as a webcam or the camera on a mobile phone is usually able to detect it.
>
> Use the camera of a mobile phone or a webcam to view a remote control and press one of the buttons on it. You should be able to detect the flashes of light even though they are invisible to your eyes.

Infrared light is emitted by warm objects. Objects with temperatures around 30°C, such as people and animals, emit wavelengths around 10 μm. As an object is heated, the wavelengths of the light emitted decrease. If something is heated to 1,000°C, most light is emitted at about 2 μm. Some of the light will even have a short enough wavelength that it is visible. As a result, a very hot object visibly glows.

Infrared light may be used in night vision equipment to enable cameras to operate at night. Monitoring buildings in infrared light can also help to assess whether they are well insulated; if heat escapes from a certain place, it will show up on a photograph taken using infrared light.

▲ This hut appears differently when viewed in infrared light on the left and visible light on the right. The window and door are cooler than the walls and the roof which shows that the hut is well insulated, although you can tell that the heater is on the right of the door, under the window. The boy standing in front of the hut appears much warmer than anything else

Although cold objects emit longer wavelengths of light, they do not emit much light beyond 100 μm. As a result, longer wavelengths of light, about 1 mm or longer, come from a different source. These are microwaves and radio waves. Microwaves have wavelengths from 1 mm to about 1 m. Those waves with wavelengths longer than a meter are radio waves, although the wavelength ranges of microwaves and radio waves are often considered to overlap.

Waves with a longer wavelength diffract more than waves with a shorter wavelength (Chapter 9, Development). As a result, microwaves and radio waves diffract easily and are able to spread out past obstacles. This makes them useful for communications as they can travel large distances and their diffraction makes them detectable when the broadcasting aerial is not visible.

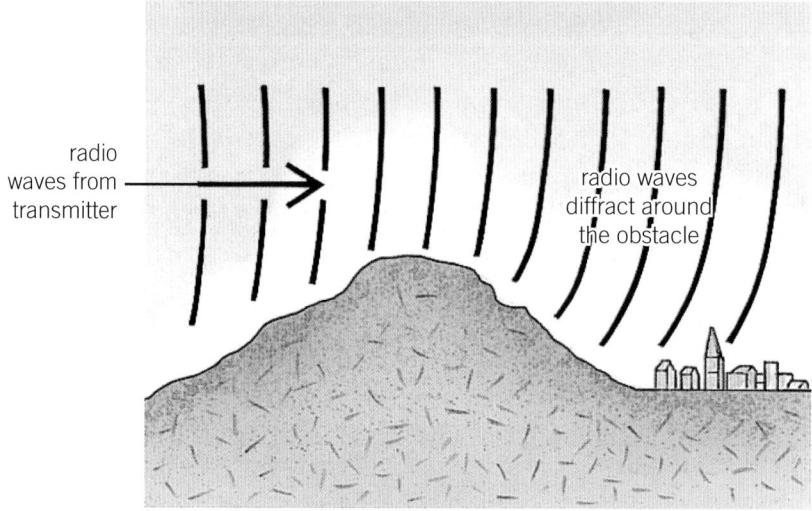

radio waves from transmitter

radio waves diffract around the obstacle

▲ Microwaves and radio waves have long wavelengths, so they diffract around obstacles. As a result, signals can be detected even if you do not have a direct line of sight to the transmitter

▲ An oven emits microwaves at a frequency of 2.45 GHz; these are absorbed by water in the food, which heats up and cooks it

Microwaves are used in mobile phone communication as well as wireless internet connections and bluetooth. Many wavelengths of microwave are absorbed by water in the air, so they are only suitable for short-range communication. However, there are some frequencies of microwaves which are not absorbed by water in the atmosphere. These can travel further through the atmosphere, so they can be used to communicate with satellites or for mobile phone communication with tall masts.

Radio waves can also bounce off a layer of the atmosphere called the ionosphere. This increases their range further and makes radio communication over thousands of kilometers possible.

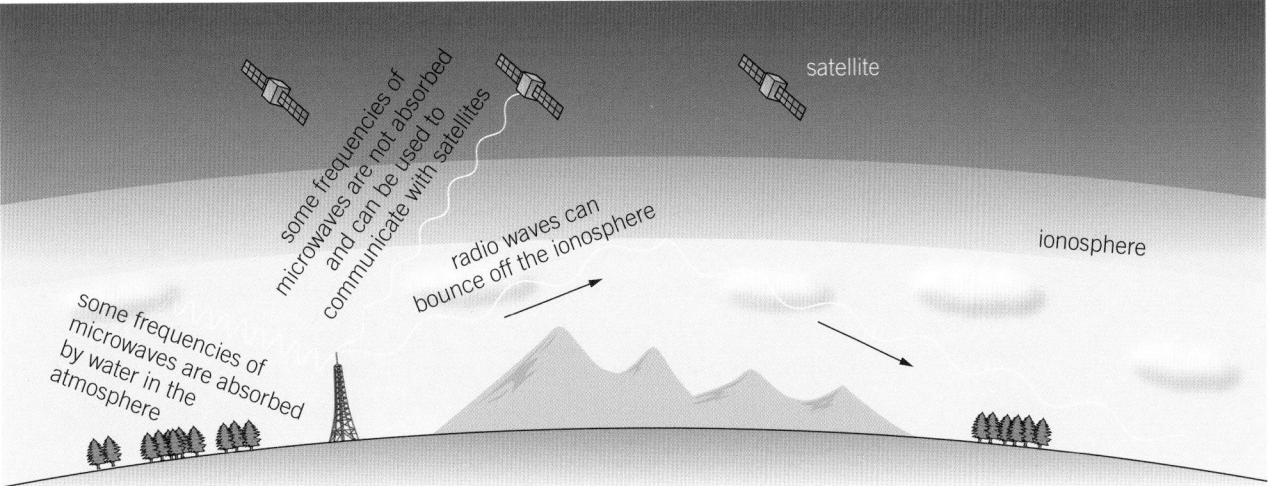

▲ Radio waves bounce off the ionosphere. This increases the range over which they can be used to communicate. Some frequencies of microwaves are absorbed by water in the atmosphere; others can pass through the atmosphere and be used to communicate with satellites

1. A radio signal is broadcast at 200 kHz. Calculate the wavelength of this broadcast. (Remember that all electromagnetic waves travel at the speed of light.)

2. Mobile phones which operate on a 4G system use wavelengths of 800 MHz, 1.8 GHz and 2.6 GHz.

   a) Which of these has the smallest wavelength?

   b) Express 800 MHz in GHz.

   c) Calculate the wavelength and time period of the 2.6 GHz frequency.

What happens at shorter wavelengths?

WAVES

Humans can perceive light with wavelengths as short as 400 nm, but if the wavelength decreases much beyond this it becomes invisible to us. This is ultraviolet light (meaning beyond violet) which is often abbreviated to UV. Ultraviolet light has wavelengths from 400 nm down to about 10 nm.

UV light which is only just outside the range of human vision is often called near ultraviolet or UVA. Some animals can see this light. Some chemicals can absorb ultraviolet light and re-emit it as visible light. This is called fluorescence. It is used in printing some banknotes to make them harder to forge; if such a banknote is held under an ultraviolet light it shows a pattern that is not normally visible.

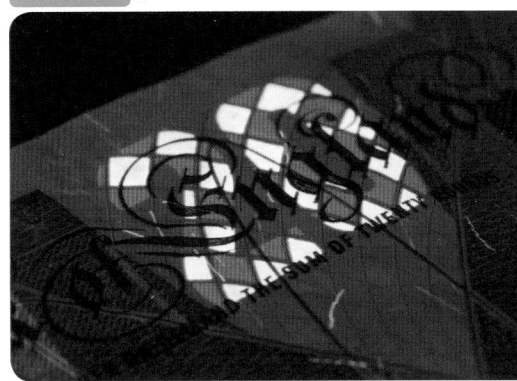

▲ The patterned 20 on this banknote is not normally visible. When UV light is shone on it, the special ink fluoresces and is visible. This makes the banknote harder to forge

1. UVA light has wavelengths of 315–400 nm and UVB has wavelengths of 280–315 nm.

   a) Which of these regions is closer to visible light?

   b) In which UV range does light with a frequency of 10^{15} Hz lie?

Below about 300 nm, the atmosphere starts to absorb UV light. This is very useful since these wavelengths of light are dangerous to humans. They can cause skin cancer (melanoma) and cataracts in the eyes. The range of wavelengths between 280 and 315 nm are of particular concern because some of the energy can get through the atmosphere and harm us. These waves are called UVB. This is why we are advised to apply sunscreen (which blocks UVB) when we are outside in strong sun. When skiing, you have a higher altitude so there is less atmosphere above you to block out UVB rays. For this reason you are advised to wear sunglasses or goggles to block UVB.

Below 280 nm, the UV light is completely absorbed by the atmosphere, so we are saved from its damaging effects.

ATL Collaboration skills

Building consensus

The layer of the atmosphere which blocks harmful UV light is called the ozone layer. Ozone is a molecule of oxygen with three oxygen atoms (O_3) in it rather than the usual two (O_2). In the 1970s, scientists noticed that the levels of ozone in the atmosphere were decreasing and the cause was found to be chlorine-based compounds, particularly chlorofluorocarbons (CFCs) which were used in aerosols and refrigerants.

In the 1980s, an international agreement called the Montreal Protocol was reached to remove CFCs from use. These chemicals stay in the upper atmosphere for a long time, and so there was no immediate change in the levels of ozone. The amount of ozone started to stabilize in the 1990s, and in the 2000s it started to recover. It will take many decades for ozone levels to fully recover, but the Montreal Protocol is regarded as the most successful intervention on climate change to date.

WAVES

What are the shortest wavelengths of light?

Light with wavelengths that are shorter than UV light, less than 10 nm, fall into the final two parts of the electromagnetic spectrum: X-rays and gamma rays. X-rays have wavelengths that are less than about 10 nm and gamma rays generally have wavelengths less than 100 pm (a picometer is 10^{-12} m).

There is an overlap between the ranges of X-rays and gamma rays. Often the distinction between these two regions of the electromagnetic spectrum depends on the source of the waves. X-rays are normally produced using high voltages whereas gamma rays are emitted from the nucleus of an atom when it decays.

X-rays with wavelengths from 10 nm down to about 0.1 nm are called soft X-rays. They are easily absorbed by air and can only travel a couple of centimeters before being absorbed.

1. If soft X-rays have wavelengths of 10–0.1 nm and hard X-rays have wavelengths less than 0.1 nm, what type of X-ray has a frequency of 3×10^{17} Hz?

X-rays with wavelengths smaller than 0.1 nm are called hard X-rays. They can travel large distances through air and can pass through many solid materials easily. Hard X-rays are useful in medical imaging. They pass through soft tissue and can be detected on the other side, but bone, metal and other dense objects absorb more of the hard X-rays and leave a shadow.

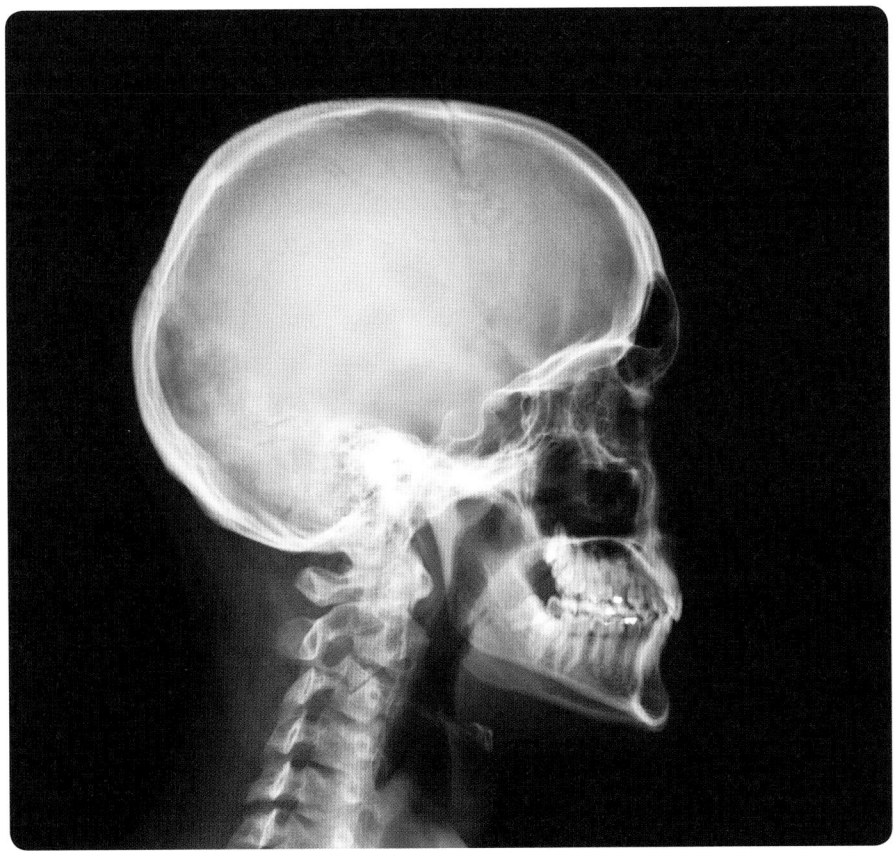

▲ An X-ray of the head. The bones show up because they absorb X-rays better than the soft tissue

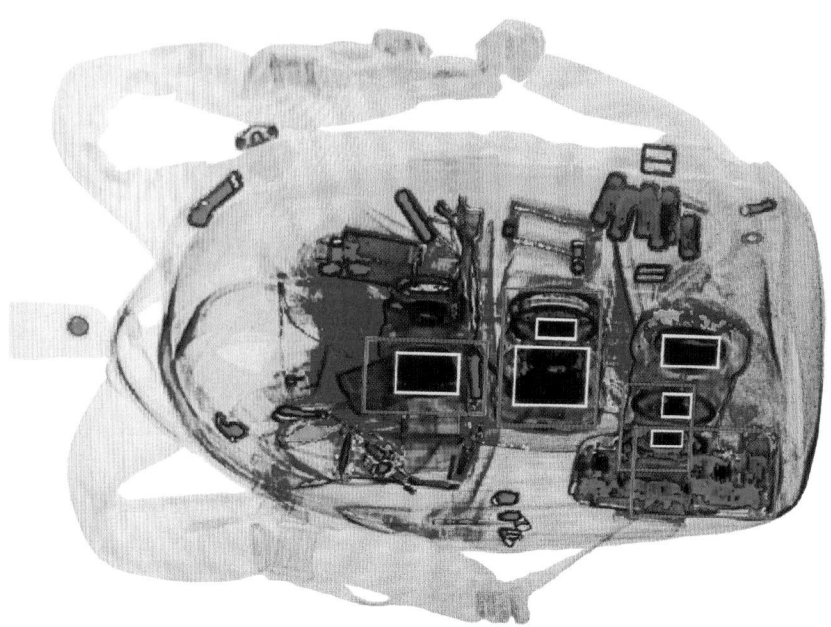

▶ At airports, luggage is scanned with an X-ray scanner before it is allowed on board. What precautions are needed to ensure that this is safe? Why are X-rays not used in the scanners that detect whether you have any metal objects on you?

Like hard X-rays, gamma rays can also travel large distances in air and pass through many solid materials. Gamma rays are used in medical imaging. A source of gamma rays can be introduced to a part of the body. The source of the rays is chosen according to the part of the body that is going to be imaged, so they might be injected, eaten or even breathed in. The gamma rays that are emitted can be detected outside the body. Unlike X-rays which create a shadow, gamma rays are emitted from the organ that is being imaged, so they can be used to see soft tissue. This makes them useful for detecting blockages, tumors and other abnormal growths.

Although X-rays and gamma rays are very useful, the photons have high energy and this can make them damaging. When photons of X-rays or gamma rays hit an atom, they have enough energy to knock an electron out of it, changing the atom into an ion. For this reason, X-rays and gamma rays are classed as ionizing radiation.

If a person is exposed to high doses of X-rays or gamma rays, molecules in their body may be ionized. In the vast majority of cases, this will not cause any ill effect; however, it is possible for the ionization to cause a mutation in a person's DNA. Even then, DNA is often able to repair these mutations. In some cases, however, a mutation might lead to cancer.

As a result of the dangers of X-rays and gamma rays, it is important to avoid unnecessary exposure to these waves. This is why, if you have an X-ray scan, the person who operates the scanner stands behind a protective screen or wears protective clothing. The risk of a

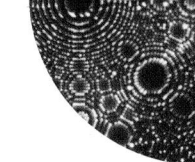

single X-ray scan to the patient is very small and such a scan is only taken if there is a medical reason to do so; however, the cumulative effects of many X-ray scans every day to the people who operate the machine is dangerous, so they must be shielded from the waves.

Why do nuclei decay?

NUCLEAR PHYSICS

Gamma rays are short wavelength rays emitted from atomic nuclei. Atoms are made up of electrons around a central nucleus (see Chapter 1, Models). So what causes a nucleus to decay?

A nucleus is tiny – about 10,000 times smaller than the atom itself and made up of protons and neutrons. The protons carry a positive charge so they repel each other. Because they are so close together in the nucleus, the repulsive force between them is quite large – 10 to 100 N, an enormous force to be acting on a tiny particle. You might expect that such a force would cause all nuclei (apart from hydrogen) to disintegrate instantly; however, there must be an attractive force which holds the protons together. This force is the residual strong force. Because the strong force only acts over very short ranges, we do not detect its effects outside of the nucleus.

If the nucleus is not able to hold itself together, or if there is a better arrangement of the protons and neutrons that has less energy and is more stable as a result, then the nucleus decays.

1. A force of 10 N is an enormous force to be exerted on a proton which has a mass of 1.67×10^{-27} kg.

   a) Using the equation $F = ma$, calculate the acceleration of a proton which experiences a 10 N force.

   b) The size of an atomic nucleus is about 10^{-15} m. If the proton is accelerated across this distance by a 10 N force, use the equation $W = Fd$ to calculate the work done by the force.

   c) As this work is transferred to kinetic energy, calculate the final speed of the proton.

   d) Why does the electrostatic repulsion of protons in the nucleus not affect a nucleus of hydrogen?

What happens if a nucleus is too big?

NUCLEAR PHYSICS

Small, stable nuclei tend to have as many protons as neutrons. The repulsive electrostatic force between the protons is balanced by the residual strong interaction of the protons and neutrons. Larger stable nuclei with more than 20 protons, on the other hand, tend to have more neutrons than protons. This is because the range of the strong force is very small. Although the repulsive interaction of the protons stretches across the entire nucleus, the attractive strong force gets considerably weaker over these distances. More neutrons are required to hold the nucleus together.

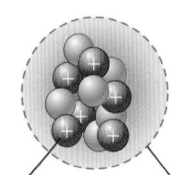
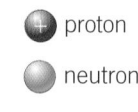
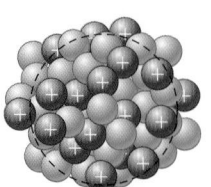

proton

neutron

Protons are repelled by other protons

Protons and neutrons are held together by the strong nuclear force. The range of the force from the central neutron is shown

Large nuclei can become bigger than the range of the strong nuclear force. More neutrons are now required to hold the nucleus together.

▲ Small stable nuclei have approximately the same number of protons and neutrons. Larger stable nuclei need more neutrons to hold them together because of the short range of the strong nuclear force. Very big nuclei become too large to be stable. These nuclei tend to decay by alpha decay

Very large nuclei become more unstable. The largest stable isotope is an isotope of lead ($^{208}_{82}$Pb, Chapter 1, Models explains this notation); any nucleus larger than this will decay. The most common way for large nuclei to decay is by emitting a helium nucleus, also known as an alpha particle. This is because a helium nucleus is very stable, and by losing a helium nucleus, the large nucleus becomes smaller and more stable. This process is called alpha decay.

When a large nucleus emits an alpha particle, the remaining nucleus, often called a daughter nucleus, is now smaller as it has lost two protons and two neutrons. This can be written as a nuclear equation. For example, the decay of americium-241 ($^{241}_{95}$Am) can be written as:

$$^{241}_{95}\text{Am} \rightarrow {}^{237}_{93}\text{Np} + {}^{4}_{2}\alpha$$

The atomic number (the number of protons) decreases by two from 95 to 93 meaning that the daughter nucleus is the element neptunium. The mass number decreases by four from 241 to 237 to account for the loss of two protons and two neutrons.

In general the equation for alpha decay is:

$$^{A}_{Z}\text{X} \rightarrow {}^{(A-4)}_{(Z-2)}\text{Y} + {}^{4}_{2}\alpha$$

The alpha particles or helium nuclei emitted when a nucleus decays by alpha emission have high energy and travel at speeds of around $1.5 \times 10^7 \, \text{m s}^{-1}$. They have a charge of $2e$ ($2 \times 1.6 \times 10^{-19} \, \text{C}$) and as a result they ionize atoms and molecules that they pass near to by attracting the electrons towards the alpha particle. This means that alpha radiation is classed as ionizing radiation. In fact, it is so good at ionizing the material that it passes through that it loses energy quickly and as a result does not travel very far. Alpha radiation only travels a few centimeters in air and is stopped by a thin sheet of paper.

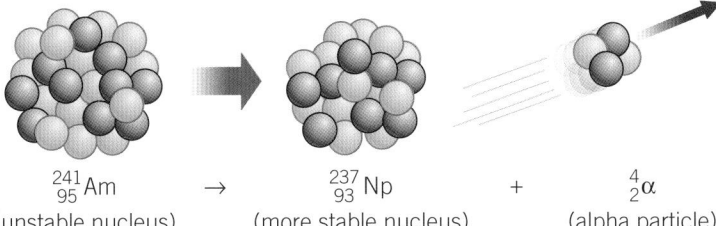

$$^{241}_{95}\text{Am} \quad \rightarrow \quad ^{237}_{93}\text{Np} \quad + \quad ^{4}_{2}\alpha$$

(unstable nucleus) (more stable nucleus) (alpha particle)

▲ A large nucleus can decay by alpha decay. It emits an alpha particle (a helium nucleus consisting of two protons and two neutrons) so it becomes smaller

1. Astatine is the rarest naturally occurring element on Earth. Nuclei of its most stable isotope $^{210}_{85}\text{At}$ only last an average of 12 hours before they decay by alpha decay. What does $^{210}_{85}\text{At}$ decay into? You may need a periodic table to find which element is formed.

2. Radon gas ($^{222}_{86}\text{Rn}$) is formed when uranium-234 ($^{234}_{92}\text{U}$) decays by a series of alpha decays. How many alpha decays are needed for uranium-234 to decay to radon-222?

How else can a nucleus be unstable?

NUCLEAR PHYSICS

Small stable nuclei tend to have similar numbers of protons and neutrons and larger nuclei have slightly more neutrons. If nuclei have too many or too few neutrons compared to the number of protons, they can become unstable. A nucleus with too many neutrons can restore the balance and become more stable if a neutron turns into a proton. If a neutron does this, it also emits a high-speed electron from the nucleus. This is called a beta particle and the process is called beta decay.

The process by which a neutron turns into a proton can be written as the equation:

$$^{1}_{0}\text{n} \rightarrow ^{1}_{1}\text{p} + ^{0}_{-1}\beta$$

The electron or beta particle is given the mass number 0 and the atomic number -1 in order to balance the equation.

An example of beta decay is the decay of carbon-14. The most abundant isotope (see Chapter 1, Models) of carbon is carbon-12 which has six protons and six neutrons. Carbon-14 is much rarer as it has two extra neutrons which make the nucleus unstable. The equation for the decay of carbon-14 into nitrogen-14 is:

$$^{14}_{6}\text{C} \rightarrow ^{14}_{7}\text{N} + ^{0}_{-1}\beta$$

The total number of protons and neutrons remains the same, but by turning one neutron into a proton, the balance in the number of protons and neutrons is restored to seven of each. The general equation for a nucleus decaying by beta emission is:

$$_Z^A X \rightarrow \,_{(Z+1)}^A Y + \,_{-1}^0 \beta$$

It is important to distinguish between the electrons which are emitted in beta decay and the electrons which orbit around the nucleus in the atom. Compared to the tiny size of the nucleus, the orbital electrons are a long way from the nucleus and do not take part in the decay. Beta particles, on the other hand, are emitted from the nucleus as part of the decay process. They travel very fast, straight out of the nucleus, and interact with the matter they pass though.

Beta particles also ionize the matter they pass through. Because of their high speeds, which can be 70% to 90% of the speed of light, they pass other atoms and molecules very quickly and do not interact with them for long. As a result, they are not as ionizing as alpha radiation, so they travel further in air. Beta particles can travel a few meters in air and pass through materials that would stop alpha particles. A metal sheet a few millimeters thick stops beta particles.

▶ An unstable nucleus with too many neutrons can decay by beta emission. A neutron in the nucleus changes into a proton and emits a beta particle (a high-speed electron) in the process

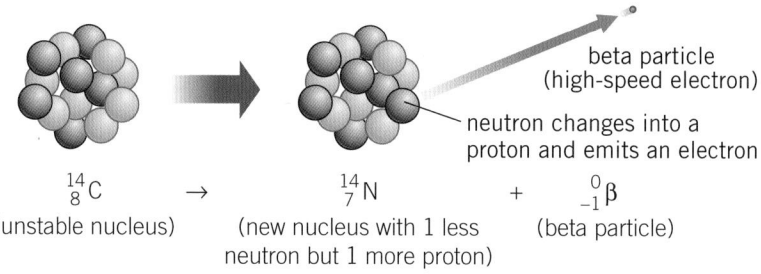

$$_8^{14} C \qquad \rightarrow \qquad _7^{14} N \qquad + \qquad _{-1}^0 \beta$$

(unstable nucleus)   (new nucleus with 1 less neutron but 1 more proton)   (beta particle)

1. Nitrogen-16 ($_7^{16}$N) is an isotope of nitrogen with two more neutrons than the more common nitrogen-14. It decays through beta decay. What will it decay into? (You may need a periodic table to find which element it decays into.)

2. Iodine-135 ($_{53}^{135}$I) is created in nuclear power plants. It decays into barium-135 ($_{56}^{135}$Ba) through a series of beta decays. How many beta decays must occur?

NUCLEAR PHYSICS

How can a nucleus emit gamma rays?

After alpha or beta decay, the nucleus can be left in an excited state. This means that it has excess energy. The nucleus can undergo a further decay process where it settles into a more stable state. In doing so it releases energy in the form of a high-energy photon. This process is called gamma decay and the high-energy photons, gamma rays, are the most energetic part of the electromagnetic spectrum with the shortest wavelengths.

Gamma decay does not involve a change in the structure of the nucleus, hence the equation for gamma decay is:

$$_Z^A X^* \rightarrow\ _Z^A X + _0^0 \gamma$$

where * indicates that the initial nucleus was in an excited state.

Like alpha and beta particles, gamma rays are ionizing. However, since the photons have no charge, they do not interact as strongly with the matter that they pass through, so they are less ionizing than alpha and beta radiation. As a result, they are harder to stop and travel further through air. Gamma rays can travel kilometers through air and are only blocked by a thick layer of dense material (often a couple of centimeters of lead).

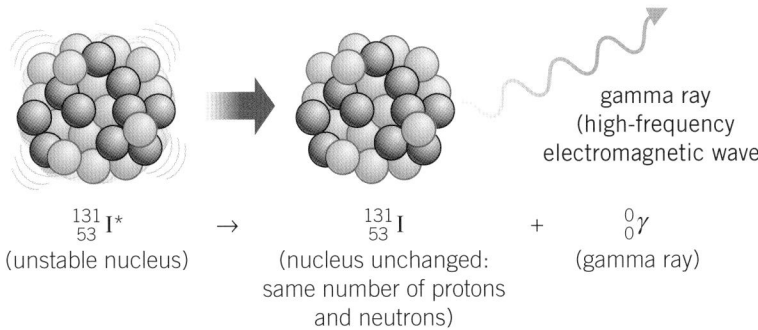

$$_{53}^{131} I^* \qquad \rightarrow \qquad _{53}^{131} I \qquad + \qquad _0^0 \gamma$$
(unstable nucleus)   (nucleus unchanged: same number of protons and neutrons)   (gamma ray)

▲ After a nuclear decay, the nucleus may be left in an excited state meaning that it has excess energy. It can release this energy by emitting a gamma ray, a high-energy photon

How do we measure nuclear decay?

Nuclear radiation can be detected with a Geiger–Müller tube. Radiation that passes into the tube ionizes the gas inside it. The positive ions that are created from this ionization are attracted to the outside of the tube which is negatively charged, and the electrons are attracted to the positively charged electrode.

When the electrons arrive at the central electrode, they create a small electrical pulse which can be counted. The counting circuit counts the number of pulses from the Geiger–Müller tube over a period of time, say 10 s. Dividing the number of counts by the period of time (10 s) gives the number of counts per second.

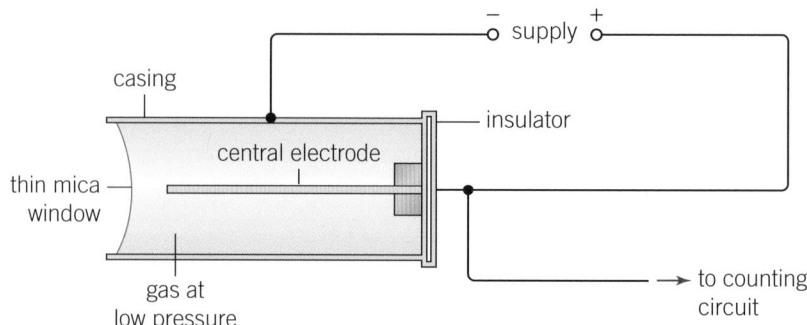

▲ A Geiger–Müller tube can be used to detect radiation

The number of counts per second is called the count rate. It is measured in becquerels (Bq) where 1 Bq is 1 count per second. The count rate is proportional to the activity of the source. The activity is the number of decays per second in the source which can also be measured in becquerels. The difference between the count rate and the activity is that the activity refers to the total number of decays whereas the measured count rate is smaller because not all the decays are detected.

1. Why is it important to design a Geiger–Müller tube to have a thin front window if it is to be used to detect alpha radiation?

2. The activity of a radioactive sample is tested with a Geiger–Müller tube. The number of counts in one minute is measured three times and found to be 277, 251 and 282. If the Geiger–Müller tube detects 25% of the radiation emitted, calculate the measured activity.

NUCLEAR PHYSICS

When will a nucleus decay?

Nuclear decay is a random process which means that it is impossible to predict when a nucleus will decay. It is also very difficult to cause a nucleus to decay since it is a tiny part of the atom at the center. Heating a substance causes the atoms to collide with each other with more energy, but this only affects the electrons on the outside of the atom. Likewise, chemical reactions, physical force and changes in pressure affect the orbital electrons, but do not influence when the nucleus might decay.

However, just because a process is random doesn't mean that there is no pattern to it. Some radioactive nuclei are very nearly stable. For example, the nuclei of bismuth-209 are likely to last longer than 2.5×10^{19} years before decaying (almost 2 billion times longer than the age of the universe), whereas the nuclei of livermorium (the element with atomic number 116) are so unstable that they are likely to have decayed within a tenth of a second.

To anticipate when nuclei are likely to decay, physicists define a quantity called half-life. The half-life of a sample of a substance is the amount of time it takes for half of the nuclei to decay. Because the activity of a sample is proportional to the number of radioactive nuclei, the activity also halves every half-life.

1. At 9.00 a.m. on a Monday, the activity of a sample of sodium-24 is measured to be 2,400 Bq. By midday the following Thursday, the activity has fallen to 75 Bq. What is the half-life of sodium-24?

2. A sample of uranium-240 has an activity of 20,480 Bq. After one week it has decayed until its activity is 5 Bq. What is its half-life?

3. Oganesson-294 ($^{294}_{118}$Og) was first synthesized in 2002. It has a half-life of 0.7 ms. What is the probability of an atom of oganesson lasting for more than 3.5 ms?

Demonstrating awareness of media interpretations of events

Many events are random, which means that the outcome is unpredictable. A good example is tossing a coin where there are two equally likely outcomes: heads or tails.

Due to the random nature of tossing a coin, it is impossible to predict the outcome. However, if the coin was tossed many times, you would expect about half the results to be heads and half to be tails, although the probability of getting exactly half the results as heads would be small.

If a coin is tossed 20 times, the probability of getting 10 heads and 10 tails is about 18%, however, if we allow for 10% deviation from this expected result (between 9 and 11 heads), the probability is about 50%. If the coin is tossed 100 times the probability of getting half the results as heads to within 10% (between 45 and 55 heads) is just over 72%. Tossing a coin 1,000 times gives a probability of 99.8% that half the results to within 10% will be heads (between 450 and 550).

The more times the coin is tossed, the closer the actual results are likely to be to the expected outcome. When considering radioactive nuclei, the numbers of atoms in a sample can be vast; a standard radioactive source used in schools might have 10^{15} atoms or more. As a result of the large numbers of nuclei, the rate at which they are likely to decay can be predicted reliably.

Probability often poses problems for media organizations who want to present information with certainty. Elections and other public votes can be particularly tricky as they are often closely tied with two similarly likely outcomes. In the months before elections, polls try to assess the likelihood of different outcomes. Between 2004 and 2016, the polls before the US presidential elections normally presented one candidate as having a 70% chance of winning with the other candidate having a 30% chance. In 2004, 2008 and 2012, the more likely candidates won but in 2016, President Trump's victory was presented as a surprise even though you would expect the polls to be wrong 3 times out of 10 if the probability is only 70%.

▶ At the beginning of a football match the referee tosses a coin to see which side starts with the ball. This is a random event and the outcome cannot be predicted

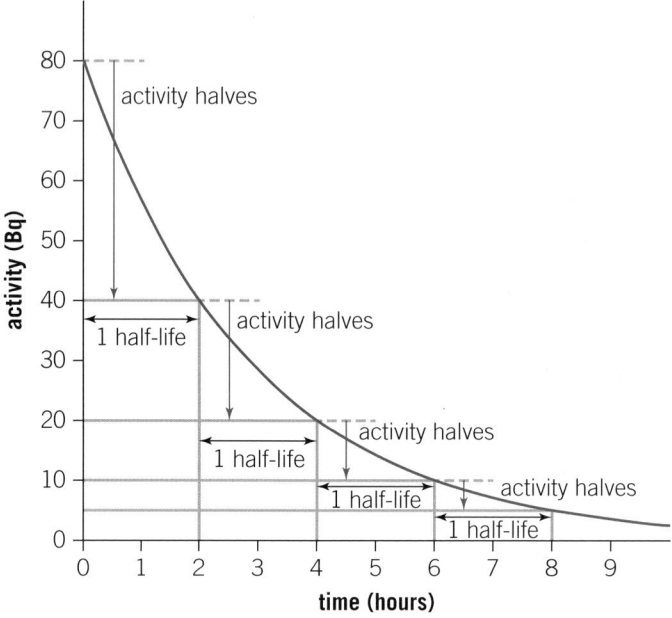

▲ This graph shows the decay of an isotope with a half-life of two hours. Every two hours the number of nuclei remaining halves, as does the activity

Worked example: Half-life

Question

Cesium-137 is an isotope that is found in nuclear waste from a power station. It has a half-life of 30 years.

a) How long will it take for 75% of the atoms of cesium-137 to decay?

b) What proportion will remain after 120 years?

Answer

a) After one half-life, 50% of the original cesium will have decayed. After a further half-life, another half will have decayed leaving only 25% remaining. At this point 75% of the atoms will have decayed. Therefore, the time is two half-lives or 60 years.

b) 120 years is four half-lives. After one half-life 50% remains, after two half-lives 25% remains, after three half-lives 12.5% remains, and so after four half-lives 6.25% remains.

Data-based question: Carbon dating

Carbon-14 is an isotope of carbon with a half-life of 5,730 years. It is formed when high energy particles from the Sun's rays strike atoms in the atmosphere and release a neutron from them. This free neutron can be absorbed by nitrogen-14 forming carbon-14. Because the Sun's intensity has remained constant for millions of years, the amount of carbon-14 in the atmosphere has remained constant at about one atom per 10^{12} atoms of normal carbon-12.

When plants photosynthesize, they absorb carbon-14 from the atmosphere and convert it into food for other organisms. Animals eat this food and in turn breathe out carbon dioxide. As a result, the same proportion of carbon-14 is contained in all living things.

When an animal or plant dies, it stops exchanging carbon with the outside world. The radioactive carbon-14 starts to decay and a long time later, it might be possible to measure how much has decayed and therefore work out how old the material is. A graph showing the proportion of ^{14}C to ^{12}C remaining in a sample is shown below.

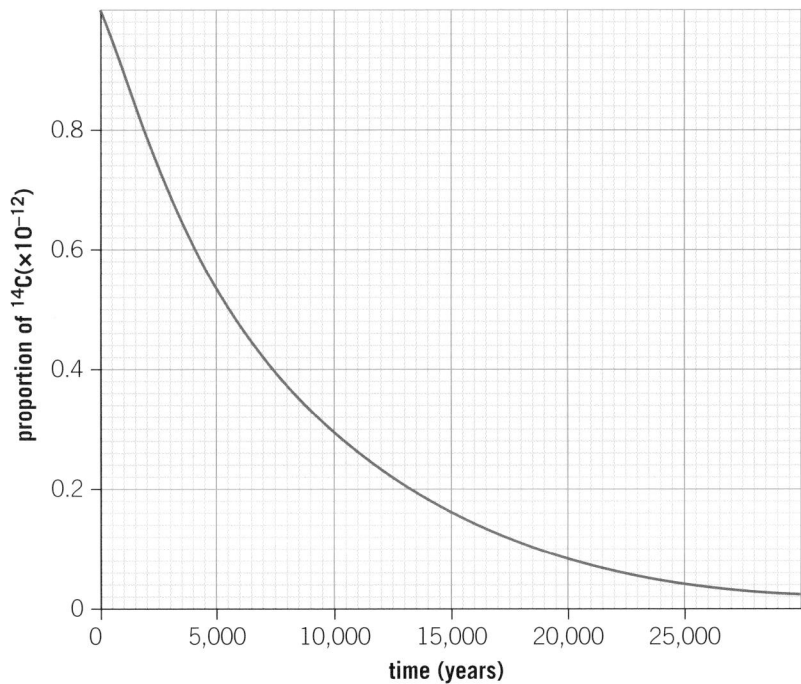

1. The equation for the formation of carbon-14 when nitrogen absorbs a neutron in the atmosphere is:

$$^{14}_{7}N + ^{1}_{0}n \rightarrow ^{14}_{6}C + ^{?}_{?}X$$

By considering what the numbers represented by question marks must be, deduce what particle X is.

2. An early human settlement is discovered and archeologists recover a stone axe, some animal bones, and some burnt wood from a fire.

   a) Which of these could be dated using carbon dating?

   b) A sample of material from the settlement contains one-fifth of the ^{14}C proportion that a modern sample would have. How old does this suggest that the settlement is?

3. Why is it not possible to use carbon dating to determine the age of a dinosaur bone from 65 million years ago?

What are the sources of radioactive nuclei?

There are radioactive isotopes which occur naturally so some exposure to radiation is inevitable. Such sources of radiation are called background radiation. Some background radiation is man-made. This includes fall-out from nuclear weapons testing and nuclear accidents; however, these account for a tiny proportion of the total background radiation. The vast majority of radiation is naturally occurring.

Heavy elements such as uranium and thorium occur in certain minerals in the ground. They have long half-lives of around a billion years, so they do not decay quickly, although the products of these decays may have shorter half-lives. Rocks account for about 10% of the background radiation that we experience. Rocks are often dug up and used for building materials, making buildings a possible source of background radiation as well.

▶ This rock contains uranium ores. As a result, it is a natural source of radioactivity

As these radioactive elements decay, they create other radioactive elements. Often these have shorter half-lives and decay underground where they are formed. An exception is radon-222 which is formed as part of the decay of uranium-238. Radon is a noble gas which means that it doesn't form chemical compounds. The gas, which gradually seeps out of rocks containing uranium, normally floats away, but buildings can trap the radon if there is not enough ventilation. As radon has a half-life of 3.8 days, it has enough time to build up before decaying. Radon decays by alpha decay which normally does not represent too much of a hazard as the alpha particles cannot travel far in air, and the radiation would likely be stopped by the outer layer of skin. However, as it is a gas, it can be breathed into the lungs. As a result, it is thought that radon gas is the second biggest cause of lung cancer (although the biggest cause, smoking, accounts for about 90% of lung cancers). In areas where radon gas is common, buildings have increased ventilation to allow the gas to escape.

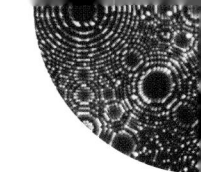

Other radioactive isotopes can be concentrated by plants. Certain nuts, seeds and fruits contain high levels of potassium, for example. About 0.01% of potassium atoms are radioactive potassium-40 which has a half-life of 1.25 billion years. Foods which contain high levels of potassium therefore have higher levels of radioactivity.

Another source of background radiation is from the sky. Cosmic rays are formed when high-energy particles from the Sun and from space strike atoms in the atmosphere. These collisions send showers of particles towards the Earth. Most of these are absorbed by the atmosphere, but some reach ground level. The amount of background radiation from cosmic rays is greater at higher altitudes and so pilots and astronauts are exposed to higher doses of cosmic rays than people remaining near sea-level.

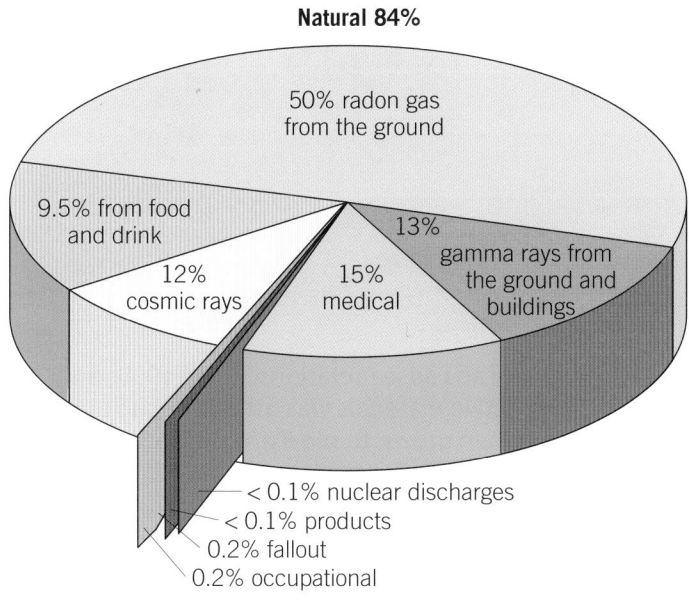

▲ The radiation that we are exposed to every day as part of our normal lives is called background radiation. The majority is from natural sources. This chart shows the sources of this background radiation

What are the dangers of radioactivity?

NUCLEAR PHYSICS

All three types of radioactive emission, alpha, beta and gamma, are ionizing. This means that the decay particles can remove electrons from atoms and molecules that they pass. If cells in animals and plants are ionized, then a mutation to their DNA may occur which can cause cancer. For this reason, it is important to minimize exposure to radiation from radioactive sources.

▲ Exposure to radiation can cause mutations. In the 1950s and 1960s, radiation from radioactive materials was used to create mutations in crops. These were then grown to see if any of the mutations were beneficial. In this picture, plants are placed at different distances from a central source of radiation. Many crop species which originate from these trials are still in use today, such as star ruby grapefruit and supersweet sweetcorn

NUCLEAR PHYSICS

How can radioactive sources be useful?

Despite the dangers of radiation, radioactive nuclei have many beneficial uses. As high doses of radiation can kill cells, this is a good way of sterilizing equipment and food. Medical tools or packed food can be exposed to doses of radiation, normally gamma rays, to kill any bacteria that are present. The gamma rays do not leave any trace on the equipment or the food, so the taste is not affected and they are not left radioactive. In this way, infection can be reduced, and the shelf life of food can be extended.

Although exposure to radiation can cause cancer, it can also be used to treat cancer. In radiotherapy, the area of the body which has the cancer is exposed to doses of radiation. Beta radiation is usually used as it can penetrate to the cancerous area and cause ionization there, damaging the cells and hopefully killing the cancer.

Radioactive sources can also be used to monitor industrial processes. The thickness of paper or plastic films can be measured by putting a radioactive source on one side and a detector on the other. If the material that passes between the source and the detector becomes thicker, the measured radiation decreases.

How can unstable nuclei be used to generate energy?

NUCLEAR PHYSICS

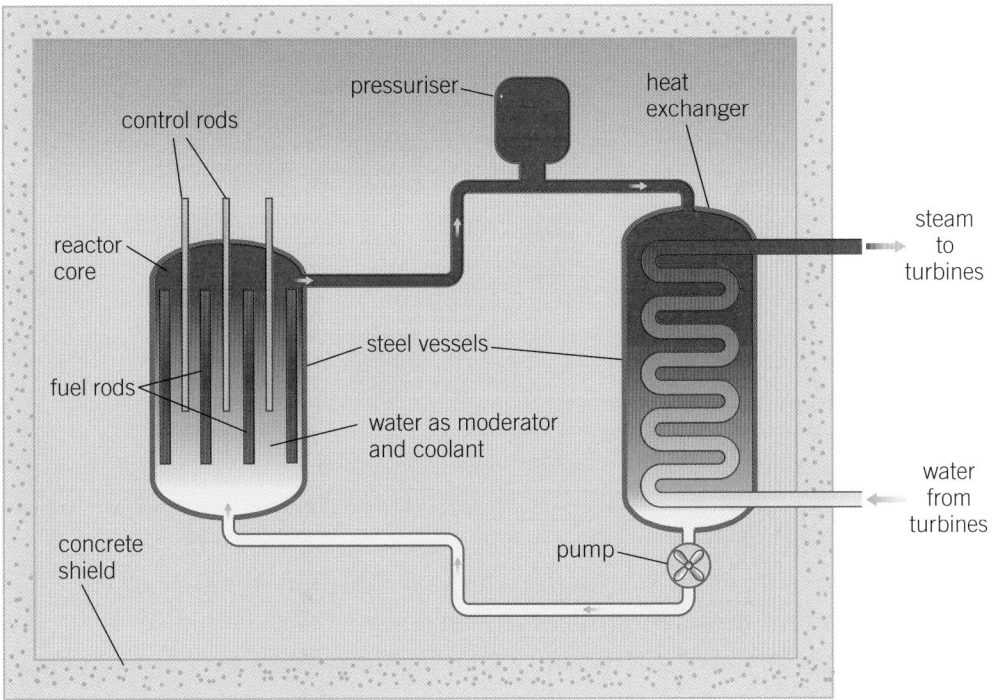

▲ Core of a nuclear reactor

The amount of energy released in nuclear decays can be very large, and if this can be controlled, it can provide a useful energy resource. Generally, elements such as uranium decay very slowly with half-lives of billions of years. Normal ways of increasing this rate, such as increasing the temperature or pressure, do not affect the rate of this decay because these factors only affect the electrons on the outside of the atom rather than the nucleus in the center.

There is, however, a way in which a uranium nucleus can be made to decay. If a slow neutron is fired at the nucleus, it can be absorbed. If uranium-235 absorbs a neutron in this way, it becomes unstable and then falls apart into two smaller nuclei. This process is called induced fission. Fission means the splitting of a nucleus into two smaller parts and induced refers to the fact that the fission was caused by a neutron. Elements which can be made to undergo induced fission in this way are called fissile.

When a uranium nucleus falls apart, it forms two smaller nuclei called daughter nuclei and about three extra neutrons. These neutrons have a lot of energy and are traveling very fast, too fast to cause another induced fission reaction. However, if they can be slowed down, they can go on to cause more fission reactions. This is a chain reaction with the products of one reaction going on to cause further ones.

▶ When neutrons from one fission reaction go on to cause other fission reactions, the result is a chain reaction

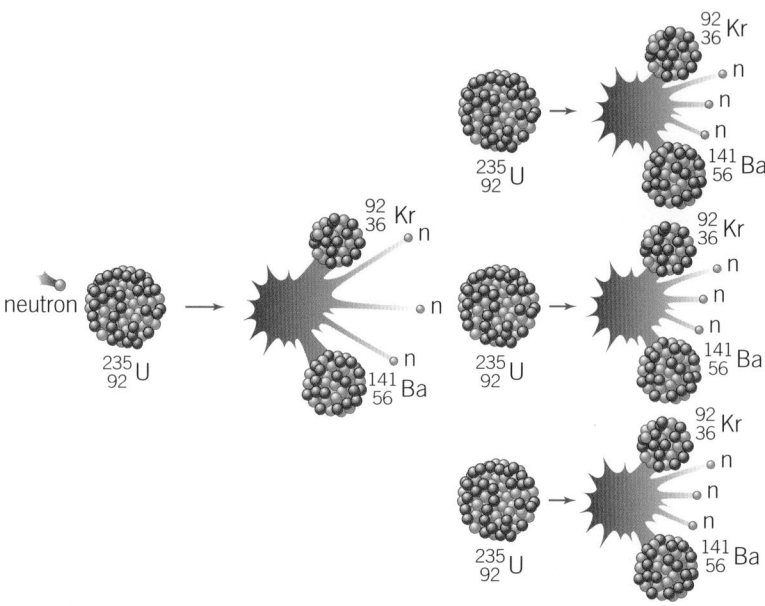

In a nuclear power station, there needs to be a way of slowing these neutrons down so that they can cause more nuclear reactions; this is the role of the moderator. The moderator is usually made of graphite or water as these substances are good at slowing down neutrons and absorbing some of their kinetic energy. In doing so, they get hot due to the energy transfer. Water can be pumped through the core of the nuclear power station carrying the heat from the center and out to turbines where the thermal energy is converted to kinetic energy and then electrical energy.

If every neutron released from a fission reaction went on to be absorbed by another nucleus of uranium-235, the reaction rate would quickly increase out of control, so it is important to have a mechanism to keep this rate of reaction under control. Control rods are made of a material which is good at absorbing neutrons, often boron or cadmium. These can be raised or lowered into the core of the reactor to change the number of neutrons they absorb. To maintain a steady rate of fission reactions, one neutron from each fission reaction should go on to cause another reaction.

ATL Reflection skills

Considering ethical implications

The knowledge of how to make a nuclear power plant can also be used to create a nuclear bomb. During the Second World War, the scientific work towards harnessing nuclear fission was increased and directed towards creating a nuclear bomb.

Consider the following questions.

1 Is war a beneficial influence on scientific progress?

2 Is scientific progress always a good thing?

▲ A nuclear explosion

What are the problems of nuclear power?

NUCLEAR PHYSICS

The waste products of nuclear power are highly radioactive and some of the substances can have long half-lives. As a result, they need to be disposed of carefully.

Some nuclear waste is placed in storage ponds. About 10 m of water above the waste shields the radiation and also provides cooling. After some years, the waste is safe for final disposal.

A disused mineshaft can provide a suitable place for disposing of the waste as the rock above shields the radiation. The rock must be stable and not prone to earthquakes or other subsidence. Care must also be taken that the radioactive waste is not able to leak into surrounding water. Nuclear waste can be sealed and left there for thousands of years until the levels of radioactivity have decreased.

Not all dangerous radioactive waste comes from power stations. There are many medical uses of radioactive isotopes and this creates radioactive waste. Scientific research and some industrial uses also create waste that needs to be disposed of.

Another problem of nuclear power stations is that accidents can be extremely dangerous. Although these are very unlikely, the possibility of releasing radioactive material into the environment is a concern. The worst accident in a nuclear power station took place at Chernobyl in 1986. About 30 people died in the accident, although the number of deaths which can be attributed to exposure to radiation from the leak of radioactive material is not yet known.

More recently, the Tohuku earthquake and subsequent tsunami in 2011 damaged the nuclear power station in Fukushima. Although there were no deaths caused by this accident, radioactive material leaked from the reactor.

Nuclear waste

Cesium-134 and cesium-135 are isotopes which are found in nuclear waste. Cesium-134 has a half-life of 2 years while cesium-135 has a half-life of 2.3×10^6 years. Both decay by beta decay into stable isotopes.

1. Use a periodic table to work out what element the cesium isotopes decay into.

2 Which of these isotopes will cause more problems for the disposal of the nuclear waste?

▲ Special measures need to be taken for the safe disposal of nuclear waste

Summative assessment

Statement of inquiry:

Patterns can demonstrate relationships between events and shed light on how they are caused.

Introduction

Knowing how radiation passes through air is important. Some types of radiation are easily absorbed and do not pass through air well whereas other types are able to travel large distances through the atmosphere. In this assessment, we look at how different types of radiation penetrate through air.

 ## The dangers of nuclear and electromagnetic radiation

1. Ultraviolet radiation can be dangerous to humans. Much of the UV light from the Sun is blocked by the atmosphere.

   a) State the name of the chemical in the atmosphere which blocks dangerous UV light. [1]

   b) What are the dangers of UV light and how can they be avoided? [3]

2. Nuclear radiation can also be dangerous.

   a) Give an example of the dangers of nuclear radiation. [2]

   b) Suggest a sensible safety precaution when handling radioactive sources. [2]

3. Dangerous radiation is often called ionizing radiation.

   a) What is meant by ionizing? [2]

   b) Which parts of the electromagnetic spectrum are ionizing? [2]

   c) Which type of nuclear radiation is the most ionizing? [1]

   d) How far through air would you expect nuclear radiation to travel? [2]

 ## Investigating beta radiation

A class experiment uses a radioactive source to investigate how far beta radiation travels through air. A detector is positioned at varying distances from the radioactive source and the number of counts in a period of 1 minute is detected.

4. Identify the independent and dependent variables for this experiment. [2]

5. Suggest a suitable detector for this experiment. [1]

6. Suggest a suitable set of distances that could be investigated in the experiment. [3]

7. There are suspicions that the radioactive source is emitting gamma rays as well as beta radiation. Explain how a thin piece of metal can help to distinguish how much of the detected radiation is gamma and how much is beta. [4]

8. It is important to take background radiation into account.

   a) Suggest one possible source of background radiation. [1]

   b) Explain how background radiation could be taken into account in this experiment. [4]

 Studying how soft X-rays pass through air

A student knows that soft X-rays are known to be blocked by air easily and that hard X-rays can travel long distances through air. She forms a hypothesis that the distance X-rays can travel is directly proportional to the frequency of the X-rays.

In order to test her hypothesis, she tries to find some data. She discovers this graph in a scientific paper. It shows the percentage of X-rays which can travel a certain distance in air. The graph shows results for different wavelengths of X-rays.

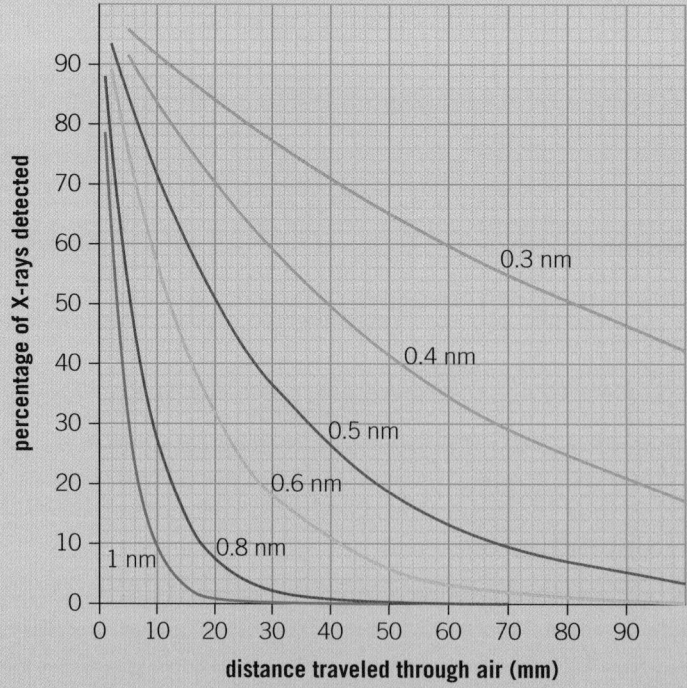

The student uses this data from this experiment to find the amount of air required to block half of the X-rays at different wavelengths.

9. Read off values from the graph to find the distance the different wavelengths of X-rays travel before half are absorbed. Record your data in a suitable table. [4]

10. Plot a graph of your data. [6]

11. Add a line of best fit to your graph. [1]

12. Describe the trend of your data. [2]

13. Use your graph to find:

a) the wavelength of X-rays for which half would be absorbed by 30 mm of air [1]

b) the distance that X-rays with a wavelength of 0.7 nm could travel before half are absorbed. [1]

14. The student's original hypothesis was that the frequency of the X-rays is directly proportional to the distance they traveled. Suggest whether the hypothesis is supported or contradicted by the data. [3]

15. The student writes a report on her findings. Explain why is it important that she references the scientific paper in which she found the original graph. [3]

16. The scientific paper from which the data came refers to the X-rays as radiation. Other pupils in her class thought that radiation referred to radioactive decay. Write a brief explanation of the similarities and differences between these two types of radiation. Try to use scientific terms correctly. [6]

17. X-rays of a similar wavelength can be used in astronomy. This is a picture of the Crab Nebula, the remnant of a supernova, taken using X-rays of frequencies between about 1×10^{17} and 2×10^{18} Hz. It shows the neutron star at the center of the nebula. Explain why the X-ray telescope had to be in space, in orbit around the Earth, rather than on the ground. [3]

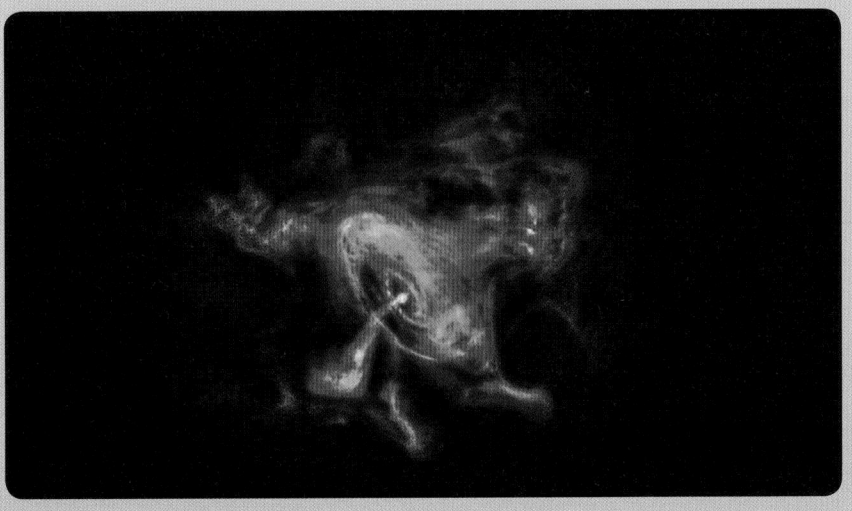

◀ The Crab Nebula is the remnant of a supernova which occurred in 1054. This image is taken in the X-ray part of the spectrum and shows the neutron star at the center

# Glossary

Absolute zero	is the lowest temperature theoretically obtainable.
Acceleration	is the rate of change of increasing velocity (or speed).
Accuracy	is the degree to which a measurement represents the actual value of the thing being measured.
Activity	is the number of decays per second of a radioactive sample.
Air resistance	is a frictional force caused by moving through the air.
Alpha decay	is the radioactive decay of a nucleus giving off an alpha particle (helium nucleus).
Alpha particle	an alpha particle is a positively-charged helium nucleus which is ejected from certain radioactive nuclei.
Alternating current (a.c.)	is an electric current which reverses its flow in periodic cycles.
Ammeter	an ammeter is an instrument used to measure the amount of electric current flowing through a particular point in an electrical circuit.
Ampere	an ampere (abbreviated to amp or A) is the unit of electric current.
Amplitude	the amplitude is the maximum displacement of an oscillating object from its mean position.
Apollo missions	the Apollo missions were a series of United States space missions in the 1960s and early 1970s. In 1969, the Apollo 11 mission successfully landed astronauts on the moon for the first time.
Archimedes can	an Archimedes can is a can with a spout that is used to measure the amount of water displaced when an object is submerged (also called a displacement can).
Archimedes principle	the Archimedes principle states that when a body is partially or totally immersed in a fluid, there is an upthrust equal to the weight of the fluid displaced.
Asteroid	the asteroids are a large number of rocks orbiting the Sun in a belt between the orbits of Mars and Jupiter.
Atmosphere	the atmosphere is the air that surrounds the Earth and is held to it by gravity.
Atmospheric pressure	is the pressure exerted by the air and is caused by the gravitational attraction of the air to the Earth.
Atom	an atom is the smallest particle of an element which can take part in a chemical reaction and remain unchanged.
Atomic notation	is a way of describing the constituents of an atomic nucleus in the form $^{A}_{Z}X$, where X is the chemical symbol of the element, A is the mass number of the nucleus and Z is the atomic number of the nucleus.

Atomic number	is the number of protons an element has in the nucleus of its atom.
Atomic theory	is the theory that all matter is made up of atoms.
Atto	is a prefix used with SI units to indicate $\times 10^{-18}$.
Background radiation	is the result of spontaneous disintegration of naturally occurring radioisotopes found in rocks and living material.
Balanced	is a term used to describe forces or moments where the total of the forces in one direction is equal in magnitude to the sum total of forces in the opposite direction. As a result, the net force is zero in that direction.
Bar magnet	a bar magnet is a magnet in a straight shape with the North and South poles at opposite ends.
Barometer	a barometer is an instrument which measures atmospheric pressure.
Battery	a battery is a number of electric cells connected together.
Becquerel	a becquerel is the SI unit for measuring radioactivity, equal to the activity in a material in which one nucleus decays on average per second.
Beta decay	is the radioactive decay of a nucleus by conversion of a neutron into a proton, giving off a beta particle (high-energy electron).
Beta particle	a beta particle is a high-energy electron emitted from certain radioactive nuclei.
Big Bang theory	the Big Bang theory suggests that the universe was formed from a highly dense central mass (the size of an atomic nucleus containing all the matter in the universe) that exploded around 15 billion years ago.
Big Crunch	the Big Crunch is a theoretical ending for the universe where the expansion of space reverses and the universe collapses into a single point.
Big Freeze	the Big Freeze is a possible fate of the universe where it keeps expanding and cooling until energy transfers are no longer possible.
Big Rip	the Big Rip is a possible fate of the universe in which its expansion accelerates until all matter is torn apart.
Biofuel	is plant material or animal waste which can be used as a fuel resource.
Biogas	is the gas which is produced from rotting organic matter.
Black hole	a black hole is a region of space where gravity is so strong that even light cannot escape.
Boiling point	is the temperature at which all of a liquid changes into a gas (or vapour) because the vapour pressure of the liquid is equal to atmospheric pressure.
Boson	a boson is a particle, such as a photon, through which the fundamental forces of nature interact.
Boyle's law	states that the volume of a given mass of gas at a constant temperature is inversely proportional to its pressure: pV = constant.
Brittle	a material which cannot be permanently deformed and instead breaks is described as brittle.
Brownian motion	is the random motion of particles in water or air caused by collision with the surrounding molecules.

Carbon dating by comparing the amounts of carbon-14 in dead material (like wooden artefacts, leather sandals, etc.) with the levels of carbon-14 in living material, we can measure the age of the dead material.

Carbon dioxide is present in very small amounts in the atmosphere (0.03%), but it is very important because it is used for photosynthesis in plants.

Cell a cell is a system in which two electrodes are in contact with an electrolyte.

Celsius scale the Celsius scale is a common temperature scale based on the lower fixed point of ice at 0°C and the upper fixed point of steam at 100°C.

Center of mass the center of mass (or center of gravity) is a point on an object through which its total weight (or mass) appears to act.

Chain reaction a chain reaction is one where the products of one reaction go on to cause further reactions.

Chemical potential energy is the energy stored in systems such as fuel and oxygen, food and oxygen, and chemicals in batteries.

Circuit an electrical circuit is a continuous conducting path along which electric current can flow.

Circuit diagram a circuit diagram represents an electrical circuit where wires are shown as lines and different components are represented by circuit symbols.

Circuit symbol a circuit symbol is used in a circuit diagram to represent an electrical component. Some common circuit symbols are shown on page 124 in Chapter 6.

Commutator a commutator in a device used in a d.c. electric motor to reverse the current direction every half turn.

Compass a compass is a navigational device used to find a direction. A simple compass consists of a freely moving bar magnet which aligns to the magnetic field of the Earth.

Compound a compound is the substance formed by the chemical combination of elements in fixed proportions, as represented by the compound's chemical formula.

Compression is the squashing together of particles (for example, those in the medium of a longitudinal wave).

Compression wave a compression wave or pressure wave is a longitudinal wave that travels through a medium.

Condensation is the change of state from gas (or vapour) to a liquid.

Conduction is the way in which heat energy is transferred through solids (and to a much lesser extent in liquids and gases).

Conductor a conductor is a substance which has a high thermal conductivity.

Conservation of energy this law states that energy cannot be created or destroyed, but can be converted from one form to another.

Constellation a constellation is a group of stars in the sky which form a fixed pattern in relation to each other, as viewed from Earth.

Constructive interference is when two waves of equal wavelength add together to give a larger wave.

Control rod	a control rod is a part of a nuclear power station. Its purpose is to absorb excess neutrons to keep the rate of reaction under control.
Control variable	a control variable is a variable in an experiment that is kept constant so that it does not affect the results.
Convection	is the way in which heat energy is transferred through liquids and gases by movement of the particles in the liquid or gas.
Convection current	the circulating movement of a heated fluid.
Conventional current direction	is from the positive terminal of the battery to the negative terminal and is shown as an arrow on the circuit diagram.
Cosmic rays	are high-energy particles that fall on the Earth from space.
Coulomb	a coulomb is the quantity of electric charge transported by an electric current of 1 amp flowing for 1 second.
Count rate	the count rate is the number of radioactive decay particles that are detected in one second.
Critical angle	the critical angle is the smallest angle of incidence at which total internal reflection occurs (in glass, about 42°; in water, about 45°).
Crust	the Earth's crust is the surface layer of rock (between 5 km and 50 km thick) which lies on top of the mantle.
Cycle	one cycle is one complete motion.
Dark energy	is a theoretical entity that is thought to be responsible for the acceleration of the expansion of the universe.
Dark matter	is a hypothesized type of matter which has mass and so has a gravitational effect but appears to not interact in any other way. Its gravitational effects have been observed but its nature is not known.
Daughter nucleus	a daughter nucleus is an atomic nucleus which is the result of a radioactive decay or the product of a nuclear process such as fusion or fission.
Deceleration	is the rate of change of decreasing velocity (speed).
Decibel	a decibel is a commonly used unit of sound intensity or loudness.
Density	the density of a material is its mass per unit volume.
Dependent variable	the dependent variable is the quantity which is measured in each trial in order to assess the outcome of an experiment.
Destructive interference	is when two waves of equal wavelength are out of phase and add together in such a way as to produce a wave of a lower amplitude or to cancel each other out.
Diffraction	is the spreading of waves which occurs when a wave goes around an obstacle or through a gap.
Direct current (d.c.)	is an electric current which is flowing in one direction only.
Directly proportional	two quantities may be described as directly proportional if doubling one quantity results in the doubling of the other (the same would be true of trebling or any other multiple). On a graph of the two quantities, a directly proportional relationship would result in a straight line through the origin.

Displacement is the distance and direction an object has moved from a fixed reference point.

Displacement can a displacement can is a can with a spout that is used to measure the amount of water displaced when an object is submerged (also called an Archimedes can).

Distance is the separation in space between two coordinates. It is a scalar quantity and so does not account for the direction of separation – the equivalent vector quantity is displacement.

Domains are regions in a magnet which, according to the domain theory of magnetism, are made up of many tiny molecular magnets called dipoles.

Ductile ability to be made into wire.

Dwarf planet a dwarf planet is an object in the Solar System which is large enough for its gravitational field to have pulled itself into a spherical shape but not large enough to dominate its orbit. Examples of dwarf planets are Ceres (the largest asteroid in the asteroid belt), Pluto (formally designated as a planet but now known to share its orbit with many other objects) and Eris (a dwarf planet slightly smaller but heavier than pluto, which has an orbit)

Dynamo a dynamo is a generator which produces electrical energy in the form of direct current.

Efficiency is the proportion of energy that is successfully transferred to the intentional or useful output.

Elastic potential energy is the energy associated with a charge at a particular point within an electric field.

Electric generator [not in dictionary]

Electrical energy is a form of energy which is carried by electric currents, and can be changed into other forms such as heat and light using various electrical appliances.

Electricity is the flow of electrons (or other charges) which can be used to transfer energy and power devices.

Electric motor an electric motor is a device which uses the motor effect to change electrical energy into mechanical energy.

Electrode an electrode is a piece of metal or carbon (graphite) placed in an electrolyte which allows electric current to enter and leave during electrolysis.

Electromagnet an electromagnet is a solenoid with a core of ferromagnetic material such as soft iron.

Electromagnetic spectrum the electromagnetic spectrum s the range of frequencies over which electromagnetic waves are propagated.

Electromagnetic waves are transverse waves produced by oscillating electric and magnetic fields at right angles to one another.

Electromagnetism is the combination of an electric field and a magnetic field and their interaction to produce a force.

Electromotive force	is equivalent to the potential difference across the terminals of a battery when it is not supplying a current.
Electron	an electron is a negatively charged subatomic particle which is found orbiting the nucleus of atoms.
Electrostatics	is the study of electric charges and the forces between them.
Element	an element is a substance that cannot be broken down into two or more simpler substances by chemical means.
Elementary charge	the elementary charge is 1.6×10^{-19} C. It is the magnitude of charge carried by an electron or proton and so all charged objects have a charge that is a multiple of this.
Energy	is the capacity of a system to do work.
Energy transfer	is a change of one energy form into another.
Equilibrium	occurs when the overall clockwise moments acting on an object are equal to the overall anticlockwise moments.
Evaporation	is the process of a liquid changing into a vapour at temperatures below its boiling point.
Exa	is a prefix used with SI units to indicate $\times 10^{18}$.
Experiment	an experiment is a series of trials designed to test a hypothesis. Different parameters are changed or controlled and the resulting changes are measured in order to deduce the effect of these changes.
Femto	is a prefix used with SI units to indicate $\times 10^{-15}$.
Filament	galactic filaments are some of the largest scale structures in the universe. They are formed of a string of galactic superclusters and can be about 200 million light years in length.
Fleming's left-hand rule	gives the direction of the motor effect.
Force	a force is a pushing or pulling action which can change the shape of an object, or make a stationary object move or a moving object change its speed or direction.
Fossil fuels	are formed from the remains of ancient buried organisms.
Free-body diagram	a free-body diagram is a diagram which shows the forces acting upon an object.
Freezing point	is the temperature at which all of a liquid changes into a solid.
Frequency	the frequency is the number of complete cycles of a motion in one second.
Friction	is the force which acts to oppose the motion between two surfaces as they move over each other.
Fulcrum	a fulcrum or pivot is the point about which a lever rotates.
Fundamental	a fundamental particle is one that is not made of smaller particles and so cannot be split into smaller fragments.
Fusion	is the change in state from a solid to a liquid of a substance which is a solid at room temperature and pressure (not to be confused with **nuclear fusion**).

Galaxy a galaxy is a giant collection of gas, dust and stars held together by gravitational attraction between its components.

Gamma decay is the process where an excited nucleus releases energy in the form of a gamma ray. The number of protons and neutrons remains unchanged.

Gamma ray a gamma ray is a high energy electromagnetic wave emitted from a radioactive nucleus. They may be used in cancer treatment and the sterilization of equipment.

Gas the particles in a gas are very far apart, randomly arranged, free to move (diffuse), moving in all directions, occasionally colliding.

Gas giant a gas giant is a large planet which consists mainly of gases such as hydrogen and helium. In our Solar System, the gas giants are Jupiter, Saturn, Uranus and Neptune.

Geiger–Marsden experiment the Geiger–Marsden experiment (also referred to as Rutherford scattering) is an experiment where alpha particles were fired at a thin gold leaf. It led to the discovery of the atomic nucleus.

Geocentric model the geocentric model was a model of the Solar System which placed the Earth at the center with the Sun and other planets orbiting around the Earth.

Geothermal energy is heat energy from hot rock deep in the Earth's crust.

Giant impact hypothesis the giant impact hypothesis is the most accepted theory for the formation of the moon. It suggests that the moon was formed when a large protoplanet crashed into the Earth early in its history.

Giga is a prefix used with SI units to indicate $\times 10^9$.

Gradient the gradient is a measure of the slope of a line on a graph or a measure of the rate of change in a quantity in space.

Gravitational field strength (g) is the measure of the force that is exerted on 1 kg of mass. It also represents the acceleration of an object in freefall at that point in space. On Earth, g = 9.8 N kg^{-1}.

Gravitational force (or gravity) is the force of attraction that objects have on one another because of their masses.

Gravitational potential energy is the stored energy an object has because of its position above the Earth.

Greenhouse effect the greenhouse effect is the trapping of heat energy in the atmosphere because of the effects of greenhouse gases.

Greenhouse gases are gases in the atmosphere which absorb infrared radiation, causing an increase in air temperature.

Hadley cell a Hadley cell is a region of the atmosphere which moves through convection.

Half-life the half-life is the time taken for half the atoms in a radioactive sample to undergo radioactive decay.

Heliocentric model the heliocentric model of the Solar System is one that has the Sun at the center and the planets orbiting around it.

Hertz is the SI unit of frequency.

Hubble's Law	is the directly proportional relationship between distant galaxies and the speed at which they are moving away from us. The constant of proportionality, Hubble's constant, is about 70 km s^{-1} Mpc^{-1}.
Hydroelectricity	is electricity produced by trapping rainwater at a high level and then allowing it to flow through electrical turbines at a lower level.
Hypothesis	a hypothesis is a testable explanation for why something happens.
Inclined plane	an inclined plane is a simple machine such as a ramp that creates a mechanical advantage by doing work against gravity over a longer distance so the required force is less than directly lifting the object to that height.
Independent variable	in an experiment, the independent variable is the property that is changed to measure its effect on the outcome.
Induced fission	is a fission reaction which is caused by an external influence such as absorbing a neutron.
Induced voltage	when a conductor experiences a changing magnetic field, an induced voltage is caused.
Induction of charge	is caused by the attraction of opposite charges and the repulsion of like charges.
Infrared radiation	from warm or hot objects (e.g. fires, living bodies), it is easily absorbed by most objects causing a rise in temperature. It is used in thermal imaging in medicine, in cameras for seeing at night and in remote controls for devices such as televisions.
Infrasound	is sound below the threshold of the human hearing range, around 20 Hz.
Insulator	an insulator is a material which allows no electrons (or very few) to pass through.
Interference	is the interaction of two or more waves of the same frequency emitted from coherent sources.
Inverse square law	waves emitted from a point source in a vacuum obey the inverse square law.
Inversely proportional	two quantities may be described as inversely proportional if doubling one quantity results in the halving of the other.
Ion	an ion is a charged particle formed when an atom (or group of atoms) gaines or loses one or more electrons.
Ionizing radiation	is a term used to describe radioactive emissions and high energy electromagnetic radiation which can cause atoms to lose an electron. Ionizing radiation is typically dangerous to humans as it can cause cancer.
Isotopes	are atoms of the same element (same number of protons and electrons) with different numbers of neutrons, and so different mass numbers.
Joule	a joule of work is done by a force of one newton moving one metre in the direction of the force.
Kelvin	is the unit of temperature on the absolute scale and is the SI unit of thermodynamic temperature.
Kilo	is a prefix used with SI units to indicate ×10^3 or a thousand.
Kilogram	a kilogram is the SI unit of mass.

Kinetic energy is the energy possessed by an object or particle because it is moving.

Kinetic theory states that matter is made up of particles which move with a vigour proportional to their absolute temperature.

Lamp a lamp is an electrical device which converts electrical energy into light energy.

Large Hadron Collider The Large Hadron Collider is a particle accelerator on the French-Swiss border which collides particles at high energy to investigate the nature of the fundamental particles and forces of physics. It is 27 km in circumference and is one of the largest and most expensive machines ever built.

Law in physics, a law is a statement which has been confirmed by many experiments and its predictions are believed to always be valid.

Lever a lever is a simple machine consisting of a rigid bar supported or pivoted at a point along its length called the fulcrum.

Lift is an upward force generated by wings.

Light is the visible part of the electromagnetic spectrum and is a form of energy emitted by luminous objects like the Sun.

Light-dependent resistor (LDR) a light-dependent resistor is a resistor made from a semiconductor (e.g. cadmium sulphides or selenium) whose resistance changes with light intensity.

Light energy is a type of energy transfer through visible light.

Linear a linear relationship between two variables is one which can be described using only multiplication and addition (no higher powers such as x^2 or complex functions). On a graph, a linear relationship is a straight line that does not necessarily go through the origin. Linear can also refer to a scale which goes up in equal increments (unlike a logarithmic scale).

Liquid the particles in a liquid are touching but further apart than in a solid, not regularly arranged, held together loosely, moving by sliding past each other.

Local group the local group is the group of galaxies which includes the Milky Way galaxy.

Logarithmic scale a logarithmic scale, often used on graphs, is a non-linear scale where intervals are separated by an order of magnitude. Hence the scale might be 1, 10, 100, 1,000 where each successive interval represents ten times the previous one.

Longitudinal wave a longitudinal wave is a progressive wave in which the oscillation or vibration is at right angles to the direction in which the wave is travelling (direction of energy movement).

Lunar eclipse a lunar eclipse occurs when the Earth moves into a position directly between the Sun and the Moon.

Magnetic field a magnetic field is a field of force that exists around a magnet or a current-carrying conductor

Magnetic force	the magnetic force acts between two objects which have a magnetic field. It can also act when one object has a magnetic field and the other has an induced magnetic field.
Magnetic poles	are regions near the ends of a magnet from which the magnetic forces appear to originate.
Magnetism	is a property of matter which produces a field of attractive and repulsive forces.
Magnitude	the magnitude of a quantity is the numerical value, not including any direction or a negative sign.
Malleable	ability to be made into sheets.
Mantle	the mantle is a thick layer of dense, semi-liquid rock which extends some 2,900 km below the Earth's crust.
Mass	is the quantity of matter in an object (or body).
Mass number	is the total number of protons and neutrons found in the nucleus of an atom.
Matter	is material in the universe that has a mass.
Mechanical advantage	for a simple machine is the ration of the load (output force) to the effort (input force).
Mega	is a prefix used with SI units to indicate $\times 10^6$ or a million.
Megaparsec (Mpc)	a megaparsec is a large unit of distance equal to 3.26 million light years or 3.09×10^{22} m.
Melting point	is the temperature at which a solid completely changes into a liquid.
Metals	are a class of chemical elements which always form positive ions (cations) when they react to form compounds.
Metre	distance light will travel in a vacuum in 1/299792458 of a second.
Micro	is a prefix used with SI units to indicate $\times 10^{-6}$ or a millionth.
Microwaves	are electromagnetic waves with a wavelength between 1 mm and 1 m. They can cause molecules to vibrate and become very hot. They are used in microwave ovens and in communication devices such as satellite televisions and mobile phones.
Milky Way	the Milky Way is the galaxy to which our Sun belongs.
Milli	is a prefix used with SI units to indicate $\times 10^{-3}$ or a thousandth.
Moderator	a moderator is part of a nuclear reactor which slows down the neutrons emitted from nuclear fission so that they are able to induce further fission reactions.
Momentum	of an object is its mass multiplied by its velocity.
Motor effect	when a wire carrying a current is brought into a magnetic field, there is repulsion between the magnetic field of the current and the field of the magnet, which causes a force on the wire.
Nano	is a prefix used with SI units to indicate $\times 10^{-9}$.
Neutral	a neutral object has no overall charge.

Neutron   a neutron is a neutrally charged subatomic particle which is found in the nucleus of atoms (except hydrogen).

Newton   the newton is the SI unit of force, defined as the force which gives a mass of 1 kilogram an acceleration of 1 m s^{-2}.

Newton pair forces   are forces, as described in Newton's third law, which are of the same type and magnitude but opposite in direction.

Newton-meter   a newtonmeter is a device to measure a force or the weight of an object.

Newton's first law   states that an object will continue in a state of rest or uniform motion unless acted upon by an external force.

Newton's second law   states that the rate of change of momentum of an object is directly proportional to the force acting on the object.

Newton's third law   states that forces always occur in equal and opposite pairs, called the action and reaction.

Nobel prize   The Nobel prizes are given every year for significant advances in a field of study. Prizes are awarded for physics, chemistry, physiology or medicine, literature, economics and peace.

Non-linear   is a relationship between two properties that cannot be described without using powers or other complex functions. A graph of the two properties would have a curved line.

Non-renewable resources   include minerals and energy sources such as fossil fuels (coal, oil and natural gas). Once such resources are used up, they cannot be replaced.

Normal   is a term meaning at right angles. When describing how waves reflect and refract, the normal line is at right angles to the surface where the waves hit.

Normal reaction   the normal reaction is the contact force between two objects. It acts on an object at right angles to the surface with which that object makes contact.

Nuclear energy   is the energy released by nuclear fission or nuclear fusion.

Nuclear fission   is the process by which a heavy, unstable nucleus is split up into two or more smaller nuclei called fission products.

Nuclear fusion   is the process by which small nuclei combine to produce a larger nucleus releasing energy.

Nuclear potential energy   is the energy that is stored in an atomic nucleus and that is released through nuclear fission (for example, in nuclear power stations or nuclear bombs) or nuclear fusion (for example, in the Sun or other stars).

Nuclear power   is an energy resource which uses the fission of heavy elements such as uranium to generate power. While nuclear fusion is also a possible source of nuclear power, it is not yet a viable energy resource.

Nucleus   a nucleus is the very small central core of an atom, containing most of the atomic mass.

Ohm   an ohm is the resistance of a conductor in which a current of one ampere flows when a potential difference of one volt is applied across its ends.

Ohm's law   states that the ratio of the potential difference across the ends of a metal conductor to the electric current flowing through the conductor is a constant.

Optical fibres	use total internal reflection to transmit light along very fine tubes of plastic or glass.
Orbit	an orbit is a circular or elliptical path around a central object such as the orbit of planets or asteroids around the Sun, or the moon around the Earth.
Paradox	a paradox is a set of two or more statements or observations that are both seemingly true but they lead to conflicting conclusions.
Parallel circuit	a parallel circuit is formed when the components are arranged so that there is more than one path for the current to take.
Particle	a particle is a very small piece of matter (or energy). Some particles are fundamental, but compound objects such as molecules can be considered as particles if their size is sufficiently small that it can be assumed to be zero.
Pascal	a pascal is the SI unit of pressure and is equivalent to a force of 1 newton acting over an area of 1 square metre: $1 \text{ Pa} = 1 \text{ N m}^{-2}$.
Period	is the time of one oscillation (one complete wave).
Periodic table	the periodic table is an arrangement of elements in order of increasing number of protons (atomic number).
Peta	is a prefix used with SI units to indicate $\times 10^{15}$.
Photoelectric effect	the photoelectric effect is when light of a sufficiently short wavelength shines on a metal and causes electrons to be freed from the surface.
Photon	a photon is a particle of light or electromagnetic energy.
Photosynthesis	is the chemical process of separating hydrogen from water (light stage or photolysis) which then combines with carbon dioxide (dark stage) to synthesize simple foodstuffs such as glucose.
Pico	is a prefix used with SI units to indicate $\times 10^{-12}$.
Pivot	a pivot or fulcrum is the point about which a lever rotates.
Planet	a planet is a major celestial body that orbits the Sun in a slightly elliptical orbit.
Plasma	is a fourth state of matter which can only exist at very high temperatures, e.g. inside the Sun.
Plum pudding model	the plum pudding model was a model of the atom which consisted of electrons dotted throughout a ball of positive charge. It was proposed at the beginning of the 20th century, after the discovery of the electron, but before Rutherford scattering led to the discovery of the atomic nucleus.
Potential difference	is the difference in potential between two charged points.
Potential energy	is energy which is stored in a body or system because of its position, shape or state.
Precision	is a measure of the variation in the results of identical trials of an experiment. If there is less variation in the range of results, the value may be expressed with a larger number of significant figures and may be more precise.
Pressure	is a continuous force applied by an object or fluid against a surface, measured as the force acting per unit area of surface.

Pressure law	states that the pressure of a fixed mass of gas at constant volume is directly proportional to its temperature (in kelvins): p/T = constant.
Proton	a proton is the positively charged subatomic particle which is found in the nucleus of an atom.
Pulley	a pulley is a simple machine for raising loads, consisting of one or more wheels with a grooved rim to take a belt, rope or chain.
Quantum mechanics	is a set of theories such as Heisenberg's uncertainty principle and wave–particle duality which govern particles on very small scales and describe them according to probabilities.
Quark	this is a fundamental particle of all atoms. Unlike protons or electrons, quarks have fractions of electronic charge $\left(+\frac{2}{3} \text{ or } -\frac{1}{3}\right)$. The proton consists of three quarks, two "ups" and one "down": $\frac{2}{3} + \frac{2}{3} - \frac{1}{3} = 1$.
Radiation	is a general term applied to anything that travels outward from its source but which cannot be identified as a type of matter like a sold, liquid or gas.
Radio wave	are electromagnetic waves with wavelengths longer than 1 m.
Radioactive decay	is the spontaneous disintegration of a radioactive nucleus, giving off alpha or beta particles, often together with gamma rays.
Radioactivity	is the spontaneous disintegration of unstable atomic nuclei and is usually accompanied by the emission of radiation.
Radiotherapy	is the use of radiation from radioisotopes to treat cancer by killing cancer cells.
Radon gas	is a gas which is formed from the radioactive decay of some rocks. It is radioactive itself and in most places accounts for the majority of background radiation.
Random	a process is random if the outcome or timing cannot be predicted exactly.
Red shift	the red shift is a lengthening of the wavelength of light from distant stars so that it seems to shift towards the red end of the spectrum.
Reflection	is the bouncing off of a wave from a barrier.
Refraction	is the change in direction of a wave as it passes from one medium to another.
Refractive index	the refractive index of a material is the ratio of the speed of light in a vacuum to the speed of light in that material.
Relativity	is a term which refers to two of Einstein's theories: special relativity and general relativity.
Reliability	is the extent to which an experiment produces similar outcomes for similar trials.
Renewable resources	include plant and animal products such as food, crops, timber and wood for fuel, and energy sources such as wind power and solar power.
Residual strong force	is the force which holds protons and neutrons together in the nucleus of an atom.
Resistance	is the ability of a conductor to resist, or oppose, the flow of an electric current through it.
Resistor	a resistor is a component of an electrical circuit that is present because of its electrical resistance.

Resultant force	a resultant force is the net or total force that is the overall effect of one or more forces adding together.
Retrograde motion	retrograde motion is when a planet appears to reverse its direction of motion against the background stars.
Rheostat	a rheostat is a variable resistor often consisting of a coil of wire and a sliding contact which determines the length of wire that a current flows through.
Right-hand grip rule	the right-hand grip rule is a way of remembering the direction of a magnetic field around a current-carrying wire. If the thumb on your right hand points in the direction of current, your fingers will curl in the direction of the magnetic field.
Rutherford scattering	is the deflection of some alpha particles when they are fired at a thin metal target. It was observed in the Geiger–Marsden experiment and led to the discovery of the atomic nucleus.
Scalar quantity	a scalar quantity is one which has magnitude (size), but not direction.
Scale model	a scale model is a representation of a system where all distances are shrunk or enlarged by a common factor.
Scientific method	the scientific method is a system of investigation where a hypothesis is tested by experiment and the results published so that they can be tested by other scientists.
Screw	a screw is a simple machine consisting of a spiral thread. It converts a turning force into a linear force.
Series circuit	a series circuit is formed when the components are arranged so that there is a single path for the current to take.
SI units	SI stands for "Système international" and is the internationally recognized system of units in which quantities are measured using the base units kilogram, meter, second, kelvin, ampere, mole and candela or units which are combinations of these.
Snell's law	is the law of refraction which states that $n_1\sin(\theta_i) = n_2\sin(\theta_r)$ where n_1 and n_2 are the refractive indices of the materials the wave passes between, and θ_i and θ_r are the angles of incidence and refraction (measured to the normal).
Solar eclipse	a solar eclipse occurs when the Moon moves into a position directly between the Sun and the Earth.
Solar system	the solar system is our Sun and the eight major planets that orbit around it: Mercury, Venus, Earth, Mars, Jupiter, Saturn, Uranus and Neptune.
Solar wind	the solar wind consists of charged particles that stream out from the Sun all the time but whose intensity varies with the month or time of year.
Solenoid	a solenoid is a long cylindrical coil of insulated wire.
Solid	the particles in a solid are very close together, arranged in regular rows, held together very tightly, not moving from their position but vibrating.
Sound	is a progressive longitudinal wave caused by the vibration of an elastic medium such as air.

Sound waves consist of compressions and rarefactions caused in a medium when it is disturbed by a vibrating object.

Specific heat capacity is the heat energy absorbed or released when 1 kg of a substance changes its temperature by 1 K.

Spectrum a spectrum is a range of wavelengths of light. The visible spectrum is the rainbow of colors (red, orange, yellow, green, blue, indigo, violet). Spectrum can also refer to the electromagnetic spectrum – a wider range of wavelengths.

Specular a specular reflection is one in which all the rays of light reflect in the same way causing an image to be reflected. The surface from which the waves reflect will appear shiny or mirrored.

Speed is the rate at which an object moves, expressed as the distance the object travels in a certain time.

Speed of light all electromagnetic waves travel at the same speed in a vacuum, which is approximately 3×10^8 m s^{-1} or 300,000 km s^{-1}.

Spring balance a spring balance is a device which measures the weight of an object (although sometimes converting the result to a mass) using the extension of a spring.

Standard form is a mathematical notation which uses powers of ten and is useful for very large or very small numbers.

Star a star is a ball of plasma which is so large and hot that nuclear fusion occurs in its center.

State of matter are the three common physical forms or phases in which matter exists: solid, liquid and gas.

Steam engine a steam engine is a device which uses steam to convert heat energy into mechanical work.

Steam turbine a steam turbine is a device which uses steam to convert heat energy into mechanical work. They are often used to drive electrical generators.

Step-down transformer is one in which the number of turns of the secondary coil is less than the primary coil, so the secondary coil is less than the primary voltage.

Step-up transformer is one in which the number of turns on the secondary coil is greater than the primary coil, so the secondary voltage is greater than the primary voltage.

Summer solstice the summer solstice is the day in which the Sun spends the longest time above the horizon. In the northern hemisphere, the summer solstice usually falls on June 21, while in the southern hemisphere the solstice usually falls on December 21.

Supercluster a supercluster is a large collection of galactic groups. A supercluster may contain hundreds of thousands of galaxies.

Supermassive black hole a supermassive black hole is a black hole with a mass of a million to a billion times the mass of the Sun. It is believed that all large galaxies have a supermassive black hole at their center.

Supernova	a supernova is an immense explosion which results when an old and very massive star uses up most of its fuel for nuclear fusion and collapses under the force of its own gravity.
Tangent	a tangent is a straight line on a graph which touches a curve and shows the gradient of the curve at that point.
Temperature	is the degree of hotness of coldness of something.
Tension	is a force caused by stretching or pulling on an object.
Tera	is a prefix used with SI units to indicate $\times 10^{12}$.
Terminal velocity	is the constant velocity reached by an object falling through a fluid (liquid or gas) when its gravitational force (weight) is equal to the frictional forces acting on it.
Theory	a scientific theory is a hypothesis that has been tested by experiment and is widely accepted by the scientific community.
Thermal energy	is the energy an object possesses because of the kinetic and potential energy of its particles.
Thermistor	a thermistor is a resistor made from a semiconductor whose resistance falls sharply when its temperature rises above room temperature.
Thermodynamics	study of laws that govern energy and energy transfers
Tidal energy	is produced by the use of tidal barrages to trap water at high tide, which is then allowed to flow through turbines set in a concrete wall.
Total internal reflection	is the complete reflection of light at a boundary between two media.
Tough	a material is tough if it requires a large force to deform it.
Transformer	a transformer is a device for changing the voltage of an alternating current without changing its frequency.
Transverse wave	a transverse wave is a progressive wave in which the oscillation or vibration is at right angles to the direction in which the wave is travelling (direction of energy movement).
Turns ration	the turns ratio is the number of turns on the primary and secondary coil of a transformer.
Ultrasound	is sound above the human hearing range, around 20,000 Hz.
Ultraviolet (UV)	ultraviolet light (or ultraviolet radiation) is a part of the electromagnetic spectrum with wavelengths between 10 and 400 nm. UV light is given off by very hot objects (the Sun, mercury vapor lamps), and it is detected by fluorescent materials which absorb rays and charge them into visible light. It is used in tanning beds and invisible markings for security.
Universe	the universe is all the matter, energy and space that exists.
Upthrust	is the upward force on an object which is immersed in fluid.
Vacuum	a vacuum is a space in which there is no matter.
Validity	is whether an experiment has been carried out in a way that produces a conclusion that can be trusted.

Variable — in an experiment, a variable is a parameter that can change between different trials. Variables are usually classified as the independent, dependent and control variables.

Variable resistor — a variable resistor is one whose resistance can be changed.

Vector quantity — a vector quantity is on which has both magnitude and direction.

Velocity — is the rate at which an object moves in a particular direction, expressed as the displacement of an object in a certain time.

Visible light — is an electromagnetic wave with a wavelength between 400 and 700 nm. It is emitted from hot objects (the Sun) and can be detected by our eyes. It is used in optic fibres and photography.

Void — a void is a large region of space, hundreds of light years across, between galactic superclusters and filaments which has very few galaxies.

Voltage — is the potential difference of the value of the electromotive force.

Voltmeter — a voltmeter is an instrument used to measure the potential difference (voltage) between any two points in an electrical circuit.

Volume — is the amount of space that an object occupies.

Wave — a wave is a regular periodic disturbance in a medium or space.

Wavelength — is the distance between two identical points on the wave, e.g. two adjacent peaks or two adjacent troughs.

Wave–particle duality — is the idea that small particles such as electrons can behave both as a wave and a particle.

Wedge — a wedge is a simple machine that can give a mechanical advantage. Driving the wedge downwards gives a large sideways force that can drive two components apart. An example is an axe.

Weight — is the gravitational force exerted on an object by the Earth (or another planet).

Wheel and axle — a wheel and axle is a simple machine that converts a rotational force into linear force. If the wheel has a larger radius than the axle, then turning the wheel gives a mechanical advantage.

Wind power — is the use of the motion of the Earth's atmosphere to drive machinery or generators to produce electricity.

Winter solstice — the winter solstice is the day when the Sun spends the shortest time above the horizon. In the Northern Hemisphere, the winter solstice usually falls on December 21 while in the Southern Hemisphere, the solstice usually falls on June 21.

Work — is the energy transfer that occurs when a force causes an object to move a certain distance in the direction of the force.

X-ray — X-rays are high frequency electromagnetic waves with wavelengths below 10 nm. They are emitted by X-ray tubes and can be detected by photographic film. They are used at low energy to take images of internal organs.

Index

The entries in **bold** are explained in the glossary.